THE CHALLENGE OF
Effective Speaking
in a Digital Age

THE CHALLENGE OF
Effective Speaking
in a Digital Age

17th Edition

Rudolph F. Verderber
University of Cincinnati

Deanna D. Sellnow
University of Kentucky

Kathleen S. Verderber
Northern Kentucky University

Australia • Brazil • Mexico • Singapore • United Kingdom • United States

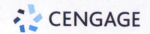

The Challenge of Effective Speaking in a Digital Age, Seventeenth Edition
Rudolph F. Verderber, Deanna D. Sellnow, Kathleen S. Verderber

Product Director: Monica Eckman

Product Manager: Kelli Strieby

Associate Content Developer: Claire Branman

Content Developer: Kassi Radomski

Marketing Manager: Sarah Seymour

Content Project Manager: Dan Saabye

Art Director: Marissa Falco

Manufacturing Planner: Doug Bertke

IP Analyst: Ann Hoffman

IP Project Manager: Erika Mugavin

Production Service: Cenveo® Publisher Services

Compositor: Cenveo® Publisher Services

Text and Cover Designer: Red Hangar Design

Cover Image: america365/Shutterstock.com

For product information and technology assistance, contact us at **Cengage Customer & Sales Support, 1-800-354-9706**

For permission to use material from this text or product, submit all requests online at **www.cengage.com/permissions**. Further permissions questions can be emailed to **permissionrequest@cengage.com**.

Library of Congress Control Number: 2016952403

Student Edition:
ISBN: 978-1-305-94819-8

Loose-leaf Edition:
ISBN: 978-1-305-94829-7

Cengage
20 Channel Center Street
Boston, MA 02210
USA

Cengage is a leading provider of customized learning solutions with employees residing in nearly 40 different countries and sales in more than 125 countries around the world. Find your local representative at **www.cengage.com**.

Cengage products are represented in Canada by Nelson Education, Ltd.

To learn more about Cengage platforms and services, register or access your online learning solution, or purchase materials for your course, visit **www.cengage.com**.

Printed at CLDPC, USA, 07-21

Brief Contents

Contents

PART ③ # Informative and Persuasive Speaking

PART **4**

Adapting to Other Occasions and Formats

Preface

I am really excited about this 17th edition of *The Challenge of Effective Speaking in a Digital Age*, and I believe you will be too. Although Rudy and Kathie Verderber no longer play an active role in revisions, you will see I have remained true to their original ideas, while updating content to reflect speechmaking as it occurs today. You will see that I continue to ground public speaking firmly in its roots—**rhetorical theory**—beginning in Chapter 1 and then throughout the book. Doing so reminds readers that public speaking concepts and skills are based on a rhetorical tradition that has stood the test of time for over 2,000 years! Of course, this book is also still organizedaround its hallmark six **Speech Plan Action Steps**.

NEW TO THIS EDITION

- This edition provides additional information and a greater emphasis on the powerful role **digital media and technology** play in all aspects of preparing, presenting, and interpreting public speeches today. For example, the first chapter opens with a discussion of how technology shapes speechmaking today. Moreover, throughout the book I offer sample speeches about technology-related topics, as well as actual examples addressing technology-related challenges in public speaking occurring in both face-to-face and online settings.

- Each **sample formal speech outline** now includes commentary in the margins, a sample preparation outline, and sample note cards or PowerPoint slides with key word outlines or notes. (See chapters 1, 2, 11, 12, and 14.)

- *New* **Public Speaking in the Real World boxes** include "What Former President Bill Clinton Can Teach Us About Listening and Success" (Chapter 3) and "Filmmakers and NASA Team Up on Research for 'The Martian'" (Chapter 6).

- *New* **Reflect on Ethics topics** include "Yahoo CEO Resigns Over Inaccurate Resume" (Chapter 2); "Jim Cramer and CNBC's Mad Money" (Chapter 4); "Academy Awards Host Chris Rock: Ethical or Not?" (Chapter 8); and "Super Bowl Ad Ethics: Where Should the Line Be Drawn?" (Chapter 13).

- Streamlined **Speech Planning boxes** now include sample Student Responses at the end, rather than in a separate box, which some readers of previous editions found confusing. The separate Speech Assignment and Speech Evaluation Checklist boxes have been simplified and combined into a single Speech Assignment & Checklist box.

Chapter-by-Chapter Updates and Revisions

- **Chapter 1, Foundations of Public Speaking**, now begins with a discussion of some of the ways digital media and technology influence public speaking today. It goes on to highlight public speaking as an empowering civic right and our responsibility to be ethical public speakers. Then I explain how public speaking functions as a form of communication whether we do so in a face-to-face or online setting. After discussing the elements in the communication process and the contexts that situate public speaking among intrapersonal, interpersonal, group, and public communication, I describe the foundational theoretical concept of the rhetorical situation as it grounds effective public speaking. Finally, I provide an overview of the major principles of effective speechmaking and sample speech outlines for a eulogy, "My Grandma Frances."

- **Chapter 2, Your First Speech**, focuses specifically on getting students up and speaking. It begins with a scenario about Kira, a first-generation college student who is terrified about giving her first classroom speech. I then use Kira as an example throughout the chapter as I discuss public speaking apprehension and the six-step speech planning process. I close the chapter with sample outlines of Kira's speech of self-introduction, "On Being First."

- **Chapter 3, Listening**, has been updated to reflect current research by prominent listening scholars. It begins by addressing why it is important to study listening in a public speaking course and then differentiates hearing from listening. I then talk about some of the reasons effective listening can be difficult and provide specific strategies for improving listening skills. The chapter concludes with a comprehensive discussion of how to listen to and constructively critique a speech, including preparing feedback for the speaker.

- **Chapter 4, Speech Topic and Goal**, opens with a vignette about Romeo, who has been asked to give a speech to students at the high school he graduated from. He is used as an example throughout the chapter. I begin by reminding readers that a good speech goal is grounded in the rhetorical situation. In other words, a good speech topic and goal is based on (a) the speaker's interest, knowledge, and expertise, (b) the knowledge and expectations of the audience, and (c) the nature of the occasion. The chapter also focuses specifically on how to collect audience demographic and subject-related data, as well as data about the occasion, and how to use that data when preparing a speech.

- **Chapter 5, Adapting to Audiences**, continues to focus specifically on tailoring speech ideas to different audiences. It opens with a scenario about Megan, who has decided to do her speech on hurricanes, and J.J., who selected the topic "cell phone distracted driving." Their situations are used as examples throughout the chapter as I discuss why and how to identify the audience's initial disposition, establish common ground, demonstrate relevance, highlight speaker credibility, and be comprehensible and memorable.

- **Chapter 6, Topic Development**, focuses primarily on how to use the Internet to locate and evaluate sources and information. It also touches on how to find multimodal supporting material that can be used in a speech. Then I address how to skim online information to determine what to select for the speech and how to keep track of information in an annotated bibliography, in electronic slide files, or on research cards. Finally, I provide examples for citing sources and information on speech outlines and transcripts, as well as for citing them orally during the speech.

- **Chapter 7, Organizing the Speech Body**, features an opening scenario about Katie and Alyssa, who are taking their public speaking class online over the summer. An updated version of Katie's speech body outline on the uses and abuses of the prescription drug Adderall is used as an extended example to demonstrate each step in the organizing process.

- **Chapter 8, The Introduction and Conclusion**, continues to feature Katie and Alyssa in the opening scenario and pieces of Katie's Adderall speech outline as she develops it throughout the chapter. I emphasize the importance of audience-centered introductions and conclusions with specific examples of rhetorical devices that can be used as attention getters and clinchers. Finally, Katie's entire updated speech outlines including the introduction and conclusion, are offered in the form of the student response to the speech planning action step.

- **Chapter 9, Presentational Aids**, reflects the increasingly prominent role of technology-enhanced visual, audio, and audiovisual presentational aids in public speeches today. More specifically, such aids not only serve as embellishments, but are actually most effective when they function as a form of supporting material for developing content. Ignite speeches and TED talks serve as examples to illustrate this point. After describing the various types of visual, audio, and audiovisual aids that might be used in a speech and offering illustrations that mirror how they might appear in computerized slideshows, I close the chapter with an explanation about how to select, create, and use them effectively.

- **Chapter 10, Language and Oral Style**, continues to focus on how oral style differs from written style, as well as how to choose language that is appropriate, accurate, clear, and vivid. It also integrates a how-to demonstration of verbal immediacy and linguistic sensitivity when speaking to diverse audiences that may or may not share the same first language as the speaker. I close with the speech Professor Nikki Giovanni gave at the memorial ceremony for the Virginia Tech shooting victims.

- **Chapter 11, Delivery**, addresses both how to rehearse effectively using the technology tools available to us and how to deliver speeches effectively to virtual audiences over the Internet. In the opening scenario, I return to Katie and Alyssa, this time focusing on Alyssa's concerns about using her voice and body to most effectively convey her great speech content about volunteering and civic engagement. Throughout the chapter, Alyssa serves as an extended example regarding use of voice, body, and presentational aids. The chapter closes with Alyssa's preparation outline, annotated formal speech outline, and speaking outline/notes on volunteering and civic engagement.

- **Chapter 12, Informative Speaking**, includes a brief discussion of the nature of informative speaking and the importance of developing material that is suited to different learning styles. I highlight the important role of using listener relevance links to gain and maintain audience interest throughout the speech and close with Anna's sample process speech outlines and speaking notes on Internet identity theft.

- **Chapter 13, Persuasive Messages**, is the first of two chapters dedicated to the subject. I have streamlined this chapter to focus specifically on the general nature of persuasion and how people process persuasive messages. The chapter is dedicated to how the rhetorical strategies of logos, ethos, and pathos are used to develop persuasive messages not only in formal speeches but whenever we are attempting to influence the attitudes, beliefs, values, or behaviors of others, as well as when others attempt to persuade us. A new Reflect on Ethics feature in the chapter highlights the pervasive nature of persuasive messages beyond formal speeches by discussing the ethics of persuasive messages in Super Bowl TV advertisements.

- **Chapter 14, Persuasive Speaking**, builds on the nature of persuasive messages by focusing specifically on how to create and organize a persuasive speech. I have revised it in ways that highlight doing so as a three-step process of (1) determining an appropriate persuasive speech goal, (2) organizing the speech content using an appropriate persuasive speech pattern, and (3) refining the speech based on ethical guidelines for persuasive speeches. The chapter closes with Adam's updated preparation and annotated formal speech outlines on cyber bullying, as well as a sample of his speaking outline/notes as they would appear in the "notes" feature of a PowerPoint slideshow.

- **Chapter 15, Ceremonial Speaking**, is chock–full of information on various types of ceremonial speeches that readers may find themselves giving at some point in their lives. These include speeches of welcome, introduction, nomination, recognition, acceptance, and tribute, among others. The general nature and guidelines for each type of speech are described, followed by a short sample speech for each. The chapter poses a number of impromptu speech challenges students might complete to practice various types of ceremonial speeches.

- **Chapter 16, Group Communication and Presentations**, which was revised dramatically for the 16th edition, continues to open by addressing the nature of effective leadership in problem-solving groups and the shared leadership responsibilities of all group members. It then discusses group conflict as it contributes to successful problem solving when managed effectively. I have devoted an entire section of the chapter to communicating effectively in virtual groups, followed by descriptions of the various formats available today for communicating group results. Communicating group deliverables can take place through written formats (e.g., written briefs and comprehensive reports), oral formats (e.g., oral briefs, oral reports, panel discussions, symposiums), and virtual formats (e.g., remote access reports, streaming videos). Finally, the chapter explains how to evaluate both group dynamics and formal group presentations using the criteria of effective communication described throughout this book.

CONTINUING FEATURES

- Each **opening vignette** focuses on multimodal (integrated oral, written, visual, and digital) communication issues; the vignettes are revisited as examples throughout the chapters.

- Each chapter opens with specific **learning outcomes**, which drive the content throughout the chapter, and closes with reflective questions pertaining to each outcome, which readers should be able to answer after completing the chapter.

- **Speech Plan Action Steps** guide students through a step-by-step preparation process, which results in significantly better speeches. The Action Step activities are streamlined for this edition and continue to be supplemented by in-text and online examples of each activity prepared by other students.

- **Sample student speech outlines** continue to be a hallmark in this edition. They have been expanded to illustrate preparation outlines, formal sentence outlines with commentary, and speaking notes/outlines as they are used to develop and then deliver the speech. Samples can be found in Chapters 1, 2, 11, 12, and 14. Additional sample speech student outlines, along with their accompanying speeches and speech transcripts, are available for viewing in the **Speech Video Library**, available on MindTap.

- **Speech Snippet** boxes throughout the book provide brief examples of speeches by student speakers working through the myriad issues they must face when preparing a speech. For example, in the Chapter 5 discussions about adapting to an audience, the Speech Snippet boxes highlight how speakers demonstrated personal impact in a speech, addressed timeliness and acknowledged listener attitudes, demonstrated their direct expertise, and established their trustworthiness.

- **Impromptu Speech Challenge** boxes, which appear in the margin throughout the text, encourage students to practice speaking with limited preparation time.

- **Public Speaking in the Real World** boxes feature successful actors, musicians, athletes, and business professionals and how they grapple with the speaking challenges addressed in the chapters; each closes with questions for students to ponder. Highlights include actors Julia and Eric Roberts and their childhood stuttering (Chapter 1); Harrison Ford on speech anxiety (Chapter 2); former President Bill Clinton on focused listening (Chapter 3); Matt Damon and the filmmakers of the move *The Martian* on conducting research (Chapter 6); Steve Jobs on organizing (Chapter 7); Lady Gaga on introductions and conclusions (Chapter 8);President Obama on language and oral style (Chapter 10); Anne Hathaway on practicing speech delivery (Chapter 11); and Charlize Theron and Brad Pitt on persuasive speaking (Chapters 13 and 14).

- **Reflect on Ethics** boxes in each chapter use contemporary situations to help students think through ethical challenges and the choices people face in public communication settings today. Each one closes with questions for students to ponder regarding the ethical dilemma posed. Several of the Reflect on Ethics case studies feature well-known people, such as Food Network chef Robert Irvine (Chapter 1), musician Kanye West (Chapter 3), *Mad Money* host and financial guru Jim Cramer (Chapter 4), football player Manti Teʾo (Chapter 5), rock band Coldplay (Chapter 6), comedian and actor Chris Rock (Chapter 8), baseball player David Ortiz (Chapter 14), and actor Steve Carell (Chapter 15).

- End-of-chapter activities include **Impromptu Speech Exercises** and **Assessment Activities**. Although students may only give three or four graded speeches per term, the impromptu speech exercises challenge students to practice speaking more often with short, quickly prepared speeches related to chapter material. Assessment activities are also tied to chapter content so that students and instructors can measure how well students understand and can apply the concepts and skills in each chapter. **Bongo**, available with **MindTap**, provides technology that can be used to assign, review, and grade these activities online.

TEACHING AND LEARNING RESOURCES

- **MindTap®** for *The Challenge of Effective Speaking in a Digital Age*, 17th edition, is a fully online, highly personalized learning experience that enhances learner engagement and improves outcomes. MindTap provides a full suite of integrated materials including readings, multimedia, activities, and assessments in a singular Learning Path that guides students through their course with ease and engagement. Activities in MindTap guide students through the process of analyzing sample speeches, creating topics, building outlines, and practicing and presenting their speech. MindTap includes access to the **Speech Video Library** of over 100 student and professional speeches, the **Bongo** video recording, delivery and grading system, and the speech preparation **Outline Builder**. Instructors can personalize the Learning Path by customizing Cengage Learning resources and adding their own content via apps that integrate into the MindTap framework seamlessly with any Learning Management System.

Note to faculty: If you want your students to have access to the online resources for this book, please be sure to order them for your course. The content in these resources can be bundled with every new copy of the text or ordered separately. Contact your local Cengage Learning Consultant. *If you do not order them, your students will not have access to the online resources.*

Student Resources in MindTap

- **Outline Builder**, available in MindTap, is a speech preparation resource that provides step-by-step support for students to select an appropriate topic, design balanced and organized main points and sub points, formulate citations that follow guidelines, and create succinct note cards. Students arrive well-prepared and confident on speech day, with a complete and well-organized outline in hand. Outline Builder can also be customized based upon instructor preferences and expectations.

- **Practice and Present available in MindTap**, powered by Bongo, is a synchronous (live capture) and asynchronous speech video delivery, recording, and grading system. It compiles student video submissions in one easy-to-access place that allows self-review, peer review and instructor grades in one system. Instructors are able to provide feedback via rubrics and time-stamped comments so that students receive contextualized, meaningful feedback on their presentations. This system allows students to practice their speech outside of class ahead of time and get feedback, providing students with the tools to help reduce speech anxiety. It gives students the ability to synchronize visual aids to videos. Finally, Bongo provides synchronous and asynchronous group presentation and delivery functionality.

- **CengageBrain.com** online store is a single destination for more than 15,000 new print textbooks, textbook rentals, eBooks, single eChapters, and print, digital, and audio study tools. CengageBrain.com provides the freedom to purchase Cengage Learning products à la carte—exactly what you need, when you need it. Visit **cengagebrain.com** for details.

- *A Guide to the Basic Course for ESL Students* (ISBN 9780534567798) can be bundled and is designed to assist the nonnative speaker. The *Guide* features FAQs, helpful URLs, and strategies for accent management and speech apprehension.

- *The Art and Strategy of Service-Learning Presentations*, 2nd edition (ISBN 9780534617547) is an invaluable resource for students in the basic course that integrates, or will soon integrate, a service-learning component. This publication provides guidelines for connecting service-learning work with classroom concepts and advice for working effectively with agencies and organizations. It also provides model forms, reports and other useful resources.

Instructor Resources

- **The Speech Video Library available in MindTap** provides instructors an easy way to keyword search, review, evaluate, and assign exemplar student speeches into their classroom and online learning environment. It includes 100+ videos, including both famous historical speeches and realistic student classroom speeches. Student speech types include informative, persuasive, invitational, impromptu, and group presentations. All speeches are accompanied by activities to help students refine and develop their speech preparation and critical thinking skills.

- **Instructor's Resource Website**. This website is an all-in-one resource for class preparation, presentation, and testing for instructors. Accessible through Cengage.com/login with your faculty account, you will find an Instructor's Manual, chapter-by-chapter PowerPoint presentations, and Cengage Learning Testing files powered by Cognero.

- The **Instructor's Resource Manual** includes sample syllabi, chapter-by-chapter outlines, summaries, vocabulary lists, suggested lecture and discussion topics, classroom exercises, assignments, and a comprehensive test bank with answer key and rejoinders.

- **Cengage Learning Testing, powered by Cognero**, is accessible through Cengage. com/login with your faculty account. This test bank contains multiple choice, true/false, and essay questions for each chapter. Cognero is a flexible, online system that allows you to author, edit, and manage test bank content, and create multiple test versions instantly and deliver through your LMS platform from wherever you may be. Cognero is compatible with Blackboard, Angel, Moodle, and Canvas LMS platforms.

- *The Teaching Assistant's Guide to the Basic Course* (ISBN 9780534567781), based on leading communication teacher training programs, covers general teaching and course management topics as well as specific strategies for communication instruction—for example, providing effective feedback on performance, managing sensitive class discussions, and conducting mock interviews.

- **Digital Course Support** provides the training, connections, and support you need for the seamless integration of digital resources into your course. This unparalleled technology service provides robust online resources, peer-to-peer instruction, personalized training, and a customizable program you can count on. Visit **cengage.com** to sign up for online seminars, first-days-of-class services, technical support, or personalized, face-to-face training. Our online and onsite trainings are frequently led by one of our Lead Teachers, faculty members who are experts in using Cengage Learning technology and can provide best practices and teaching tips.

ACKNOWLEDGMENTS

The book you are holding is the result of a team effort, and I have been privileged to work with the best. First, I want to acknowledge the wonderful students whose speeches appear in this book. I also want to thank my colleagues around the world who have used previous editions of the book and have graciously shared their experiences in teaching from these texts. I would like to single out the following people who participated in the review process for this edition: Diane Badzinski, Colorado Christian University; Katherine Dawson, University of Louisiana at Monroe; Elizabeth Desnoyers-Colas, Armstrong Atlantic State University; Jenny Hodges, St. John; and Tarsha Rogers, Elizabeth City State University.

As I prepared this revision, I enjoyed working with Kelli Steiby, product manager; Dan Saabye, content project manager; Lauren MacLachlan, production manager; Eve Malakoff-Klein, copyeditor; and Karolina Kiwak, associate content developer. Special thank yous are due to two people. First, thank you to Monica Eckman, senior product director, whose belief in this book is only outweighed by her enthusiasm and hard work. And second, to Kassi Radomski, content developer, who not only keeps me on task, but also offers great advice to improve the quality of the book. As always, she has been a godsend on this project.

Finally, I want to acknowledge Rudy Verderber for his innovative vision in conceiving the step-by-step process approach to public speaking that continues to ground this book. I also want to thank both Rudy and Kathie Verderber for entrusting me with the privilege of taking these ideas forward in ways that now also address the digital age we live in today. Lastly, I ask you to keep them both in your thoughts and prayers as they continue to fight Rudy's ongoing battle with Alzheimer's disease. As always, to God be the glory!

THE CHALLENGE OF

Effective Speaking

in a Digital Age

1
Foundations of Public Speaking

WHAT'S THE POINT?
WHEN YOU'VE FINISHED THIS CHAPTER, YOU WILL BE ABLE TO:

- Explain why technology is so important to effective public speaking today

- Describe the nature, power, and ethical responsibilities of public speaking as a liberal art

- Explain how public speaking fits within the realm of communication

- Define the components of the rhetorical situation

- Examine effective content, structure, and delivery speech components

MindTap®

Review the chapter **Learning Objectives** and **Start** with quick warm-up activity.

Ethical communicators are honest, fair, responsible, and respectful of others.

Dominic just returned from a 2-day training and development workshop where he learned how to use a new online purchase order requisition submission and tracking program. Dominic's supervisor now wants him to lead a series of training sessions for the other 50 to 60 full- and part-time purchasing clerks at the company where he works.

Chen Chen was awarded "server of the month" three times since she started working at the restaurant. Customers really like her and several have begun to request that they be seated in her section. Her manager asked her to give a pep talk to the managers and other servers about "how she does it" at the next companywide meeting. She felt a bit nervous, but she agreed to do it.

Although her grandmother had been sick for some time, Diana was heartbroken when she learned her grandmother had passed away. She was caught off guard when her mother asked her to represent the family by delivering the eulogy at the funeral, but of course, Diana graciously agreed to do it.

Jediah landed an interview for his dream job as an electrical engineer. The interview is going to be conducted via videoconference. To prepare for the interview, Jediah was asked to create a 10- to 15-minute webinar explaining why he is the best candidate for the position.

Which of the situations above illustrates someone who will be giving a "speech"? Actually, because the definition of **public speaking** is "a sustained formal presentation by a speaker to an audience," each is an example of public speaking. Public speaking today might occur in a face-to-face professional setting, as it will for Dominic and Chen Chen; in a nonprofessional setting, as it will for Diana; or in an online environment, as it will for Jediah. In this course, you will learn how to give effective speeches, a skill that will help you to be more successful in both your personal and professional lives.

This chapter provides an overview of the fundamentals of effective public speaking as it pertains to the digital age in which we live. We begin with a preview of the opportunities and challenges technology has given rise to for public speaking. Next, we describe the nature of public speaking as a liberal art, as well as the ethical responsibilities of public speakers. Then, we describe public speaking broadly as a form of communication and more specifically as an audience-centered endeavor rooted in the rhetorical situation. Finally, we highlight the major speech components of content, structure, and delivery. By the time you finish reading this chapter and applying what you learn, you will have begun the exciting journey toward becoming an effective audience-centered public speaker in a digital age.

public speaking:
a sustained formal presentation by a speaker to an audience

PUBLIC SPEAKING IN A DIGITAL AGE

As you see on the front cover, the name of the book you're reading is *The Challenge of Effective Speaking in a Digital Age*. Without a doubt, the technology explosion we have witnessed since the dawn of the 21st century influences what and how we communicate. Wireless technology, for instance, makes it possible to access information about and from anywhere in the world; watch TV programs and movies; participate in meetings, classes, and webinars; and interact with friends and family via social networks at any time and place. Smartphones and tablets fit easily into a backpack, purse, or pocket, making technology access portable. What scholars have termed *information communication technology* (ICT) is exploding as an academic field of study in colleges and universities all over the world. And this growth is for good reason. According to a report released in March of 2015 by the US Census Bureau, US businesses spent $330.9 billion on ICT in 2013 alone.[1]

But what does all this mean for public speaking? In short, it means we must embrace technology in ways that turn its potential challenges into opportunities if we are to be effective public speakers when we share information, as well as when we instruct and attempt to influence others in this digital age. Although the fundamentals of effective speaking are just that—fundamentals—regardless of the technological channels we choose to use, various technologies do pose unique challenges. Thus, each chapter in this book describes the fundamentals and expands on them in relation to ICT. We are excited that you are taking this journey with us to become effective public speakers in this age of information and technology.

PUBLIC SPEAKING AS A LIBERAL ART

When we say public speaking is a liberal art, we mean that public speaking knowledge and skills are fundamental to participating effectively in society regardless of your major or profession. That's why a course devoted to public speaking is often required in a general education curriculum.[2] Public speaking is a powerful right for engaged citizens—a right that also carries with it several important ethical responsibilities.

The Civic Right of Public Speaking

Civic rights are the essential conditions that individuals need to live happy and successful lives. Public speaking has been revered as a civic right in democratic civilizations since ancient times. Historically, public speaking was at the center of a liberal arts education because it was the means by which free men conducted business, made public decisions, and gained and maintained power.[3] Today, effective public speakers continue to reap rewards in personal relationships, the work world, and the public sphere.[4] However, effective public speakers in the 21st century not only must communicate in face-to-face settings like the orators in ancient Greek and Rome, but also do so through and with various technologies.

Certainly, the formal study of public speaking equips us to give effective presentations; however, the process of preparing these speeches also teaches us not *what* to think but *how* to think—a central skill for responsible citizens in the sound-bite–saturated, image-managed, technology-flooded, politically divisive information world in which we live. We must carefully consider why we think a certain topic is important for our audience. We must critically evaluate the credibility, validity, and reliability of the information we collect. We must thoughtfully organize our ideas and choose words that will be both clear and compelling. In face-to-face settings, we must perceptively adjust to the nonverbal reactions of our audience members as we speak to ensure they are getting the meaning we intend. When delivering our messages virtually, we must devise alternative ways to check for mutual understanding, such as live tweeting. Learning to think critically as we prepare and present our own speeches also equips us to analyze the messages offered by others, enhancing our ability to critically evaluate their information and arguments, identify reasoning flaws, and recognize unethical communication practices.

Photo 1.1 Public speaking is a civic right in democracies. In what ways can you demonstrate ethics as you exercise your civic right to speak publicly about issues important to you?

The Power of Public Speaking

Effective public speaking is empowering. First, public speaking skills empower us to participate in democratic processes. Free speech is a hallmark of democracy. The policies a democratic government adopts are a direct result of the debates that occur across the nation: in living rooms, over pizza at the local hangout, on blogs and social networking sites, in the media, and in the executive, legislative, and judicial branches of government. Effective public speaking skills give us the confidence to voice our ideas on important public issues.

Second, public speaking skills empower us to communicate our ideas and opinions in ways that all audience members can understand. Most of us have had an unfortunate experience with a teacher who "talked over our heads." The teacher understood the material but was unable to express it clearly to us. When we can express our ideas clearly, we are more likely to share them. When others understand our ideas, they learn from us.

Third, public speaking skills empower us to persuade others. We can convince others to agree with us or to take action regarding important issues ranging from personal (e.g., practicing a heart-healthy diet) to local (e.g., supporting a local nonprofit) to global (e.g., climate change or violent extremism terrorism).

Fourth, public speaking skills empower us to achieve our career goals. Research shows that, for almost any job, one of the most highly sought-after skills in new hires is oral communication skills.[5] So, whether you aspire to a career in business, industry, government, the arts, or education, good communication skills are a prerequisite to your success. Certainly, Dominic, Diana, and Chen Chen (from the chapter opener) will have to draw upon their public speaking skills to prepare their speeches. Jediah will also need to do so as he prepares the "job talk" he will deliver via videoconference.

The Ethical Responsibilities of Public Speaking

Ethics are a set of moral principles held by a society, group, or individual that differentiate right from wrong. In other words, ethics reflect what we believe we "ought to" and "ought not to" think and do. Ethical communication involves both speaking

ethics: moral principles that a society, group, or individual hold that differentiate right from wrong

and listening. As audience members, we expect speakers to behave ethically. Likewise, as speakers, we expect audience members to behave ethically. Five generally agreed-upon ethical standards for public speaking are honesty, integrity, fairness, respect, and responsibility. Let's look at how public speakers and listeners meet each of these responsibilities.

plagiarize: presenting the ideas, words, or created works of another as one's own by failing to credit the source

cyberplagiarism: presenting material found on the Internet as one's own by failing to credit the source

1. **Ethical communicators are honest.** In other words, ethical communicators tell the truth in ways that demonstrate empathy for others. To do so, effective public speakers research a topic carefully and accurately present all sides of controversial issues. In addition, honest speakers do not **plagiarize** by presenting others' ideas as their own. Instead, they properly credit the ideas of others they use in their speech. Sadly, surveys conducted in countries around the world report plagiarism on the rise among college students; much of this comes from students who fail to reference material they find on the Internet, something we now refer to as **cyberplagiarism**.[6] As a result, many college and university instructors now use plagiarism-detection software programs regularly when grading student work. Here are some tips to remember so you don't plagiarize unintentionally:

   - If you change a few words at the beginning, in the middle, or at the end of material, but copy much of the rest and don't cite the source of the information, you are plagiarizing.

   - If you completely paraphrase the unique ideas of another person and do not credit that person, you are plagiarizing.

   - If you purchase, borrow, or use a speech or essay in part or in whole that was prepared by another and present it as original, you are plagiarizing.[7]

   Ethical listeners are expected to give honest feedback in a tactful way. This includes their nonverbal expressions of attention, questions and comments they offer after the speech, and written critiques they might follow up with later.[8]

2. **Ethical communicators act with integrity.** In other words, ethical communicators "practice what they preach." The person who says, "Do what I say, not what I do," lacks integrity. For example, a speaker who implores listeners to quit smoking and then goes outside and lights up lacks integrity. A listener who espouses the importance of civility but then interrupts and heckles speakers lacks integrity.

3. **Ethical communicators behave fairly.** Fair communicators attempt to act impartially and acknowledge any potential bias they might have regarding a topic. For speakers, behaving fairly means researching and accurately reporting all sides of an issue. For listeners, it means considering all of the evidence a speaker presents, even when that evidence contradicts the listeners' beliefs.

4. **Ethical communicators demonstrate respect.** Behaving respectfully means showing regard for others, including their point of view, their rights, and their feelings. Speakers show respect for their audience by choosing language and humor that is inclusive and not offensive. Listeners demonstrate respect by giving their undivided attention to the speaker. For example, it is disrespectful to send or read texts/emails, use Facebook or other social media, or in any other way "multitask" during a speech.

5. **Ethical communicators are responsible.** Responsible communicators recognize the power of words. So ethical speakers only advocate for things that they believe are in the best interest of audience members. Similarly, ethical listeners critically evaluate the positions that speakers advocate and do not blindly accept positions that may not be in their best interest (Photo 1.2).

Photo 1.2 Ethical communicators act with integrity by "practicing what they preach." Leonardo DiCaprio, an avid environmentalist, shows up at Hollywood events on a bicycle and lives in a green home powered by solar energy. What is an example of how *you* act with integrity in your daily life?

Throughout this book, we elaborate on how these ethical communication principles should guide you as you both present and listen to speeches. We also challenge you to reflect on the ethical choices presented in each chapter's feature, "Reflect on Ethics."

PUBLIC SPEAKING AS COMMUNICATION

Because public speaking is a specialized type of communication, to become effective public speakers, we need to understand what communication is. **Communication** is the process of creating shared meaning. To understand how the communication process works, let's look at its essential elements: participants, messages, feedback, channels, interference/noise, and contexts/settings.

Participants

Participants are the individuals who assume the roles of senders and receivers during an interaction (see Exhibit 1.1). As **senders**, participants form and transmit messages using verbal symbols (words), nonverbal behaviors, and, sometimes, visual images. **Receivers** interpret the messages sent by others. Although all participants act as both senders and receivers, in public speaking contexts, one participant acts primarily as sender and presents an extended message to which other participants listen, interpret, and provide feedback. So when Dominic presents his training workshop, he will act as the sender and his coworkers will be the receivers. And when Jediah presents his online "job talk," he will act as the sender and the interviewers observing the videoconference will be the receivers.

Messages

Messages are the verbal utterances, visual images, and nonverbal behaviors used to communicate. We refer to the process of creating messages as **encoding** and the process of interpreting them as **decoding**. In public speaking situations, messages are typically speeches that are prepared beforehand and presented by one participant.

communication: the process of creating shared meaning

participants: individuals who assume the roles of senders and receivers during an interaction

senders: participants who form and transmit messages

receivers: participants who interpret messages sent by others

messages: the verbal utterances, visual images, and nonverbal behaviors used to communicate

encoding: the process of creating messages

decoding: the process of interpreting messages

1.1 Model of Communication

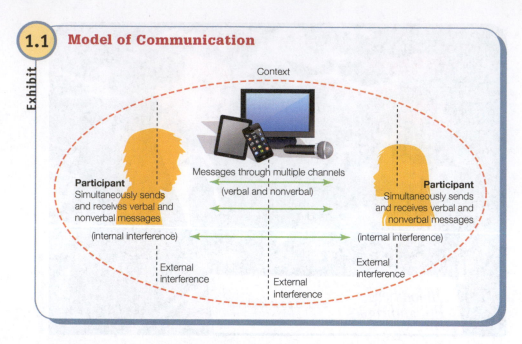

Context

Messages through multiple channels
(verbal and nonverbal)

Participant
Simultaneously sends
and receives verbal and
nonverbal messages

(internal interference)

External
interference

Participant
Simultaneously sends
and receives verbal and
nonverbal messages

(internal interference)

External
interference

External
interference

---

feedback: the receivers'
reactions and responses that
indicate how a message is
interpreted

channels: both the route
traveled by a message and
the means of transportation

mediated channels:
technology-enhanced
auditory and visual channels

virtual presence: simulated
presence made possible
through the use of digital
technology

interference/noise: any
stimulus that interferes with
the process of achieving
shared meaning

> **SPEECH SNIPPET**
>
> Jediah practiced his
> videoconference in
> advance for his mother
> back in his hometown.
> He was glad he did
> because he realized there
> was sometimes a delay
> in getting feedback. He
> made a note to himself
> where to pause for a
> moment to try to account
> for this challenge.

Feedback

Feedback consists of the messages sent by receivers to let the sender know how the message is being interpreted. We can express feedback verbally or nonverbally. When audiences listen to a speech, usually most of the feedback is nonverbal. So as Dominic conducts his workshop, he observes the facial expressions of his coworkers for feedback about whether his message is making sense. He also periodically stops and asks for feedback in the form of actual questions.

Channels

Channels are both the route traveled by a message and the means of transportation. We send and receive messages primarily through auditory (speaking and hearing) and visual (seeing) channels. Sometimes these channels are enhanced by technology. We call these technology-enhanced auditory and visual (or audiovisual) channels **mediated channels**. Chen Chen, Dominic, and Diana send and receive verbal and nonverbal messages when they speak in a face-to-face setting. Jediah's videoconferencing software allows him and his presentational aids to be both seen and heard, even though he is not physically present in the room with his interviewers. This software also allows him to see his interviewers' feedback on the computer screen as he speaks. We call this phenomenon of simulated presence made possible through the use of digital technology **virtual presence**.

Interference/Noise

Interference, also referred to as **noise**, is any stimulus that interferes with the process of achieving shared meaning. Noise can be physical or psychological. *Physical* noise is any external sight or sound that distracts us from the message. For example, when someone enters the room or a cell phone goes off while a speaker is talking, or when we get an email or Facebook update while listening to a speaker online, we might be distracted from the message. *Psychological* noise refers to the thoughts and feelings we experience that compete with the sender's message for our attention. So when we daydream about what we have to do at work today or feel offended when a speaker uses foul language, we are being distracted by psychological noise.

Reflect on Ethics

CELEBRITY CHEF CONCOCTS IMPRESSIVE PAST

Celebrity chef Robert Irvine went to St. Petersburg, Florida, in 2007 with a plan to turn it into "the next Monaco." He claimed to be a royal knight and asked to be introduced as Sir Robert Irvine. He said he owned a castle in Scotland and had cooked for presidents and royalty.[9]

However, it's difficult to separate fact from fiction when it comes to "Sir" Robert Irvine. What is known to be true is that he is an excellent chef, and he starred on the Food Network's *Dinner: Impossible* series until July 20, 2008, when he was replaced by *Iron Chef America's* Michael Symon amidst a controversy about assertions Irvine had made in his biography as posted on the Food Network website. For example, Irvine claimed:

- he had a BS degree in food and nutrition from the University of Leeds. Officials from the University of Leeds have no record of Irvine having been a student there.

- to have worked on the wedding cake for Prince Charles and Princess Diana. He was at the school where the cake was made, but did he actually help make it? Does "picking fruit and things like that" count?

- he received several Five Star Diamond Awards from the American Academy of Hospitality Sciences. The "academy" is actually housed in a Manhattan apartment, and recipients pay for the honor.

- he was a royal knight. According to Jenn Stebbing, press officer at Buckingham Palace, "He is not a KCVO [Knight Commander of the Royal Victorian Order] and he wasn't given a castle by the queen of England." Irvine now admits that was a lie.

- to have trained White House military cooks and served presidents and heads of state. White House spokespersons claim he has never had anything to do with planning, preparing, or serving at any public or private White House food function.

The Food Network rehired Irvine in November 2008, and he continued to host the program through its eighth season, which ended in 2010. Irvine currently hosts *Restaurant: Impossible*. His newest book is *Fit Fuel*. Although the "facts" about Irvine's past remain unclear, his career does not seem to have suffered any negative consequences as a result of the controversy.

1. Did Irvine violate any ethical communication principles, and, if so, how?

2. When, if ever, is it OK to stretch the truth about your qualifications?

Contexts/Settings

Communication context refers to the environment in which communication occurs.[10] Communication contexts differ based on the number of participants and the balance of roles among them.[11] Let's briefly look at four of these.

1. **Intrapersonal communication**, also referred to as self-talk, is communicating with yourself. Usually this is done by thinking through choices, strategies, and the possible consequences of taking action. When you sit in class and consider what you'll have for dinner tonight, you are communicating intrapersonally. Much of our intrapersonal communication occurs subconsciously.[12] When we drive into the driveway "without thinking," we're communicating intrapersonally but at a subconscious level. When we give a speech and notice confused looks on listeners' faces, we might communicate intrapersonally as we recognize the need to rephrase our explanation.

2. **Interpersonal communication** is communication between two people who have an identifiable relationship with each other.[13] Talking with a friend on the sidewalk between classes, visiting on the phone with your mother, and texting or chatting online with a family member or friend are all examples of interpersonal communication. Interpersonal communication sometimes occurs in a public speech setting when, during a question-and-answer session, a speaker directs remarks to one audience member.

communication context: the environment in which communication occurs

intrapersonal communication: communicating with yourself (self-talk)

interpersonal communication: communication between two people who have an identifiable relationship with each other

3. **Small group communication** typically occurs with approximately three to ten people.[14] Examples of small groups include a family, a group of friends, a group of classmates working together on a class project, and a management team in the workplace.[15] Some research suggests there are more small groups in the United States than there are people. Small group communication occurs in a public speech setting when a team is asked to work together to research, prepare, and deliver a presentation on a particular topic.

4. **Public communication** occurs with more than ten people by one primary sender to multiple receivers. This communication may occur face-to-face or via mediated, technology-driven channels. One form of public communication is **mass communication**, which is communication produced and transmitted via mass media to large segments of the population. Examples include newspapers, magazines, books, blogs, listservs, TV programs, movies, websites, Facebook posts, and Twitter feeds, as well as Tumblr, Instagram, Snapchat, and YouTube posts. Another form is public speaking, which is a sustained, formal, oral presentation delivered to an audience that is typically physically present at the time. As technology and media become increasingly accessible, however, the lines between mass communication and public speaking are blurring (Photo 1.3). For example, when the president gives a State of the Union address, some people are there, others watch on TV or stream the address over the Internet, and still others view it later in the form of televised snippets or as a website video (e.g., YouTube).

Photo 1.3 Thanks to the technology explosion, the distinction between mass communication and public speaking is becoming blurred. When have *you* engaged in public speaking via a technology (mass communication) channel?

Fabrizio Costantini/The New York/Redux Pictures

AUDIENCE-CENTERED SPEAKING AND THE RHETORICAL SITUATION

The discipline of communication as a formal field of study in colleges and universities is fairly young.[16] The study and practice of public speaking, however, has a long and rich history dating back more than 2,000 years to ancient Greek (e.g., Aristotle and Plato) and Roman (e.g., Cicero and Isocrates) philosophers. They were, in fact, the ones who coined the terms *rhetoric* and *oratory* to describe the processes of preparing, presenting, and critiquing public speeches.

Fundamental to public speaking then and now is *audience*. The ancient Greek philosopher, teacher, and public speaker Aristotle is often credited with claiming, "The audience is the end and object of the speech."[17] What he meant was that the eloquence of your words is irrelevant if the words are not heard by, are not understood by, or do not affect the people to whom you are speaking. Frankly, whether conveyed in written, oral, or visual form, or some combination of them, and whether delivered in a face-to-face setting or via a mediated channel, a message is only effective if it is understood and internalized by the people being addressed. Today, we recognize that the effectiveness of any speech depends not just on understanding the audience but also on how well the message addresses the entire rhetorical situation. Let's turn now to a discussion of the rhetorical situation generally and then to the specific effective speech principles of content, structure, and delivery.

The Rhetorical Situation

The **rhetorical situation** is the intersection of the speaker, audience, and occasion. Exhibit 1.2 illustrates the rhetorical situation in a Venn diagram. As you can see, the rhetorical situation is the place where the speaker, audience, and occasion overlap. Lloyd Bitzer, the rhetorical scholar who introduced the concept of the rhetorical situation, believed that the particular speech given by an individual to an audience on a specific occasion is also the result of some real or perceived specific need that a speech might help address.[18] Bitzer referred to this as the **exigence**.[19] According to the Encarta dictionary, *exigence* is "something that a situation demands or makes urgently necessary and that puts pressure on the people involved."[20]

On December 14, 2012, a lone gunman charged into Sandy Hook Elementary School in Newtown, Connecticut, and massacred 26 defenseless children and adults before killing himself. This unfathomable heinous mass murder of innocent children created an exigence that led many people to speak out about the dire need to do something, ranging from tightening gun control laws to arming teachers to increasing support for mental health care facilities to banning violent video games. In the United States, from President Obama's televised speeches to simple calls to action heard in classrooms across the country to thousands of Facebook posts, Twitter feeds, blogs, vlogs, and YouTube videos, individuals felt compelled to speak out and do something to help the families of the victims and to stop school violence.

The massacre created an exigence that motivated speakers to seek an occasion and audience where a speech they would give could help accomplish positive change. For example:

- high school senior Perry Rockwood gave a 10-minute speech at a schoolwide assembly urging fellow classmates to purchase bracelets for $1, with the money to be donated to Sandy Hook. He also asked his classmates to wear the bracelets as a visual memorial of solidarity throughout the school. And he encouraged them to engage in 26 acts of kindness toward others in an attempt to change the way they perceive and interact with one another.

- Newtown, Connecticut, community members were also motivated to form a grassroots organization called the Sandy Hook Promise (SHP), which they

rhetorical situation: the intersection of the speaker, audience, and occasion

exigence: a real or perceived specific need that a speech might help address

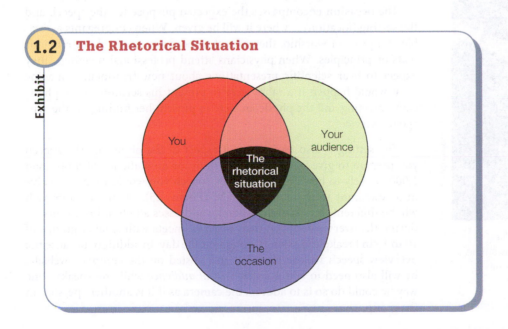

Exhibit 1.2 The Rhetorical Situation

You

Your audience

The rhetorical situation

The occasion

announced in public speeches at the Edmund Town Hall on January 13, 2013. The mission of SHP is to bring people together all over the world to do everything we can to "encourage and support common sense solutions to make [our] communit[ies] and our country safer from similar acts of violence."[21]

- Similarly, Jeremy Anthony, a high school junior in Iowa City, wanted to shift focus from the negative things that happen in school to the positive. So he started a Twitter feed (@westhighbros) as a place to post uplifting messages and compliments to encourage others.

As time passes, exigence may diminish or even disappear as an issue is resolved or the perception of it as demanding an urgent response wanes. In the case of Sandy Hook, the topics it brought to the forefront continue to be the subject of much debate in politics, in the media, in classrooms, and in living rooms. Sandy Hook Promise Facebook pages, Twitter feeds, and TV public service announcements, as well as political campaign platforms, serve as evidence of the issue's ongoing exigence.

The **speaker** is the originator of the speech. As the speaker, what you discuss, and how well you do so will depend on your interests, beliefs, background, and public speaking skills. You will choose topics that you care about, know something about, and want to inform or persuade others about. Dominic, for example, will be training his coworkers to use the new purchase order requisition submission and tracking program based on personal knowledge he gained earlier. Diana will share stories about her grandmother, someone she knew well and loved dearly, in ways that will likely lead her audience to feel warmly about her grandmother.

The **audience** is the specific group of people to whom the speech is directed. **Audience analysis** is the study of the diverse characteristics of the intended audience members and **audience adaptation** is the process of tailoring the message to address exigence in terms of the audience's unique interests, needs, and expectations. For example, organizers of benefit concerts today recognize that many audience members are tech savvy, so they appeal for donations online and via text messages in addition to staffing toll-free phone lines (Photo 1.4).

The **occasion** encompasses the expected purpose for the speech and the **setting** (location) is where it will be given. When congregants assemble at a place of worship, they expect to hear a message about religious texts or principles. When physicians attend professional meetings, they expect to hear scientific presentations about new treatments. Imagine what would happen if a rabbi were to present his sermon to the physicians' meeting and the physician were to present her findings at the synagogue service!

The setting is also an important aspect of the occasion. The speech you prepare to give in a large auditorium for an audience of more than 1,000 is likely to be different than the speech you would prepare to give in a restaurant to an audience of 20 (Photo 1.5). Dominic's approach will be different, for example, when he addresses all 60 of his coworkers during the overview session than when he meets with smaller groups of 10 to 15 in breakout sessions throughout the day. In addition, because the overview speech will be recorded and posted on the company website, he will also need to address that *virtual audience* while he speaks. One way he could do so is to address the camera as if it is another "person" in the group.

speaker: the originator of the speech

audience: the specific group of people to whom the speech is directed

audience analysis: the study of the intended audience for your speech

audience adaptation: the process of tailoring a speech to the needs, interests, and expectations of its listeners

occasion: the expected purpose of and setting (location) for the speech

setting: the location where the speech will be given

Photo 1.4 Many fundraising drives make their appeals for donations online or via texts. What organizations have appealed for support from you via such technologies?

Photo 1.5 Speakers tailor their speech to adapt to the size of the audience. What are some ways this speaker should adapt to this large audience?

Although effective speeches are tailored to address audience exigence, they do so in ways that adhere to the overlapping elements and constraints of the entire rhetorical situation. Now let's consider how effective public speakers tailor their addresses via the primary components of effective speeches: content, structure, and delivery.

EFFECTIVE SPEECH COMPONENTS

When we give a speech, our goal is to create and achieve shared meaning with our audience members. We do so through the rhetorical appeals of ethos, pathos, and logos.[22] **Ethos** includes everything we say and do to convey competence and good character. Dressing appropriately, being poised as we speak, citing credible sources, and speaking within the time parameters allotted, for instance, convey ethos. **Pathos** consists of everything we say and do to appeal to emotions, which can range from negative emotions such as fear or dread to positive emotions such as adventure or joy. **Logos** includes everything we say and do to appeal to logic and sound reasoning. Essentially, effective speeches use ethos, pathos, and logos in content, structure, and delivery.

Content

Content comprises the information and ideas you present. It includes your speech's purpose and main points as well as the evidence and reasoning used to develop each main idea. Evidence consists of all the facts, examples, and other supporting material you include to help explain your main ideas. Evidence can come from your own experiences as well as from research materials you collect.

Effective evidence has sufficient breadth and depth. *Breadth* refers to the amount and types of evidence you use. *Depth* is the level of detail you provide from each piece of evidence. Evidence is effective when it is logically linked to the main idea it supports. The ideas you choose to present depend on what is appropriate for

ethos: everything you say and do to convey competence and good character

pathos: everything you say and do to appeal to emotions

logos: everything you say and do to appeal to logic and sound reasoning

content: the information and ideas you present

listener relevance links: statement alerting listeners about how a main point or subpoint is relevant to them

your audience and the occasion. You adapt your content so that it includes **listener relevance links**, which are statements alerting listeners about how a main point or subpoint is relevant to them. Doing so makes the exigence of your ideas transparent. Diana's purpose was to praise her grandmother's attributes. She decided to focus on two main values her grandmother both preached and practiced: a positive attitude and perseverance. She planned to begin each main point with a listener relevance statement about the universal nature of her grandmother's values. She would then develop each main point with several brief examples to provide breadth and one more detailed story to add depth.

Structure

structure: the framework that organizes the speech content

macrostructure: the overall organizational framework of your speech content

Structure is the framework that organizes the speech content. Clear structure helps listeners follow your ideas as they listen. Effective structure consists of both macrostructure and microstructure elements. **Macrostructure** is the overall organizational framework used to present your speech content. Effective macrostructure comprises four elements: the introduction, body, conclusion, and transitions. You may not realize it, but you have already studied macrostructure—you use it when you write formal papers for school. Now you will learn how to adapt what you have already learned to formal oral messages.

Careful attention to macrostructure is even more important when you craft a speech than when you write an essay. A reader can easily reread a poorly written essay to try to understand the author's intent, but an audience does not usually have the opportunity to listen to a speech again, unless it is being recorded and posted to an accessible website. Your introduction should build audience interest in your topic and preview your main points (tell them what you are going to tell them). Your speech body should contain the main ideas and supporting material used to develop each one (tell them). Your conclusion should remind the audience of your main ideas and motivate them to remember what you have said (tell them what you told them). Speech macrostructure also includes **transitions**—words, phrases, or sentences that bridge two ideas.

transition: words, phrases, or sentences that bridge two ideas

microstructure: the specific language and style you use within your sentences

Whereas macrostructure is the overall framework for your speech, **microstructure** is the specific language and style you use within your sentences. Effective speeches are understandable and memorable when speakers use appropriate, accurate, clear, and vivid language, as well as rhetorical style devices such as alliteration, onomatopoeia, personification, similes, metaphors, and analogies.

Delivery

delivery: communicating through the use of voice and body to convey your message

Delivery—how you use your voice and body to convey your message—can dramatically affect your audience's ability to understand, remember, and possibly act on your message. Effective speakers are conversational, intelligible, poised, and expressive in their delivery. Being conversational means sounding as though you are having a spontaneous conversation with your audience, rather than simply reading to or performing in front of them. Intelligible speakers use a rate, volume, and pitch that are easily understood. If you are speaking in a second language or have a pronounced accent or a speech impediment, you might find that speaking somewhat slower improves your intelligibility. (See "Public Speaking in the Real World" to learn how Oscar-winning actress Julia Roberts learned to manage her tendency to stutter.) Poised speakers stand confidently without fidgeting, swaying, or using any other potentially distracting bodily action. Being poised also means making eye contact with your audience members in face-to-face settings, or with the camera when delivering ideas via mass media, rather than focusing solely on your notes. Being expressive means changing your pitch, volume, rate, and so forth to emphasize the emotional intent of your ideas. Generally, you

Kevin Mazur/WireImage/Getty Images

PUBLIC SPEAKING IN THE REAL WORLD

Julia and Eric Roberts Overcome Their Childhood Stutter

Julia Roberts is an Oscar-winning actress, but what few know about her is that she was born with a genetic predisposition to stutter. Both Julia and her brother Eric, who is also an actor, appear on the Stuttering Foundation of America's (SFA) list of "Famous People Who Stutter." According to SFA, over three million Americans stutter.[23] However, stuttering can be managed effectively with the help of speech therapy and does not need to limit your intelligibility or success when speaking in public. Certainly, Julia and her brother Eric serve as evidence of that, and they are not alone. Other actors who once stuttered and went on to lead successful lives in fields where public speaking skills are paramount include James Earl Jones, Bruce Willis, Marilyn Monroe, and Emily Blunt. What do they suggest doing to reduce stuttering and increase intelligibility? (1) Slow down your thoughts and think about what you are saying now rather than three or four sentences ahead. (2) Read out loud and even in front of a mirror where you can watch yourself as others will see you. (3) When you stumble, remember that everyone makes mistakes. Stop and then simply start again. As former basketball star, sportscaster, and SFA spokesperson Bill Walton says, "It's what you do after those mistakes that will determine your ultimate success."[24]

1. What are some speaking challenges you deal with or have dealt with?

2. What strategies, if any, have you used to help you overcome them?

want to sound a bit more dramatic than you would in casual conversation. For example, you might speak more quickly or loudly to underscore your emotional convictions or to stress key words or phrases, or you might pause strategically to call attention to important ideas. Being expressive also means using appropriate facial expressions to reflect your conviction about the topic and gestures to reinforce important points.

What follows is an outline of Diana's speech of tribute to her grandmother with commentary. As you read, consider how you might address the rhetorical situation effectively as you develop the content and structure, as well as practice the delivery, of your speech. Then, answer these questions about Diana's content and structure.

1. **Content:** What are Diana's main points? What kinds of evidence does she use to support them? What are some examples of breadth, depth, and listener relevance in the body of her speech?

2. **Structure:** What does Diana do to get the attention of her listeners? What does she say to lead listeners from one main point to the next? How does she provide a sense of closure and motivate listeners to remember the speech? What wording seems to demonstrate inclusion, provide clarity, and evoke vivid images?

Speech Assignment & Checklist

Speech of Personal Significance

Prepare a 2- to 3-minute speech about a hero in your life. Offer two or three main points about the values that person holds that you admire and why. Offer specific personal examples and stories to support each of your main points. Use Diana's speech outline as a guide to help you prepare, as well as the Speech Evaluation Checklist that follows as you practice, to make sure your speech includes all the elements of an effective speech.

Speech Evaluation Checklist

General Criteria

You can use this checklist to critique a speech you hear in class. (You can also use it to critique your own speech.)

Content

_____ 1. Were all main points addressed per the assignment?

_____ 2. Were two to three pieces of evidence provided for each main point (breadth)?

_____ 3. Was one extended piece of evidence provided for each main point (depth)?

_____ 4. Were listener relevance links provided for each main point?

_____ 5. Did the speech fall within the time constraints of the assignment?

Structure

1. Did the speech provide all the basic elements (*macrostructure*) of an effective speech: introduction, body, conclusion, and transitions? _____

2. Did the introduction catch the audience's interest? _____ identify the speech topic/goal? _____ preview the main points? _____

3. Were transitions provided between each main point? _____

4. Did the conclusion remind the audience of the main points? _____ motivate the audience to remember the main ideas of the speech? _____

5. Did the speaker use words (*microstructure*) that were appropriate and inclusive? _____ accurate and clear? _____ vivid and expressive? _____

Delivery

1. Was the speaker intelligible in terms of volume? _____ rate? _____ pronunciation? _____ enunciation? _____

2. Was the speaker conversational? _____

3. Did the speaker look up from his or her notes most of the time and make eye contact with the audience? _____

4. Did the speaker appear professional, poised, and confident? _____

5. Was the speaker expressive in term of changes in rate and volume? _____ strategic pauses? _____ appropriate facial expressions? _____ appropriate gestures? _____

DIANA'S EULOGY

Grandma Frances: My Hero

Preparation Outline

Notice how Diana's preparation outline doesn't necessarily use complete sentences and that some elements still need to be developed. However, it does give a basic structure for the main points and supporting material she will use in the speech. In a sense, a preparation outline serves as a rough draft of the speech.

INTRODUCTION

I. (maybe ask audience members who they consider heroes) — **Attention getter**

II. We all have/need heroes (role models). — **Listener relevance and speaker credibility**

III. I have known Grandma Frances my entire life and even lived with her for three summers.

IV. — **Thesis statement**

V. Today we are going to talk about my hero, Grandma Frances. (positive attitude and perseverance) — **Main point preview**

BODY

I. Modeled a positive attitude — **First main point**

   A. link attitude to improved physical and mental health — **Listener relevance**

   B. Share story about grandma's positive attitude when we went on a fishing trip to Canada.

   (I still need to figure this out. Something like this: Now that you understand how my grandma modeled a positive attitude, let's talk about her perseverance, both within herself and in encouraging me to persevere.) — **Transition**

II. Perseverance and encouragement

   A. Talk about perseverance as a cultural norm in the United States. — **Listener relevance**

   B. Share the story about grandma's vocabulary.

   C. Share the story about singing with my brothers.

CONCLUSION

I. Now you know why my Grandma Frances is my hero. — **Thesis restatement**

II. Her positive attitude and perseverance — **Main point summary**

III. (I still need to figure this out.) — **Clincher**

Formal Outline

INTRODUCTION

I. [Show slide of several well-known superheroes from popular culture.] What makes someone a hero? Do you have any? Who are they and why do you consider them heroes? — **Attention getter**

Notice how Diana uses a series of questions to pique curiosity, then motivates listeners by addressing listener relevance before previewing the main points.

II. A simple definition of a hero is someone who is admired for noble qualities. So a hero doesn't have to be someone famous. — **Listener relevance and credibility**

Based on this definition, I bet most of us in this room can identify at least one hero, one person we admire and look up to. When I think of my heroes, one important person always comes to mind: my Grandma Frances. [show slide of photograph of Grandma Frances]

Thesis statement with main point preview

III. In the next few minutes, let's talk about my Grandma Frances as a hero who taught me by her example of how to maintain a positive attitude and to persevere through good times and bad.

BODY

First main point

I. I consider Grandma Frances a hero because she modeled a positive attitude in all situations.

Subpoints (listener relevance)
Diana provides listener relevance by pointing out how a positive attitude can actually make us healthier.

   A. We all want to be happy and healthy. Did you know that study after study shows a direct link between a positive attitude and improved mental and physical health? Who wouldn't want that?

Subpoints
Here Diana provides a detailed story to provide depth in terms of content.

   B. When it came to having a positive attitude, Grandma Frances was a "rock star." You couldn't get to her.

      1. One story that really shows how grandma would "turn lemons into lemonade" with a smile on her face the whole time occurred one summer when I was about 9 years old and my parents and two brothers joined grandma and grandpa on a week-long fishing expedition in Canada. [show slide of our family just before leaving for the trip]

      2. As we packed for the trip, grandpa announced that we wouldn't need to pack food because we were going to eat what we caught and really live off the land (or in this case off the water, I suppose). I don't know whether grandpa knew it at the time, but grandma packed a few things just to be safe. With that, we headed out on our family fishing adventure from our comfortable homes in central Minnesota to the rugged countryside of Saskatchewan, Canada.

      3. As luck would have it, we couldn't catch a fish to save our souls. We tried fishing early in the morning, throughout the day, and into the evening. We hired guides who took us to "secret spots" where they claimed we would be sure to catch fish. We had pretty much exhausted the food supplies Grandma Frances had packed, having just finished the last package of hot dogs. We wondered what we would eat for the next 4 days, as grandma was saving the water we had used to boil the franks. [show slide of kettle of water with one wiener in it.] When my mom asked Grandma Frances what she was doing with the water, grandma responded, "Well, we might need to make wiener water soup." So you see when I talk about grandma as an eternal optimist, I don't necessarily think about making lemonade from lemons, but I surely do think about making soup out of leftover wiener water.

      4. After doing the dishes, Grandma Frances said she was going to try her luck fishing right off the dock. No one from our group had tried fishing from the dock because we were told that nobody catches anything that way. Well, all I can say is they didn't know my Grandma Frances! When the fish started biting for grandma, the whole family joined her catching our limit right off the dock. In fact, we caught so many fish for the next three days that we ate fish for every meal and still came home from our adventure with coolers full. [show slide of our family holding a stringer of fish standing on the dock]

TRANSITION

A good transition statement can be as simple as Diana's is here. It works because it reminds listeners of the main point she just finished talking about—a positive attitude—and introduces the next one—perseverance.

> *Not only do I consider grandma a hero for teaching me to have a positive attitude but also for teaching me to persevere.*

II. Grandma Frances was always doing things that demonstrated her will to persevere and encouraging me to do so, as well.

    A. Throughout our lives, most of us have been inundated with messages—about the importance of believing in ourselves and persevering, whether from children's stories like *The Little Engine That Could*, songs like "I Will Survive," movies like *Rocky*, or even symbols like Nike's "Just Do It" brand [show slide of the Nike symbol]. In fact, perseverance could even be considered a cultural norm about how we ought to live.

    B. One way Grandma Frances taught me the value of perseverance was through modeling what to do when people discouraged her. When people made fun of her for using unusual words as way to improve her vocabulary, she didn't let it get to her. She kept on doing so. For example, she would do the crossword puzzle in the newspaper every day and then use at least two words she learned doing it in conversation that day. I remember one time she used an unfamiliar word and her friends responded by teasing her with a made up word: "polly-go." Grandma Frances just smiled and kept on doing puzzles and using new words every day.

    C. Another way Grandma Frances taught the value of perseverance was by encouraging me when others discouraged me. One example that stands out happened when I was in grade school. As many of you know, I come from a family of singers, and one time my brothers and I were singing. I guess I didn't hit all the right notes, and I recall a family member saying my brothers were really good singers, but I didn't seem to have the "gene." Grandma responded with "she just has a smaller range right now. It will get larger as she gets older." I never forgot what Grandma Frances said. I kept singing and practicing and luckily for my music professors in college and the kids I work with in the choirs I direct now, my range did expand. I sometimes wonder about what I would be doing today if I would have listened to the discouragers rather than Grandma Frances.

CONCLUSION

  I. We all have heroes we admire for their noble qualities. Grandma Frances, who taught me the value of a positive attitude and perseverance, was my hero.

  II. [Show slide again of superheroes from popular culture] Grandma Frances may not be able to fly through the air like Superman, scale buildings like Spider-Man, or even wield a Lasso of Truth like Wonder Woman, but she will always be a superhero to me.

Second main point

Supporting material (listener relevance)

Supporting material

Supporting material

Thesis restatement and main point review
Notice how quickly Diana reviews her thesis and main points in one short sentence.

Main point review and clincher
Diana does a nice job of clinching by tying her closing back to her attention getter in a meaningful way.

Speaking Outline Note Cards

Speaking outlines are brief notes that remind you of main points, macrostructure, and delivery cues when you speak. Sometimes speakers use the "notes" feature on PowerPoint slideshows, but using a few 3" × 5" index cards (below) is preferred because it affords a better opportunity for eye contact with the audience. Notice how few notes Diana uses for her speech.

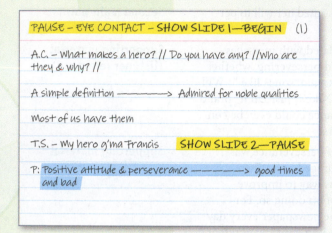

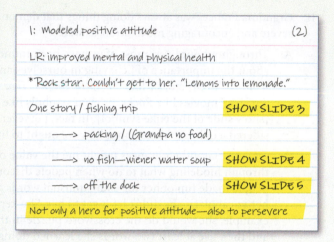

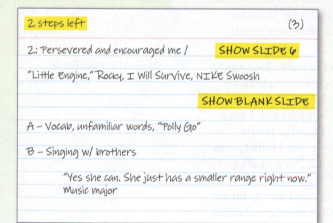

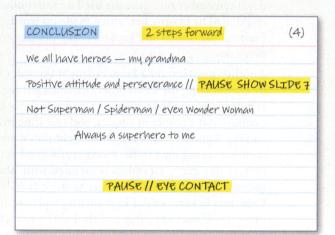

Reflection and Assessment

Public speaking is important to achieving success in nearly every walk of life. Effective public speaking makes it possible to enact our civic engagement responsibility actively and ethically. To assess how well you've learned what we've discussed in this chapter, answer the following questions. If you have trouble answering any of them, go back and review that material. Once you can answer each question accurately, you are ready to move ahead to the next chapter.

1. Why is technology so important to effective public speaking today?
2. What is the nature of public speaking as a liberal art? What are your ethical responsibilities in public speaking?
3. What is communication and how is public speaking a form of it?
4. What is the rhetorical situation and how can it help you determine an appropriate speech goal?
5. What are the components of an effective audience-centered public speech?

Challenge Resource and Assessment Center

MindTap®

Now that you have read Chapter 1, go to your MindTap Communication for *The Challenge of Effective Speaking in a Digital Age* for quick access to flashcards, chapter quizzes, and more.

Applying What You've Learned

1. **Impromptu Speech Activity:** Identify one of your heroes. Your hero may or may not be famous. Identify one of the five ethical principles your hero's life adheres to and why. In your 2- to 3-minute impromptu speech, provide at least two incidents that serve as evidence regarding how this person demonstrates/demonstrated the principle.
2. **Assessment Activity A:** Visit Facebook. If you don't have an account, you might make one to observe while completing this course. Read through the postings on the "news feed" and identify which of them adhere to and do not adhere to the ethical communication principles proposed in this chapter.
3. **Assessment Activity B:** Visit a local retail store in a nearby mall. Spend time observing what you see. Describe what you observe according to the elements of the rhetorical situation (occasion, speaker, audience). Do you think the sales clerk you observed was effective? Again, based on what you observed regarding the rhetorical situation, why or why not?

2

Your First Speech

WHAT'S THE POINT?

WHEN YOU'VE FINISHED THIS CHAPTER, YOU WILL BE ABLE TO:

- Describe the nature of public speaking apprehension
- Practice several public speaking apprehension management methods and techniques
- Identify the six steps in an effective speech action plan
- Employ the steps to prepare and present a speech of self-introduction

MindTap®

Review the chapter **Learning Objectives** and **Start** with quick warm-up activity.

Ethical communicators behave responsibly by thoroughly preparing and practicing their speeches.

Kira had been staring at the computer screen for over an hour. Every time she started to type some ideas for her self-introduction speech assignment, her heart would start to race and she would freeze with thoughts of fear. "What if my classmates think my speech is boring? What if I make a mistake and they laugh at me or think I'm stupid? I'm too shy to give a speech. I'm just not good at it. I'm sure my voice will crack. If I do get up the nerve to do this, I hope I don't faint." She thought about dropping the class, but it is a required course that she'd registered for and dropped twice already. She knew she would eventually have to complete this class, but in her mind it had no real value. "I'm certainly not planning to be a public speaker in real life." She couldn't ask any of her family members for advice. None of them went to college, so they had no experience with public speaking classes. She didn't want to admit to her friends that she was so terrified. She sighed, shut down her computer, and picked up a textbook for another class.

You might be thinking, "Poor Kira. If she's that nervous, her school should really let her opt out of the course." Or you might relate to Kira. You might even be thinking that people like you and Kira who suffer from severe public speaking apprehension—or stage fright—should not be put through such turmoil.

What you might not know, however, is that according to the National Institute of Mental Health, as many as 75 percent of us suffer from some speech anxiety.[1] For example, did you know that actors Meryl Streep, Hayden Panettiere, and Harrison Ford; singers Barbra Streisand and Adele; and evangelists Billy Graham and Joel Osteen all experience fear of public speaking? Yet all are effective public speakers because they employ strategies for managing their nervousness—strategies we will discuss in this chapter.

We begin by explaining the nature of public speaking apprehension. Then we discuss the causes and benefits–yes, *benefits*—of it. Finally, we propose several strategies for managing anxiety successfully. Perhaps most important is the role careful preparation plays in managing anxiety, which we'll describe by walking you through Kira's step-by-step process of preparing and practicing her speech of self-introduction.

UNDERSTANDING THE NATURE OF PUBLIC SPEAKING APPREHENSION

Glossophobia, which is the technical term for public speaking apprehension or speech anxiety, is simply the fear of public speaking. We may experience it before or while delivering a classroom speech, a workplace presentation, a wedding toast, or a job interview. To be honest, almost all of us have some level of public speaking apprehension, and about 15 percent of the US population experiences high levels of it.[2] However, even people with high levels of apprehension can be effective and confident public speakers. In fact, having some public speaking apprehension actually makes us better public speakers than having none at all. Why? Because these feelings are really signs of the adrenaline boost that helps us perform at our best. Just as an adrenaline boost helps athletes, musicians, and actors perform better, so can it also help us deliver better

glossophobia: the fear of public speaking

public speeches.[3] So, if you are lackadaisical about giving a speech, you probably will not do a good job.[4] Because at least some tension is constructive, the goal is not to eliminate nervousness but to learn how to manage it.[5]

Symptoms

The symptoms of public speaking apprehension vary from individual to individual and range from mild to debilitating. Symptoms can be cognitive, physical, or emotional. Cognitive symptoms include negative self-talk, which is also the most common cause of public speaking apprehension.[6] For example, a highly apprehensive person might do what Kira did in the opening vignette and dwell on thoughts such as "I'm going to make a fool of myself," or "I just know that I'll blow it." Physical symptoms may be stomach upset (or butterflies), flushed skin, sweating, shaking, light-headedness, rapid or pounding heartbeats, stuttering, and vocalized pauses ("like," "you know," "ah," "um"). Emotional symptoms include feeling anxious, worried, or upset.

Luckily, public speaking apprehension gradually decreases for most of us as we speak. Researchers have identified three phases we proceed through: anticipation, confrontation, and adaptation (see Exhibit 2.1).[7]

The *anticipation phase* is the anxiety we experience before giving the speech, both while preparing it and waiting to speak. The *confrontation phase* is the surge of anxiety we feel as we begin delivering the speech. The *adaptation phase* is the period during which our anxiety level gradually decreases. It typically begins about 1 minute into the presentation and tends to level off after about 5 minutes.[8] So, it's normal to be nervous before you speak and, when managed effectively, can result in a better speech than having no nervousness at all.

There are many ways to measure your level of public speaking apprehension. Exhibit 2.2 presents a short self-assessment survey you can complete to gauge your level of apprehension.

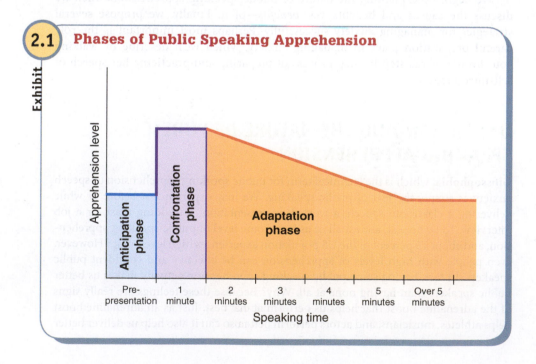

Exhibit 2.1 Phases of Public Speaking Apprehension

Exhibit 2.2

Personal Report of Public Speaking Apprehension[9]

These statements give you a chance to express how you feel about speaking in public. Please indicate in the space provided the degree to which each statement applies to you by marking whether you:

1 = strongly agree;   2 = agree;   3 = are undecided;   4 = disagree;   5 = strongly disagree

_____ 1. I have no fear of giving a speech.
_____ 2. Certain parts of my body feel very tense and rigid while giving a speech.
_____ 3. I feel relaxed while giving a speech.
_____ 4. My thoughts become confused and jumbled when I am giving a speech.
_____ 5. I face the prospect of giving a speech with confidence.
_____ 6. While giving a speech, I get so nervous I forget the facts I really know.
_____ TOTAL

SCORING: Begin by reversing the numbers you assigned to statements 2, 4, and 6 (1 = 5, 2 = 4, 3 = 3, 4 = 2, 5 = 1). Then, add all six numbers.

INTERPRETING: If your total is more than 24, you may experience a high level of public speaking apprehension. People who are highly apprehensive will benefit most from applying the techniques designed to reduce anxiety.

Causes

Public speaking apprehension is most commonly caused by negative self-talk.[10] **Self-talk** is defined as intrapersonal communication regarding perceived success or failure in a particular situation. Negative self-talk increases anxiety. Negative self-talk about public speaking generally focuses on a fear of being stared at, a fear of the unknown, a fear of failure, or a fear of becoming fearful. Where do these negative thoughts come from? Research suggests three common roots: biologically based temperament, previous experience, and level of skills.

self-talk: intrapersonal communication regarding perceived success or failure in a particular situation

Biologically Based Temperament

According to this theory, people who are extroverted tend to experience lower levels of public speaking apprehension than people who are introverted.[11] Does this mean that naturally introverted people are doomed to be ineffective public speakers? Absolutely not! Remember the successful celebrities we mentioned earlier? Many of them are introverted, yet all of them enjoy a great deal of public speaking success. Believe it or not, even though one of the authors of this textbook is introverted, she has won multiple national titles in competitive collegiate speech tournaments.

Previous Experience

Our level of apprehension may also result from our experiences with public speaking while growing up. In other words, some of us actually learned to fear public speaking! Research tells us that we may be socialized to fear public speaking as a result of modeling and incidents of negative reinforcement.[12] *Modeling* has to do with observing how your friends and family members react to speaking in public.[13] If they tend to be reserved and avoid speaking in public, your fears might stem from modeling. *Negative reinforcement* concerns how others have responded to your public speeches in the past. If you experienced negative reactions, you might be more apprehensive about public speaking than if you were praised for your efforts.[14]

Consider your past. How might modeling have influenced your current fears about public speaking? Did family and friends talk openly with each other a great deal, or were they quiet and reserved? What was it like around the dinner table or at

Photo 2.1 Tina Fey learned the public speaking behaviors she observed from family members when growing up. What public speaking behaviors did your family model? How might they have influenced your beliefs about yourself as a public speaker?

lev radin/Shutterstock.com

community events? Did any of your family members do much public speaking? What were their experiences? Emmy-winning actress, writer, and comedian Tina Fey was once asked what it was like around her dinner table growing up. She remarked that "the whole family played to each other"; her "mom's a dry wit," and her dad "has a good sense of silliness." Their modeling not only rubbed off on her as a comedian, but also helped her eventually overcome being a "shy, nerdy" teenager (Photo 2.1).[15]

How others have reinforced our public speaking efforts also influences how apprehensive we feel about public speaking. We have all had many "public speaking" experiences, from reading aloud in elementary school, to giving an oral report in science class, to accepting a sports award at a banquet. If the responses to your speaking in the past were generally positive, you probably learned to feel confident about your ability. If, on the other hand, the responses were negative, you probably learned to feel fearful of public speaking. If your elementary school teacher humiliated you when you read aloud, if you flubbed that science report, or if friends laughed at your acceptance speech, you will probably be more apprehensive about speaking in public than if you had been praised for your efforts. Kira, for example, kept thinking about the time she gave a short speech in her eighth-grade social studies class. The entire class chuckled when she mispronounced "synonym" as "cinnamon." The teacher reprimanded the class and asked Kira to continue, but she couldn't do it. The instructor allowed her to return to her seat without finishing the speech. Embarrassed and shaking, Kira was convinced she was not a good public speaker and vowed never to do another speech (Photo 2.2).

Level of Skills

An important source of public speaking apprehension comes from having underdeveloped speaking skills. This "skill deficit" theory suggests that most of us become apprehensive because we don't know how to (or choose not to) plan or prepare effectively for our public presentations. Some current research even suggests that, thanks to the growing reliance on technology to communicate (e.g., texts, emails, social networking), the number of people with skill deficits is increasing exponentially, particularly among millennials.[16] As you become skilled at using the six-step speech-planning and preparation process we introduce in this chapter, you will gain confidence and become a more effective public speaker.

MANAGING PUBLIC SPEAKING APPREHENSION

Because public speaking apprehension has multiple causes, we describe a few general anxiety-reduction methods, several specific techniques, and a six-step speech-planning and preparation process you can employ to manage anxiety and boost your confidence about public speaking.

General Methods

1. **Communication orientation motivation (COM)** helps reduce anxiety by adopting a "communication" rather than a "performance" orientation when giving speeches.[17] According to communication researcher Michael Motley, speakers with a **performance orientation** believe they must impress a

IMPROMPTU SPEECH CHALLENGE

Think of a time in your childhood when you spoke in front of more than 10 people. Describe what you spoke about, as well as when, where, and to whom. Then talk about how you felt about yourself as a public speaker afterward and why.

communication orientation motivation (COM): adopting a "communication" rather than a "performance" orientation toward speeches

performance orientation: believing in the need to impress a hypercritical audience with knowledge and delivery

hypercritical audience with their knowledge and delivery.[18] When you approach public speaking with a performance orientation, your self-talk tends to focus on a fear of failing, which increases your anxiety. On the other hand, speakers with a **communication orientation** view public speaking as an opportunity to engage in conversation with a number of people about an important topic. When you have a communication orientation, you focus on getting your message across rather than on how people might be judging your performance.

Chuck Savage/Flirt/CORBIS

Photo 2.2 Effective speakers demonstrate integrity not by eliminating nervousness but by managing it effectively. What methods and strategies will you use to manage public speaking anxiety?

2. **Visualization** helps reduce anxiety by assisting you in picturing yourself giving a masterful speech. Like COM techniques, visualization helps you overcome cognitive and emotional symptoms of apprehension arising from a fear of failure. If you visualize yourself going through an entire speech preparation and delivery process successfully, you are more likely to be successful when you actually deliver the speech.[19]

Visualization has been used extensively to improve athletic performances. In a study of basketball players trying to improve their foul-shooting percentages, for example, players were divided into three groups. One group never practiced, another group practiced making foul shots, and a third group "practiced" by visualizing themselves making foul shots. As you might expect, those who physically practiced improved far more than those who didn't practice at all. But those who simply *visualized* practicing improved almost as much as those who actually practiced.[20] Imagine what happens when you both visualize *and* practice (Photo 2.3)!

3. **Relaxation exercises** can help reduce anxiety through the use of breathing techniques and progressive muscle relaxation. To be effective, however, the exercises must be practiced regularly until they eventually become habitual. Then you will be able to use them to calm yourself in the moments before you speak.

Let's take a closer look at breathing techniques. You were born breathing correctly—using the muscles in your abdomen to draw air into and push air out of your lungs. But when you become anxious, the muscles in your abdomen become tense and you take shallower breaths, often raising your shoulders to get air into your lungs and dropping them to expel the air. Shallow breathing contributes to anxiety, depression, and fatigue.[21] Instead, think of your lungs as balloons that fill up with air. Have you ever seen someone making balloon animals? If so, you probably noticed that, when the artist wanted part of the balloon to remain uninflated, he or she squeezed that area off. Shallow breathing is like filling only the top half of the balloon because, when your abdominal muscles tighten, you stop air from filling the bottom half of your lungs. Fortunately, you can retrain yourself to breathe from the abdomen and thereby reduce your anxiety. Exhibit 2.3 offers some suggestions.

Similarly, we can train our bodies to relax by practicing progressive muscle relaxation exercises. Essentially, you systematically tense certain muscle groups for about 10 seconds and then relax them for another 10 seconds while focusing

communication orientation: viewing public speaking as a conversation with a number of people about an important topic and getting the message across

visualization: a method to reduce anxiety by picturing yourself giving a masterful speech

relaxation exercises: the use of breathing techniques and progressive muscle relaxation to reduce anxiety

SPEECH SNIPPET

Kira had been successful using visualization before swim meets. She thought this technique might work to help her prepare for her speeches too. She pictured herself in front of the class comfortably giving her speech.

Exhibit 2.3

Breathing and Relaxation Exercises

1. **Abdominal breathing:** Lie on the floor and place your hand on your abdomen. Consciously focus on filling your abdomen with air when you inhale by watching your hand rise. Then, as you release the air, watch your hand lower again.

2. **Sighing:** By sighing right before it is your turn to speak, you can release tension and lower your anxiety level, allowing the inevitable rush of adrenaline to work for you, not against you.[22]

3. **Progressive muscle relaxation exercises:** Consciously tense and relax each of these muscle groups twice and then move on to the next group: hands, arms, shoulders, neck, lips, tongue, mouth, eyes and forehead, abdomen, back, midsection, thighs, stomach, calves, feet, and toes.

systematic desensitization: an anxiety-reduction method of gradually visualizing and then engaging in increasingly more frightening speaking events while remaining calm

cognitive restructuring: an anxiety-reduction method of systematically replacing negative self-talk with positive coping statements

on what the relaxed state feels like.[23] Once you teach your body to relax on command, you can call on it to do so before beginning to give your speech.

4. **Systematic desensitization** can help reduce anxiety as you gradually visualize and then engage in increasingly more frightening speaking events while remaining calm.[24] Research tells us that more than 80 percent of those who try this method reduce their level of anxiety.[25] Essentially, once you are in a relaxed state, imagine yourself in successively more stressful speech-planning and speech-making situations—for example, researching a speech topic in the library, practicing the speech out loud in front of a roommate, and delivering the final speech to your audience. Once you can maintain a relaxed state while visualizing yourself in each event, you try performing each event while maintaining the learned state of calmness. The ultimate goal of systematic desensitization is to transfer the calm feelings you attain while visualizing to the actual speaking event. Calmness on command—and it works.

5. **Cognitive restructuring** helps reduce anxiety by replacing anxiety-arousing negative self-talk with anxiety-reducing positive self-talk. The process consists of four steps.

   - **Identify your fears.** Write down all the fears that come to mind when you know you must give a speech.

   - **Determine whether or not each fear is rational.** Most fears are, in fact, irrational because public speaking is not life threatening.

   - **Develop positive coping statements to replace negative self-talk.** No one list of coping statements will work for everyone, so you must develop a list that works for you. Exhibit 2.4 is an example of how Kira used this process to help manage her anxiety. Psychologist Richard Heimberg of the State University of New York at Albany reminds his clients that most listeners don't notice or even care if the clients do what they're afraid of doing when giving a speech. Ultimately, he asks them, "Can you cope with the one or two people who [notice or criticize or] get upset?"[26]

   - **Incorporate positive coping statements into your life so they become second nature.** You can do this by writing your statements down and reading them aloud to yourself each day, as well as before giving a speech. The more you repeat your coping statements to yourself, the more natural they will become and the more unnatural your negative thoughts will seem.

All of these methods have helped people successfully reduce their anxiety. If you think you'll experience public speaking apprehension in

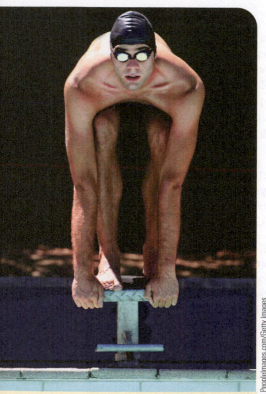

Peopleimages.com/Getty Images

Photo 2.3 If people can visualize themselves going through an entire process, they will have a much better chance of succeeding when they are in the actual situation. When have you used positive visualization to gain confidence about succeeding?

Exhibit 2.4

2.4 Negative Self-talk Versus Positive Coping Statements

Kira decided to try cognitive restructuring to reduce her anxiety about giving speeches in front of her classmates. Here is how she worked through the process:

Negative self-talk
1. I'm afraid I'll stumble over my words and look foolish.
2. I'm afraid everyone will be able to tell that I'm nervous.
3. I'm afraid my voice will crack.
4. I'm afraid I'll sound boring.

Positive coping statements
1. Even if I stumble, I will have succeeded as long as I get my message across.
2. They probably won't be able to tell I'm nervous, but as long as I focus on getting my message across, that's what matters.
3. Even if my voice cracks, as long as I keep going and focus on getting my message across, I'll succeed at what matters most.
4. I won't sound bored if I focus on how important this message is to me and to my audience. I don't have to do somersaults to keep their attention because my topic is relevant to them.

this course, which of these techniques do you think might help you? Have you already tried some of them in other situations? If they helped, do you think you could apply them to reduce your anxiety about giving a speech? For most people, using several of them yields the best results.[27]

Specific Techniques

In addition to these five general anxiety-reduction methods, we recommend several specific techniques to employ in the days before you deliver your speech and on the day you actually give it.

1. **Allow sufficient time to prepare.** As soon as you know the day you are to give your speech and the expectations for it, identify the topic and begin to prepare. At minimum, you should spend at least 10 days to 2 weeks researching, organizing, and practicing your speech. The more time you spend doing so, the more confident you will become and the better your speech will ultimately be.

Pascal Le Segretain/Getty Images

PUBLIC SPEAKING IN THE REAL WORLD

Harrison Ford and Public Speaking Anxiety

Although actor Harrison Ford is one of the highest grossing movie stars of all time, he struggles with public speaking anxiety. In his own words, public speaking is "a mixed bag of terror and anxiety."[28] Not only that, he even feels fear when a character he is playing must give a speech.[29] The former philosophy major and Sigma Nu fraternity member at Ripon College in Wisconsin manages his anxiety using a modified version of Motley's communication orientation motivation (COM) method. As Ford says, "I don't want to be a movie star. I want to be in movies that are stars. For me, it's not about performance. It's about storytelling."[30]

1. How does Harrison Ford's storytelling technique help him focus on the message rather than the performance?

2. How might thinking about your speeches as storytelling help manage anxiety?

2. **Use presentational aids.** Recall that one of the major fears that increase public speaking anxiety is the fear of being stared at. Although it is human nature to enjoy being recognized for things we've done well, it is not human nature to be the constant center of attention for a prolonged amount of time.[31] When you give a speech, all eyes are focused constantly on you, and you can feel conspicuous. Using presentational aids allows you to direct the audience's attention toward something else at carefully placed points during your speech, which can diminish your sense of being constantly stared at and the anxiety that can accompany it.

3. **Practice your speech aloud.** When you practice your speech aloud, you get comfortable hearing yourself talk about your topic. You identify sections of the speech where your ideas may not flow and where you need to do additional preparation. By the third or fourth time you have practiced aloud, you will notice your delivery becoming easier, and you will gain confidence in your ability to present your ideas to others.

Many successful speakers not only practice aloud alone but also practice in front of trusted friends or family members who give them feedback (Photo 2.4). If possible, practice your speech in the room where you'll ultimately deliver it. Hearing your voice in the room where you'll speak reduces anxiety that can arise from fear of the unknown, as you will know what it will feel like to present your speech in that room. If you will be giving your speech online, practice recording and then watching yourself on the recording several times to get comfortable with making virtual eye contact with the camera and speaking into the microphone with ease. Finally, on the night before your speech, review your speech plan immediately before you go to sleep. That way, as you sleep, your mind will continue to prepare.[32]

4. **Dress up.** We tend to feel more confident when we know we look good. By dressing up a bit for your speech, you'll reduce anxiety about being stared at because you will feel good about how you look. Not only that, dressing up enhances credibility (ethos) because doing so sends a message that you care about the audience, the occasion, and the message you want to get across to your listeners. Even if you are going to deliver your speech online as a voiced-over slide show presentation, dressing up will still reduce anxiety by boosting your confidence.

5. **Choose an appropriate time to speak.** If you have a choice, pick the time that works best for you. In face-to-face speech classes, for example, some speakers become more nervous when they listen to others, so they are better off speaking early in the class period. Others find that listening to their peers calms them, so they are better off speaking later in the class period. When given a choice, choose to speak at the time that is optimal for you. If you are recording your speech for an online presentation, do so when your creative energy is highest. If you are a "morning person," record your speech early in the day. If you get your best bursts of energy in the evening, do it later in the day.

6. **Use positive self-talk.** Immediately prior to getting up to speak, coach yourself with a short "pregame pep talk." Remind yourself about the importance of your message. Remember how hard you prepared and visualize how good you are when you are at your best. Remind yourself that nervousness is normal and useful. Tell yourself that you are confident and ready.

David Young-Wolff/PhotoEdit

Photo 2.4 Effective public speakers practice their speeches aloud several times before they actually deliver them in person or online. Where and how will you practice your speeches?

7. **Face the audience.** Face your audience with confidence. In face-to-face settings, walk purposefully to the front of the room. Plant yourself firmly yet comfortably. Review your opening statement in your head. Make eye contact with the audience. Take a deep breath and begin your well-rehearsed introduction. For your online speech, follow the same pattern: situate yourself comfortably but professionally, review your opening statement in your head, take a moment to look directly into the camera, take a deep breath, and then begin your well-rehearsed speech.

8. **Focus on sharing your message.** Although you may feel nervous, your audience rarely "sees" it. Employ a communication-orientation by focusing on getting your ideas across rather thinking about your nerves.

DEVELOPING AN EFFECTIVE SPEECH PLAN

Whether you are a marketing account manager presenting an advertising campaign idea to clients, a coach trying to motivate your team for its game with your arch rival, or a student giving a speech in class, you can manage anxiety, demonstrate confidence, and be more effective when you develop and follow an effective **speech plan**—a strategic method for achieving your effective speech goal.

speech plan: a strategic method for achieving your effective speech goal

In this section and throughout the chapters that follow, we will work through a six-step process for planning and preparing speeches, a process grounded in the works of major speech scholars across the ages. Ancient Roman philosophers actually clarified the five general rules for effective public speeches more than 2,000 years ago. These rules, known as the **canons of rhetoric**, still hold true today.[33] The five canons are invention (well-developed content), arrangement (clear organization), style (appropriate language), delivery (use of voice, body, and strategic presentation aids), and memory (creativity and polish). Although classical approaches to speech planning were speaker focused, scholars now recognize that effective speeches are audience centered and address the rhetorical situation.[34] So, the speech-making skills we propose are both rooted in ancient wisdom and informed by contemporary research.

canons of rhetoric: Five general rules for effective public speeches

The six speech action plan steps are:

1. Select a specific speech goal that is appropriate to the rhetorical situation.

2. Understand your audience and adapt to it.

3. Gather and evaluate information.

4. Organize ideas into a well-structured outline.

5. Choose, prepare, and use appropriate presentational aids.

6. Practice oral language and delivery style.

Exhibit 2.5 illustrates these steps. Let's briefly preview what each step entails by describing how Kira worked through each one to prepare her speech of self-introduction.

Step 1: Select a Specific Speech Goal That Is Appropriate to the Rhetorical Situation

Your **speech goal** is a specific statement of what you want your audience to know, believe, or do. To arrive at an appropriate speech goal, you need to consider the rhetorical situation, that is, yourself as the speaker, your audience, and the occasion. Doing so will encourage your audience to pay attention because they will perceive your speech as relevant to them.

speech goal: a specific statement of what you want your audience to know, believe, or do

Exhibit 2.5

An Effective Speech Plan Is the Product of These Six Action Steps

Goal

1. Select a specific speech goal that is appropriate to the rhetorical situation.

Audience

2. Understand your audience and adapt to it.

Research

3. Gather and evaluate information.

Organization

4. Organize ideas into a well-structured outline.

Presentational Aids

5. Choose, prepare, and use appropriate presentational aids.

Delivery

6. Practice oral language and delivery style.

Audience icon, Sielan/Shutterstock.com; all other icons, CoraMax/Shutterstock.com

Begin by selecting a topic that you may know something about, that interests you, and that is important to you. Although you might occasionally speak on a topic that is unfamiliar to you, you will usually speak on topics that meet these three criteria. Kira's speech topic was herself.

Next, analyze your audience so you can address the topic in ways that will be relevant to their needs, interests, and desires. Who are they? What do they need to know about your topic? What might they already know about it?

Kira's audience included her classmates and her instructor. Because she didn't know any of them before enrolling in the course, pretty much everything about her would be new to them. She counted 14 females and 11 males. Almost everyone appeared to be 18 to 24 years old except for one woman who had mentioned having a 13-year-old daughter. She was probably in her 30s. Kira didn't know about her classmates' religion or ethnicity. Although most of her classmates appeared to be Caucasian, she wasn't really sure if that was true. She assumed two students—Xialing and Min—were of Asian descent, but she didn't know if they were international students or Asian Americans. She did know, however, that everyone was pursuing an undergraduate degree at the same school in the same state. She decided to talk about why she decided to go to college, to attend this university, and to pursue her major. She figured everyone could relate to that in some way.

You also need to consider the occasion. What is the size of the audience? When will the speech be given? Where will the speech be given? Will you give the speech in a room or online? If you will give the speech in a face-to-face setting, are there any peculiarities of the room? If you will give the speech online in real time or recorded, are you familiar with the technology you will be using? What is the time limit for the speech? What are the particular expectations for the speech?

The room Kira will be speaking in is pretty typical for a speech class. Kira is expected to introduce herself in a 2- to 3-minute speech using the lectern and including at least two presentational aids. Her instructor will be recording all the speeches, so students can critique and assess their performances later.

Once you determine a topic based on your interest and expertise, the audience, and the occasion, you are ready to phrase your speech goal. Every speech has a general and a specific goal. For most classroom speeches, the general goal is usually either to inform, where your goal is shared understanding, or to persuade, where your goal is to convince your audience to believe something or persuade them to take action. We will discuss several other general goals, which Aristotle called "ceremonial speeches" (e.g., to introduce, to entertain, and to celebrate), in later chapters.[35]

Your specific speech goal articulates exactly what you want your audience to understand, believe, or do. For instance, Gina, who is majoring in health and nutrition, might phrase her informative speech goal as, "I want the audience to understand three methods for ridding our bodies of harmful toxins." And Glen, a bioengineering major, might phrase his persuasive speech goal as, "I want to convince my audience of the value of genetic engineering." Kira was glad the instructor told everyone to focus on the same three main points for this speech. She phrased her specific speech goal as, "I want my audience to understand a bit about my personal background, what I am majoring in, and what I plan to do when I graduate."

Step 2: Understand Your Audience and Adapt to It

Once you have a clear and specific speech goal based on the speaker, audience, and occasion, you should begin working on understanding your audience more fully and then adapting your speech to address their needs, interests, and expectations. We refer to this process of tailoring your speech to the needs, interests, and expectations of your listeners as **audience adaptation** (Photo 2.5).

For any speech, you should consider your audience's initial level of interest in your goal, their ability to understand the content of your speech, and their attitude toward your topic. If you believe your audience has very little interest in your topic, adapt

audience adaptation: the process of tailoring a speech to the needs, interests, and expectations of listeners

Photo 2.5 Suppose you were giving a speech on genetic engineering. How would you adapt your speech for this audience versus an audience made up of your classmates?

by explaining how and why the topic is important or relevant to them. If you believe your audience doesn't know much about your topic, provide the basic information they need to understand your speech. Kira decided that not everyone would know what a "first-generation student" is. So she would define it for them as "an undergraduate student whose parents never attended college."

Finally, you need to adapt to your audience's initial attitude toward your topic. Kira's postgraduation goal is to return to Eastern Kentucky to help develop college readiness skills in children whose parents never attended college. Although she assumed none of her classmates would be opposed to this idea, they also might not really care one way or another. So, she would work hard on ways to overcome apathy by identifying common values of college students in her listener-relevance links.

Step 3: Gather and Evaluate Information

In addition to drawing on material from your own knowledge and experiences, you can draw on the expertise of others by perusing published written, visual, and audio-visual materials about your topic, as well as conducting interviews and surveys yourself. Kira, for example, gathered photographs of her hometown, including friends and family, photographs of her cohort of first-generation students at college, as well as college preparation and readiness checklists for grades 9, 10, 11, and 12 she found online. You also need to evaluate the information and sources you collect and select only the items you deem to be truthful and credible. Kira, who is a first-generation student herself, can speak from personal experience about the additional challenges such students must overcome to succeed, as well as from information she collected from First Generation Organization websites.

Step 4: Organize Ideas into a Well-Structured Outline

Begin organizing your speech by identifying the two to four major ideas you want your audience to remember, then turn each major idea into a complete sentence. These sentences will become the main points for the body of your speech. Next, combine your speech goal with each major idea into a succinct thesis statement with a main point preview that describes specifically what you want your audience to understand, believe, or do when you have finished speaking. This process provides the overarching framework, or macrostructure, of your speech. Kira's first draft of a thesis statement with main point preview looked like this:

> Today, I'm going to tell you a bit about who I am by focusing on my personal background, what I am majoring in, and what I plan to do after I graduate.

Arrange your main points using an organizational framework that will help your audience understand and remember them. Two common organizational frameworks are chronological and topical. **Chronological** means following an order that moves from first to last. You can see by looking at Kira's thesis statement with main point preview that her speech will be organized chronologically. **Topical** means following an order of interest. For instance, Gina, who decides to inform her audience about the three proven methods for removing harmful toxins from the body, may begin with the simplest one—keeping hydrated—and end with the most difficult one—eating more natural whole foods.

chronological: following an order that moves from first to last

topical: following an order of interest

Having identified and ordered your main points, you are ready to outline the speech body. You do so by adding information as subpoints to support each of your two to four main points. At least one subpoint used to elaborate on each main point should provide listener relevance by articulating why or how the information relates to the audience's needs, interests, or desires. After you have outlined the speech body, outline the introduction and conclusion. Kira decided to get attention in her introduction and provide a memorable conclusion by using the popular sporting event chant: "We're number one!" in reference to being a first-generation college student.

Step 5: Choose, Prepare, and Use Appropriate Presentational Aids

As a result of the plethora of technological sources available today—computers, tablets, MP3 players, smartphones, etc.—we need to present public speeches via multimodal (visual, oral, written) messages and channels (face-to-face, print, technology enhanced). Whereas presentational aids were once considered optional embellishments, today they are integral to your speech content and making it memorable. So, even for a very short speech, you may decide to use a presentational aid to clarify, emphasize, or dramatize your goal and main points. You might convey various ideas through models, charts, graphs, pictures, audios, videos, or audiovisuals—usually using computer technology to assist you. Note in your outline precisely where you will use them and practice using them when you rehearse your speech.

Step 6: Practice Oral Language and Delivery Style

In your practice sessions, you need to choose the wording of main points and supporting materials carefully. If you have not practiced various ways of phrasing your key ideas, you risk missing a major opportunity for communicating your ideas effectively. In practice sessions, work on the appropriateness, accuracy, clarity, and vividness of your wording. Recall that these language choices make up the microstructure of your speech.

How effective you will be is also largely a matter of how well you use your voice and body to deliver your speech. Present your speech intelligibly, conversationally, and expressively. Use good posture and eye contact (look at members of the audience and/or the camera while you are speaking) to appear confident and comfortable. Use facial expressions and gestures that emphasize emotional intentions and clarify structure.

Very few people can present speeches effectively without considerable practice. Practicing out loud gives you confidence that you can talk conversationally and

Reflect on Ethics

YAHOO CEO RESIGNS OVER INACCURATE RESUME

Scott Thompson was hired to lead Yahoo as CEO in January 2012. Just four months later, however, he was forced to tender his resignation.[36] What happened between January and May that forced him to resign?

Essentially, the downward spiral toward his forced resignation began when the board of directors learned that Thompson's biographical statement, which had been submitted in a regulatory filing, indicated that he had earned a bachelor's degree in both computer science and accounting when, in fact, he did not have a degree in computer science at all. He responded at first that it was an "inadvertent error" but when pressed further, claimed he had no knowledge of the error and that a search firm actually altered the material. A special investigation

revealed that Thompson had used the same biography to get hired at PayPal, his previous employer.

1. Do you think Thompson should have had to resign over this issue? Why or why not?
2. Some people justify exaggerating and even lying because not doing so will hurt their chances of getting a good job or getting promoted. In fact, according to CareerBuilder.com, 38 percent of those surveyed admitted to embellishing their job responsibilities on their resumes, and 18 percent admitted to lying about their skill sets.[37] Given these numbers, are the justifications reasonable? Why or why not?

expressively to accomplish your speech goal within the time limit. Don't try to memorize the speech, which is likely to increase anxiety because you may fear forgetting what you planned to say. Instead, practice delivering your speech extemporaneously based on speaking notes composed of key words and phrases that remind you of structure, main points, and delivery cues.

What follows is an outline of Kira's speech of self-introduction. As you read, consider how you might address the rhetorical situation effectively as you develop a speech of self-introduction for your audience. How will you organize your ideas and practice your delivery? What presentational aids will you include? Then, answer these questions about Kira's content and structure.

1. **Content:** What are Kira's main points? What kinds of evidence does she use to support them? What are some examples of breadth, depth, and listener relevance in the body of her speech?

2. **Structure:** What does Kira do to get the attention of her audience? What does she say to lead her audience with her from one point to the next? How does she wrap up the speech to help her audience remember her ideas? What wording seems to demonstrate inclusion, provide clarity, and evoke vivid images?

Speech Assignment & Checklist

Speech of Self-Introduction

Prepare a 2- to 3-minute speech of self-introduction. Use the following as your main points:

1. Your personal background.
2. Your academic major.
3. What you hope to do after you graduate.

Speech Assignment & Checklist (*continued*)

Remember that an effective speech is based on audience-centered content (breadth, depth, listener relevance), structure (macro- and micro-), and delivery (use of voice, body, and presentational aids). As you prepare, use the checklist that follows and Kira's sample speech to guide you.

Speech Evaluation Checklist

General Criteria

You can use this checklist to critique a speech of self-introduction that you hear in class. (You can also use it to critique your own speech.) As you listen to the speaker, consider what makes a speech effective. Then, answer the following questions.

Content

_____ 1. Were all main points addressed per the assignment?

_____ 2. Were two to three pieces of evidence provided for each main point (breadth)?

_____ 3. Was one extended piece of evidence provided for each main point (depth)?

_____ 4. Were listener-relevance links provided for each main point?

_____ 5. Did presentational aids enhance clarity, embellish key ideas, or dramatize an important point?

_____ 6. Did the speech fall within the time constraints of the assignment?

Structure

1. Did the speech provide all the basic elements (*macrostructure*) of an effective speech: introduction, body, conclusion, and transitions? _____

2. Did the introduction catch the audience's interest? _____ identify the speech topic/goal? _____ preview the main points? _____

3. Were transitions provided between each main point? _____

4. Did the conclusion remind the audience of the main points? _____ motivate the audience to remember the main ideas of the speech? _____

5. Did the speaker use words (*microstructure*) that were appropriate and inclusive? _____ accurate and clear? _____ vivid and expressive? _____

6. Were the presentational aids constructed and displayed effectively? _____

Delivery

1. Was the speaker intelligible in terms of volume? _____ rate? _____ pronunciation? _____ enunciation? _____

2. Was the speaker conversational? _____

3. Did the speaker look up from his or her notes most of the time and make eye contact with the audience? _____

4. Did the speaker appear professional, poised, and confident? _____

5. Was the speaker expressive in terms of changes in rate and volume? _____ strategic pauses? _____ appropriate facial expressions? _____ appropriate gestures? _____

6. Did the speaker integrate presentational aids gracefully? _____

KIRA'S SPEECH OF SELF-INTRODUCTION

On Being First

Preparation Outline

Notice how Kira's preparation outline doesn't necessarily use complete sentences and that some elements still need to be developed. However, it does give a basic structure for the main points and supporting material she will use in the speech. In a sense, a preparation outline serves as a rough draft of the speech.

INTRODUCTION

Attention getter I. "We're number one!"

Speaker credibility II. I'm also number one in my family—first one to go to college

Thesis statement with main point preview III. Introduce myself to you—first-generation college student, academic major, goals after graduation

BODY

First main point I. Personal background and decision to attend University of Kentucky

Listener relevance A. Listener relevance about growing up a Kentucky Wildcats fan

B. First-generation college student

Transition *[need to add a transition between main points]*

Second main point II. Majoring in teacher education

Listener relevance A. Listener relevance about how we all want to better ourselves

B. Social studies education

Transition *[need to add a transition here.]*

Third main point III. Goals after graduation

Listener relevance A. Listener relevance about wanting to make a difference

B. Move back to Eastern Kentucky and Harlan County

CONCLUSION

Thesis restatement with main point summary I. So now you know a little bit about me as a first-generation college student, why I chose to major in teacher education, and how I hope to pay it forward when I graduate from UK.

Clincher II. [refer to "We're number one!" again.]

Formal Outline

INTRODUCTION

Attention getter

Notice how Kira piques interest by asking a question about a chant most of her audience is likely to be familiar with and then leads them to her topic gradually by offering another meaning.

I. [Show slide of Wildcats fans cheering] What comes to mind when someone shouts "We're number one! We're number one!"? If you're like most people I know, that chant probably conjures up images about winning a sporting event.

Listener relevance and speaker credibility

II. Like you, I too think about winning games. But that's not the only thought that comes to mind for me. I also think about the fact that I'm "number one" because I am the first person in my family to attend college. As a first-generation college student, I can't help but think about what a tremendous opportunity all of us have to pursue our dreams because we are here in college today.

III. Today, I'd like to introduce myself to you by talking about my unique personal background as a first-generation college student, my choice of majors, and my goals after graduation.

BODY

I. To begin, let's talk about my personal background and how it shaped my decision to apply to the University of Kentucky.

    A. [show presentational aid/photo of fans cheering at a UK sporting event] Like most of you, I grew up in Kentucky cheering for the Wildcats and daydreaming about what it would be like to attend college here someday.

    B. [blank slide] Unlike most of you, though, I am also a first-generation college student, which means I am the first person in my family to attend college.

        1. [slide with photo of my family] I was raised in Harlan County where my dad works as a miner, my mom works as a server at a local café, and my brother attends high school.

        2. Although my parents supported my dream to go to college, they couldn't afford to pay for it; to give me advice about what college would be like; to help me prepare for it, including how to study for the ACT; or to help me fill out my college application.

        3. [presentational aid of collage of books/websites/teachers] Instead, I had to seek out information and advice from books, websites, teachers, and school counsellors.

        4. I learned that I would need to develop a strong resume. So I put extra effort into doing so by studying hard to earn good grades, volunteering as a Sunday school teacher, singing in the school choir, and participating on the swim team.

        5. [blank slide] Knowing I would have to pay for school myself, I also worked part-time throughout high school and applied for every scholarship, grant, and low interest loan I was eligible for.

Now that you know a little bit about my personal background as a first-generation college student, you probably also understand why I never take for granted the fact that I am a student here at UK. What you probably don't know, however, is what I am majoring in and why.

II. I am pursuing a major in teacher education.

    A. If you're like me, you are pursuing a college degree for reasons beyond the fact that we'll probably make more money as a result.

        1. Many of us want to learn knowledge and skills in a particular field of study.

        2. Many of us want to gain self-confidence about our abilities.

        3. Many of us want to develop strong leadership skills.

        4. These reasons help each of us pick a major.

    B. I am pursuing my degree in social studies education because the teacher education program here has a great reputation for preparing students to be effective teachers.

        1. Coursework in the teacher education program will help me develop leadership skills to work effectively with middle school and high school students in an educational setting.

Thesis statement and main point review
Kira very simply states her thesis with main point preview so her audience can get her main points firmly in mind.

First main point

Subpoint (listener relevance)
Kira knows most of her classmates are Wildcat fans so she decides to play on that to keep them listening.

Subpoint
Kira defines what a first-generation college student is in case some of her listeners are unfamiliar with the phrase.

Listing several examples is a way to add breadth.

Transition
Kira offers a complete transition statement that both restates the main point she finished discussing and introduces the upcoming main point.

Second main point

Subpoint (listener relevance)
Kira's use of "us" rather than "I" is an example of inclusive language.

Subpoint

Kira points to the fact about the program placement statistics for supporting material. She could have also used a visual aid showing the actual job placement statistics to add depth.

Transition

2. Becoming certified as a K–12 teacher will provide the credentials needed for me to obtain employment in a K–12 educational system.

3. The experiences I will gain by working in the innovative P-20 initiative in the UK College of Education will set me apart from other job seekers when I graduate. [show graph of the P-20 program offerings and explain how it works, then conceal it]

4. The teacher education program's job placement rate statistics are remarkable.

So I chose to earn my degree in teacher education to gain the confidence and skills I will need to make a difference in the world. Let's look more specifically at how I hope to make a difference after I graduate.

Third main point

III. I have several goals for my life after graduation.

Subpoint (listener relevance)

Again Kira uses inclusive "we" language and the phrase "and I assume for many of you too" to help her listeners feel included in the public speaking conversation with her.

A. Because we can all expect to spend more time at work than anywhere else once we graduate, we all aspire to being in a career that we love. For me, and I assume for many of you too, that means being in a career where I can make a difference. I know I want to pay it forward by helping other potential first-generation college students achieve their college preparation and placement goals and dreams.

Subpoint

B. When I graduate, I want to return to Eastern Kentucky, maybe even to Harlan County, to teach social studies to middle school students, high school students, or both.

Kira adds depth to this point by showing the first of her step-by-step long-term goals.

1. I plan to embed activities focused on career planning that will encourage students to discover and then have the courage to pursue their dreams.

2. I also plan to develop after-school programming for students who would be first-generation college students like me to provide them with the information and skills they need to succeed.

3. I hope to ultimately turn the program into a nonprofit organization where I train others to create similar programs across the state.

Subpoint

C. My long-term goal is to return to UK to pursue a master's degree in counselling psychology.

1. In doing so, I can learn more about how to make a difference in the lives of students who may face a variety of potential barriers to success.

2. I can then use that knowledge and those skills to broaden my goals from helping potential first-year college students to also helping other students with special needs overcome obstacles to success.

CONCLUSION

Thesis restatement with main point review

I. So now you know a little bit about me as a first-generation college student, why I chose to major in teacher education, and how I hope to pay it forward when I graduate from UK.

Clincher

Kira offers a visually reinforced clincher that ties back to the emotion-arousing attention catcher to motivate listeners to remember her speech.

II. [show UK fans cheering "We're number one"] And even more than that, whenever you find yourself chanting "We're number one" you'll think about my speech today, not just in terms of what it means to be a first-generation college student, but also in terms of how each of us can achieve our career *goals* by landing a good job AND our career *dreams* by making a difference.

Speaking Outline Note Cards

Notice how Kira's speaking outline reduces her formal sentence outline to brief notes that identify only key words/phrases and delivery cues.

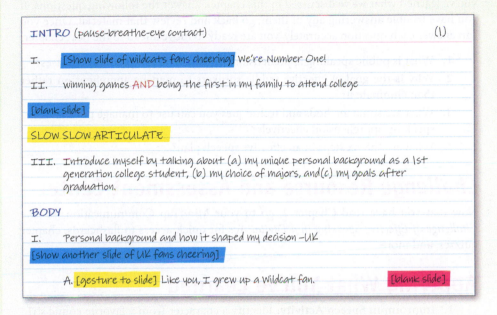

INTRO (pause-breathe-eye contact)   (1)

I.   [Show slide of wildcats fans cheering] We're Number One!

II.   winning games AND being the first in my family to attend college

[blank slide]

SLOW SLOW ARTICULATE

III. Introduce myself by talking about (a) my unique personal background as a 1st generation college student, (b) my choice of majors, and (c) my goals after graduation.

BODY

I.   Personal background and how it shaped my decision –UK
[show another slide of UK fans cheering]

      A. [gesture to slide] Like you, I grew up a Wildcat fan.   [blank slide]

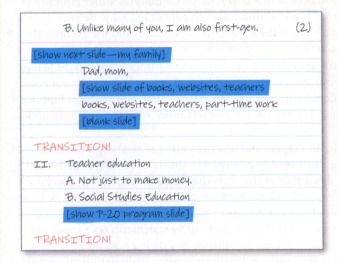

      B. Unlike many of you, I am also first-gen.   (2)

[show next slide—my family]
      Dad, mom,
      [show slide of books, websites, teachers]
      books, websites, teachers, part-time work
      [blank slide]

TRANSITION!
II.   Teacher education
      A. Not just to make money.
      B. Social Studies Education
      [show P-20 program slide]

TRANSITION!

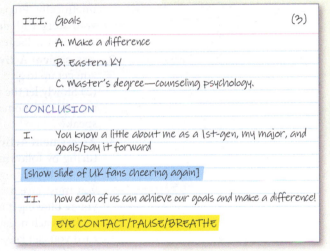

III. Goals   (3)
      A. Make a difference
      B. Eastern KY
      C. Master's degree—counseling psychology.

CONCLUSION

I.   You know a little about me as a 1st-gen, my major, and goals/pay it forward

[show slide of UK fans cheering again]

II.   how each of us can achieve our goals and make a difference!

EYE CONTACT/PAUSE/BREATHE

Reflection and Assessment

This chapter focused on public speaking apprehension and how to manage it in ways that will help you become a confident and effective public speaker. To assess how well you've learned what we've discussed in this chapter, answer the following questions. If you have trouble answering any of them, go back and review that material. Once you can answer each question accurately, you are ready to move ahead to the next chapter.

1. What is public speaking apprehension? What are its symptoms and causes?
2. Why is the goal of effective public speakers to manage apprehension rather than eliminate it?
3. What are some methods and techniques you can use to manage public speaking apprehension effectively?
4. What are the six steps in an effective speech plan?

MindTap®

Challenge Resource and Assessment Center

Now that you have read Chapter 2, go to your MindTap Communication for *The Challenge of Effective Speaking in a Digital Age* for quick access to flashcards, chapter quizzes, and more.

Applying What You've Learned

1. **Impromptu Speech Activity:** Identify a character from a favorite comic strip or cartoon where you believe that character communicates either ethically or unethically. Prepare a 2- to 3-minute speech explaining why. Be sure to tell your story with details about the setting, the characters, and the event(s) that support the life lesson or moral of your story.

2. **Assessment Activity A:** Practice a calming sigh to reduce anxiety right before you get up to give your speech. (1) Inhale deeply but gently through your nose. (2) Slowly let the air out while saying "Ahhhh." (3) Let your body go limp for a couple of moments. (4) Repeat. Do you feel more relaxed as you get up to speak?

3. **Assessment Activity B:** Prepare and practice your personal cognitive restructuring by following this five-step process. (1) Create your own negative self-talk list by writing down four or five fears that come to mind when you know you must give a speech. (2) Identify why each fear is irrational, that is, how you're blowing it out of proportion. (3) Create a positive self-talk statement to replace each negative one. (4) Place these positive statements on a small note-card you can keep in your pocket or wallet or as a digital note on your smartphone. (5) Practice your positive self-talk statements daily until they become second nature.

3

Listening

WHAT'S THE POINT?
WHEN YOU'VE FINISHED THIS CHAPTER, YOU WILL BE ABLE TO:

- Explain what listening is and why it's important to study it in a public speaking course
- Describe why effective listening is so challenging
- Employ specific strategies to improve your listening skills
- Practice providing constructive speech critiques

MindTap®

Review the chapter **Learning Objectives** and **Start** with quick warm-up activity.

Ethical listeners hear speakers out even when they present an opposing point of view.

B Busco/Getty Images

Traffic was horrible today during Bart's morning commute, so he got to the office later than usual. He rushed into his office and quickly logged into the webinar that was already in session. He quietly exhaled a sigh of relief after he realized he had only missed the first 5 minutes. He placed his microphone on mute and proceeded to get organized for the day while listening. He hung up his jacket, got the papers he worked on the night before out of his satchel, and decided to do a quick check of email messages to see if there was anything that needed his urgent attention. At that moment, Bart heard his supervisor say, "Bart will catch us up on that. Right Bart?" Bart thought, catch them up on what? Yikes!

Does this sound familiar? Do you ever find yourself trying to multitask when attending a meeting online or even in person? If we are completely honest with ourselves, most of us have probably found ourselves in a predicament like Bart's on at least one occasion. We shouldn't underestimate the importance of listening; it can provide clarification, help us understand and remember material, improve our personal and professional relationships, and increase our ability to evaluate information effectively.[1] In fact, survey after survey reports that listening is one of the most important skills employers seek in job candidates. So the skills you learn and apply from this chapter will set you apart in ways that will benefit you both personally and professionally.

We begin with a discussion of what listening is and some challenges we must overcome to listen effectively. Then we offer several specific strategies to improve listening skills related to each of the steps in the active listening process. Finally, we provide guidelines to follow as you prepare effective and ethical constructive speech critiques.

WHAT IS LISTENING?

Recall that communication is the process of creating shared meaning. So to be effective, *speakers* must present messages clearly and compellingly and *listeners* must accurately interpret what is said.

People sometimes make the mistake of thinking that hearing and listening are the same thing, but they're not. **Hearing** is a physiological process. **Listening**, on the other hand, consists of complex affective, cognitive, and behavioral processes. *Affective* processes are those that motivate us to attend to a message. *Cognitive* processes include understanding and interpreting its meaning.[2] *Behavioral* processes are those related to responding with verbal and nonverbal feedback.[3] Listening is important because studies show that, even when we factor in the use of technology such as social media, email, and texting, listening is still "the most widely used daily communication activity."[4] Not only that, even when we try to listen carefully, most people remember only about 50 percent of what they hear shortly after hearing it and only about 25 percent 2 days later.[5] Some suggest this is getting even worse in this age of technology-enhanced communication.[6]

As we've already mentioned, effective listening is a key to success in most occupations. One survey of top-level North American executives revealed that 80 percent believe listening is one of the most important skills needed in the corporate environment.[7] Listening skills (or the lack thereof) are often at the root of company success or failure. When employees fail to listen effectively to instructions, they usually make mistakes. Mistakes cost organizations time and money. And when

hearing: the physiological process that occurs when the brain detects sound waves

listening: the cognitive process of receiving, attending to, constructing meaning from, and responding to messages

supervisors don't listen effectively to employees when they share concerns about potential problems or their creative ideas and solutions, the result may again be lost time and money. Results of one large study of more than 6,000 organizational crisis events revealed that, in nearly every instance, employees and others had warned management repeatedly about potential problems. Had management listened effectively, the crises may have been avoided.[8] Of course, when the employees of a company do not listen and respond to customers, they are bound to fail. So it simply makes sense to improve listening skills.

We choose to listen for various reasons depending on the situation. For example, when we listen to music for enjoyment and to speakers because we like their style, we engage in *appreciative listening* (Photo 3.1). When we listen to infer what more a speaker might mean beyond the actual words being spoken, we engage in *discriminative listening*. When a doctor is explaining test results, for example, we might also try to discern whether the results are troubling or routine. When our goal is to understand, remember, and recall information—for example, material a professor shares during a classroom lecture—we engage in *comprehensive listening*. When we listen to provide emotional support, we engage in *empathic listening*. Finally, when we want to really understand and critically evaluate the worth of a message, we engage in *critical listening*. Because we need to hear, understand, evaluate, and assign worth to the message, as well as remember and recall it, critical listening requires more psychological processing than the others.

Photo 3.1 Listening to music for enjoyment is a form of appreciative listening. What kinds of music do you enjoy listening to and why?

Bubbles Photolibrary/Alamy Stock Photo

LISTENING CHALLENGES

To become effective listeners in any situation, we need to first overcome three key challenges. These challenges are rooted in (1) our listening apprehension, (2) our preferred listening style, and (3) the approach we take to processing what we hear.

listening apprehension: the anxiety we feel about listening

Listening Apprehension

Listening apprehension is the anxiety we feel about listening. Listening apprehension may increase when we worry about misinterpreting the message, or when we are concerned about how the message may affect us psychologically.[9] For example, if you're in an important meeting or job training session, you may worry about trying to absorb all the important technical information needed to do your job well. Or you might feel anxiety when the material you need to absorb is difficult or confusing. Likewise, your anxiety may increase when you feel ill, tired, or stressed about something else going on in your life. Listening apprehension makes it difficult to focus on the message (Photo 3.2).

Photo 3.2 Listening apprehension that arises in stressful situations can make it difficult to focus on the message. What might you do to reduce listening apprehension during stressful situations?

iStockphoto.com/Dean Mitchell

Listening Style

listening style: the favored and usually unconscious approach to listening

Listening style is our favored and usually unconscious approach to listening.[10] Each of us favors one of four listening styles. However, we also may change our listening style based on the situation and our goals for the interaction.[11]

content-oriented listeners: focus on and evaluate the facts and evidence

1. **Content-oriented listeners** focus on and evaluate the facts and evidence. Content-oriented listeners appreciate details and enjoy processing complex messages that may include a good deal of technical information. Content-oriented listeners are likely to ask questions to get even more information.

people-oriented listeners: focus on the feelings the speakers may have about what they are saying

2. **People-oriented listeners** focus on the feelings their conversational partners may have about what they are saying. For example, people-oriented listeners tend to notice whether their partners are pleased or upset and will encourage them to continue by using nonverbal cues like head nods, eye contact, and smiles.

action-oriented listeners: focus on the ultimate point the speaker is trying to make

3. **Action-oriented listeners** focus on the ultimate point their conversational partner is trying to make. Action-oriented listeners tend to get frustrated when ideas are disorganized and when people ramble. Action-oriented listeners also often anticipate what the speaker is going to say and may even finish the speaker's sentences.

time-oriented listeners: prefer brief and hurried conversations

4. **Time-oriented listeners** prefer brief and hurried conversations and often use nonverbal and verbal cues to signal that their conversational partner needs to be more concise. Time-oriented listeners may tell others exactly how much time they have to listen; interrupt when feeling time pressures; regularly check the time on smartphones, watches, or clocks; and may even nod their heads rapidly to encourage the speaker to pick up the pace.

Each of these listening styles has advantages and disadvantages. Content-oriented listeners are likely to understand and remember details, but miss the overall point of the message and be unaware of the speaker's feelings. People-oriented listeners are likely to understand how the speaker feels, empathize, and offer comfort and support. However, they might become so focused on the speaker's feelings that they miss important details or fail to evaluate the facts offered as evidence. Action-oriented listeners may notice inconsistencies but, because they tend to anticipate what will be said rather than hearing the speaker out, may miss important details. Finally, time-oriented listeners are prone to only partially listen to messages while also thinking about their time constraints; thus, they might miss important details and be insensitive to their partner's emotional needs. In our opening scenario, Bart fell victim to the consequences of being too action- and time-oriented when he should have been listening more closely to his webinar.

With these challenges in mind, let's turn now to some specific techniques we can employ to improve our active listening skills in both face-to-face and virtual settings.

Processing Approach

passive listening: the habitual and unconscious process of receiving messages

active listening: the deliberate and conscious process of attending to, understanding, remembering, evaluating, and responding to messages

Research suggests that we tend to process information in two ways—passively or actively—based on the rhetorical situation. In other words, we listen more carefully when the topic seems important (exigence) to us (audience), when we trust and respect the sender, and during times when we are not constrained by other distractions or obligations (occasion). **Passive listening** is the habitual and unconscious process of receiving messages. When we listen passively, we are on autopilot. We may attend only to certain parts of a message and assume the rest. We tend to listen passively when we aren't really interested or when we are trying to multitask, as Bart did in the opening scenario. By contrast, **active listening** is the deliberate and conscious process of attending to, understanding, remembering, evaluating, and responding to messages. Active listening requires practice. The rest of this chapter focuses on helping you become a better active listener.

ACTIVE LISTENING STRATEGIES

Active listening is a complex psychological process made up of five steps. In this section, we offer techniques to improve listening related to each step (see Exhibit 3.1).

Attending

Effective active listening begins with attending. **Attending** is the process of intentionally perceiving and focusing on a message.[12] Poor listeners have difficulty exercising control over what they attend to, often letting their focus drift to thoughts unrelated to the topic. One reason for this is that people typically speak at a rate of about 120 to 150 words per minute, but our brains can process between 400 and 800 words per minute.[13] This means we usually assume we know what a speaker is going to say before he or she finishes saying it. So our minds have lots of time to wander from the message.

attending: process of intentionally perceiving and focusing on a message

Not only does the gap between speaking rate and processing create opportunities for inattention, but research suggests, thanks in part to the Internet, smartphones, and other technologies, our attention spans continue to get shorter and shorter.[14] Consider your own experiences. Do you ever find yourself daydreaming or checking Facebook in class or when participating in an online conference or meeting?

The first step to becoming a good active listener, then, is to train ourselves to focus on or *attend* to what people are saying regardless of potential distractions (Photo 3.3). Let's consider four techniques for doing so.

1. **Get physically ready to listen.** Good listeners create a physical environment that reduces potential distractions and adopt a listening posture. For example, you might turn off background music, your smartphone, and computer so you won't be tempted to turn your attention to email and social media sites when you are trying to listen. You can adopt a listening posture by sitting upright in your chair, leaning slightly forward, and looking directly at the speaker or

Exhibit 3.1 — Ineffective and Effective Listening Behaviors

	Ineffective listening behavior	Effective listening behavior
Attending to the speech	Seeming to listen but looking out the window and letting your mind wander	Physically and mentally focusing on what is being said, even when information doesn't seem relevant
	Listening the same way regardless of type of material	Adjusting listening behavior to the specific requirements of the situation
Understanding/ remembering speech information	Listening to individual bits of information without regard for structure	Determining organization by identifying goals, main points, and supporting information
	Seldom or never reconsidering what was said	Asking yourself questions to help identify key aspects of the speech
	Seldom or never paraphrasing	Silently paraphrasing to solidify understanding
	Ignoring nonverbal cues	Seeking out subtle meanings based on nonverbal cues
	Relying on memory alone	Taking good notes
Evaluating and responding	Relying on gut reactions	Assessing quality of content, structure, and delivery

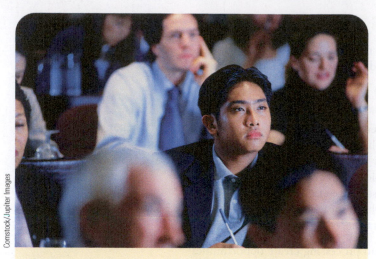

Comstock/Jupiter Images

Photo 3.3 Effective listeners train themselves to focus on the message regardless of potential distractions. What will you do to stay focused when listening?

computer screen (if you are watching and listening to a speaker online).[15]

2. **Resist mental distractions.** While listening to a speech or webcast, work consciously to block out wandering thoughts that might come from visual distractions (e.g., a classmate entering the room when the professor is lecturing), auditory distractions (e.g., coworkers chatting beside you while your supervisor is giving instructions), or physical distractions (e.g., wondering what you'll eat for lunch because your stomach is growling).

3. **Hear the speaker out.** Far too often, we stop listening because we disagree with something a speaker says, we assume we know what the speaker is going to say, or we become offended by an example or word used. To be effective at attending, you must train yourself not to interrupt or even mentally argue with a speaker and to stay focused throughout the message.

4. **Find personal relevance.** Speakers sometimes articulate relevance for us. For example, your professor may say, "Pay attention because this will be on the test." But you can also discover relevance for yourself by consciously considering how you might benefit from learning the information to improve some aspect of your life.

Understanding

Understanding is accurately interpreting a message. Four strategies can improve listening to understand.

1. **Identify the goal and main points.** Sometimes people's thoughts are well organized and easy to follow. Other times, however, we must work hard to decode the speaker's goal and main points. To be an effective listener, ask yourself, "What does the speaker want me to know or do?" (goal) and "What are the main points?" Try not to get bogged down with the details (e.g., specific examples, statistics) so much that you miss the speaker's goal and main points.

2. **Ask questions.** A **question** is a statement designed to clarify information or get additional details. Although ethical listeners demonstrate respect by waiting until the speaker is finished with the formal presentation to ask questions, you can make notes of any questions you have as you listen. Some questions may eventually be answered as the speaker moves through the presentation. However, others may not. You can pose your unanswered questions during the question-and-answer period that often follows a presentation, privately approach the speaker after the presentation, or use the questions to do additional research about the topic later.

3. **Paraphrase silently. Paraphrasing** is putting a message into your own words. It is not simply repeating what is said. After listening, try to summarize your understanding. So, after the speaker explains the criteria for selecting the best smartphone plan, you might say to yourself, "In other words, the key to deciding whether an unlimited plan is cost effective depends on how many minutes I'm likely to spend talking and texting on the phone each month."

understanding: accurately interpreting a message

question: a statement designed to clarify information or get additional details

paraphrasing: putting a message into your own words

KANYE WEST STEALS TAYLOR SWIFT'S MOMENT

At the 2009 MTV Video Music Awards (VMA), Kanye West jumped on stage and interrupted Taylor Swift's acceptance speech, saying, "Yo, Taylor. I'm happy for ya. I'm gonna let you finish. But Beyoncé had one of the best videos of all time. One of the best videos of all time." West's outburst quickly went viral[16] and can still be easily found online today.

Many have offered their opinions about how West was an unethical communicator at that moment because he violated the ethical principle of demonstrating respect for others. Similarly, many have commented about how Swift and Beyoncé reacted to the situation ethically because they adhered to that same principle. West has retorted that his actions were OK because he was adhering to the ethical principle of honesty—he believed he was telling the truth. Three years after the incident, stories like the one published at *hollywoodlife.com* entitled "Kanye West Will Not Apologize to Taylor Swift at VMAs" continue referring to it. In that article, a source for West said, "Kanye don't make no apologies . . . even when he's in the wrong."[17] One commenter, "Down n TX," posted a comment on Alison Bonaguro's CMT blog that he or she wished Swift had hit West over the head with the award. Another commenter, "Bree," said "As for Pink, and all the other celebs bad-mouthing Kanye, more power to you!! What he did was cold, and he deserves everything he's gonna get."

Years later, West again stormed the stage when Beck won a Grammy. West again thought Beyoncé should have won.[18] Though some thought the instant replay was a joke, West clarified that it was no joke. In a post-Grammy interview, West said Beck should have respected inspiration and given the award to Beyoncé.[19]

1. How would you respond to West's contentions about ethics, honesty, and respect?

2. What advice would you give to someone who disagreed as vehemently as West did to a public message such as the selection of a Grammy award winner?

---

4. **Observe nonverbal cues.** We interpret messages more accurately when we observe the nonverbal behaviors that accompany the words. Good speakers use their tone of voice, facial expressions, and gestures to emphasize important points and clarify structure. You can improve your listening skills by noticing where and how the speaker is attempting to emphasize or clarify points and then keying in on those comments.

Remembering

Remembering is being able to retain and recall information later. We may find remembering difficult, for instance, if we filter out information that doesn't fit our listening style, our listening anxiety prevents us from recalling what we have heard, we engage in passive listening, we practice selective listening and remember only what supports our position, or we fall victim to the primacy-recency effect of remembering only what is said at the beginning and end of a message. Let's consider three techniques to improve our ability to remember information.

1. **Repeat the information. Repetition**—saying something mentally two, three, or four times—helps store information in long-term memory.[20] If a speaker makes an important point or offers a key statistic, repeat it in your head two or three times to help make it "stick."

2. **Construct mnemonics.** A **mnemonic device** associates a special word or very short statement with new and longer information. One of the most common mnemonic techniques is to form a word with the first letters of a list of items you are trying to remember (Photo 3.4). For example, most beginning music students learn the mnemonic "*every good boy deserves fudge*" for the notes on the lines of the treble clef (E, G, B, D, F) and the word *face* for the notes on the spaces of the treble (F, A, C, E). You might try to construct a mnemonic to help remember the two to four main points in a speech.

> **SPEECH SNIPPET**
>
> When the webinar host flashed the words "STOP!" and "TAKE NOTE!" on the computer screen, Nancy refocused her attention to listen carefully to what the host was about to say.

remembering: retaining and recalling information at a later time

repetition: repeating words, phrases, or sentences for emphasis

mnemonic device: associates a special word or very short statement with new and longer information

Photo 3.4 Some people remember the color spectrum using the mnemonic device "Roy G. Biv" for red, orange, yellow, green, blue, indigo, and violet. What are some mnemonic devices you use to help remember something?

evaluating: critically analyzing the message

facts: statements whose accuracy can be verified as true

inferences: assertions based on the facts presented

3. **Take notes.** Note-taking is a powerful method for improving your recall of what you have heard in a speech. Not only does note-taking provide a written record that you can go back to, but by taking notes, you take a more active role in the listening process.[21]

What constitutes good notes varies by situation. For a short speech, good notes may consist of a statement of the goal, a brief list of main points, and a few of the most significant details. Or your notes might be a short summary of the entire concept (a type of paraphrase). For lengthy presentations, good notes will also include more detailed statements of supporting material, as well as questions that arise while listening.

Evaluating

Evaluating is the process of critically analyzing a message to determine its truthfulness, utility, and trustworthiness. Critical analysis is especially important when being persuaded to believe, support, or act on what was said. If you don't critically analyze messages, you risk going along with ideas that violate your values.

To evaluate messages effectively as you listen, try to separate facts from inferences. **Facts** are statements whose accuracy can be verified as true. If a statement is offered as a fact, analyze it thoughtfully to determine if it is true. **Inferences** are assertions based on the facts presented. When a speaker makes an inference, you need to determine whether the inference is valid. You should ask:

- What are the facts that support this inference?
- Is this information really central to the inference?
- Is there other information that would contradict this inference?

Separating facts from inferences helps us realize the difference between a verifiable observation and an opinion related to that observation. Separating facts from inferences is important because inferences may be false, even if they are based on verifiable facts.

Responding

responding: providing feedback to the speaker

Responding is providing feedback. You might respond during a speech through nonverbal behaviors (e.g., smiling, head nodding, brow furrowing). Sometimes, however, you need to prepare a formal written evaluation or critique of a presentation by a classmate, colleague, or employee. Typically, a critique is based on your critical analysis of how well the speech and speaker performed on specific key criteria. In the next section, we focus on techniques for responding effectively and ethically in constructive speech critiques.

constructive critique: an evaluative response that identifies what was effective and what could be improved in a speech

CONSTRUCTIVE CRITIQUES

A **constructive critique** is an evaluative response that identifies what was effective and what could be improved in a speech. Constructive critiques comprise statements that evaluate content, structure, and delivery.

Constructive Critique Statements

Constructive critique statements follow four guidelines.

1. **Constructive critique statements are specific.** Comments like "great job" or "slow down" are too vague to truly help a speaker improve. Instead, describe specific things the speaker did to make you conclude that the speech was great, or provide feedback on areas where some improvement might be needed. For example, did the speaker use transitions in a way that helped you follow the train of thought? Were there specific places where you would have liked the speaker to present the material at a slower pace?

2. **Constructive critique statements begin with observations about what was effective or done well.** Begin with positive observations so that you reinforce what the speaker did well. When we receive reinforcement for what we have done well, we are more likely to continue doing it. By the same token, any speech has room for improvement. Because the goal of a critique is to help the speaker improve, describe the specific problems you observed in the speech and then offer suggestions for overcoming them.

3. **Constructive critique statements explain how and why the observed behavior affected the speech.** For example, if you suggest that the speaker slow down while previewing the speech's main points, your statement will be more helpful if you also explain that the speaker's rate made it difficult for you to get the points firmly in your mind.

4. **Constructive critique statements are phrased as personal perceptions.** You can ensure this by using "I" rather than "you" language. For example, instead of

Josh Brasted/Getty Images

PUBLIC SPEAKING IN THE REAL WORLD

What Former President Bill Clinton Can Teach Us About Listening and Success

According to a *Huffington Post* article, "Bill Clinton Has a Superpower, and Mastering It Can Make You Successful Beyond Belief," the secret to Bill Clinton's success then and now is simple: "Clinton gives everyone he meets his full, undivided attention."[22] With all the potential distractions we face today, however, paying attention isn't easy. Studies report we spend nearly half of our waking hours thinking about something other than what we're doing and tend to check our smartphones every 6½ minutes.[23] Here are five key things Bill Clinton teaches us about mastering the skill of focused listening:

- **Paying attention is about empathy.** In his book, *My Life*, Clinton writes "All my life I've been interested in other people's stories . . . I wanted to know them, understand them, feel them."
- **Paying attention can be the difference between a strong and weak communicator.**
- **People can tell when you're listening and they love it.**

- **Eye contact matters.** In fact, it is considered the strongest form of nonverbal communication and Clinton is a master. Actress Gillian Anderson clarified his approach this way. "When he gets to you, he takes your hand and makes eye contact. After he leaves and he moves on to the next person, he looks back at you and seals the deal."
- **You can improve your listening skills.** Just as we have explained in this chapter, good listeners aren't born, they're made. And as Clinton has shown, mastering active listening can make you more effective and successful.

1. Do you think Bill Clinton is an effective listener? Why or why not?
2. What are some reasons you find it difficult to listen attentively to someone?

using "you" language to say, "You need to slow down," use "I" language: "During the preview of main points, I had trouble listening because the points were presented faster than I could understand and remember them."

Constructive Critique Elements

Constructive critiques comprise statements about a speech's content, structure, and delivery.

1. **Content critique statements focus on the goal, main points, and supporting material used to develop them.** For example, you might comment on how effectively the speaker used reasoning to tie a piece of evidence to the main point it supports. Or you might comment on the breadth and depth of the information used to develop each main idea. You might observe how relevant, recent, or credible the speaker's evidence seemed to be. Or you might talk about how effective content offered in a presentational aid was or could have been. Exhibit 3.2 illustrates ineffective and effective constructive critique statements regarding content.

2. **Structure critique statements focus on macrostructure (overall framework) and microstructure (language and style).** You might provide feedback on elements of the introduction (e.g., attention grabber, listener relevance, speaker credibility, thesis statement with main point preview), body (e.g., organizational pattern, transitions), or conclusion (e.g., thesis restatement with main point review, clincher, call to action). You might also offer statements about the speaker's language and style choices (e.g., appropriate, inclusive, accurate, clear, vivid, expressive). And you might offer statements about the construction of presentational aids (e.g., size, color, labels, layout, design). Exhibit 3.3 offers examples of ineffective and effective constructive critique statements regarding structure.

3. **Delivery critique statements focus on use of voice and body.** In commenting on voice, you might consider intelligibility (e.g., understandable rate, volume, pronunciation, enunciation), conversational style (e.g., fluent, spontaneous), and emotional expression (e.g., changes in rate, pitch, or volume; strategic pauses; stresses on key words). In commenting on body, you might consider attire, poise, posture, eye contact, facial expressions, gestures, and movement. You can consider if the speaker's mannerisms distracted you from the message or enhanced it. You can comment on how well the speaker used voice and body to integrate presentational aids (e.g., conceal, reveal, reference). Exhibit 3.4 provides examples of ineffective and effective constructive critique comments regarding delivery.

Certainly, you can help other speakers improve by offering constructive critiques. You can also help yourself by completing a self-critique after each speech you give, using the same approach you use to critique others. This self-critique approach is actually a form of cognitive restructuring that can help reduce your anxiety because it forces you to temper negative self-talk with positive self-talk immediately after your speech. Exhibit 3.5 presents a list of general criteria for preparing a constructive critique.

IMPROMPTU SPEECH CHALLENGE

Draw a card from a pile supplied by your instructor. Each card will have a different speech evaluation observation statement on it (e.g., the statistics were difficult [or easy] to understand, the organization was easy [or hard] to follow, the speaker talked fast). Prepare an effective constructive critique statement for the comment listed on your card. Then share it for the class in the form of a 1- to 2-minute impromptu speech. Be sure to explain why your critique statement is effective in your speech.

Exhibit 3.2 Ineffective and Effective Comments about Speech Content

Ineffective	Effective
• Interesting stories.	• I liked the story about your trip to the carnival. The many details you provided made it sound really fun!
• Too short.	• I would have liked to hear another example for each main point. This would have helped me better understand why the carnival was so significant to you.

Exhibit 3.3

Ineffective and Effective Comments about Speech Structure

Ineffective	Effective
• Nice transitions.	• Because you finished one main point and introduced the upcoming main point in your transition, I found it easy to follow your ideas.
• Boring introduction.	• I would have tuned in to the speech more quickly if you had begun with a great story about the carnival to capture my attention before stating your thesis.

Exhibit 3.4

Ineffective and Effective Comments about Speech Delivery

Ineffective	Effective
• Great gestures!	• I really liked how you gestured while you stated your transitions. It made it even clearer to me that we were moving to the next main point.
• Slow down.	• It would have been helpful for me if you slowed down while previewing your main points. I had a hard time catching them. Slowing down would have helped me follow the structure throughout the body of your speech.

Exhibit 3.5

General Criteria for a Constructive Critique

1. **Content**
   - Does the speaker establish common ground and adapt the content to the audience's interests, knowledge, and attitudes?
   - Does the speaker seem to have expertise in the subject areas?
   - Does the speaker have high-quality sources for the information given in the speech?
   - Does the speaker reveal the sources of the information?
   - Are the sources relevant? recent? varied? distributed throughout the speech?
   - Does the information presented explain or support each of the main points?
   - Are presentational aids appropriate and well used?
   - Is each main point supported with breadth? depth? listener relevance?

2. **Structure**
   - Does the introduction of the speech get attention, establish listener relevance and credibility, and lead into the topic?
   - Has the speaker stated a clear goal for the speech?
   - Are the main points of the speech clearly stated, parallel, and meaningful?
   - Do transitions lead smoothly from one point to another?
   - Does the information presented explain or support each of the main points?
   - Does the speaker use language that is appropriate, accurate, clear, and vivid?
   - Does the speaker use a compelling style?
   - Does the conclusion summarize the main points and end with a clincher?

3. **Delivery**
   - Does the speaker sound intelligible? conversational? expressive?
   - Is the presentation fluent?
   - Does the speaker look at the audience?
   - Does the speaker use appropriate facial expressions?
   - Were the pronunciation and articulation acceptable?
   - Does the speaker have good posture?
   - Does the speaker have sufficient poise?

Speech Assignment & Checklist

Preparing a Constructive Critique

Prepare a constructive critique of a speech, using the general criteria offered in this chapter.

Speech Evaluation Checklist

General Criteria

You can use this checklist to critique a speech you hear in class. (You can also use it to critique your own speech.)

Content

_____ **1.** Did you offer specific statements?

_____ **2.** Did you begin with statements about what the speaker did well?

_____ **3.** Did you offer statements for improvement?

_____ **4.** Did you provide an explanation *(why)* for each statement?

_____ **5.** Did you use "I" language to phrase each statement as a personal perception?

_____ **6.** Did you offer statements about content?

_____ **7.** Did you offer statements about structure?

_____ **8.** Did you offer statements about delivery?

_____ **9.** Did you offer statements about presentational aids?

Reflection and Assessment

Effective active listening takes conscious effort. Being an effective listener is crucial to the communication process and to creating shared meaning. To assess how well you've learned what we've discussed in this chapter, answer the following questions. If you have trouble answering any of them, go back and review that material. Once you can answer each question accurately, you are ready to move ahead to the next chapter.

1. What is listening and why should you study it in a public speaking course?
2. Why is effective listening challenging and what makes it most challenging for you?
3. What are some specific strategies you will employ to improve your listening skills?
4. What makes an effective and ethical constructive critique statement?

Challenge Resource and Assessment Center   MindTap®

Now that you have read Chapter 3, go to your MindTap Communication for *The Challenge of Effective Speaking in a Digital Age* for quick access to flashcards, chapter quizzes, and more.

Applying What You've Learned

1. **Impromptu Speech Activity:** Consider the last time you listened to music. Prepare and present a 2- to 3-minute impromptu speech describing the situation, the type of listening you engaged in, and what you remember about the song(s) you heard.

2. **Assessment Activity A:** Dale Carnegie once said "You can make more friends in 2 months by becoming interested in other people than you can in 2 years by trying to get other people interested in you."[24] Try this experiment at your workplace or after class: Ask a coworker, classmate, or friend his or her opinion about something and really listen to the response. Follow up with a "why" or "how" question, and really listen again. Write a short one- to two-page reflection paper about how you are received.

3. **Assessment Activity B:** Keep a log of three conversations you have with a friend, family member, or coworker. Try to limit how much talking you do. Keep the other person talking by asking "how" and "why" questions. Assess the experience in written form by answering the following questions: (a) How much of the conversations can you describe here? (b) Was it difficult to keep quiet? Why or why not? (c) Were you able to stay focused? If so, how? If not, why? (d) Do you think the other person noticed your efforts to listen rather than speak? Explain.

4 Determining an Appropriate Speech Goal

WHAT'S THE POINT?

WHEN YOU'VE FINISHED THIS CHAPTER, YOU WILL BE ABLE TO:

- Generate potential speech subjects and topics
- Analyze the rhetorical situation
- Select a speech topic appropriate to the rhetorical situation
- Write a specific speech goal statement tailored to the rhetorical situation

MindTap®

Review the chapter **Learning Objectives** and **Start** with quick warm-up activity.

Steve Jennings/Stringer/WireImage/Getty Images

ℯ Ethical communicators demonstrate respect by selecting a speech goal that is appropriate for the rhetorical situation.

CoraMax/Shutterstock.com

ACTION STEP 1

Determine a speech goal that is appropriate to the rhetorical situation.

A. Brainstorm and concept map for subjects and topics.

B. Analyze the rhetorical situation.

C. Develop a specific speech goal statement that is tailored to the rhetorical situation.

Several years ago, Romeo was voted "most likely to succeed" among his graduating high school classmates. Today he is making a good living as a professional musician and tours the country with his band. He has just accepted an invitation to speak to a student assembly at the inner-city high school he attended. He was asked to talk about the role his education played in helping him become a successful professional musician. He wonders how he can tailor his ideas to generate interest in what he has to say.

Whenever we are invited to give a speech, whether in the classroom or in some other setting, the first thing we have to do is determine a speech topic and goal. At times, this can feel pretty daunting, but it doesn't have to be. In this chapter, we'll walk you through an efficient process for determining a specific speech goal that is appropriate to the rhetorical situation.

Recall from Chapter 1 (and as reiterated in Exhibit 4.1), the elements of the rhetorical situation. They include you (and your knowledge and intentions), your audience (and their knowledge and expectations), and the occasion (the setting, purpose, and constraints). Because the audience is a crucial component of the rhetorical situation, effective speech goals are based on **audience analysis**, the study of the intended audience for your speech, and **audience adaptation**, the process of tailoring your speech to your listeners' unique needs, interests, and expectations. This step in the speechmaking process is rooted in what communication scholars refer to as "uncertainty reduction theory."[1] Although effective speakers adapt to their audience throughout the speechmaking process, they begin at the point of determining a specific speech goal.

To determine a specific speech goal adapted to the rhetorical situation, begin by identifying the many subjects and topics that interest you. Then, based on your analysis of both the audience and the occasion, narrow your topic list down to include only those that (a) interest you; (b) you know something about or would like to know more about; (c) can be adapted to address the needs, interests, and expectations of the audience; and (d) are appropriate for the occasion.

MindTap®

Read, highlight, and take notes online.

audience analysis: the study of the intended audience for your speech

audience adaptation: the process of tailoring a speech to the needs, interests, and expectations of your listeners

Exhibit 4.1 The Rhetorical Situation

You

Your audience

The rhetorical situation

The occasion

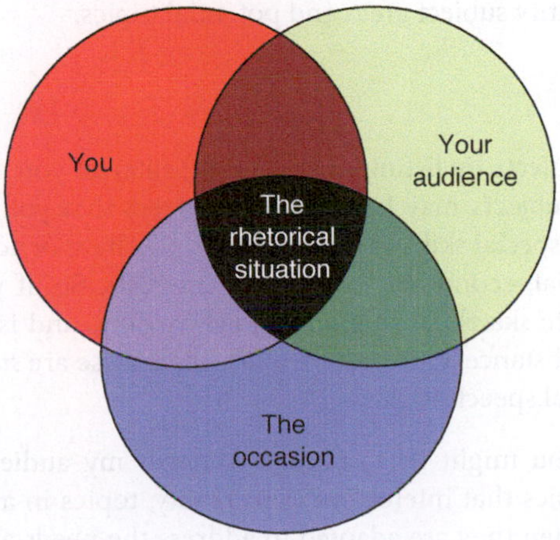

PUBLIC SPEAKING IN THE REAL WORLD

Aaron Sorkin's Attention to the Rhetorical Situation

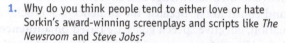

Even speeches by characters on TV and film are most compelling when they address the rhetorical situation. Oscar and Emmy award-winning screenwriter Aaron Sorkin is responsible for monumental films and TV programs such as *A Few Good Men*, *The American President*, *Charlie Wilson's War*, *The Social Network*, *The West Wing*, *Steve Jobs*, and *The Newsroom*. He intentionally writes character monologues that address exigence because they focus on real events. In *Steve Jobs*, for instance, the film opened in the Jobs' family garage in Silicon Valley. Doing so made it feel real, not only because that was Steve Jobs' home, but also because it captured the essence of the technology-saturated world we live in and Steve Jobs' role in creating it.[2]

When asked about what he was thinking when creating *The Newsroom*, Sorkin said, "I like writing about heroes [who] don't wear capes or disguises. You feel like, 'Gee, this looks like the real world and feels like the real world—why can't that be the real world?'" He goes on to discuss how he deliberately focuses on events that really occurred in the recent past because "writing fictional news . . . would take us too far from reality." Thus, as Sorkin's mouthpiece, Will McAvoy (played by Jeff Daniels) vows to cover stories because they're important and not for the ratings. Whether or not you like *The Newsroom* or Sorkin's other works, he certainly seems to understand how to identify a specific goal tailored to the rhetorical situation.[3]

1. Why do you think people tend to either love or hate Sorkin's award-winning screenplays and scripts like *The Newsroom* and *Steve Jobs*?

2. Where should the line be drawn between fact and fiction when telling a dramatized story about real people or events? Why?

BRAINSTORM AND CONCEPT MAP FOR POTENTIAL SPEECH SUBJECTS AND TOPICS

subject: a broad area of knowledge

topic: a narrow aspect of a subject

Good speech topics come from subjects we have some knowledge about and interest in. A **subject** is a broad area of knowledge, such as contemporary cinema, renewable energy, computer technology, or the Middle East. A **topic** is a narrow aspect of a subject. So, if your broad area of expertise is contemporary cinema, you might feel qualified to speak on a variety of narrower topics such as how the Academy Awards nomination process works; the relationships among movie producers, directors, and distributors; or how technology is changing movie production. Let's look more closely at how you can identify subject areas and potential topics.

Subjects

You can identify subjects by listing those that (a) interest you and (b) you may know something about. Subjects may be related to careers that you are considering, your major area of study, special skills or competencies you have or admire, or your hobbies, as well as your social, economic, or political interests. So, if your major is marketing, your hobbies are skateboarding and snowboarding, and issues that concern you include illiteracy, substance abuse, and obesity, then these are *subjects* from which you can identify potential speech topics.

At this point, you might be thinking, "What if my audience isn't interested in the subjects and topics that interest me?" In reality, topics in any subject area can be made interesting when they are adapted to address the needs and expectations of the audience.

Exhibit 4.2 **Kameron's Subject Lists**

Career Interests	Hobbies	Issues of Concern
Website designer	Bouldering	Climate change
Teacher	Bird watching	Human rights
Computer programmer	Disc golf	Civil rights
Event planner	Video games	Fracking

Exhibit 4.2 contains subject lists that Kameron came up with for his upcoming classroom speech. He chose to organize the subjects under three broad headings: (1) career interests, (2) hobbies, and (3) issues of concern.

Brainstorming, Concept Mapping, and Internet Searches

Because a topic is a specific aspect of a subject, you can identify many topics related to one subject. Three methods for doing so are brainstorming, concept mapping, and Internet searching. **Brainstorming** is an uncritical, nonevaluative process of generating associated ideas. When you brainstorm, list as many ideas as you can without evaluating them. If the subject for Kameron's speech was civil rights, he could brainstorm to come up with a list of potential topics, such as the role of women suffragists in gaining the right to vote, the rise and fall of Jim Crow in the American South, the pro-life/pro-choice debate, gun control, and same-sex marriage.

Concept mapping is a visual means of exploring connections between a subject and related ideas.[4] To generate connections, you might ask yourself questions about your subject, focusing on who, what, where, when, and how. In Exhibit 4.3, you can see an example of what Kameron's concept map looked like for the gun control topic.

brainstorming: an uncritical, nonevaluative process of generating associated ideas

concept mapping: a visual means of exploring connections between a subject and related ideas

Exhibit 4.3 **Kameron's Concept Map**

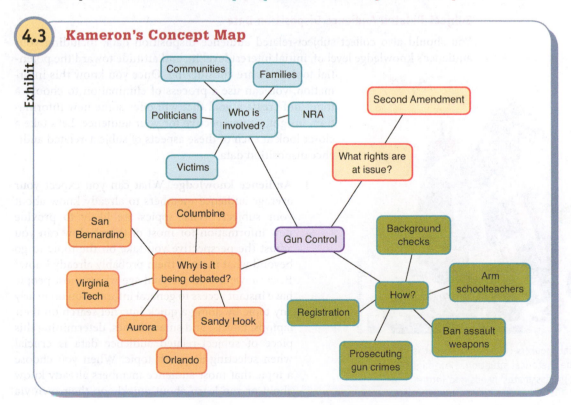

Notice how concept mapping allowed him to think more deeply about a general topic idea.

Internet search: a way to generate a variety of potential topic ideas on a subject area

If you find it difficult coming up with ideas, you might also do an **Internet search** on a subject area. If you do use this technique, however, be sure to set parameters, such as a time limit of 30 to 60 minutes to come up with 8 to 10 topics of interest. Because the Internet makes an unlimited supply of information available, you need to set these kinds of parameters to protect your time.

Speech-Planning Action Step 1, Activity 1A, will help you develop a list of topic ideas for speeches you could do in this course.

ANALYZE THE RHETORICAL SITUATION

Once you have generated a variety of potential subject areas and topics that interest you, consider how to tailor them to the rhetorical situation. To do so, examine who your audience is by collecting both demographic and subject-related data as well as the occasion and its potential constraints.

Analyze Your Audience

To analyze your audience, consider what types of demographic and subject-related audience data you might collect, data-gathering methods you might use to do so, and specific things to consider for using audience data ethically in your speeches (Photo 4.1).

Demographic Data

Helpful demographic information includes, for example, each person's approximate age, education level, sex, occupation, socioeconomic status, race, ethnicity, religion, geographic uniqueness, and first language. Exhibit 4.4 presents a list of questions that may help you uncover important demographic information.

Subject-Related Audience Disposition Data

You should also collect subject-related audience disposition data, including your audience's knowledge level of, initial interest level in, and attitude toward the potential topics you are considering. Once you know this information, you can use a process of elimination to choose a topic and create a goal that will offer some new information, insight, or perspective for your audience. Let's take a closer look at each of these aspects of subject-related audience disposition data.

1. **Audience knowledge.** What can you expect your average audience members to already know about your subject? What topics are likely to provide new information for most of them? How can you adjust the perspective you take on the topic to go beyond what most of them probably already know? Because we live in a digital age where most people have instant access to general information on nearly any topic by doing a quick Internet search on their laptops, tablets, and smartphones, determining this piece of subject-related audience data is crucial when selecting a speech topic. When you choose a topic that most audience members already know about or can learn about quickly on their own via

Photo 4.1 Ethical speakers select a topic that is appropriate to the rhetorical situation. How might you discover what your classmates' needs and interests are?

Stokkete/Shutterstock.com

Exhibit 4.4 — Demographic Audience Analysis Questions

Age. What is the age range of your audience, and what is the average age?

Education. What percentage of your audience has a high school, college, or postgraduate education?

Sex. What percentage of your audience is male? female?

Socioeconomic background. What percentage of your audience comes from high-, middle-, or low-income families?

Occupation. Is a majority of your audience from a single occupational group or industry, or do audience members come from diverse occupational groups?

Race. Are most members of your audience of the same race, or is there a mixture of races?

Ethnicity. What ethnic groups are in the audience? Are most audience members from the same cultural background?

Religion. What religious traditions are followed by audience members?

Geographic uniqueness. Are audience members from the same state, city, or neighborhood?

Language. What languages do a significant number of audience members speak as a first language? What language (if any) is common to all audience members?

Knowledge of subject. What can you expect the audience already knows about your subject? How varied is the knowledge level of audience members?

Attitude toward subject. What can you expect your audience's feelings to be about your subject?

---

an Internet search, you will bore them if you are not really creative. On the other hand, if you choose a topic for which your audience has insufficient background knowledge, you will have to provide the background or risk confusing them. For instance, if your subject is music, you can expect that an audience of traditional-age college students will know the general history of hip-hop music, including the major performers. So the topic "A Brief History of Hip-Hop" might bore them because you aren't offering new information or insight or perspective. However, a speech on the contributions of female artists to the development of hip-hop might draw on the audience's background knowledge but offer new information to most audience members.

2. **Audience interest.** How likely are audience members to be interested in your topic? You can actually make educated guesses about this piece of subject-related data based on the demographic data you collect.

   For instance, suppose you would like to speak on the subject of cancer drugs. If your audience is made up of health-care professionals, they might well be interested in the topic, but also might already know a good deal about it. You would need to delve deeper into the topic to ensure interest. On the other hand, if your audience is a beginning public speaking class made up mostly of 18- and 19-year-old students, then unless they have had personal experience with cancer, they may not naturally be interested in the topic. So make an extra effort to determine why 18- and 19-year-olds ought to know about cancer drugs and articulate this relevance throughout your speech.

3. **Audience attitude.** What might your audience's initial disposition be toward your topic? Audience attitude is especially important when trying to influence beliefs or move your audience to take action. You can determine your audience's attitudes toward your topic directly by surveying them, which we will

SPEECH SNIPPET

Laura wanted to give a speech on the prevalence of unnecessary hysterectomies. Because her audience included males and females, she took care to make her speech relevant for all by talking about how everyone is affected by the increases in insurance rates that result from unnecessary operations, and how a patient's emotional trauma caused by an unnecessary hysterectomy can have a profound effect on family and friends.

1A SPEECH PLANNING

Identifying Potential Speech Topics

Step 1: Develop a subject list.

    a. Divide a sheet of paper into three columns. Label column 1 "major and career interests," label column 2 "hobbies and activities," and label column 3 "issues of concern."

    b. Working on one column at a time, identify subject areas that interest you. Try to identify at least three subjects in each column.

    c. Place a check mark next to one subject in each list that you would enjoy speaking about.

    d. Keep the lists for future use in choosing a topic for an assigned speech.

Step 2: For each subject you checked, brainstorm a list of narrower topics that relate to it. Which of the topics do you have the most interest in? Place a check mark beside one or two of them.

Step 3: Develop a concept map for those topics you checked to identify smaller topic areas and related ideas that might be developed into future speeches.

SAMPLE STUDENT RESPONSE

Identifying Potential Speech Topics

Step 1: Develop a subject list

Major and career interests	Hobbies and activities	Issues of concern
Teaching	Singing	School violence
✓ Early childhood education	✓ Volunteering	Breast cancer research
Chef	Rock climbing	Cyberbullying
Coaching	Swimming	✓ Childhood obesity

Step 2: Brainstorm a list of narrower topics for "early childhood education"

Parental care	✓ Professional group day care
Family care	✓ Parent cooperatives
✓ Nannies	

(continued)

Activity

1A **SPEECH PLANNING** (continued)

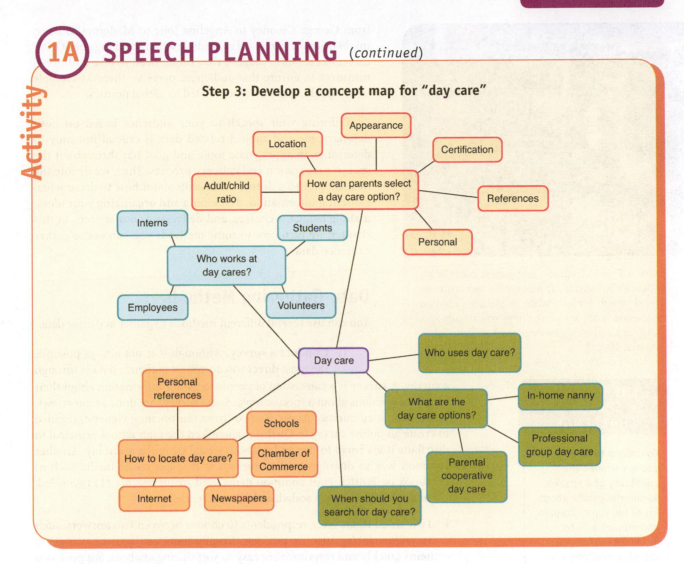

Step 3: Develop a concept map for "day care"

discuss in the next section. If you cannot survey the audience directly, you might try to see if published opinion polls related to your subject are available. Then you can estimate your audience members' attitudes by studying these opinion polls and extrapolating their results to your audience.

Once you have an idea about your audience's initial attitude toward your topic, you can tailor your specific goal in ways that will allow you to influence rather than alienate them (Photo 4.2). For example, one reason the gun control debate tends to be so heated stems from different attitudes based on personal experiences. Friends and family members of those killed at places such as Columbine, Virginia Tech, Aurora, and Sandy Hook Elementary School would likely come to the speaking occasion with a different initial attitude than those who are avid hunters living in rural areas where they appreciate the sense of protection owning a firearm provides them.

4. **Audience perception.** Will your audience recognize you as a subject-matter expert? Will you need to establish your credibility as you speak? **Credibility** is the audience's perception of you as knowledgeable about the topic, trustworthy (honest, dependable, and ethical), and personable (friendly; sincere; genuinely committed to the topic, occasion, and audience). Consider, for example, transnational celebrity activism. Although superstars

credibility: the perception of a speaker as knowledgeable, trustworthy, and personable

Photo 4.2 Even Stephen Colbert must consider his audience's knowledge of, interest in, and attitudes toward various subjects when he plans his opening monologue. What are some things you already know about your audience's knowledge of and interest in potential topics?

IMPROMPTU SPEECH CHALLENGE

Consider a time when you questioned the credibility of a speaker as knowledgeable about his or her topic. Prepare and present a 2- to 3-minute impromptu speech explaining why.

survey: a canvassing of people to get information about their ideas and opinions about a specific topic

two-sided items: survey items that force respondents to choose between two answers

multiple-response items: survey items that give respondents several alternative answers from which to choose

from George Clooney to Angelina Jolie to Madonna to Bono might be easily perceived as credible when speaking about their careers as actors or singers, they might need to take additional measures to ensure that audiences perceive them as credible when speaking about issues related to global politics.

Tailoring your speech to your audience based on both demographic and subject-related data is crucial not only to determine an appropriate topic and goal but throughout the speech preparation and delivery process. Thus, we devote the next chapter to a deeper discussion about how to do so when gathering information, developing and organizing your ideas, making language choices, and delivering your speech. In this chapter, we turn now to some methods you can use to gather audience data.

Data-Gathering Methods

You can use several different methods to gather audience data.

1. **Conduct a survey.** Although it is not always possible, the most direct way to collect audience data is through a survey. A **survey** is a canvassing of people to gather information about their ideas and opinions about a specific topic. Some surveys are done as interviews, others as written questionnaires. Romeo (from our opening vignette) decided to create an online survey in Qualtrics and asked the high school principal to distribute it via email to the students who would be in the assembly. Another common way to distribute online surveys is through social media such as Facebook or Twitter. Four common items used in surveys are (1) two sided, (2) multiple response, (3) scaled, and (4) open ended.

-   **Two-sided items** force respondents to choose between two answers, such as yes/no, for/against, or pro/con. Respondents can answer two-sided items quickly and responses are easy to sort during analysis. Suppose you wanted to understand your audience members' attitudes on violence in adult video games. You might ask:

    Do you play adult video games (e.g., Bioshock, Grand Theft Auto)?

    _____ *Yes* _____ *No*

    Romeo asked:

    Do you ever attend live concerts?

    _____ *Yes* _____ *No*

-   **Multiple-response items** give respondents several alternative answers from which to choose and are especially useful for gathering demographic data. For example:

    What is the highest level of education you have completed?

    _____ *Some high school* _____ *High school diploma* _____ *Some college*

    _____ *Associate's degree* _____ *Bachelor's degree* _____ *Master's degree*

    _____ *Doctorate* _____ *Post-doctorate* _____ *Other*

- **Scaled items** measure the direction or intensity of respondents' feelings or attitudes toward something (e.g., on a scale from 1 to 5 with 5 being "very likely"). For example:

Indicate the extent to which you agree or disagree with the following statement:

Adult video games contain too much violence.

____ *Strongly agree* ____ *Agree* ____ *Neutral* ____ *Disagree*
____ *Strongly disagree*

Scaled items can also be used to assess audience interest. For example:

Please place a check next to the response that best describes your interest in learning about each of the following.

What is it like to travel on a bus for weeks at a time?

____ *Very interested* ____ *Somewhat interested* ____ *Uninterested*

How do musicians practice while touring?

____ *Very interested* ____ *Somewhat interested* ____ *Uninterested*

What challenges do musicians face when performing the same songs night after night?

____ *Very interested* ____ *Somewhat interested* ____ *Uninterested*

- **Open-ended items** encourage respondents to elaborate on their opinions without forcing them to answer in a predetermined way. These items yield rich information, but the wide variety of responses can be difficult to analyze. For example, to determine what you would need to do to establish your credibility on the subject of video game violence, you might ask:

How can you tell if someone is an expert on video game violence?

2. **Observe informally.** If you are familiar with your audience members, you can learn a lot through informal observation. For instance, after being in class for even a couple of sessions, you should be able to estimate your classmates' approximate age or age range and the ratio of men to women. As you listen to your classmates talk, you will learn more about their interest in, knowledge of, and attitudes toward many issues.

3. **Question a representative.** When you are invited to speak to a group you are unfamiliar with, ask your contact person for demographic and subject-related audience data related to your topic (Photo 4.3). Romeo made an appointment to visit with the principal and with one of the academic counselors to get perspectives on demographic and subject-related data about the students who would be at the assembly.

4. **Make educated guesses.** If you can't get information any other way, you can

scaled items: survey items that measure the direction and/or intensity of an audience member's feeling or attitude toward something

open-ended items: survey items that encourage respondents to elaborate on their opinions without forcing them to answer in a predetermined way

Photo 4.3 Sometimes you can find out about an audience by questioning a representative. Who could you question to find out more about your classmates and their interest in your topic?

make educated guesses based on indirect data such as the general makeup of the people who live in a specific community, belong to a certain or similar organization, or are likely to attend the speech event. For example, Romeo could infer that his audience members would range in age from 14 to 18 years old, that there would be males and females, and that some would be very interested in learning more about the life of a professional musician and others might not be interested at all.

Ethical Use of Audience Data

Once you have collected audience data, you can use it to tailor your speech to your audience's interests, needs, and expectations. To demonstrate respect for everyone, avoid making inappropriate or inaccurate assumptions based on the data you collect. Two potential pitfalls to avoid are marginalizing and stereotyping.

marginalizing: ignoring the values, needs, and interests of some audience members, leaving them feeling excluded

Marginalizing is the practice of ignoring the values, needs, and interests of some audience members, leaving them to feel excluded. For example, if you discover that most of your audience members have played adult video games, to avoid marginalizing the few members who have never done so you might quickly show a brief demonstration of a game in your speech introduction.

stereotyping: assuming all members of a group have similar knowledge, behaviors, or beliefs simply because they belong to that group

Stereotyping is assuming all members of a group have similar knowledge, behaviors, or beliefs simply because they belong to that group. If, for example, you find out that the average age of your audience is 65, you might stereotype by assuming that most of them know nothing about video games when, in fact, many have either played them or observed family members doing so. To avoid stereotyping based on demographic data, you need to collect subject-related data as well.

audience diversity: the range of demographic and subject-related differences represented in an audience

You can also reduce your chances of marginalizing or stereotyping by recognizing and acknowledging the diversity represented in your audience. **Audience diversity** is the range of demographic and subject-related differences represented in an audience. So while the average age of your audience may be 65, there may also be some in the audience who are much younger.

You can use Exhibit 4.5 to summarize the demographic and subject-related audience data you collect. Now that you understand audience analysis, you can complete Speech-Planning Action Step 1, Activity 1B.

Analyze the Occasion

occasion: the expected purpose of and setting (location) for the speech

The **occasion** is made up of the expected purpose of and setting (location) for the speech. Answers to several key questions about the occasion should guide you when selecting your topic and throughout the speech-making process.

1. **What is the intended purpose (exigence) of the speech?** In other words, why does the audience think this speech is being given? At a religious service, for example, the congregation expects the sermon to have a religious theme. At a national sales meeting, the field representatives expect to hear about new products. Romeo's audience expects him to talk about why and how to prepare for college. For your classroom speeches, a major expectation is that your speech will meet the assignment criteria.

2. **What is the expected length?** Time limits for classroom speeches are usually quite short, so choose a topic that is narrow enough to be accomplished in the brief time allotted. "Three Major Causes of the Declining Honeybee Population" could probably be presented in 5 minutes, but "A History of Human Impact on the Environment" could not. Time-limit expectations are not unique to classroom

4.5 **Audience Analysis Summary Form**

My subject is _____

Data were collected:

_____ by survey

_____ by direct observation

_____ by questioning the person who invited me

_____ by educated guessing

Demographic Data

1. The average audience member's education level is _____ high school _____ college _____ postgraduate.

2. The ages range from _____ to _____. The average age is about _____.

3. The audience is approximately _____ percent male and _____ percent female.

4. My estimate of the average income level of the audience is _____ upper _____ middle _____ lower.

5. Most audience members are of _____ the same occupation/major (which is _____) _____ different occupations/majors.

6. Most audience members are of _____ the same race (which is _____) _____ a mixture of races.

7. Most audience members are of _____ the same religion (which is _____) _____ a mixture of religions.

8. Most audience members are of _____ the same nationality (which is _____) _____ a mixture of nationalities.

9. Most audience members are from _____ the same state _____ the same city _____ the same neighborhood _____ different areas.

10. Most audience members speak _____ English as their first language _____ English as a second language (ESL).

Subject-Specific Data

1. The average audience member's knowledge of the subject is likely to be _____ extensive _____ moderate _____ limited because _____

2. The average audience member's interest in this subject is likely to be _____ high _____ moderate _____ low because _____

3. The average audience member's atitude toward my subject is likely to be _____ positive _____ neutral _____ negative because _____

4. My initial credibility with the audience is likely to be _____ high _____ medium _____ low because _____

Conclusion

Based on these data _____
_____
_____

which relate to my speech topic in the following ways: _____
_____

I will tailor my speech in the following ways: _____
_____
_____

Ian's classmates ranged from first-year 18-year-old students to 30-somethings, some of them married. To be audience-centered, Ian realized he needed to adapt to audience diversity regarding fire safety. So he decided to talk about fire safety measures that would be appropriate not only for students living in residence halls but also for people who own their own homes.

Activity

Analyzing Your Audience

Step 1: Decide on a method for gathering audience data and collect it.

Step 2: Use the information gathered to complete the Audience Analysis Summary Form (Exhibit 4.5).

Step 3: Write two short paragraphs to describe what these audience demographics and subject-related data might suggest about your audience's knowledge, interests, attitudes, and expectations toward your topic.

SAMPLE STUDENT RESPONSE

Analyzing Your Audience

Step 1: Decide on a method

I gathered audience data through informal observation.

Step 2: Complete the Audience Analysis Summary Form

My subject is *day care options*

Data were collected:

___X___ by survey

_____ by direct observation

_____ by questioning the person who invited me

_____ by educated guessing

Demographic Data

1. The average audience member's education level is _____ high school __X__ college _____ postgraduate.

2. The ages range from __19__ to __24__ The average age is about __20__.

3. The audience is approximately __65__ percent male and __35__ percent female.

4. My estimate of the average income level of the audience is _____ upper __X__ middle _____ lower.

5. Most audience members are of _____ similar occupations/majors __X__ different occupations/majors.

6. Most audience members are of _____ the same race __X__ a mixture of races.

7. Most audience members are of _____ the same religion __X__ a mixture of religions (because I can't really tell).

8. Most audience members are of __X__ the same nationality (*which is American*) _____ a mixture of nationalities.

(continued)

1B SPEECH PLANNING *(continued)*

Activity

9. Most audience members are from __X__ the same state ____ the same city ____ the same neighborhood ____ different areas.

10. Most audience members speak __X__ English as their first language ____ English as a second language (ESL).

Subject-Specific Data

1. The average audience member's knowledge of the subject is likely to be ____ extensive ____ moderate __X__ limited because *my audience members are mostly first and second year college students without children of their own.*

2. The average audience member's interest in this subject is likely to be ____ high __X__ moderate ____ low because *without encouragement, they have no need to know about this subject. I will help them consider their futures in my listener relevance links.*

3. The average audience member's attitude toward my subject is likely to be ____ positive __X__ neutral ____ negative because *the audience doesn't really have any information about the topic.*

4. My initial credibility with the audience is likely to be ____ high ____ medium __X__ low because *this is our first speech and they don't know I am a single parent.*

Step 3: Write summary paragraphs

Conclusion

From these data, I conclude that most audience members are similar to one another and to me. We are all students at U.K. Most of us are around 20 years old, which suggests that we have a common generational view. There are more men than women in the class, and we are a mixture of different races. I can't really tell if we are similar or different in terms of religious affiliation. I would have to probe more specifically for that information if it seems pertinent for my ultimate topic and speech goal. Although most audience members speak English as their first language, there are also two international students who do not speak English as their first language. I will want to avoid marginalizing them by using visual aids to help them comprehend important information throughout the speech.

Most audience members don't know a lot about day care and probably have only a moderate interest in the subject. I will need to make sure to explain how and why this information may be important to them throughout the speech. Since they don't know about my experience as a single parent, I will need to establish my credibility during the introduction and periodically throughout the speech.

Photo 4.4 Even musicians ought to demonstrate respect for their audiences by adhering to time-limit expectations. Have you ever felt offended when a concert seemed too short or too long?

speeches (Photo 4.4). Adhering to audience time-limit expectations demonstrates respect. For example, consider when you paid a hefty ticket price to attend a live concert or other public event. If the main event was shorter than you expected it to be, you probably felt cheated. Or consider when a teacher kept you in class longer than the allotted time. You may have become frustrated because it seemed the instructor failed to respect the other commitments (e.g., other classes, jobs) you juggled along with that particular course. Speakers who speak for more or less time than has been allotted can seriously interfere with event programming and lose the respect of both their hosts and their audiences.

3. **Where will the speech be given?** Rooms vary in size, lighting, and seating arrangements. Some are single level, some have stages or platforms, and some have tiered seating. The space affects the speech. For example, in a long, narrow room, you will need to speak loudly to be heard in the back row. If you are speaking in an auditorium to a large group of people, you will need to speak loudly and perhaps use a microphone. You will also need to use large gestures and presentational aids that can be seen and heard easily in all parts of the room. The brightness of the room and the availability of room darkening shades may impact what kinds of presentational aids you can use. If possible, visit the room in advance either physically or virtually via online photo galleries or virtual tours posted on the venue's website. The more you know about the location where you will be giving your speech, the better you will be able to tailor it to be most effective in that setting.

Today we often give speeches online via live video streaming or by recording ourselves and uploading the speech to YouTube or some other website. To prepare for giving speeches virtually, practice recording and critiquing yourself until you appear and sound spontaneous and natural even when speaking only to the camera.

4. **When will the speech be given?** A speech given early in the morning requires a different approach from one given right after lunch or in the evening. If your speech is scheduled after a meal, for instance, your audience may be lethargic, mellow, or even on the verge of sleep. So you may want to plan to insert more material designed to gain and regain audience interest throughout. Similarly, where you are placed on the schedule of events should influence your speech planning. For example, if you are first, you may need to "warm up" the audience and be prepared to deal with the distraction of latecomers entering the room while you are speaking. If you speak later in the program, you may need to integrate attention-catching material to keep the interest of a weary audience.

5. **What equipment is necessary and available?** Would you like to use a microphone, lectern, flip chart, smartboard, or computer and LCD projector to display visuals or audiovisuals? If so, does the room have an adequate means for displaying visuals and projecting audio? Do you plan to use the Internet? If so, is the room wired for Internet or Wi–Fi enabled? It is your responsibility to check with your host to make sure the equipment can be made available or to make alternative arrangements. Regardless of the arrangements made, however, experienced speakers realize that something

may go wrong and always prepare a backup plan. So if you plan to use a computerized slide show, you might also prepare handouts of key slides in case the equipment fails.

Speech-Planning Action Step 1, Activity 1C will help you understand the occasion so that you take into consideration your purpose, audience expectations, and location as you choose your topic and develop your speech.

SELECT A TOPIC

As you review your topic list, compare each topic to your audience profile. Are any topics too simple or too difficult for the audience's knowledge base? If so, eliminate those topics. Are some topics likely to bore the audience and you can't think

1C SPEECH PLANNING

Activity

Analyzing the Occasion

Fill in answers to the following questions:

1. What is the intended purpose (exigence) for the speech? _____

2. What is the expected length? _____

3. Where will the speech be given? _____

4. When will the speech be given? _____

5. What equipment is necessary and available? _____

Write a short paragraph mentioning which aspects of the occasion are most important to consider as you prepare your speech and why.

_____

_____

SAMPLE STUDENT RESPONSE
Analyzing the Occasion

1. What is the intended purpose (exigence) for the speech? _An informative speech_

2. What is the expected length? _4–6 minutes_

3. Where will the speech be given? _In my public speaking classroom_

4. When will the speech be given? _I am the first of six speakers to begin at 9:30 a.m. on Monday morning._

5. What equipment is necessary and available? _LCD projector, computer, and screen_

Time is certainly important: Four to six minutes is not very long. I plan to time my speech when I practice to make sure I stay within the expected time limits.

of any way to pique their interest with new insight or a new perspective on them? Eliminate those, as well. How might the audience's age range, ethnicity, and other demographic features mesh with each topic? By asking these and similar questions, you will be able to identify topics and perspectives on topics that are appropriate for your audience.

Next, consider the occasion. Are some topics inappropriate for the intended purpose? Are some too broad to cover adequately in the time allotted? Would any require equipment that cannot be made available where you will be speaking? Answers to these kinds of questions will help you identify topics appropriate to the occasion.

WRITE A SPEECH GOAL STATEMENT

Once you have chosen your topic, you are ready to identify and write the general goal of your speech and then to write your specific goal statement tailored to your audience and occasion.

General and Specific Speech Goals

general goal: the overall intent of the speech

The **general goal** is the overall intent of the speech. Most speeches intend to entertain, inform, or persuade, even though each type can include elements of other types. Consider the following examples:

- Stephen Colbert's opening monologue on *The Late Show with Stephen Colbert* is generally intended to entertain, even though it also includes information about real-life events and even attempts to persuade audience members to agree with his opinions about certain issues.

- Presidential campaign speeches are generally intended to persuade, even though they also include informative material.

- Classroom lectures are generally intended to inform, even though they may include entertaining anecdotes and stories. The general goal is usually dictated by the occasion. (In classroom speeches, the instructor usually specifies it.)

Speech-Planning Action Step 1, Activity 1D will help you select your topic.

Reflect on Ethics

JIM CRAMER AND CNBC'S MAD MONEY

Jim Cramer hosts CNBC's *Mad Money*, a program devoted to providing financial advice to its viewers. In an interview on Comedy Central's *The Daily Show*, former host Jon Stewart claimed both Stewart and Cramer were "snake oil salesmen" but that *The Daily Show* was labeled as such. Stewart was essentially arguing that CNBC's *Mad Money* was duping viewers by claiming to offer sound financial advice, when actually it was not. For example, Stewart showed footage of Cramer recommending that his viewers buy Bear Stearns stock just before it collapsed.

If you are personally unfamiliar with the show, watch at least one episode before answering the following questions. Then, with regard to *Mad Money*, consider the elements of the rhetorical situation we've discussed in this chapter (purpose, audience expectations, and location).

1. How would you respond to Stewart's claim that *Mad Money*'s host is being unethical?

2. Why might the fact that *Mad Money* is shown on CNBC (and not Comedy Central) influence your decision about its host as an ethical communicator?

(1D) SPEECH PLANNING

Activity

Selecting a Topic

Use your responses to Action Step Activities 1A, 1B, and 1C to complete this activity.

Step 1: Look over the concept map you prepared in Activity 1A. List each of the specific topics that you generated:

_____   _____   _____

_____   _____   _____

_____   _____   _____

Step 2: Using the information you compiled in Activity 1B (audience analysis), compare each topic to your audience profile. Eliminate topics that seem less appropriate for this specific audience. List the remaining topics:

_____   _____   _____

_____   _____   _____

Step 3: Compare each of the remaining topics to the information you compiled in Activity 1C (analysis of the occasion). Eliminate topics that seem less appropriate for this occasion. List the remaining topics:

_____   _____   _____

Step 4: The remaining topics are appropriate to the rhetorical situation (you, the audience, and the occasion). Select the topic from this list that you are most excited about sharing with others.

My topic will be: _____

SAMPLE STUDENT RESPONSE

Selecting a Topic

Step 1: Look over the concept map you prepared in Activity 1A. List each of the specific topics that you generated:

Who works at day cares?   *How do parents locate a day care?*

How can parents select a day   *When should parents search for a*
care option?   *day care?*

(continued)

Activity

Step 2: Using the information you compiled in Activity 1B (audience analysis), compare each topic to your audience profile. Eliminate topics that seem less appropriate. List the remaining topics:

How can parents select a day care option?   *How do parents locate a day care?*

Who works at day cares?

Step 3: Compare each of the remaining topics to the information you compiled in Activity 1C (analysis of the occasion). Eliminate topics that seem less appropriate for this occasion. List each of the remaining topics:

How can parents select a day care option?   *Who works at day cares?*

Step 4: The remaining topics are appropriate to the rhetorical situation (you, the audience, and the occasion). Select the topic from this list that you are most excited about sharing with others.

My topic will be *How can parents select a good day care option?*

---

specific goal: a single statement that identifies the exact response the speaker wants from the audience

Whereas the general goal is typically determined by the occasion, the **specific goal** (or specific purpose) is a single statement that identifies the desired response a speaker wants from the audience. For a speech about "Vanishing Honeybees," if your general goal is to inform, you might state the specific goal as "I would like the audience to understand the four reasons honeybees are vanishing" (Photo 4.5). If your general goal is to persuade, you might instead state the specific goal as "I intend to convince the audience to donate money to Honeybee Advocacy International, a group trying to solve the problem and stop the crisis."

Phrasing a Specific Speech Goal Statement

A specific speech goal statement must be carefully crafted because it lays the foundation for organizing your speech. The following guidelines can help you craft specific goal statements.

1. **Write a first draft of your speech goal in one complete sentence.** Romeo drafts his speech goal this way:

   I want my audience to understand my life as a professional musician.

   Romeo's draft is a complete sentence, and it specifies the response he wants from the audience: *to understand* the life of a professional musician. Thus, he is planning to give an informative speech.

2. **Make sure the goal statement contains only one idea.** Suppose Romeo had written:

   I would like the audience to understand my lifestyle as a music student and as a successful professional musician.

This goal statement would need to be revised because it includes two distinct ideas: the lifestyle of a music student and of a professional musician. Either one could be a worthy goal—but not both in one short speech. If your goal statement includes the word *and*, you probably have more than one idea and need to narrow your focus.

3. **Revise the statement until it clearly articulates the precise focus of your speech tailored to the audience.** Romeo's draft "I want my audience to understand my life as a professional musician" is a good start, but it is fairly broad. Romeo narrows the statement to: "I want my audience to understand some important challenges I overcame in school that helped me become a successful professional musician." This version is more specific, but still does not clearly capture his intention, so he revises it again to: "I would like the audience to understand three challenges I overcame as a high school music student that helped me become a successful professional musician." Now the goal is limited by Romeo's focus not only on the specific number of challenges but also on a specific situation as a high school music student. A good specific speech goal statement will guide you as you research your speech. Once you have completed your research, you will revise your specific speech goal into a thesis statement, which will be the foundation on which you will organize the speech. Exhibit 4.6 gives several additional examples of general and specific informative and persuasive goals.

zlikovec/Shutterstock.com

Photo 4.5 For his informative speech on the vanishing honeybee population, Justin decided to focus on the four major reasons attributed to it. What other specific goal statements could he use for a speech on vanishing honeybees?

Speech-Planning Action Step 1, Activity 1E will help you develop a well-written specific goal statement for your speech.

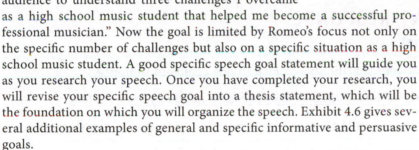

Exhibit 4.6 **General and Specific Speech Goals**

Informative Goals

General goal: To inform the audience about e-books

Specific goal: I want the audience to understand the differences between the Kindle and the Sony/iPad approaches to electronic books.

General goal: To inform the audience about forms of mystery stories

Specific goal: I want the audience to be able to identify the three basic forms of mystery stories.

Persuasive Goals

General goal: To persuade the audience that saving for retirement is important

Specific goal: I want the audience to begin a personal ROTH IRA funded this year with at least 2 percent of their income.

General goal: To persuade the audience to get involved with the food bank

Specific goal: I want to persuade the audience to volunteer to work on the campus food drive for our local food bank.

1E SPEECH PLANNING

Writing a Specific Goal

1. Write a first draft of your specific speech goal in one complete sentence.

2. If the statement contains more than one idea, select one and rewrite the statement.

3. Revise the statement until it clearly articulates the precise focus of your speech tailored to your intended audience.

4. Write the final draft of the specific speech goal.

   _____

   _____

   _____

SAMPLE STUDENT RESPONSE
Writing a Specific Goal

1. Write a first draft of your specific speech goal in one complete sentence.

   I want the audience to understand how to choose a good day care option.

2. If the statement contains more than one idea, select one and rewrite the statement.

   I want my audience to recognize the choices they have for day care.

3. Revise the statement until it clearly articulates the precise focus of your speech tailored to your intended audience.

   I want to teach my audience about three popular day care options.

4. Write the final draft of the specific speech goal.

   I want to teach my audience about the advantages and disadvantages of at-home day care, professional group day care, and parental cooperative day care.

Reflection and Assessment

The first step in preparing an effective speech is to identify a topic and goal. An appropriate topic is one that addresses the rhetorical situation (you, your audience, and the occasion). To assess how well you've learned what we've discussed in this chapter, answer the following questions. If you have trouble answering any of them, go back and review that material. Once you can answer each question accurately, you are ready to move ahead to the next chapter.

1. How do you go about brainstorming for potential speech subject areas and topics?
2. What are some kinds of data you should collect as you examine the rhetorical situation?
3. How do you use the rhetorical situation data you collect to select a speech topic?
4. What are the characteristics of an effective specific speech goal statement?

Challenge Resource and Assessment Center   MindTap®

Now that you have read Chapter 4, go to your MindTap Communication for *The Challenge of Effective Speaking in a Digital Age* for quick access to flashcards, chapter quizzes, and more.

Applying What You've Learned

1. **Impromptu Speech Activity:** Identify a pet peeve and prepare a 2- to 3-minute impromptu speech describing the pet peeve and why it bothers you. Include in your reasons which ethical communication principle(s) your pet peeve violates in your opinion and why.
2. **Assessment Activity A:** Complete Speech-Planning Action Step 1, Activities 1A through 1E, for one of the speeches you may give this semester.
3. **Assessment Activity B:** Suppose you were asked to give a speech about some aspect of your work to a group of your coworkers and managers. Explain what demographic and subject-specific information you would need, how you would collect it, and how you might use it in your speech planning. How would your approach differ if your audience was your fellow students in your speech class?

5

Adapting to Audiences

WHAT'S THE POINT?
WHEN YOU'VE FINISHED THIS CHAPTER, YOU WILL BE ABLE TO:

- Address initial audience disposition toward your topic
- Highlight common ground with your audience
- Articulate the relevance of your speech to your audience
- Establish your credibility as knowledgeable, trustworthy, and personable
- Employ strategies to enhance comprehension and retention
- Overcome potential language and cultural differences
- Create your own audience adaptation plan

MindTap®

Review the chapter **Learning Objectives** and **Start** with quick warm-up activity.

Ethical communicators demonstrate respect by adapting their message to the audience at all points in the speech-making process.

ACTION STEP 2
Understand your audience and adapt to it.

A. Understand audience diversity.
B. Tailor your speech to address their needs, interests, and expectations.

Megan decided to do her speech on the causes and effects of hurricanes. Hurricane Katrina had destroyed her family's home several years ago. They still hadn't fully recovered from it. When she watched news reports of Superstorm Sandy, the awful memories came flooding back. Her heart ached for the victims. She really wanted her classmates to better understand the physical and emotional havoc raised by hurricanes. But how would she gain and maintain the interest of classmates who live in a landlocked state nowhere near a coastline? How could she help them see the relevance of an event that happened years ago? Her instructor said nearly any topic can be tailored to address the needs, interests, and expectations of the audience. Still, Megan couldn't help but think this was going to pose quite a challenge.

J.J. chose to do his speech on cell phone distracted driving. Audience analysis had confirmed his assumption that most of his classmates realized they shouldn't talk or text while driving, yet their survey responses revealed that 90 percent of them did so anyway. Many of them indicated they were very careful. They did not believe they were likely to get in an accident while texting and most certainly not while merely talking on the phone. He knew better. But he also knew that convincing them to agree with him and to stop engaging in this dangerous behavior would be a real challenge.

In the previous chapter, we talked about how to conduct an audience analysis and then use it to narrow your topic and determine your speech goal. Recall, however, that effective speakers don't stop there. Effective speakers use *audience adaptation*—the process of tailoring their speech to the needs, interests, and expectations of the audience—to inform everything from researching the topic to organizing the main points to developing them with supporting material to making language choices and practicing delivery. In this chapter, we offer guidelines for adapting to your audience by acknowledging initial audience disposition, establishing common ground, demonstrating relevance, gaining credibility, enhancing information comprehension and retention, and overcoming potential language and cultural differences.

INITIAL AUDIENCE DISPOSITION

Initial audience disposition is the knowledge and opinions your audience have about your topic before they hear you speak. Recall that this information helped you narrow the topic and determine your speech goal. You also want to consider initial audience disposition when determining your main points, selecting supporting material, and making language choices. For example, if you are giving a speech on refinishing wood furniture, you may face an audience whose initial attitude is that refinishing furniture is complicated and boring. On the other hand, you may face an audience of young homeowners who love HGTV and are really looking forward to your talk. Although the process you describe in both situations will be the same, your approach to explaining the steps will differ somewhat. If your audience thinks refinishing furniture is boring and complicated, you will need to pique their interest and convince them that the process is really simpler than they initially thought. And if you know your audience enjoys watching HGTV, you can play upon these interests by making reference to some popular HGTV shows (Photo 5.1).

initial audience disposition: the knowledge and opinions listeners have about your topic before they hear you speak

Photo 5.1 Effective speakers analyze initial audience disposition toward their topic and then tailor their speech to the audience's needs and expectations. How do home improvement shows address initial audience disposition?

COMMON GROUND

People are unique, with different knowledge, attitudes, philosophies, experiences, and ways of perceiving the world. As a speaker, your goal is to identify and highlight **common ground**—the perception that you are knowledgeable, trustworthy, and personable. You can do so by using personal pronouns, asking rhetorical questions, and drawing on common experiences.

Use Personal Pronouns

One way to establish common ground is to use the **personal pronouns** "we," "us," and "our." For example, in her speech about hurricanes, Megan used personal pronouns to establish common ground in this way:

Let's discuss how hurricanes form and the varying degrees of intensity of them.

By using "let's discuss" rather than "I'll explain," Megan created a sense of common ground that she and her audience would work together to form a common understanding about hurricanes.

Ask Rhetorical Questions

A second way to establish common ground is to pose **rhetorical questions**—questions phrased to stimulate a mental response from the audience. Rhetorical questions are often used in speech introductions but can also be used effectively in transitions and other parts of the speech. For instance, notice how this transition, phrased as a rhetorical question, creates common ground:

When watching a particularly violent TV program, have you ever asked yourself, "Did they really need to be this graphic to make the point?"

Used in this way, rhetorical questions highlight similar attitudes between the speaker and audience and pique interest about the content that is to come.

common ground: the perception of a speaker as knowledgeable, trustworthy, and personable

personal pronouns: "we," "us," and "our"—pronouns that directly link the speaker to members of the audience

rhetorical questions: questions phrased to stimulate a mental response from the audience

Draw from Common Experiences

Another way to establish common ground is to share personal stories and examples. In her speech about hurricanes, Megan tried to establish common ground in her introduction in this way:

> Close your eyes and think about a time when you were absolutely terrified. Maybe it was when you were a child and afraid of a bully on the playground. Or maybe it was a time when you were scared about getting in an accident while driving during a terrible snow, sleet, or hailstorm. Or maybe you were terrified as a child when you got lost in a crowd at the shopping center or county fair. In any case, all you wanted to do was to get home where you would be safely surrounded by family and friends. Now imagine feeling that petrified AND having no idea if your home would even be there when you arrived. Well, that's exactly how I felt when Hurricane Katrina hit the Louisiana coastline when I was a kid.

Although Megan realized that very few, if any, of her classmates had probably ever experienced a hurricane, she drew upon a common experience she knew they could all relate to: that of being afraid.

RELEVANCE

Another important way to tailor your speech to your audience is by demonstrating **relevance**—adapting information in ways that help audience members realize its importance to them. Listeners pay attention to and are interested in ideas that affect them personally in some way ("What does this have to do with me?") and lose interest when they don't see how a speech relates to them. You can demonstrate relevance by emphasizing the timeliness, proximity, and personal impact of the ideas you share throughout your speech (Photo 5.2).

relevance: adapting information in ways that help audience members realize its importance to them

Emphasize Timeliness

Information has **timeliness** when it is useful now or in the near future. For example, in a speech about the hazards of cell phone distracted driving, J.J. demonstrated relevance via timeliness with this introduction:

timeliness: showing how information is useful now or in the near future

> Most of us in this room, as many as 90 percent of us in fact, are a danger to society. Why? It's because we talk on our phones or text while driving. According to the National Safety Council's Injury Facts 2015, distracted driving is the third most common cause of traffic fatalities today. Did you know that when you talk on the phone when you're driving—even if you do so on a hands-free set—you're four times more likely to get into a serious crash than if you're not doing so? This issue is far from harmless and is certainly one each of us should take seriously.

Photo 5.2 Although we all know it's not safe to text while driving, many people admit doing so anyway. How might you establish relevance in a speech about driving while phoning or texting?

By referencing recent statistics, J.J. uses timeliness to demonstrate the relevance of his topic. Megan did so by talking not only about her own experiences with Hurricane Katrina, which may not

Matthew Rambo/Photodisc/Getty Images

proximity: the relevance of information to the listener's personal space

credibility: the perception of a speaker as knowledgeable, trustworthy, and personable

Photo 5.3 Sometimes speakers, such as Warren Buffet, a well-known and successful business investor and philanthropist, come to the occasion with established credibility as an expert on a topic. What speakers have you heard that come to the occasion with established credibility?

seem timely to her listeners, but also more recent stories of those attempting to recover from Superstorm Sandy.

Emphasize Proximity

Listeners are more likely to be interested in information that has **proximity**, that is, a relationship to their personal "space." Psychologically, we pay more attention to information related to our "territory"—to us, our family, our neighborhood, or our city, state, or country. You have probably heard speakers say, "Let me bring this close to home for you" and then make their point by using a local example. As you do research, look for statistics and examples that emphasize proximity for your audience. For example, J.J. used the latest cell phone distracted driving accident statistics in his state and a story reported in the local paper of a young mother who was killed as a result of cell phone distracted driving.

Emphasize Personal Impact

When you emphasize a serious physical, economic, or psychological impact of your topic, audience members are interested in what you have to say. Consider, for example, how you perk up when your instructor says, "You might want to jot this down because it will be on the test." That's an example of emphasizing personal impact because remembering it will help you earn a better grade. Megan emphasized personal impact by highlighting ripple effects of hurricanes such as skyrocketing gasoline prices and energy costs. J.J. emphasized personal impact by showing how much higher everyone's auto insurance is today as a result of cell phone distracted traffic accidents.

SPEAKER CREDIBILITY

Credibility is the audience's perception of a speaker as knowledgeable about the topic, trustworthy, and personable. The impact of credibility on speaker success has been a fundamental concept in public speaking since Aristotle described it as *ethos* more than 2,000 years ago. Having been understood as a key concept for so long, it is no wonder that several theories exist about how speakers develop credibility.

Some people are widely known as experts on a particular topic (Photo 5.3). When these people give a speech, they don't have to do much to establish their credibility. When the president of the United States speaks, for example, he or she has a certain degree of established credibility.

However, most of us need to adapt our remarks to help establish credibility with our audience. We can do so by articulating our knowledge and expertise, conveying trustworthiness, and displaying personableness.

Articulate Knowledge and Expertise

Your audience's assessment of your knowledge and expertise depends on how well you convince them that you are qualified to speak on this topic. You can do so directly and indirectly.

You can articulate your expertise directly by disclosing your personal experiences with your topic, including formal education, special study, demonstrated skill, and your "track record." For example, in his cell phone distracted driving speech, J.J. explained:

I became interested in the issue of cell phone distracted driving after being involved personally in an accident caused by a driver who was texting while

iStockphoto.com/GYI NSEA

driving. Since then, I've done a great deal of research on the subject and am involved in a grassroots organization devoted to passing legislation in our state to make driving while phoning or texting illegal.

Megan articulated knowledge and expertise by sharing her personal stories about experiencing Hurricane Katrina and the things she and her family did and continue to do to live according to what she described as a "new normal." When you articulate personal experience with your topic, your audience will perceive you as knowledgeable about the material.

Similarly, when you develop your ideas through specific statistics and high-quality examples, audience members are more likely to view you as knowledgeable. J.J. did so by citing the most recent statistics release by the National Safety Council and Megan did so by citing reports she found in *The Washington Post* and statistics published by the National Weather Service.

Audience members also assess knowledge and expertise through indirect means. Audiences have an almost instinctive sense of when a speaker is "winging it." Most audiences will perceive speakers who do not appear to have command of the material as less knowledgeable and speakers who are confident, fluent, and easy to follow as more knowledgeable.

Convey Trustworthiness

Trustworthiness is the extent to which the audience believes what you say is accurate, true, and in the audience's best interests. People assess trustworthiness by judging a speaker's character and motives.

As you prepare, consider how you will demonstrate good character—that you are honest, industrious, dependable, and ethical (Photo 5.4). For example, when you credit the source of your information as you speak, you demonstrate good character. You are confirming you did not make up the information (honesty), and you are not plagiarizing (ethics).

How trustworthy you seem also depends on how the audience views your motives. If people believe that what you are saying is self-serving rather than in their best interests, they will be suspicious and view you as less trustworthy. Early in your speech, you should show how audience members will benefit from what you are saying. For example, in his speech on toxic waste, Brandon described how one community's ignorance of toxic waste disposal allowed a toxic waste dump to be located in the community, which led to serious health issues. He then shared his motive by saying, "My hope is that this speech will give you the information you need to thoughtfully participate in decisions like these that may face your community."

trustworthiness: the extent to which the audience can believe that what you say is accurate, true, and in their best interests

personableness: the extent to which you project a pleasing personality

The Washington Post/Getty Images

Photo 5.4 Ethical speakers are fair in that they present all sides of an issue, not just the one they favor. Would you describe Donald Trump as ethical in this regard? Why or why not?

Display Personableness

Personableness is the extent to which one conveys a pleasing personality. Quite simply, we have more confidence in people we like. We quickly decide how much we like a person based on our first impressions. This fact is based on a communication concept known as impression formation and management, which is rooted in the theory of symbolic interactionism.[1] Our first impressions are

In his *Sports Illustrated* interview in 2012, University of Notre Dame football player Manti Te'o was clearly devastated. Why? Both his grandmother and his girlfriend, Lennay Kekua, had died ten days earlier. During the interview, Te'o described his girlfriend as having graduated from Stanford and living in Carson, California. He explained that she discovered she had leukemia while recovering from injuries incurred from being hit by a drunk driver on April 28, 2012. At the time, Te'o was described as a hero: the "physical and emotional center" of the team who somehow found inspiration in the memories of his grandmother and girlfriend and persevered.

The public later learned that Lennay Kekua never existed. She was fake. Some said she was a hoax created to help Te'o's chances to win the Heisman trophy. (He ultimately came in second.) Some said Te'o was "in on it" all along and others said he had been duped. In an interview with Katie Couric in January 2013, Te'o said he wasn't lying. He was in love with a girl he met online and had never met in person. As he himself said, "What I went through was real. You know, the feelings, the pain, the sorrow—that was all real, and that's something that I can't fake."[2] While we may never know the truth, some speculate that Te'o's teammates were inspired to play harder because of his resilience in the face of what appeared to be the tragic deaths of two loved ones.

1. Is it ethical to adapt in a way that resonates with your audience even if it is not entirely true?
2. How (if at all) did Te'o's perceived credibility change among various audiences (e.g., teammates, fans) after learning that Kekua didn't exist?

based on what we infer about people from what we see, such as how they dress, how physically attractive we find them, how well they speak, whether they smile and appear friendly, and even how they carry themselves.

You can also demonstrate personableness by using appropriate humor. By appropriate humor, we mean humor that demonstrates respect for diverse listeners by not potentially offending a particular group (i.e., it is not sexist, ageist, racist, etc.) or the values held by them.

INFORMATION COMPREHENSION AND RETENTION

You also need to adapt your speech to ensure comprehension and retention throughout it. Five ways to do so are (1) appealing to diverse learning styles, (2) using transitions, (3) choosing specific and familiar language, (4) using vivid language and examples, and (5) comparing unfamiliar ideas with familiar ones.

Appeal to Diverse Learning Styles

learning style: a person's preferred way of receiving information

A **learning style** is a person's preferred way of receiving information. Because people differ in their preferred learning styles, you should present your ideas in ways that make it easy for all audience members to understand and remember what you are saying. Models for understanding learning styles have been developed by many scholars.[3] One prominent model, called Kolb's cycle of learning, conceptualizes learning preferences along four dimensions: feeling, thinking, watching, and doing.[4] Kolb's model is actually rooted in John Dewey's experiential learning theory.[5] Exhibit 5.1 illustrates the watching, doing, feeling, and thinking dimensions of the learning cycle.

Some people prefer to learn by "watching" and easily understand and remember things they see and relate to well-designed visual aids and vivid examples they can picture in their minds. Others prefer to learn by doing. For these people, hands-on activities aid their comprehension and memory. People who prefer to learn by doing relate well to speakers who provide real-life applications and clearly state how the speech topic is relevant to the audience's personal or professional lives.

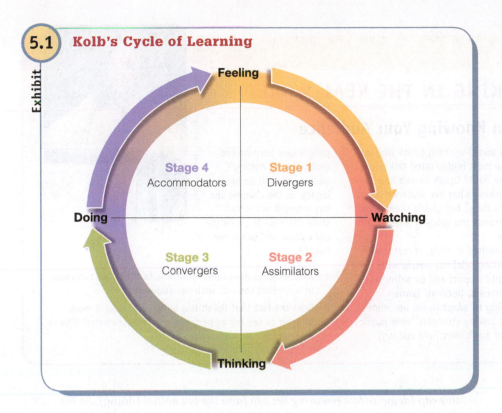

5.1 **Kolb's Cycle of Learning**

Exhibit

Feeling

Stage 4
Accommodators

Stage 1
Divergers

Doing

Watching

Stage 3
Convergers

Stage 2
Assimilators

Thinking

Some people learn best when their feelings are engaged. These people learn well from stories and other supporting material that appeal to their emotions or senses. Other people learn best by thinking about factual material and connect well when ideas are supported with detailed definitions, explanations, facts, and statistics.

Although each of us has a preferred learning style, research also reveals that all people learn most effectively when ideas are presented in ways that "round" the entire cycle of learning.[6] So as you develop your speech, adapt to diverse learning styles by presenting information in ways that appeal to each of the four dimensions (watching, feeling, doing, and thinking).

For example, suppose you are trying to make the point that understanding simple directions can be a problem for functionally illiterate people. You could do so by saying:

For instance, a person who is functionally illiterate might not be able to read or understand a label that says, "Take three times a day after eating."

Now look at how much richer this explanation becomes when it is developed in ways that appeal to different learning styles:

Many Americans are functionally illiterate. In fact, about 35 million people, or 20 percent of the adult population, have serious difficulties with common reading tasks (thinking). That means that one of every five people cannot read well enough to understand how to bake a frozen pizza, how to assemble a child's bicycle from printed instructions, or which bus to catch from the signs at the stop (feeling).

Many functionally illiterate people don't read well enough to follow the directions on this bottle [show an enlarged image of the label on a medicine bottle that reads, "Take three times a day after eating"] (watching). Not only that, they wouldn't know they need to "press down while turning" to remove

SPEECH SNIPPET

In her speech about hurricanes, Megan appealed to both feeling and watching by showing photos of her hometown after it was ravaged by a hurricane. She appealed to both watching and thinking by explaining hurricane categories with the help of a visual aid chart. She appealed to doing by having the audience look through a box of hurricane-tossed articles to search for a baby's ring.

this cap [*demonstrate removing the cap from the pill bottle*] (*doing*). *So the directions on a prescription bottle like this* [*show visual aid of enlarged prescription bottle with directions written in garbled nonsense words*] *are basically meaningless.*

Use Transitions

When listeners have trouble following a speaker's organization, they have difficulty understanding the message. So you should use transitions to help your audience follow along. Recall from Chapter 1 that a transition is a sentence or two that summarizes one main point and introduces the next. Suppose your goal is to explain the three phases of a clinical trial a cancer drug must pass through to earn FDA approval. After explaining the goals of the first phase, you might use a transition like this: "So the goal of the first phase is to see whether a drug that is safe in animals is also safe in humans. Phase I trials are not designed to determine whether or not the drug works; that is actually the goal in Phase II trials."

Choose Specific and Familiar Language

Because words have many meanings, you want to make sure your listeners understand the meaning you intend. You can do so by using specific language and choosing familiar terms. Specific words clear up the confusion caused by general words by narrowing the focus in some way. For example, saying "a feisty little year-old Yorkshire terrier" is more specific than referring to "a dog."

You also want to use familiar words. Avoid jargon and slang terms unless (1) you define them clearly the first time you use them, and (2) they are central to your speech goal. For instance, in a speech on the four major problems faced by functionally illiterate people in the workplace, your audience will need to understand what you mean by "functionally illiterate." You should offer your definition early in the speech: "By 'functionally illiterate,' I mean people who have trouble accomplishing simple reading and writing tasks."

Use Vivid Language and Examples

Vivid examples help audience members understand and remember abstract, complex, and novel material. One vivid example can help us understand a complicated concept. As you prepare, find or create real or hypothetical examples and illustrations to help your audience understand new and complex information. For example, in the functionally illiterate definition, the description "people who have trouble accomplishing simple reading and writing tasks" can be made more vivid by adding: "For instance, a functionally illiterate person could not read and understand the directions on a prescription label that states, 'Take three times a day with a glass of water. Do not take on an empty stomach.'"

Compare Unfamiliar Ideas with Familiar Ones

An easy way to adapt material to your audience is to compare new ideas with ones the audience already understands (Photo 5.5). As you prepare, identify places where you can use comparisons. For example, in a speech on functional illiteracy, if you want the audience of literates to sense what functionally illiterate people experience, you might compare it to the experience of surviving in a country where one is not fluent in the language:

> Many of us have taken a foreign language in school. So we figure we can visit a place where that language is spoken and "get along," right? But when we get to the country, we are often appalled to discover that even the road signs are written in this "foreign" language. And we can't quite make the signs out, at least not at 60 kilometers an hour. I was in France last summer, equipped with my 3 years of high school French, and I saw a sign that indicated that the train station I was looking for was "à droit"—"to the right," or is it "to the left"? I knew it was one or the other. Unfortunately, I couldn't remember and took a shot that it was to the left. Bad move. By the time I figured it out, I was 10 miles in the wrong direction and ended up missing my train. At that moment, I could imagine how tough life must be for functionally illiterate people. So many "little details" of life require the ability to comprehend written messages.

Blair Fethers/Getty Images

Photo 5.5 One way to enhance comprehension is to compare unfamiliar ideas with familiar ones. How might you do so when talking about an unfamiliar country?

LANGUAGE AND CULTURAL DIFFERENCES

Western European speaking traditions inform the approach to public speaking we discuss in this book. However, public speaking is a social act that varies across cultures. So when your audience comprises people from cultural and language groups different from your own, you should make two adaptations: try to be understandable when speaking in a second language, and show respect by choosing culturally appropriate supporting material.

Work to Be Understood When Speaking in Your Second Language

When you speak to an audience in a language that is not your native language, your audience members may have difficulty understanding you because you may speak with an accent, mispronounce words, choose inappropriate words, or misuse idioms. You can help your audience understand by speaking more slowly and articulating as clearly as you can. By slowing your speaking rate, you give yourself additional time to pronounce difficult sounds and choose words whose meanings you know. You can also use visual aids to reinforce key terms and concepts as you move through your speech. Doing so assures listeners that they've understood you correctly.

One of the best ways to improve is to practice in front of friends who are native speakers of the language in which you'll be presenting. Ask them to take note of words and phrases that you mispronounce or misuse. Then, they can work with you to correct your pronunciation or to help you choose better words to express your ideas. Also, keep in mind that the more you practice speaking the language, the more comfortable you will become with it.

Choose Culturally Appropriate Supporting Material

When speaking to audiences who are vastly different from you, it will take work to find out about their culture and experiences so you can adapt your ideas and information to them. This may mean conducting additional research to find relevant supporting material, or it may require you to elaborate on ideas that might be self-explanatory in your own culture. For example, suppose that Maria, a Mexican-American exchange student, was giving a narrative/personal experience speech for her speech class at Yeshiva University in Israel on the *quinceañera* party she had when she turned 15 years old. Because students in Israel probably don't have any experience with the Mexican coming-of-age tradition of *quinceañera* parties, they may have trouble understanding the significance of this event unless Maria uses her knowledge of the bar mitzvah and bat mitzvah coming-of-age ritual Jewish celebrations as a comparison.

FORMING A SPECIFIC AUDIENCE ADAPTATION PLAN

Now that you understand the challenges speakers face in developing and maintaining audience interest and understanding, you can develop your own adaptation plan by answering the following questions:

1. **What is my audience's initial disposition toward my topic?** What can I do to enhance audience interest?

2. **What common ground do my audience members share with one another and with me?** How and where can I use personal pronouns, rhetorical questions, and common experiences to enhance the perception of common ground?

3. **How relevant will my audience find this material?** How can I demonstrate that my material is timely, proximate, and has personal impact for my audience?

4. **What can I do to enhance my credibility?** How did I develop my knowledge of and expertise on this topic, and how can I share that with my audience? How can I demonstrate my trustworthiness as I speak? What will I do to help my audience perceive me as personable?

5. **How can I make it easier for my audience to comprehend and remember the information?** What types of material can I use to appeal to different learning style preferences? What key terms will I need to define? What new concepts might I develop with vivid language and examples? What new ideas might I want to compare to ones my audience is already familiar with?

6. **What language or cultural differences do my audience members have with one another and with me?** If I will be speaking in a second language, how will I increase the likelihood that my audience will understand me? What cultural differences do I need to be sensitive to, and what culturally appropriate material might I search for and use?

Speech-Planning Action Step 2, Activity 2 will help you identify opportunities for audience adaptation as you develop your speeches. See the student response, which shows how one student completed this exercise, in the Activity 2 Speech Planning box that follows.

Activity

2 SPEECH PLANNING

Recognizing Opportunities for Audience Adaptation

To identify opportunities for audience adaptation, state your potential topic and then answer the following questions.

Potential topic: _____

1. What is my audience's initial disposition toward my topic?

2. What common ground do my audience members share with one another and with me?

3. How relevant will my audience find this material? How can I demonstrate that my material is timely, proximate, and has personal impact for my audience?

4. What can I do to enhance my credibility?

5. How can I make it easier for my audience to comprehend and remember the information?

6. What language or cultural differences do my audience members have with one another and with me?

SAMPLE STUDENT RESPONSE
Recognizing Opportunities for Audience Adaptation

Potential topic: *The overall effects of hurricanes*

1. What is my audience's initial disposition toward my topic?

   Most audience members will be only mildly interested in and not well informed about hurricanes when I begin. I hope to pique and maintain their interest by using vivid language and examples, as well as graphic photos.

   (continued)

2. What common ground do my audience members share with one another and with me?

    Because most audience members are my age and are from the same national culture, we share areas of common ground I can draw on. First, hurricanes occur every year and affect weather patterns throughout the country. I should also be able to use personal pronouns and rhetorical questions to create common ground. We are different in that I have actually lived through the devastation of a hurricane in my hometown, so I'll have to keep in mind that most of my listeners have not. That means I'll have to be careful not to assume they know more than general facts about hurricanes.

3. How relevant will my audience find this material? How can I demonstrate that my material is timely, proximate, and has personal impact for my audience?

    Initially, since they don't live on a coast, they are not likely to see it as relevant. I can make the information timely by talking about Superstorm Sandy, a fairly recent hurricane that most people are aware of, which affected many people, and which even affected the weather in other states.

4. What can I do to enhance my credibility?

    I will build credibility through solid research and oral citations of sources. Early in my introduction, I'll mention where I live on the Gulf Coast and the fact that I've lived through several hurricanes.

5. How can I make it easier for my audience to comprehend and remember the information?

    I will round the cycle of learning by talking about my personal experiences (feeling), showing photographs (watching), offering facts and statistics about the effects of hurricanes (thinking), and providing clear instructions about how to categorize hurricanes and act appropriately to ensure safety (doing). I'll also describe the effects using vivid language and examples, and I'll compare them to other natural disasters my audience members may have experienced such as thunderstorms, tornados, and floods.

6. What language or cultural differences do my audience members have with one another and with me?

    I will not be speaking in a second language, but I will need to be careful not to use too many technical terms that may be "jargon" to my audience, and, when I do, I need to be sure to define them clearly. Although most audience members are US nationals, there are three international students in class. I will do some research to see if any of them live in a country that experiences hurricanes, and, if so, I'll include some examples from their countries as well.

Reflection and Assessment

Audience adaptation is the process of tailoring your speech to the needs, interests, and expectations of your specific audience. To assess how well you've learned what we've discussed in this chapter, answer the following questions. If you have trouble answering any of them, go back and review that material. Once you can answer each question accurately, you are ready to move ahead to the next chapter.

1. How can you find out about and then address initial audience disposition toward your topic?
2. What techniques can you use to emphasize common ground you share with your audience?
3. What are some ways you can point out the relevance of your speech to your audience?
4. How can you establish yourself as a credible speaker?
5. In what ways might you promote audience comprehension and retention?
6. What might you do to overcome potential language and cultural differences?

Challenge Resource and Assessment Center   MindTap®

Now that you have read Chapter 5, go to your MindTap Communication for *The Challenge of Effective Speaking in a Digital Age* for quick access to flashcards, chapter quizzes, and more.

Applying What You've Learned

1. **Impromptu Speech Activity:** Identify a common practice that is taken for granted in your family or your community but that may be an unusual or unique practice for other families or in other communities. (For example, one family celebrated Hanukkah-like birthdays where a present was received each day of the birthday week.) Prepare and present a 2- to 3-minute impromptu speech describing the practice in ways that employ the audience adaptation guidelines proposed in this chapter.

2. **Assessment Activity A:** Identify a cultural group in your community with which you have limited experience. Learn more about this group by (1) observing an event or other gathering, (2) participating in a cultural practice, (3) interviewing a member of the culture, and (4) doing some secondary source research. Then write a two- to three-page paper in which you begin by comparing and contrasting what you have learned about this culture. In the second part of the paper, imagine that you were going to give a speech to an audience composed of members of this cultural group. Based on what you have learned about this culture, which three of the six issues of adaptation would be the most important for you to address? Describe how you might do that.

3. **Assessment Activity B:** Volunteer at a local service organization regularly (at least twice per week) for 4 weeks. Before doing so, consider some specific things you will do to seek common ground and gain credibility. Keep a journal throughout the experience, noting what worked and did not work. After 4 weeks, prepare a two- to three-page reflection paper regarding your adaptation experience. Focus on what you expected the experience to be like, what it was like (rewards and challenges), and what you learned about others and yourself as a result.

4. **Assessment Activity C:** Complete Action Step 2 for one of the speeches you may give this semester.

6

Topic Development

WHAT'S THE POINT?

WHEN YOU'VE FINISHED THIS CHAPTER, YOU WILL BE ABLE TO:

- Locate and evaluate information sources about your topic
- Select relevant information about your topic
- Record information accurately
- Cite sources appropriately

MindTap®

Review the chapter **Learning Objectives** and **Start** with quick warm-up activity.

Adrian Sherratt/Alamy Stock Photo

CoraMax/Shutterstock.com

ACTION STEP 3

Gather and evaluate information

- **A.** Examine areas where you need additional information.
- **B.** Locate, evaluate, and select a variety of information types and sources.
- **C.** Record information.
- **D.** Cite sources.

Ethical speakers ensure that what they say is truthful by carefully researching their topic and evaluating information and source credibility.

Justin was concerned. He was scheduled to give his speech in a week, but he hadn't even begun to conduct any research. A couple of months ago, he had read a magazine article about the vanishing honeybees while in a doctor's waiting room and decided that would be an interesting topic for his informative speech. Although he couldn't remember the name of the magazine, he pulled out his laptop and Googled "vanishing honeybees." To his surprise, he got 92,000 hits. He wondered how in the world he would go about sorting through all this information and all these sources to determine which ones would be best for his speech.

Justin's experience is not unusual. Most of us have formed opinions about a variety of subjects based on our personal experiences, interactions with others, and things we've read or watched online or on television. But when it comes to presenting our ideas in a public forum, we need to do research to find evidence to support them. **Evidence** is essentially any information that clarifies, explains, or otherwise adds depth or breadth to a topic. What is particularly challenging in the digital age in which we live is not the inability to find the information we're looking for, but sorting through the array of information at our fingertips to evaluate and select the best information for our speeches. In this chapter, we explain how to locate and evaluate a variety of information types and sources, identify and select the best information, and then cite the sources of that information appropriately in your speech.

LOCATE AND EVALUATE INFORMATION SOURCES

How can you quickly find the best information related to your specific speech goal? You can start by assessing your own knowledge and experience. Then you can move to **secondary research**, which is the process of locating information discovered by other people. This includes doing Internet and library searches for relevant books, articles, general references, and websites. Information (a.k.a. evidence) can come in written, visual, audio, and audiovisual forms. Justin, for example, discovered an interview with actress Ellen Page done by Bill Maher that was posted on YouTube, an informative video posted on the US Department of Agriculture (USDA) website, and a chart showing the progression of this crisis over the past decade posted by the National Agricultural Statistics Service. If the information you find from secondary sources doesn't answer all your questions, you may need to conduct **primary research**, which is the process of collecting data about your topic directly from the real world.

Personal Knowledge and Experience

One form of evidence can be personal knowledge and experiences. For instance, saxophone players know how to select and care for a reed, entrepreneurs know the key features of a good business plan, and dieticians know a good deal about healthy diets. So Diane, a skilled long-distance runner, can draw from her own knowledge and experience to develop her speech on "How to Train for a Marathon." If you have personal knowledge and experience about the topic, however, you should also share your **credentials**—your experience or education that qualifies you to speak with authority on a specific subject. For Diane, establishing her credentials means briefly mentioning her training for and running in marathons before launching into her speech about training for one (Photo 6.1).

MindTap®
Read, highlight, and take notes online.

evidence: any information that clarifies, explains, or otherwise adds depth or breadth to a topic

secondary research: locating information that has been discovered by other people

primary research: collecting data about a topic directly from the real world

credentials: experiences or education that qualifies a presenter to speak with authority on a specific subject

Photo 6.1 Someone who runs marathons would have credibility when speaking about running injuries. Can you think of topics where you would have similar credibility?

Secondary Research

Most of us usually begin to develop a topic by searching online for sources and information. For example, we can search websites, blogs, YouTube, and discussion boards, as well as online libraries and databases. Some sources are available digitally, either free or for a fee. Some might require a visit to a library to pick up hard copies or through interlibrary loan. We can also ask librarians for help online via "ask the librarian" links or in person at a library. Because most of us do research online these days, we begin this section with a discussion of some guidelines for doing so effectively, efficiently, and ethically. We focus specifically on using search engines, encyclopedias such as Wikipedia, commercial and nonprofit organization websites, personal and corporate blogs, and online social networks. Then we talk about different types of sources you can find both online and in local libraries and how to skim and evaluate them.

Internet Sources

Thanks to ongoing advances in computer technology—including laptops, tablets, and smartphones, as well as wireless and personal hot spot Internet accessibility—we literally have instant access to a plethora of information about any topic. The challenge comes in sifting through all this information and evaluating it to select the best information for your speech.

We typically begin online searches by typing key words into a general search engine such as Google or Bing. These searches reveal hits, which are links to all sorts of websites, images, videos, articles, and other sources that include material about the key words. In our opening vignette, recall that Justin typed the words "vanishing honeybees" into Google and got 92,000 hits.

Many times one of the hits will be to an online encyclopedia entry in *Wikipedia*. These entries can be a good starting point for learning general information and for locating additional references about a given topic. Justin read the *Wikipedia* entry that came up from his "vanishing honeybees" search and learned that the official name for the phenomenon is colony collapse disorder. He also perused the "Reference List" and "Further Reading List," where he found articles published in the *New York Times*, *Science News*, and *Proceedings of the National Academies of Science*, among others. And he discovered several helpful websites listed under "External Links" from organizations such as the USDA and the National Honey Board. There is nothing wrong with starting the research process by reading a *Wikipedia* entry. In fact, doing so can be quite helpful.

Other hits may include commercial websites, which are created and maintained by for-profit organizations. Commercial website URLs typically end in .com. Commercial websites can be helpful for locating information about a company such as the National Honey Board, for finding current or popular culture material, and for finding presentational aids. Through one such commercial website, Justin found a short audiovisual clip to use in his speech about the vanishing honeybee phenomenon.

Nonprofit organization websites can be distinguished from commercial ones because their URLs will usually end in .org. These organizations are dedicated to issues or causes and can often be a source of emotional appeal examples. Justin found some startling statistics about the $15 billion in crops the United States would lose without the bees needed to pollinate plants.

Blogs are websites that provide a forum for the personal viewpoints of their authors. They can be created and maintained by an individual or an organization. They might be focused on a particular subject and include images, audios, and audiovisuals. Because they are often biased toward the opinion of the blogger, information on them may have to be verified with other sources. However, they can be a good source for finding public opinion examples and to humanize a topic. The most efficient way to find blogs is to use a blog search engine such as Google Blog Search or Blogarama. (Justin found some interesting opinions on Dady Cherie's blog posts on *News Junkie Post*.) Because blogs can be written by anyone, you will need to determine whether the author is a credible source by locating his or her credentials. If you cannot determine the author's credentials, you should not use the information in your speech.

blogs: websites that provide a forum for the personal viewpoints of their authors

Online social networks are websites where communities of people interact with one another. Some popular examples include Facebook, LinkedIn, Twitter, and Instagram. Like blogs, postings on these sites can be used to find supporting material to humanize a topic, appeal to emotions, and serve as presentational aids.

online social networks: websites where communities of people interact with one another

Other Types of Sources

You can also find pertinent information in sources that can be found online or in a local library. These include, for example, encyclopedias, books, articles in academic journals and magazines, news media, statistical sources, biographies, quotation books, websites, and government documents.

1. **Encyclopedias.** Encyclopedia entries (including Wikipedia) can serve as a good starting point by providing an overview about your topic. But because encyclopedias provide only overviews, they should never be the only source you rely on. General encyclopedias contain short articles about a wide variety of subjects. In addition, specialized encyclopedias focus on areas such as art, history, religion, philosophy, and science (e.g., *African American Encyclopedia, Latino Encyclopedia, Asian American Encyclopedia, Encyclopedia of Computer Science, Encyclopedia of Women,* and *Encyclopedia of Women in American Politics*).

2. **Books.** If your topic has been around for a while, books have likely been written about it. Although books are excellent sources of in-depth information about a topic, keep in mind that most of the information in a book is likely to be at least 2 years old by the time it is published. So books are not a good resource if your topic is very recent or if you're looking for the latest information on a topic. If you visit a library, you can use the call number for one book to physically locate other books on the same subject. For example, when Diane went to the shelves to locate a book called *Improving Sports Performance in Middle and Long-Distance Running*, she discovered a number of related books located in the same area, including one she would also use in her speech called *Advanced Sports Nutrition* by Dr. Dan Benardot.

3. **Articles.** Articles, which may contain more current or highly specialized information on your topic than a book might, are published in **periodicals**—magazines and journals published at regular intervals. The information in periodical articles is often more current than that published in books because many periodicals are published weekly, biweekly, or monthly. So a periodical article is likely to be a better source if a topic is one that's currently "in

SPEECH SNIPPET

For his speech on bioluminescence, Dan consulted a bulletin board maintained by the Association of Biogenetic Engineers. He was able to quote several issues being debated by experts in the field even before their works had been published. This complemented the information he had located in books, which was not as up to date.

periodicals: magazines and journals published at regular intervals

the news." Most libraries subscribe to electronic databases that index periodicals and many articles can be found via a general online search (Photo 6.2). Justin's general search using Google, for example, revealed articles in online periodicals by *Time, Newsweek,* and *Science News.*

4. **News media.** News media articles can provide facts about and interpretations of both contemporary and historical issues. They can also provide information about local issues and perspectives. Keep in mind, however, that most authors of news media articles are journalists who are not themselves experts on the topics they write about. So it is best not to rely solely on news media articles for your speech. Today, most traditional news media publications are available online (e.g., *New York Times, Wall Street Journal*), which makes them very accessible. You might also find good information in media sources that you can only find online, such as the *Huffington Post* and the *Drudge Report.*

5. **Statistical sources.** Statistical sources present numerical information on a wide variety of subjects. When you need facts about demography, continents, heads of state, weather, or similar subjects, access one of the many single-volume sources, such as *The Statistical Abstract of the United States,* that report such data. Justin, for example, consulted the *National Agricultural Statistics Service* to gather statistics about the declining honeybee population in the United States.

6. **Biographies.** When you need an account of a person's life, from thumbnail sketches to reasonably complete essays, you can consult a biographical reference source. Some examples include *Who's Who in America* and *International Who's Who, Contemporary Black Biography, Dictionary of Hispanic Biography, Native American Women, Who's Who of American Women,* and *Who's Who among Asian Americans.* Many famous people also have some of their biographical information posted on websites. For her speech about running, Diane found biographical information about Paula Radcliff by reading several websites about the famous female marathoner.

7. **Quotation books and websites.** A good quotation can be especially provocative as well as informative, and there are times you want to use a quotation from a respected person. *Bartlett's Familiar Quotations* (an app version is available) is a popular source of quotes from both historical and contemporary figures. Other sources are *The International Thesaurus of Quotations; Harper Book of American Quotations; My Soul Looks Back, 'Less I Forget: A Collection of Quotations by People of Color; The New Quotable Woman;* and *The Oxford Dictionary of Quotations.* Some popular quotation websites are *The Quotations Page* (www.quotationspage .com/) and *Quoteland.com.*

8. **Government documents.** If your topic is related to public policy, government documents may provide useful information. The *Federal Register* (www.federalregister.gov) publishes daily regulations and legal notices

Photo 6.2 Have you ever taken a course on conducting online research? If not, consider doing so. You will save yourself a lot of time and will locate great sources of useful information.

REB Images/Blend Images/Getty Images

PUBLIC SPEAKING IN THE REAL WORLD

Filmmakers and NASA Team Up on Research for *The Martian*

Most of us realize good research is required to develop effective research papers and public speeches. Did you know, however, that the best filmmakers (e.g., producers, directors, actors, costume designers) also do good research to create believable stories and characters? For example, film director Ridley Scott consulted with NASA's key figures in current Mars exploration efforts to get the science right. According to an article published on August 19, 2015, in the *Los Angeles Times*,[1] NASA officials took the filmmakers on a guided tour of their Houston facility, shared their current research discoveries, and consulted on the accuracy of everything they know about the planet.

1. Do you think science fiction movies ought to do research like the filmmakers did for *The Martian*? Why or why not?

2. Can you name a science fiction movie that didn't seem believable? What role could research have played in making it more plausible?

Bill Ingalls/NASA / Getty Images News/ Getty Images

issued by the US executive branch and all federal agencies. It is divided into sections, such as rules and regulations and Sunshine Act meetings. Of special interest are announcements of hearings and investigations, committee meetings, and agency decisions and rulings. The *Catalog of U.S. Government Publications* (http://catalog.gpo.gov/) covers publications of all branches of the federal government.

Skim Sources

Because your search is likely to uncover far more information than you can use, you will want to skim potential sources and resources to determine whether or not to read them in full. **Skimming** is a method of rapidly going through a work to determine what is covered and how.

As you skim an article, think about whether the source really presents information on the area of the topic you are exploring and whether it contains any documented statistics, examples, meaningful visuals, or quotable opinions. You can start by reading the **abstract**—a short paragraph summarizing the research findings. As you a skim a book, read the table of contents carefully, look at the index, and review the headings and visuals in pertinent chapters, asking the same questions as you would for a magazine article. A few minutes spent skimming will save hours of time.

Evaluate Sources

The validity, accuracy, and reliability of sources vary. **Valid sources** report factual information that can be counted on to be true. Tabloid and gossip magazines are generally considered less valid sources than mainstream news publications that use "fact-checkers" before publishing articles. **Accurate sources** attempt to present unbiased information and often include a balanced discussion of controversial topics. For example, the *Congressional Record* presents an accurate account of what each member of the US Congress said on the House or Senate floor. A newspaper account of a member's speech, however, may only report part of what was said and may even distort the remark by taking it out of context. **Reliable sources** are those that have a history of presenting valid and accurate information. Four criteria can help you evaluate the validity, accuracy, and reliability of sources.

1. **Authority.** The first test of a source is the expertise of its author and/or the reputation of the publishing or sponsoring organization. When an author is

skimming: rapidly going through a work to determine what is covered and how

abstract: a short paragraph summarizing the research findings

valid sources: report factual information that can be counted on to be true

accurate sources: attempt to present unbiased information and often include a balanced discussion of controversial topics

reliable sources: have a history of presenting valid and accurate information

listed, you can check the author's credentials through biographical references or by seeing if the author has a home page listing professional qualifications. You can use electronic periodical indexes or check the Library of Congress to see what else the author has published in the field.

On the Internet, you will sometimes find information that is anonymous or credited to someone whose background is not clear. In these cases, your ability to trust the information depends on evaluating the qualifications of the sponsoring organization. URLs ending in ".gov" (government), ".edu" (education), and ".org" (organization) are noncommercial sites with institutional publishers. The URL ".com" indicates that the sponsor is a for-profit organization. If you do not know whether you can trust the source, do not use the information.

stance: an author's attitude, perspective, or viewpoint on a topic

2. **Objectivity.** Although all authors have a **stance**—an attitude, perspective, or viewpoint on a topic—be wary of information that seems excessively slanted. Documents published by businesses, government, or public interest groups should be carefully scrutinized for obvious biases or good public relations fronts. To evaluate the stance of articles and books, read the preface or identify the thesis statement. These often reveal the author's point of view. When evaluating a website, look for its purpose. Most home pages contain a purpose or mission statement (sometimes in a link called "About"). Armed with this information, you are in a better position to evaluate stance and recognize excessive source bias regarding the topic.

3. **Currency.** In general, more recent information is preferred. Be sure to consult the latest information you can find. One reason for using Internet-based sources is that they can provide more up-to-date information than printed sources.[2] To determine how current the information is, you need to find out when the book was published, the article was written, the study was conducted, or the article was placed online or revised. Website dates are usually listed at the end of the article. If no dates are listed, you have no way of judging how current the information is.

4. **Relevance.** During your research, you will likely come across a great deal of interesting information. Whether that information is appropriate for your speech is another matter. Relevant information is directly related to your topic and supports your main points, making your speech easier to follow and understand. Irrelevant information will only confuse listeners, so you should avoid using it no matter how interesting it is.

Primary Research

When there is little secondary research available on your topic or on a main idea you want to develop in your speech, or when you wonder whether what you are reading about is true in a particular setting, consider doing primary research, which is conducting your own study in the real world. Keep in mind, however, that primary research is much more labor intensive and time consuming than secondary research, and in the professional world, much more costly. You can conduct fieldwork observations, surveys, interviews, original artifact or document examinations, or experiments.

Fieldwork Observations

ethnography: a form of primary research based on fieldwork observations

You might choose to learn about a group of people and their practices by conducting fieldwork observations, a method also known as **ethnography**. You can conduct fieldwork as a participant observer by engaging in interactions and activities with the people you are studying or as a nonparticipant observer by observing but not engaging with them. If, for instance, you are planning to talk about how social service agencies help homeless people find shelter and job training, or the process involved in adopting a pet, you can learn more by visiting or even volunteering for a period of time at a homeless shelter or humane society. By focusing on specific behaviors and taking notes on your observations and interpretations of them, you will have a record of specific information to use in your speech.

Surveys

Recall that a *survey* is a canvassing of people to get information about their ideas and opinions. Surveys may be conducted in person, over the phone, via the Internet, or with paper-and-pencil documents. At times, your secondary research will reveal publications that summarize findings from surveys that have been conducted by other people or organizations. At other times, you may want to conduct your own survey. For example, you might prepare a brief survey using SurveyMonkey or Qualtrics and post a link to it on Facebook or Twitter.

Interviews

Like media reporters, you may get some of your best information from an **interview**— a highly structured conversation where one person asks questions and another answers them. You might conduct your interview in person, over the phone, or online using software such as Skype or Adobe Connect. To be effective, you'll want to select the best person to interview, prepare a solid **interview protocol** (the list of questions to be asked), and adhere to several ethical guidelines when conducting and then processing the actual interview.

1. **Selecting the best person.** Somewhere on campus or in the larger community are people who have expertise in the topic area of your speech. Usually a bit of research and a few emails or phone calls will lead you to a good person to talk with about your topic. For instance, for a speech on "how to get a music recording contract," you might begin by asking a professor in the music department for the name of a nearby music production agency. Or you could find one by searching online. When you find a website, you can usually locate an "About Us" or "Contact Us" link on it, which will offer names, titles, email addresses, and phone numbers. Once you have identified a potential interviewee, contact the person to make an appointment. You can do so by email, phone, or text. Be forthright in your reasons for the interview and how long you expect the interview to take. Then suggest several dates and time ranges so the person can select the one that works best for him or her. If you make the appointment more than a few days in advance, contact your interviewee again the day before the interview to confirm the date, time, and location.

   Before your interview, do your research on the topic and anything the interviewee has written about it. Likewise, do your research to understand the expert's credentials. Interviewees are more likely to talk with you if you appear informed, and being informed will ensure that you ask better questions. You don't want to waste the interviewee's time by asking questions you could find the answers to elsewhere.

2. **Preparing the interview protocol.** The heart of an effective interview is the **interview protocol**, which is a list of good questions you plan to ask. How many questions you ask depends on how much time you will have for the interview. Begin by listing the topics you want to cover. Exhibit 6.1 presents a list of topics for an interview with a music producer when the goal is to learn about how to find and sign new talent. Next, prepare a couple of **rapport-building questions**, which are nonthreatening questions designed to put the interviewee at ease and demonstrate your respect for him or her. For his speech on vanishing honeybees and colony collapse disorder (CCD), Justin began his interview with "How did you get interested in doing research on CCD?"

SPEECH SNIPPET

Lauren wanted to know what addicts experience as they go through recovery, so she arranged to volunteer at a local treatment center to observe while she helped out.

interview: a highly structured conversation where one person asks questions and another answers them

interview protocol: the list of questions to be asked

SPEECH SNIPPET

For his speech on vanishing honeybees, Justin looked at his university's Biology Department website and discovered a faculty member who had published two papers on vanishing honeybees. He read the papers and learned the phenomenon is referred to as colony collapse disorder (CCD). He decided to try to set up an interview with the professor to learn more.

rapport-building questions: nonthreatening questions designed to put the interviewee at ease and demonstrate respect

primary questions:
introductory questions about each major interview topic

secondary questions:
follow-up questions designed to probe the answers given to primary questions

open questions: broad-based queries

closed questions: narrowly focused questions that require only very brief answers

neutral questions:
questions phrased in a way that does not direct a person's answers

leading questions:
questions phrased in a way that suggests the interviewer has a preferred answer

A good interview protocol is structured into primary and secondary questions. **Primary questions** are introductory questions about each major interview topic. **Secondary questions** are follow-up questions designed to probe the answers given to primary questions. Some follow-up questions probe by simply encouraging the interviewee to continue ("And then?" "Is there more?"). Others probe into a specific detail the interviewee mentioned or failed to mention. For the music producer interview, for example, you might probe with: "You didn't mention genre. What role might that play in your decision to offer a contract?" And finally, some probe into feelings: "How did it feel when her first album went platinum?"

Open questions are broad-based queries that allow freedom regarding what specific information or opinions the interviewee may provide ("Why do you think the vanishing honeybee crisis is happening so quickly and dramatically today?" "What are some kinds of behaviors you have seen bees exhibit when afflicted with this disease?" "What would you recommend people like me who aren't scientists or beekeepers do to help?" "What research studies are you working on next?").[3]

Closed questions are narrowly focused and require very brief (one- or two-word) answers. Some require a simple yes or no ("Do you believe we can stop the CCD crisis?"); others need only a short response ("What do you believe to be the most significant cause of CCD?"). By asking closed questions, interviewers can control the interview and obtain specific information quickly. But the answers cannot reveal the nuances behind responses, nor are they likely to capture the complexities surrounding the topic.[4]

Open and closed questions may also be neutral or leading. **Neutral questions** do not direct a person's answers. "What can you tell me about your work with Habitat for Humanity?" and "What criteria do you use in deciding whether or not to offer an artist a contract?" are neutral questions. By contrast, **leading questions** guide respondents toward providing certain types of information and imply that the interviewer prefers one answer over another. "What do you like about working for Habitat for Humanity?" and "Having a 'commercial sound' is an important criteria, isn't it?" are leading questions.

Exhibit 6.2 lists some of the questions you might ask in an interview with a music producer.

3. **Conducting the interview.** Best practices for conducting effective and ethical interviews, whether online, over the phone, or in person, include the following:

   - **Dress professionally.** Doing so sends a message that you *respect* the time the interviewee is giving and take the interview seriously.

   - **Be prompt.** You also demonstrate *respect* by showing up prepared to begin at the time you have agreed to. If you are conducting the interview in person, remember to allow enough time for potential traffic or parking problems. If

6.2 **Sample Music Producer Interview Questions**

Rapport-Building Opener

How did you get interested in becoming a music producer?

Major Topic Questions

Primary Question #1: How do you find artists to consider for contract?

> *Secondary Question:* Is this different from the methods used by other producers?

> *Secondary Question:* Do artists ever come to you in other ways?

Primary Question #2: Once an artist has been brought to your attention, what course of action follows?

> *Secondary Question*: Do you ever just see an artist or band and immediately sign them?

> *Secondary Question*: What's the longest period of time you "auditioned" an artist or band before signing them?

Primary Question #3: What criteria do you use in deciding to offer a contract?

> *Secondary Question*: Are there any criteria you feel are more important than others?

Primary Question #4: Can you tell me the story of how you came to sign one of your most successful artists?

> *Secondary Question*: What do you think made the artist so successful?

Primary Question #5: Can you tell me the story of an artist you signed that was not successful?

> *Secondary Question*: Why do you think this artist failed?

> *Secondary Question*: Do you think it was a mistake to sign this artist?

> *Secondary Question*: In retrospect, what could you or the artist have done differently that might have helped him or her succeed?

you are conducting the interview virtually, be sure to do a practice call in advance to make sure the technology is working properly.

- **Be courteous.** Begin by introducing yourself and thanking the person for taking the time to talk to you. Remember, interviewees most likely have nothing to gain from the interview. So let them know you are grateful for their time. Most of all, *respect* what the interviewee says regardless of what you may think of the answers.

- **Ask permission to record the interview.** If the interviewee says "no," *respect* his or her wishes and take careful notes instead.

- **Listen carefully.** At key places in the interview, repeat what the interviewee has said in your own words to be sure you really understand. This will assure the person that you will report the answers *truthfully* and *fairly* during your speech.

- **Keep the interview moving.** You do not want to rush the person, but you do want to behave *responsibly* by getting your questions answered during the allotted time.

- **Monitor your nonverbal reactions.** Demonstrate *integrity* by maintaining good eye contact. Nod to show understanding, and smile occasionally to maintain a friendly persona. How you look and act is likely to determine whether the person will warm up to you and give you an informative interview.

- **Get permission to quote.** Doing so demonstrates that you *respect* the interviewee and want to report the ideas provided *honestly* and *fairly*. Doing so also communicates that you have *integrity* and strive to act *responsibly*. You might even offer to let the person see a copy of the formal outline

Rob Loud/Getty Images

Photo 6.3 Ethical interviewers demonstrate honesty, respect, integrity, fairness, and responsibility by following several "best practices" for conducting interviews. Which "best practice" do you think is most challenging to achieve and why?

transcribe: word-for-word translation into written form of the interview

hypothesis: an educated guess about a cause-and-effect relationship between two or more things

before you give your speech. That way, the interviewee can double-check the accuracy of direct quotations.

- **Confirm credentials.** Before you leave, be sure to confirm your interviewee's professional title and affiliation (company or organization). Doing so is acting *responsibly* because you'll need these details when explaining why you chose to interview this person.

- **End on time.** As with arriving promptly, ending when you said you would demonstrates *respect* for the interviewee and for the valuable time provided (Photo 6.3).

- **Thank the interviewee.** Always close the interview by thanking the interviewee. This closure leads to positive rapport should you need to follow up later. You may even follow up with a short thank-you note after you leave.

4. **Processing the interview.** Because your interview notes were probably taken in an outline or bullet-point form, the longer you wait to translate them, the more difficult doing so will be. Sit down with your notes as soon as possible to make more extensive notes of the information you may want to use in your speech. If you recorded the interview, take some time to **transcribe** the responses by translating them word for word into written form. If at any point you are not sure whether you have accurately transcribed what the person said, take a minute to phone or email and double check.

Original Artifact or Document Examinations

Sometimes the information you need has not been published. Rather, it may exist in an original unpublished source, such as an ancient manuscript, a diary, personal correspondence, or company file. Or you may need to view an object, such as a geographic feature, a building, a monument, or an artifact in a museum, to get the information you need (Photo 6.4). Today, many original artifacts and documents or illustrations of them can be found online.

Experiments

You can design a study to test a **hypothesis**, which is an educated guess about a cause-and-effect relationship between two or more things. Then you can report the results of your experiment in your speech. Keep in mind that experiments take time, and you must understand the principles of the scientific process to be able to trust results of a formal experiment (Photo 6.5). However, sometimes you can do an informal experiment to test the results of a study you learn about elsewhere.

MAHMOUD ZAYYAT /AFP/Getty Images

Photo 6.4 Primary research can involve viewing original artifacts or documents. What original artifacts might you study for a speech?

SELECT RELEVANT INFORMATION

Once you have collected a variety of sources, you need to identify different types of information to use as evidence in your speech. These include factual statements, expert opinions, and elaborations. You may find the information written in narrative form, presented as a graphic or other visual, or in an audiovisual recording such as a TED talk or recorded interview.

Factual Statements

Factual statements are those that can be verified. "A recent study confirmed that preschoolers watch an average of 28 hours of television a week" and "The microprocessor, which was invented by Ted Hoff at Intel in 1971, made the creation of personal computers possible" are both statements of fact that can be verified. The chart Justin found illustrating decreasing honeybee populations in the United States over time is an example of factual evidence that can be verified.

One way to verify factual information is to check it against other sources on the same subject. Never use any information that is not carefully documented unless you have corroborating sources. Factual statements may come in the form of statistics, examples, and definitions.

Speech Planning Action Step 3, Activity 3A, will help you evaluate and compile a list of potential sources for your speeches in this course. The Sample Student Response provides an example of how one student completed this exercise.

Photo 6.5 Each episode of the television program *MythBusters* is actually made up of a series of simple experiments. What simple informal experiments have you tried?

Discovery Channel/Everett Collection

factual statements: information that can be verified

Statistics

Statistics are numerical facts. Statistical statements, such as, "Only five of every ten local citizens voted in the last election" or "The national unemployment rate for January 2016 was 4.9 percent" can provide impressive support for a point, but when statistics are poorly used in a speech, they may be boring and, in some instances, downright deceiving. Here are some ethical guidelines for using statistics.

statistics: numerical facts

1. **Use only statistics you can verify as reliable and valid.** Taking statistics from only the most reliable sources and double checking any startling statistics with another source will guard against the use of faulty statistics.

2. **Use only recent statistics so your audience will not be misled.**

3. **Use statistics comparatively.** You can show growth, decline, gain, or loss by comparing two numbers. For example, according to the US Bureau of Labor Statistics, the national unemployment rate for January 2016 was 4.9 percent. This statistic is more meaningful when you compare it to 5.7 percent in January 2015, 6.6 percent in January 2014, 8 percent in January 2013, and 8.3 percent in January 2012.

4. **Use statistics sparingly.** A few pertinent numbers are far more effective than a battery of statistics.

5. **Display statistics visually.** Your audience is more likely to understand statistics when you illustrate them on a chart, graph, or some other visual aid (Exhibit 6.3).

Activity

Gathering and Evaluating Information Sources

1. Brainstorm a list of keywords related to your speech goal.

2. Identify gaps in your current knowledge about the topic.

3. Do an Internet search to identify potential information sources.

4. Use a library database (either at the library or online) to identify additional potential information sources.

5. Skim the sources to decide which are likely to be the most useful.

6. Evaluate each source for validity, accuracy, and reliability.

7. Determine what (if any) primary research you might conduct to fill remaining gaps.

SAMPLE STUDENT RESPONSE
Gathering and Evaluating Information Sources

Speech goal: *I would like the audience to understand why honeybees are vanishing.*

1. Brainstorm a list of keywords related to your speech goal.

   honeybees, bumblebees, beekeepers, colony collapse disorder

2. Identify gaps in your current knowledge about the topic.

   Because I'm a biology major and have done an 8-week internship in the field, I am familiar with the kinds of work I'll need to seek out to fill any gaps in my knowledge.

3. Do an Internet search to identify potential information sources.

   I searched using Google and found a Wikipedia entry I used as a starting point to locate other websites, a YouTube video by the USDA, an interview with a beekeeper, and an interview by Bill Maher with Ellen Page I could use in my speech.

4. Use a library database (either at the library or online) to identify additional potential information sources.

   Journal of Bee Biology, Science, Biology Quarterly, Entomol

5. Skim the sources to decide which are likely to be the most useful.

   Journal of Bee Biology and Entomol are really helpful.

6. Evaluate each source for validity, accuracy, and reliability.

   Both of these journal articles pass the accuracy, validity, and reliability tests.

7. Determine what (if any) primary research you might conduct to fill remaining gaps.

   I will interview my adviser, who has been studying the vanishing honeybees since 2006.

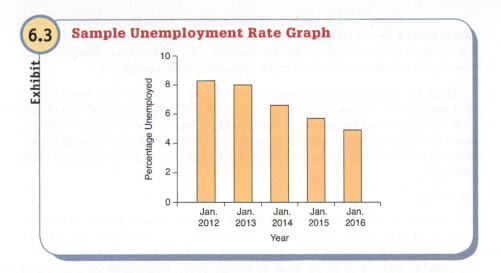

Exhibit 6.3 **Sample Unemployment Rate Graph**

6. **Remember that statistics are biased.** Mark Twain once said there are three kinds of lies: "lies, damned lies, and statistics."[5] Not all statistics are lies, of course, but consider the source of the statistics you'd like to use, what that source may have been trying to prove with the data, and how that situation might have influenced the way the data were collected and interpreted. In other words, evaluate the source thoughtfully for validity, accuracy, and reliability.[6]

Examples

Examples are specific instances that illustrate or explain a general factual statement. One or two short examples such as those that follow provide concrete details that help make a general statement more meaningful.

> *One way a company increases its power is to acquire another company. When Delta bought out Northwest Airlines it became the world's largest airline company.*

> *Professional figure skaters practice many long hours every day. 2014 Olympic Gold medalist Yuzuru Hanyu practices 5 to 6 hours per day.*

Examples can be real like these, or hypothetical. **Hypothetical examples** are specific illustrations based on reflections about future events. They develop the idea "What if . . . ?" Science fiction books and feature films such as *San Andreas*, which is about a devastating earthquake in California, and *The Martian*, which is about an astronaut surviving alone on Mars, are built around hypothetical "what if" scenarios.

Because hypothetical examples are not themselves factual, you must carefully check that the facts on which they are based are accurate. Three principles should guide your use of examples. First, use at least one example to support every generalization. A generalization without an example (or other piece of evidence to support it) can be judged by the audience as nothing more than your opinion.

Second, the examples should be clear and specific enough to create a picture the audience can understand. Consider the following generalization and supporting example.

> **Generalization:** Electronics is one of the few areas in which products are significantly cheaper today than they were in the 1980s.
>
> **Supporting example:** In the mid-1980s, Motorola sold cell phones for US$5,000 each; today, the average price of a smartphone ranges from US$200-$300 worldwide and a basic cell phone costs less than US$50, according to the International Data Corporation.[7]

examples: specific instances that illustrate or explain a general factual statement

hypothetical examples: specific instances based on reflections about future events

With this single example, the listener has a vivid picture of the tremendous difference in about a 30-year period. You can often achieve this first guideline best by sharing it in the form of a presentational aid. For example, you could show an enlarged advertisement for a Motorola cell phone in the 1980s along with a recent one.

Third, the examples you use should be representative. If cell phones were the *only* electronics product whose prices had dropped so much over that same period, this vivid example would be misleading and unethical. Any misuse of data is unethical, especially if the user knows better. To extend our thinking about illustrating examples, you might show several advertisements for different electronic devices from the 1980s and today.

Definitions

A **definition** is a statement that clarifies the meaning of a word or phrase. Definitions serve to clarify in three ways. First, definitions clarify the meaning of terminology that is specialized, technical, or otherwise likely to be unfamiliar to your audience. For example, when Dan talked about bioluminescence, he clarified the meaning of the word *bioluminescence* with the following definition: "According to *Encyclopaedia Britannica Online*, bioluminescence is the emission of visible light by living organisms like fireflies." Although dictionaries and encyclopedias contain definitions, your speech topic might be such that you have to find definitions through prominent researchers or professional practitioners. For example, in a speech about eating disorders, you might go to the website of the Academy of Nutrition and Dietetics (www.eatright.org) for your definition of the term *eating disorders*.

Second, definitions clarify words and terms that have more than one meaning. For example, because *child abuse* is a term that encompasses a broad range of behaviors, you might choose to define it in a way that acknowledges which behaviors you intend to focus on in your speech.

Third, particularly with controversial subjects, definitions clarify your stance on the subject. For example, in a speech about domestic violence against women, Donna Shalala, former Secretary of the US Department of Health and Human Services, defined such violence as "terrorism in the home."[8]

Expert Opinions

Expert opinions are interpretations and judgments made by an authority in a particular subject area at a particular time. They can help explain what facts mean or put them in perspective. "Watching 28 hours of television a week is far too much for young children" and "Having a firewire port on your computer is absolutely necessary" are opinions. Whether they are expert opinions or not depends on who made the statements. An **expert** is a person recognized as having mastered a specific subject, usually through long-term study. When you use expert opinions in your speech, remember to cite the expert's credentials.

Elaborations

Both factual statements and expert opinions can be elaborated on through anecdotes and narratives, comparisons and contrasts, or quotations.

Anecdotes and Narratives

Anecdotes are brief, often amusing stories; **narratives** are accounts, personal experiences, tales, or lengthier stories. Because holding audience interest is important and because audience attention is likely to be captured by a story, anecdotes and narratives are worth looking for or creating (Photo 6.6). The key to using them is to be sure the point of the story directly addresses the point you are making in your speech. Good stories may be humorous, sentimental, suspenseful, or dramatic. Speakers often find anecdotes and brief narratives on social media sites such as YouTube. As with all sources, however, be sure to verify that the source is credible, valid, and reliable.

Comparisons and Contrasts

One of the best ways to give meaning to new ideas is through comparison and contrast. **Comparisons** illuminate a point by showing similarities, whereas **contrasts** highlight differences. Although comparisons and contrasts may be literal, like comparing and contrasting the murder rates in different countries or during different eras, they may also be figurative.

> **Figurative Comparison:** *Friendship is like a bank account. You can't keep drawing from it without also making deposits.*

> **Figurative Contrast:** *How do participation and commitment differ? If this morning you had bacon and eggs for breakfast, I think it illustrates the difference. The eggs represent "participation" on the part of the chicken. The bacon represents "total commitment" on the part of the pig![9]*

Quotations

At times, information you find will be so well stated that you want to quote it directly in your speech. Because audiences want to listen to your ideas and arguments, they do not want to hear a string of long quotations. Nevertheless, a well-selected quotation may be perfect in one or two key places.

Quotations can both explain and enliven. Look for quotations that make a point in a particularly clear or vivid way. For example, in his speech "Enduring Values for a Secular Age," Hans Becherer, executive officer at Deere & Company, used this Henry Ford quote to show the importance of enthusiasm to progress:

> *Enthusiasm is at the heart of all progress. With it, there is accomplishment. Without it, there are only alibis.[10]*

Historical or literary quotations can help reinforce a point vividly. Cynthia Opheim, chair of the Department of Political Science at Southwest Texas State University, in her speech "Making Democracy Work," used this quote from Mark Twain on the frustration of witnessing legislative decision making:

> *There are two things you should never watch being made: sausage and legislation.[11]*

When you use a direct quotation, you need to verbally acknowledge the person it came from. Using any quotation or close paraphrase without crediting its source is **plagiarism**, the unethical act of representing another person's work as your own.

Diverse Cultural Perspectives

When identifying supporting material, be sure to include a variety of cultural perspectives. For example, when Carrie was preparing her speech on proficiency testing

Photo 6.6 Much of the success of actor and stand-up comedian Jamie Foxx can be attributed to his ability to tell great stories. What other celebrities can you think of who tell good stories?

Handout/Getty Images

comparisons: illuminate a point by showing similarities

contrasts: illuminate a point by highlighting differences

plagiarism: the unethical act of representing another person's work as your own by failing to credit the source

Reflect on Ethics

WHAT WOULD *YOU* DO?

COLDPLAY ADMITS TO PLAGIARISM

In 2005, the popular British rock band Coldplay admitted to *Rolling Stone* magazine that they plagiarized from various musical sources on their 2005 album *X & Y*. After admitting it, they also admitted that the album should have included a bibliography, discography, or references for the "borrowed" material. Despite their admission, they suffered no repercussions. Then, according to a report published in the December 5, 2008, issue of *Rolling Stone*, songwriter and guitarist Joe Satriani sued Coldplay for "ripping off his 2004 track, 'If I Could Fly,'" for their own Grammy-nominated hit "Viva La Vida." The case was dismissed on September 14, 2009. Although Satriani's lawyer would not say whether a financial settlement was involved, one thing was clear: "Under terms of the dismissal, Coldplay won't have to admit to any wrongdoing."[12] Today Coldplay is still going strong as evidenced by its halftime performance at the 2016 Super Bowl where they even performed a mashup of "Yellow" and "Viva La Vida."

1. Given the lack of repercussions, do you think Coldplay will plagiarize from other artists again? Why or why not? Be sure to point to ethical principles in your answer.

2. Do you think imitating a musical sound is truly plagiarism? Why or why not?

---

in grade schools, she purposefully searched for articles written by noted Hispanic, Asian, and African American, as well as European American, authors. In addition, she interviewed two local school superintendents—one from an urban district and another from a suburban district. Doing so boosted Carrie's confidence that her speech would accurately reflect diverse perspectives on the issue of proficiency testing.

RECORD INFORMATION AND SOURCES

As you find information, you need to record it accurately and keep a careful account of your sources so you can cite them appropriately during your speech. One way to do so is to compile an annotated bibliography of the sources you believe are relevant and create a research card for each piece of information you might use in the speech.

Annotated Bibliography

annotated bibliography: a preliminary record of relevant sources

An **annotated bibliography** is a preliminary record of the relevant sources you find as you conduct your research. It includes a short summary of the information in each source and how it might be used in your speech. A good annotated bibliography includes:

- A complete bibliographic citation for each source using an appropriate style (e.g., APA, MLA);

- Two or three sentences summarizing pertinent information;

- Two or three sentences explaining how the information might support your speech; and

- Any direct quotations you might want to include verbatim in your speech.

Research Cards

research cards: individual index cards or electronic facsimiles identifying a piece of information, the key word or theme it represents, and its bibliographic data

Research cards are individual 3" × 5" or 4" × 6" index cards or electronic facsimiles that identify (a) one piece of information relevant to your speech, (b) a key word or theme the

Part 2 | Principles

6.4 Sample Research Card

Exhibit

Topic: Fracking

Key Term/Main Idea: Health issues

Theo Colborn, president of The Endocrine Disruption Exchange in Paonia, Colorado, believes that some drilling and fracking additives that can end up in produced water are neurotoxic; among these are 2-butoxyethanol. "If you compare [such chemicals] with the health problems the people have," Colborn says, "they match up."

information represents, and (c) the bibliographic data identifying where you found it. Then you can easily find, arrange, and rearrange individual pieces of information according to key word or theme while you prepare your speech. Exhibit 6.4 shows a sample research card.

Today most speakers create file folders on their computers for each major point in their speech. Then they place word document "research cards" in each folder to be sorted later when they are ready to organize their speech content (Photo 6.7).

Speech Planning Action Step 3, Activity 3B, will help you prepare paper or electronic research cards for the sources you compiled in Activity 3A.

CITE SOURCES

You must acknowledge the sources from which you draw information to develop your speeches. Specifically mentioning your sources not only helps your audience evaluate the content but also adds to your credibility. Frankly, failure to cite sources constitutes plagiarism. Just as you would provide internal references or footnotes in a written document, so must you provide oral footnotes during your speech. **Oral footnotes** are references to an original source, made at the point in the speech where information from that source is presented. The key to preparing oral footnotes is to include enough information for listeners to access the sources themselves and to offer enough credentials to enhance the credibility of the information you are citing. You need to cite oral footnotes for any information including visuals, audiovisuals, and interviews. For example, Justin provided this oral footnote for his interview with the honeybee expert: "I had the privilege of interviewing one of the nation's leading colony collapse disorder scholars, Dr. Susan Stromme. She explained that the radiation emitted from cell phones is one cause of death for the bees." Exhibit 6.5 gives several examples of appropriate speech source citations.

oral footnotes: references to an original source, made at the point in the speech where information from that source is presented

Photo 6.7 Today, most researchers keep electronic research cards in a file on their computer that they can draw from when organizing a speech. Which method (paper or electronic) do you prefer and why?

Ermolaev Alexander/Shutterstock.com

3B SPEECH PLANNING

Recording Relevant Information

1. Carefully read all sources and information you have identified and evaluated as appropriate for your speech.

2. As you review an information item you think might be useful in your speech, record it on a research card.

SAMPLE STUDENT RESPONSE
Record Relevant Information

Speech goal: *I would like the audience to agree that domestic violence is a problem, realize some of its underlying causes, and be convinced of strategies to reduce domestic violence in the United States today.*

Card #1

Topic: The problem
Heading: Scope

More than three million women per year are physically abused by their husbands or boyfriends. Nearly one in four American women experience violence by a male partner during her lifetime. (In other words, of the 20 women in this speech class, about five will be assaulted by a male partner during her lifetime!)

Source: Futures without Violence website (2016). "Get the Facts." Retrieved February 26, 2016, from http://www.futureswithoutviolence.org/resources-events/get-the-facts/

Card #2

Topic: The problem
Heading: Severity

An average of 293,066 rapes and sexual assaults take place each year, which is more than one sexual assault every 107 seconds. Yet sexual assault has actually dropped by 49 percent in recent years.

Card #3

Topic: Causes

Heading: Power and control

Men often resort to violence for various reasons, including anger and to maintain a sense of control.

Card #4

Topic: Causes
Heading: Power and control

Many abused women would leave if human capital such as housing and employment were more readily available to them.

Source: Khazan, O. (2014, September 14). Why they stayed. *The Atlantic*. Retrieved from http://www.theatlantic.com/health/archive/2014/09/why-they-stayed/379843/.

Exhibit 6.5

Appropriate Speech Source Citations

Books

Cite the title of the book and the name of its author. You may cite the book's publication date or the author's credentials if doing so boosts credibility.

> "Thomas Friedman, noted international editor for the *New York Times*, stated in his book *Hot, Flat, and Crowded* . . ."
>
> "But to get a complete picture we have to look at the statistics. According to the 2015 *Statistical Abstract*, the level of production for the European Economic Community rose from . . ."

Journal or magazine articles

Cite the name and date of the publication in which you found the article. You may cite the article's author and title if doing so adds credibility.

> "According to an article about the Federal Reserve in last week's *Newsweek* magazine . . ."
>
> "In the latest Gallup poll cited in the February 10 issue of *Newsweek* . . ."
>
> "Timothy Sellnow, professor of communication at The University of Kentucky, wrote in an article published in 2016 in the *Journal of Applied Communication* that . . ."

Newspapers

Cite the name of the newspaper and date of the article. You may cite the article's author and his or her credentials if it adds credibility.

> "According to a May 2016 article in the *Washington Post* . . ."

Interviews

Cite the name and credentials of the person interviewed and the date the interview took place. If you cite the interview more than once, you need only cite the interviewee's name in subsequent oral footnotes.

> "In an interview on April 21st, 2016 with Dr. Cynthia Stromm, a music professor here at our university . . ."
>
> "In my telephone interview on September 29 with Dr. Susan Nissen, internal medicine physician in Phoenix, Arizona, I learned that . . ."

Internet sources

Cite the website's author, his or her credentials, and the date of the site's most recent revision. If there is no author, cite the credentials of the website's sponsoring organization. Do not cite the URL as part of your oral footnote.

> "According to a January 2016 posting on the official website of the American Heart Association . . ."

Television programs

Cite the name of the program and the date of the original broadcast. You may also cite the name of the reporter for news programs if it boosts credibility.

> "According to an October 2009 CNN special broadcast called 'Latino in America' . . ."

Public speeches

Cite the name and credentials of the speaker, as well as the occasion and date of the speech.

> "In a speech on the state of financial education for vulnerable Americans delivered at the 50th Annual Leaders Conference on September 28, 2015, Susan C. Keating, president of the National Foundation for Credit Counseling, stated . . ."

Speech Planning Action Step 3, Activity 3C, will help you prepare oral citations for the sources you recorded in Activity 3B.

③C SPEECH PLANNING

Citing Sources

On the back of each research card, write a short phrase you can use as an oral footnote during your speech.

SAMPLE STUDENT RESPONSE

> *According to Judith Gordon in her book,* Routledge Library Editions: Helping Survivors of Domestic Violence: The Effectiveness of Medial, Mental Health, and Community Services, *domestic violence is the number one reason for emergency room visits by women.*

Activity

Reflection and Assessment

Effective speeches are developed by doing good research. To do good research, you need to know where to locate different types of information and sources, as well as how to evaluate them. You also need to know how to integrate the information into your speech effectively and ethically. To assess how well you've learned what we've discussed in this chapter, answer the following questions. If you have trouble answering any of them, go back and review that material. Once you can answer each question accurately, you are ready to move ahead to the next chapter.

1. How do you locate and evaluate information sources to develop your topic?
2. What types of information might you use as evidence to support your topic?
3. How can you go about recording information accurately?
4. How do you cite sources appropriately?

Challenge Resource and Assessment Center

MindTap®

Now that you have read Chapter 6, go to your MindTap Communication for *The Challenge of Effective Speaking in a Digital Age* for quick access to flashcards, chapter quizzes, and more.

Applying What You've Learned

1. **Impromptu Speech Activity:** Draw an information source from a box in the front of the room. It might be a book; magazine or academic journal article; printout from a discussion board, blog, or website; and so forth. Read or skim the source. Then prepare a proper APA-style reference citation. Go to the front of the room and write the citation on the board. Then present a 2- to 3-minute informative speech on how well the source meets each of the four evaluation criteria for a speech on a related topic. Provide evidence for your assessments. Be sure to quote something from the information source using a proper oral footnote during the speech.

2. **Assessment Activity A:** Go to the VS Video Productions website (http://www.vsvideoproductions.com) and click on Corporate Videos. What kinds of information and information sources are used to compel viewers to use this company's services? Which are most compelling to you and why?

3. **Assessment Activity B:** Watch an opening story on a local or national news broadcast. Identify what information types and sources are used to support the story. Do they meet the criteria for good sources? Why or why not?

7 Organizing the Speech Body

WHAT'S THE POINT?

WHEN YOU'VE FINISHED THIS CHAPTER, YOU WILL BE ABLE TO:

- Organize your speech body into two to four main points using an appropriate main point pattern
- Construct a clear thesis statement with main point preview
- Develop each main point with subpoints and supporting material
- Create effective transitions
- Outline your speech body

MindTap®

Review the chapter **Learning Objectives** and **Start** with quick warm-up activity.

ACTION STEP 4

Organize ideas into a well-structured outline (the body).

A. Identify two to four main points.

B. Write a thesis statement with main point preview.

C. Develop your main points with subpoints and supporting material.

D. Outline your speech body (with transitions).

Ethical communicators behave responsibly by taking the time to organize the material they plan to share in their speeches.

leungchopan/Shutterstock.com

CoraMax/Shutterstock.com

Katie and Alyssa are taking a public speaking course online over the summer. That way, they can still make progress toward graduation while living at home where they both have great summer jobs. Most of the class is conducted asynchronously; but every Monday afternoon from 1:00 p.m. to 3:00 p.m., all students are required to "attend class virtually" using Adobe Connect. That's when students deliver their formal speeches. Matt had just finished delivering his speech when Alyssa got a text from Katie:

"Matt's speech was awesome! So many powerful stories!"

Alyssa replied: "Great stories but hard to follow. What were his main points?"

Katie responded, "Hmmm . . . Not sure. I hope mine will be easier to follow."

"Mine too," Alyssa exclaimed. "Uh oh. Late for work. CU."

MindTap®
Read, highlight, and take notes online.

Katie and Alyssa's experience is not that unusual. Even well-known speakers sometimes give speeches that are hard to follow. Yet when your speech is well organized, you are far more likely to achieve your goal. In this chapter and the next, we explain the fourth speech plan action step: Organize your ideas into a well-structured outline.

A well-organized speech has three identifiable parts: an introduction, a body, and a conclusion. This chapter focuses on the speech body; the next chapter will look at introductions and conclusions. Here we describe how to: (1) identify **main points** and arrange them using an appropriate main point pattern; (2) use main points to construct a clear thesis statement with main point preview; (3) develop each main point with appropriate supporting material (evidence and reasoning); (4) create transitions that move the speech smoothly from one main point to the next; and (5) outline the speech body.

main points: complete sentence statements of the two to four central ideas the audience needs to understand to achieve the speech goal

ORGANIZE MAIN POINTS

Organizing, the process of arranging your speech content, is guided by what you learned from your audience analysis. Begin by identifying two to four main points that will help you achieve your speech goal. The length of time allotted does not determine the number of main points to use. In fact, the difference between an effective 5-minute speech and an effective 25-minute speech with the same speech goal is not the number of main points, but the extent to which each one is developed with supporting material.

organizing: the process of arranging the speech content

Identify Main Point Ideas

For some goals, identifying main point ideas is easy. For example, if your goal is to demonstrate how to create a website, your main ideas will likely be the steps involved in developing a very basic one. Most times, however, determining main point ideas is more complex. Here is a five-step strategy to help you identify the main ideas when they aren't so obvious:

1. Begin by listing all the ideas you believe relate to your specific goal. You might list as many as nine or more.

2. Eliminate ideas that you believe your audience already understands.

3. Eliminate any ideas that might be too complicated or too broad for your audience to comprehend in the time allotted.

4. Check to see if some of the ideas can be grouped together under a broader theme

5. From the ideas that remain, choose two to four that will help you accomplish your specific speech goal.

Let's look at how Katie used these steps to identify the main point ideas for her speech to inform about the growing problem of the abuse of the prescription drug Adderall among college students. To begin, Katie listed ideas she discovered while doing her research.

What is a prescription drug

What is Adderall

What are the ingredients in Adderall

How is Adderall made

What is the history of Adderall

Who takes Adderall

Why is Adderall prescribed

What are Adderall's benefits

What are Adderall's risks

How many college students take Adderall without prescription

What are the demographics of college students who take Adderall without a prescription

Why do college students who don't have a prescription take Adderall (perceived benefits)

What are the benefit myths

What are the actual results and/or consequences of taking Adderall without a prescription

Second, Katie eliminated the idea "what is a prescription drug" because she knew her audience already understood this. Third, Katie decided the ingredients, history, and how Adderall is made were ideas too broad to cover adequately in the time allotted and were not directly related to her goal. Fourth, Katie noticed that several ideas seemed to be related. What is Adderall, why is it prescribed, and who takes it, as well as its risks and benefits, seemed to go together. How many take it, demographics of its users, and perceived benefits by college students who take Adderall without a prescription also seemed to be related. And benefit myths and actual results/consequences could be grouped together. Finally, Katie decided that her main point ideas would be (1) understanding the nature and purpose of Adderall as a prescription drug, (2) understanding Adderall's growing popularity as a study aid among college students, and (3) problems involved with nonprescribed use of Adderall. This process left Katie with three broad main point ideas she could focus on to develop her speech. The figure on the next page illustrates what Katie's list looked like after she finished her analysis and synthesis. Use Speech Planning Activity 4A to identify main point ideas for your speeches in this course.

Word the Main Points

Once you have identified your two to four main point ideas, shape each one into a complete sentence. Let's look at how Katie did this.

Recall that Katie's main point ideas are understanding Adderall's nature and purpose as a prescription drug, Adderall's growing popularity as a study aid among college

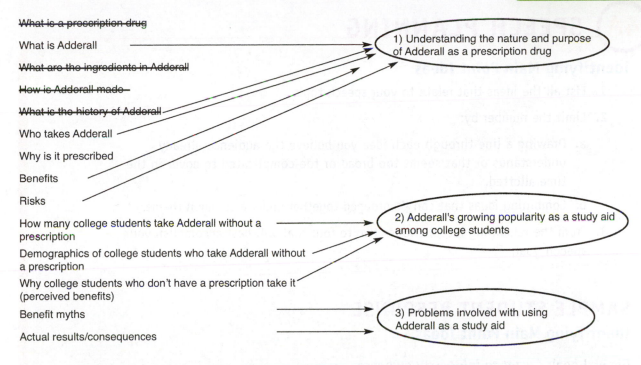

What is a prescription drug

What is Adderall ──────────────────→ 1) Understanding the nature and purpose
of Adderall as a prescription drug

What are the ingredients in Adderall

How is Adderall made

What is the history of Adderall

Who takes Adderall

Why is it prescribed

Benefits

Risks

How many college students take Adderall without a ──────→ 2) Adderall's growing popularity as a study aid
prescription   among college students

Demographics of college students who take Adderall without
a prescription

Why college students who don't have a prescription take it
(perceived benefits)

Benefit myths ──────────────────→ 3) Problems involved with using
Adderall as a study aid

Actual results/consequences

students, and the risks involved in Adderall's misuse. Suppose she wrote her first draft
of main points as follows:

    I. *What exactly is Adderall, and why is it prescribed?*

    II. *College student use*

  III. *Risks*

Some people refer to this first version of the main points as a **preparation outline**.
It provides a draft of main points but doesn't specify clearly how each main point is
related to the speech goal. To begin clarifying these relationships, Katie next creates a
complete sentence for each main point:

    I. *What exactly is Adderall?*

    II. *An increasing number of American college students are using Adderall as a
study aid.*

  III. *Nonmedical use of Adderall is risky.*

Although these statements are now complete sentences, they are still a bit vague.
To assure herself that she has worded her main points clearly, Katie applies two test
questions to them.

    1. **Is the relationship between each main point statement and the goal state-
ment clearly specified?** Katie's first main point statement doesn't indicate what
purposes Adderall serves as a prescription medicine. So she improved this
statement by saying:

    What exactly is Adderall prescribed for?

    Similarly, she improved the second main point statement by saying:

    *Nonmedical Adderall use is becoming increasingly popular as a study aid
among American college students.*

    And she revised the third main point to state:

    Nonmedical use of Adderall as a study aid is dangerous.

preparation outline:
a draft of main points and
supporting ideas

(4A) SPEECH PLANNING

Identifying Main Point Ideas

1. List all the ideas that relate to your speech topic.

2. Limit the number by:

   a. Drawing a line through each idea you believe the audience already understands or that seems too broad or too complicated to cover in the time allotted.

   b. Combining ideas that can be grouped together under a common theme.

3. From the remaining ideas, choose two to four that will best accomplish your speech goal.

SAMPLE STUDENT RESPONSE

Identifying Main Point Ideas

General goal: *I want to inform my audience.*

Specific goal: *I want my audience to understand the basics of seasonal affective disorder (SAD).*

1. List all the ideas that relate to your speech.

   What is SAD

   Symptoms

   Causes

   Historical background

   Discoverer

   Types of depression

   Vitamin deficiencies

   Locations and prevalence

   Diagnoses

   Medical treatments

   Organic treatments

   Therapeutic treatments

   Role of sunshine

   Light therapy

   Myths

   Realities

(4A) SPEECH PLANNING *(continued)*

Activity

2. Limit the number by:

   a. Drawing a line through each idea you believe the audience already understands or that seems too broad or too complicated to cover in the time allotted.

   b. Combining ideas that can be grouped together under a common theme.

3. From the remaining ideas, choose the two to four that will best accomplish your speech goal.

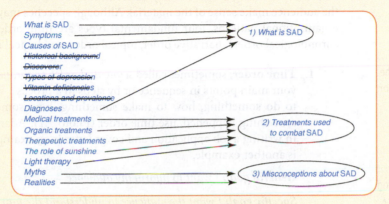

Main point ideas:

  Causes

  Symptoms

  Treatments

---

2. **Are the main points parallel in structure? Parallel structure** means the main points follow the same structural pattern, often using the same introductory words. Parallel structure is not a requirement, but it can help your audience recognize your main points when you deliver your speech. So Katie made one more small adjustment:

   I. *First, what exactly is Adderall and why is it prescribed?*

   II. *Second, a growing number of American college students are using Adderall without a prescription.*

   III. *Third, there are serious risks in nonmedical Adderall use.*

Parallel structure can be achieved in many ways. Katie used numbering: "first . . . second . . . third." Another way is to start each sentence with an active verb. Suppose Adam wants his audience to understand the steps involved in writing an effective job application cover letter. Adam's first draft of his main points was as follows:

   I. *Format the heading elements correctly.*

   II. *The body of the letter should be three paragraphs long.*

   III. *When concluding, use "sincerely" or "regards."*

   IV. *Then you need to proofread the letter carefully.*

> **parallel structure:** when the main points follow the same structural pattern, often using the same introductory words

Adam revised his main points to make them parallel by using active verbs (italicized):

I. *Format* the heading elements correctly.

II. *Organize* the body into three paragraphs.

III. *Conclude* the letter with "sincerely" or "regards."

IV. *Proofread* the letter carefully.

Select a Main Point Pattern

A speech can be organized in many different ways. Remember, your objective is to help the audience make sense of the material. Although speeches may follow many different organizational patterns, four fundamental types are time order (a.k.a. sequential or chronological order), narrative order, topical order, and logical reasons order.

time order: organizing the main points in sequence or by steps in a process

1. **Time order**, sometimes called *sequential order or chronological order*, arranges your main points in sequence or by steps in a process. When you explain how to do something, how to make something, how something works, or how something happened, use time order (Photo 7.1). Adam's speech on the *steps in writing a job application and cover letter* is an example of time order. Here is another example.

General goal: I want to inform my audience.

Specific goal: I want the audience to understand the four steps involved in developing a personal network.

Main Points:

I. First, analyze your current networking potential.

II. Second, position yourself in places for opportunity.

III. Third, advertise yourself.

IV. Fourth, follow up on contacts.

narrative order: organizing the main points as a story or series of stories

2. **Narrative order** conveys ideas through a story or series of stories. Narrative order is rooted in narrative theory, which suggests that one important way people communicate is through storytelling. We use stories to teach and to learn, to entertain, and to make sense of the world around us.[1] Although a narrative may be presented in chronological order, it may also use a series of flashbacks or flash-forwards to increase dramatic effect. Each main point may be an event in a single story or each main point may be a different story that illustrates the thesis. Lana shared her story about having anorexia using three stories as main points.

General goal: I want to inform my audience.

Specific goal: I want my audience to understand how anorexia nervosa affects the lives of its victims and their loved ones.

Main points:

I. First, let's talk about the story of a typical day as a recovering anorexic.

II. Next, let's focus on a historical account about how I became anorexic.

III. Finally, let's discuss an inspirational story about two people who basically saved my life.

Photo 7.1 Time order is appropriate when you are showing others how to do or make something or how something works. For which speech topic(s) could you use time order?

Jeff Greenberg/AGE Fotostock

PUBLIC SPEAKING IN THE REAL WORLD

The Role of Clear Organization in Steve Jobs' Speechmaking Success

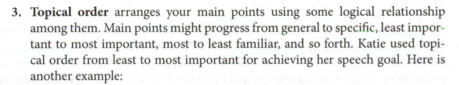

Richard Lewisohn/Alamy Stock Photo

Steve Jobs—the entrepreneur, innovator, and former CEO of Apple Inc.—died on October 5, 2011. But his legacy lives on—not only in terms of inventions like the iMac, iPod, iPad, and iPhone—but also in the form of many inspirational speeches he delivered to thousands of audiences around the globe—speeches that are forever accessible thanks in part to the technological advances he helped accomplish. In March 2012, *Fortune* named this inspirational speaker and visionary "the greatest entrepreneur of our time."[2]

Arguably one of Jobs' most inspiring speeches was the commencement address he gave to 23,000 people on June 12, 2005, at Stanford University. The speech, which earned him a standing ovation, has been and continues to be watched by millions more on YouTube. Why is this speech so memorable? Critics contend that, beyond the fascinating stories he tells, Jobs uses an engaging structure focused clearly on three main points. In essence, his speech is a textbook example of a clear speech outline.[3]

If you are not familiar with Jobs' speech, watch it on YouTube before answering these questions:

1. What are Jobs' main points of advice to the students in the audience?

2. How did the preview of main points and section transitions help you follow along and remember them?

3. **Topical order** arranges your main points using some logical relationship among them. Main points might progress from general to specific, least important to most important, most to least familiar, and so forth. Katie used topical order from least to most important for achieving her speech goal. Here is another example:

General goal: I want to inform my audience.

Specific goal: I want the audience to understand three methods for ridding our bodies of harmful toxins.

Main Points:

   I. *One method for ridding our bodies of harmful toxins is keeping well hydrated.*

   II. *A second method for ridding our bodies of harmful toxins is reducing our intake of animal products.*

   III. *A third method for ridding our bodies of harmful toxins is increasing the proportion of natural whole foods we eat.*

4. **Logical reasons order** organizes the main points according to reasons for accepting the thesis as desirable or true. Logical reasons order is often used when your general goal is to persuade (Photo 7.2).

General goal: I want to persuade my audience.

Specific goal: I want my audience to donate money to the United Way.

Main points:

   I. *When you donate to the United Way, your one donation covers many charities.*

topical order: organizing the main points by categories or divisions of a subject

logical reasons order: organizing the main points according to reasons for accepting the thesis as desirable or true

Kevork Djansezian/Getty Images

Photo 7.2 Logical reasons order is often used when trying to persuade others to agree with you or to take action. When have you been persuaded to give money to a campaign and why?

II. When you donate to the United Way, you can stipulate which charities you wish to support.

III. When you donate to the United Way, you know that a high percentage of your donation will go directly to the charities you've selected.

These four organizational patterns are the most basic ones. We will introduce you to several additional patterns in later chapters. Use Speech Planning and Response Activity 4B to organize your main points.

CONSTRUCT A CLEAR THESIS STATEMENT

thesis statement: one- or two-sentence summary of the speech that incorporates the general and specific goals and previews the main points

Once you have identified and worded your main points using an appropriate organizational pattern, you are ready to construct your thesis statement. A **thesis statement** is a one- or two-sentence summary of your speech that incorporates your general and specific goals and previews the main points of your speech. A thesis statement provides a blueprint of the speech body organization. Exhibit 7.1 provides several examples of specific speech goals and thesis statements.

DEVELOP MAIN POINTS

subpoints: statements that elaborate on a main point

supporting material: evidence and reasoning used to develop the main points

Once you have identified the main points and used them to form your thesis statement, you need to develop each one with subpoints and supporting material. **Subpoints** are statements that elaborate on a main point. A main point may have two or more subpoints depending on its complexity and the time allotted for your speech. Each subpoint is developed further with **supporting material**—evidence you gathered through secondary and primary research along with the logical reasoning you use to link it to the main point it supports. You can identify subpoints by sorting through the research you compiled in your annotated bibliography and/or on research cards to find evidence (e.g., definitions, examples, facts, statistics, stories) that supports each of your main points. Once you have listed the items that support a main point, look for relationships between and among ideas. As you analyze your information, draw lines connecting items that fit together logically and cross out those that seem irrelevant. Finally, one subpoint under each main point should be a **listener relevance link**, a statement alerting listeners to why the main point is important to them.

listener relevance link: statement alerting listeners about how a main point or subpoint is relevant to them

After drafting your subpoint ideas in a preparation outline, write them out in full sentences in your formal outline. We will talk more about the wording for these in Chapter 10. You should also include internal references for information you found in secondary sources. Doing so will remind you to cite the references during your speech, which will enhance your listeners' perception of you as credible and help you avoid plagiarism.

CREATE TRANSITIONS

transitions: words, phrases, or sentences that bridge two ideas

Transitions are words, phrases, or sentences that bridge two ideas. Transitions act like tour guides—leading the audience from point to point throughout the speech. Good transitions are certainly important in writing; however, they are crucial for formal public speeches. If listeners get lost or think they've missed something, they can't go back

4B SPEECH PLANNING

Organizing Main Points

1. Write your general and specific speech goal statements.

2. Write down the two to four main point ideas you identified in Activity 4A.

3. Write one sentence that summarizes what you want your audience to know about each idea.

4. Review the main points as a group.

   a. Is the relationship between each main point statement and the goal statement clearly specified? If not, revise.

   b. Are the main points parallel in structure? If not, consider why and revise.

5. Identify the organizational pattern you used.

SAMPLE STUDENT RESPONSE
Organizing Main Points

1. Write your general and specific goal statements.

   General goal: *I want to inform my audience.*

   Specific goal: *I want my audience to understand the three tests to determine whether a diamond is real.*

2. Write down the two to four main point ideas identified in Activity 4A.

   Acid test

   Streak test

   Hardness test

3. Write one sentence that summarizes what you want your audience to know about each idea.

   I. *One way to identify a diamond is by using the acid test.*

   II. *The streak test can also be used to identify a diamond.*

   III. *You can also identify a diamond by using the hardness test.*

4. Review the main points as a group.

   a. Is the relationship between each main point statement and the goal statement clearly specified? If not, revise.

   No. The purpose of each test is to identify whether the diamond is real. The following revision puts emphasis in the right place.

(continued)

Activity

Revision:

    I. *One way to identify whether a diamond is real is by using the acid test.*

    II. *The streak test can also be used to identify whether a diamond is real.*

    III. *You can also identify whether a diamond is real by using the hardness test.*

b. Are the main points parallel in structure? If not, consider why and revise.

Revision:

    I. *One way to determine whether a diamond is real is to use the acid test.*

    II. *A second way to determine whether a diamond is real is to use the streak test.*

    III. *A third way to determine whether a diamond is real is to use the hardness test.*

5. Identify the organizational pattern you used.

Topical

Exhibit 7.1

Sample Speech Goals and Thesis Statements

General goal: I want to inform my audience.

Specific goal: I want my audience to understand how to improve their grades in college.

Thesis statement: Three proven techniques for improving test scores in college are to attend classes regularly, develop a positive attitude, and study efficiently.

General goal: I want to inform my audience.

Specific goal: I want my audience to understand the benefits of volunteering.

Thesis statement: Some important benefits of volunteering include helping underprivileged populations, supporting nonprofit organizations, and improving your self-esteem.

General goal: I want to persuade my audience.

Specific goal: I want my audience to believe that parents should limit the time their children spend viewing television.

Thesis statement: Parents should limit the time their children spend viewing television because heavy television viewing increases violent tendencies in children.

General goal: I want to persuade my audience.

Specific goal: I want my audience to believe that they should learn to speak Spanish.

Thesis statement: You should learn to speak Spanish because it will benefit you personally, economically, and practically.

---

section transitions:
complete sentences that bridge the major parts of a speech

and check as they can when reading. Transitions come in the form of section transitions and signposts.

    Section transitions are complete sentences that bridge the major parts of your speech. They typically summarize what has just been said in one main point and preview the one coming up next. Essentially, section transitions are the glue that holds the

4C SPEECH PLANNING

Activity

Constructing a Thesis Statement

1. Write the general and specific goals you identified in Activity 4A.

2. List the main point ideas you identified in Activity 4B.

3. Now write one or two complete sentences that combine your general and specific goals with your main point ideas.

SAMPLE STUDENT RESPONSE
Constructing a Thesis Statement

1. Write the general and specific goals you identified in Activity 4A.

   General goal: *I want to inform my audience.*

   Specific goal: *I want my audience to understand the nature of seasonal affective disorder.*

2. List the main point ideas you identified in Activity 4B.

   Causes

   Symptoms

   Treatments

3. Now write one or two complete sentences that combine your general and specific goals with your main point ideas.

   Seasonal affective disorder, also known as SAD, is a fairly common mood disorder people experience regularly in winter, summer, spring, or autumn. To better understand the nature of this form of depression, let's look at some causes, symptoms, and treatment methods.

macrostructure of your speech together. Section transitions are critical for effective speeches because they help the audience follow the speech organization and remember information.

For example, suppose Adam has just finished the introduction of his speech on creating a cover letter and is now ready to launch into his main points. Before stating his first main point, he might say, "Creating a good cover letter is a four-step process. Now let's consider the first one." When his listeners hear this transition, they are signaled to mentally prepare to listen to and remember the first main point. When he finishes his first main point, he may say: "Now that we understand what is involved in creating the heading elements, we can move on to discuss what to include in the body of the letter."

Signposts are words, phrases, or visual cues that connect pieces of supporting material to the main point or subpoint they address. Whereas section transitions are complete sentences, signposts are usually one-word references. Sometimes, signposts highlight numerical order: "first," "second," "third," or "fourth" (Photo 7.3). Sometimes, they help the audience focus on a key idea: "foremost," "most important," or "above all." They can also be used to signify an explanation: "to illustrate," "for example," "in other

signposts: words, phrases, or visual cues that connect pieces of supporting material to the main point or subpoint they address

Photo 7.3 Sometimes signposts are used to highlight numerical order. Where might you add a signpost for clarity in your speech?

formal speech outline:

a full sentence representation of the hierarchical and sequential relationships among the ideas presented in the speech

words," "essentially," or "to clarify." Signposts can also signal that an important idea, or even the speech itself, is coming to an end: "in short," "finally," "in conclusion," or "to summarize." Just as section transitions serve as the glue that holds your macrostructure together, signposts serve as the glue that holds your subpoints and supporting material together within each main point.

OUTLINE THE SPEECH BODY

Once you have developed each main point with supporting material and formed transition statements to link them together, you are ready to begin putting your formal speech outline together. A **formal speech outline** is a full sentence representation of the hierarchical and sequential relationships among ideas in the speech. In other words, it is a diagram of your speech material. For most speeches, you will use main points (Roman numerals: I, II, III, etc.), subpoints (capital letters: A, B, C, etc.), and sometimes sub-subpoints (Arabic numerals: 1, 2, 3, etc.). Exhibit 7.2 shows a diagram of this general form for formal speech outlines. Use Speech Planning and Response Activity 4D to complete the outline of your speech body.

Exhibit 7.2

General Form for a Speech Outline

I. **Main point one**
  A. Subpoint A for main point one
    1. Sub-subpoint one
      a. Elaboration material (if needed)
      b. Elaboration material (if needed)
    2. Sub-subpoint two
      a. Elaboration material (if needed)
      b. Elaboration material (if needed)
  B. Subpoint B for main point one
    1. Sub-subpoint one
      a. Elaboration material (if needed)
      b. Elaboration material (if needed)
    2. Sub-subpoint two
      a. Elaboration material (if needed)
      b. Elaboration material (if needed)

Transition

II. **Main point two**
  A. Subpoint A for main point two
    1. Sub-subpoint one
      a. Elaboration material (if needed)
      b. Elaboration material (if needed)
    2. Sub-subpoint two
      a. Elaboration material (if needed)
      b. Elaboration material (if needed)
  B. Subpoint B for main point two
    1. Sub-subpoint one
      a. Elaboration material (if needed)
      b. Elaboration material (if needed)

SPEECH SNIPPET

In her speech about disciplining children, Darla used this section transition between her first and second main point:

Certainly, the behavioral modification approach based on B. F. Skinner's work can be an effective method for disciplining children. It is not the only method, however, which leads us to a second method, based on Sigmund Freud's work.

Exhibit 7.2

General Form for a Speech Outline (continued)

      2. Sub-subpoint two
        a. Elaboration material (if needed)
        b. Elaboration material (if needed)
      3. Sub-subpoint three
        a. Elaboration material (if needed)
        b. Elaboration material (if needed)
   C. Subpoint C for main point two
      1. Sub-subpoint one
        a. Elaboration material (if needed)
        b. Elaboration material (if needed)
      2. Sub-subpoint two
        a. Elaboration material (if needed)
        b. Elaboration material (if needed)
      3. Sub-subpoint three
        a. Elaboration material (if needed)
        b. Elaboration material (if needed)
      . . . etc.

IMPROMPTU SPEECH CHALLENGE

Select a favorite YouTube video. Prepare a 2- to 3-minute speech explaining why it is a favorite. Your speech should consist of a thesis statement as the introduction, two to four main points linked with section transitions for the body, and a thesis restatement for the conclusion. Be sure to consider the wording of your thesis statement and the best organizational pattern for your main points. Finally, support each main point with one or two subpoints.

4D SPEECH PLANNING

Activity

Outlining the Speech Body

Using complete sentences, write the following:

1. The general and specific speech goals you identified in Activity 4A.

2. The thesis statement you developed in Activity 4C.

3. A transition to the first main point.

4. The first main point you developed in Activity 4B.

5. The subpoints and supporting material for your first main point.

6. A transition from your first to second main point.

7. Your other main points, subpoints, support, section transitions, and signposts. Use the format shown in the Student Response to Activity 4D.

SAMPLE STUDENT RESPONSE
Outlining the Speech Body

General goal: *I want to inform my audience.*

Specific goal: *I would like the audience to understand the nature of seasonal affective disorder.*

(continued)

Activity

Thesis statement: *Seasonal affective disorder, also known as SAD, is a fairly common mood disorder people experience regularly in winter, summer, spring, or autumn. To better understand the nature of this form of depression, let's look at some of its causes, symptoms, and treatments.*

Body

I. **Several factors may contribute to seasonal affective disorder.**

    A. *Listener relevance link: Since as many as 20% of the US population may experience some form of SAD, knowing what these factors are may help you understand why you or your loved ones become depressed during a certain season.*

    B. *One factor that may cause SAD is circadian rhythm.*

      1. **Circadian rhythms are the physical, mental, and behavioral changes that follow a roughly 24-hour cycle.**

      2. **This factor is generally linked to winter-onset SAD.**

      3. **The decrease in sunlight during winter months disrupts one's internal clock, which leads to feelings of depression.**

    C. *A second factor that has been linked to SAD is serotonin levels.*

      1. **Serotonin is a brain chemical that affects mood.**

      2. **Reduced sunlight can lower serotonin levels, which then leads to feelings of depression.**

    D. *A third factor that may cause SAD is melatonin levels.*

      1. **Melatonin is a natural hormone that regulates sleep.**

      2. **Changing seasons can disrupt the balance of melatonin in the body.**

      3. **This change can affect both sleep patterns and mood.**

Transition: *Now that we understand the factors that may cause seasonal affective disorder, let's identify some of the symptoms.*

II. **Seasonal affective disorder is a form of depression that comes and goes with the changing seasons**

    A. *Listener relevance link: Because the symptoms of SAD can range from mild to major, knowing what they are may empower us to seek appropriate life-saving help for ourselves and for others.*

    B. *Symptoms that have been linked to winter-onset SAD include irritability, low energy, fatigue, oversleeping, craving carbohydrate-rich foods, and weight gain.*

    C. *Symptoms that have been linked to summer-onset SAD include insomnia, anxiety, poor appetite, and weight loss.*

Transition: *Now that we understand what the symptoms of winter-onset and summer-onset SAD are, let's discuss some treatment methods.*

4D SPEECH PLANNING (continued)

III. **Doctors typically prescribe one or more of the following methods for patients with seasonal affective disorder.**

    A. *Listener Relevance Link: When you or a loved one experiences SAD, you have several options for treating this condition successfully.*

    B. *One effective treatment method for SAD is light therapy.*

       1. **Light therapy has you sit in front of a special light box that mimics natural sunlight.**

       2. **Light therapy is often used on patients with winter-onset SAD.**

       3. **Light therapy results usually appear within a few days of using the box.**

    C. *A second treatment method for SAD is antidepressant medication.*

       1. **One common medication is an extended release version of bupropion.**

       2. **It may take several weeks to notice the effects of taking an antidepressant.**

    D. *A third treatment method for SAD is psychotherapy.*

       1. **Psychotherapy helps patients replace negative thinking and behaviors with positive coping strategies.**

       2. **Psychotherapy also helps patients learn to manage stress.**

    E. *A fourth treatment method for SAD is lifestyle adjustments.*

       1. **Make your home environment sunnier and brighter.**

       2. **Spend time outside every day.**

       3. **Exercise regularly.**

Reflect on Ethics

WHAT WOULD *YOU* DO?

A SNAKE IN THE GRASS

Harriet Ziefert's children's book, *A Snake is Totally Tail,* was to be published in early 2006 when a New York public librarian, John Peters, noticed that more than half of the text exactly matched a book by Judi Barrett. First published in 1983, Barrett's book was by then out of print. Peters posted his observation to a listserv, and Ziefert responded with, "I have no recollection of ever seeing Ms. Barrett's book—though it would be foolish of me not to consider the possibility that I might have seen it decades ago and that its structure and some of its language imprinted somewhere on my subconscious."[4] Although no formal suit was ever filed against Ziefert, the publisher decided not to publish the book after Peters' listserv posting was made public.[5] Since then, Ziefert has gone on to publish dozens of new children's books.

1. Do you believe Ziefert's explanation? Why or why not?

2. Suppose that Ziefert's book did not match the earlier book word for word but instead just followed a very similar plotline that was organized the same way and used the same narrative voice. Would your opinion of Ziefert change?

3. How does this incident influence your opinion about the originality of Ziefert's books published since 2006?

Reflection and Assessment

Effective public speeches are well organized. The speech body includes main points and subpoints that should be written in complete sentences and checked to make sure that they are clear, parallel in structure, meaningful, and limited in number to four or fewer. To assess how well you've learned what we've discussed in this chapter, answer the following questions. If you have trouble answering any of them, go back and review that material. Once you can answer each question accurately, you are ready to move ahead to the next chapter.

1. Why organize your speech body into two to four main points using an appropriate main point pattern?
2. How do you construct a clear thesis statement?
3. How do you go about developing main points?
4. How are effective section transitions constructed and why are they important in public speeches?
5. What is a formal speech outline?

MindTap®

Challenge Resource and Assessment Center

Now that you have read Chapter 7, go to your MindTap Communication for *The Challenge of Effective Speaking in a Digital Age* for quick access to flashcards, chapter quizzes, and more.

Applying What You've Learned

1. **Impromptu Speech Activity:** Identify a favorite toy or game you enjoyed as a child. Come up with a goal statement and two to four main points you could talk about concerning that toy or game. Present a short speech consisting of a thesis statement as the introduction, the two to four main points linked with section transitions for the body, and a thesis restatement for the conclusion. Be sure to consider the wording of your thesis statement and the best organizational pattern for your main points. Be prepared to defend your choices if asked to do so.
2. **Assessment Activity A:** Complete Speech Planning Activities 4A, 4B, 4C, and 4D for a speech you may give this semester.
3. **Assessment Activity B:** Watch a speaker—in person, on television, or online—who demonstrates how to make or do something. Try to identify the thesis statement and main points. Does the speaker use parallel phrasing, section transitions, and/or signposts? How does using or not using these elements influence your ability to follow along?

8

The Introduction and Conclusion

WHAT'S THE POINT?

WHEN YOU'VE FINISHED THIS CHAPTER, YOU WILL BE ABLE TO:

- Create an effective speech introduction
- Create an effective speech conclusion
- Complete your formal speech outline and reference list

MindTap®

Review the chapter **Learning Objectives** and **Start** with quick warm-up activity.

ⓔ Ethical communicators demonstrate integrity when they begin and end their speeches with an introduction and conclusion that meets all the goals intended in them.

ACTION STEP 4

Organize ideas into a well-structured outline.

E. Create the speech introduction.
F. Create the speech conclusion.
G. Compile the reference list.
H. Complete the formal speech outline.

Katie asked Alyssa to listen to her speech rehearsal. As she stood in front of the room where she was practicing, she began, "Adderall—a psychostimulant prescription drug— is becoming more and more popular as a study aid among college students today and this is a real problem. In the next few minutes, I'll explain why."

"Whoa, Katie," Alyssa said. "That's your introduction?"

"Yes," Katie replied. "I've got a lot of information to share and don't have a lot of time to say it. So, I don't want to waste any more time than necessary on my introduction."

Katie's response might sound reasonable at first. But what she is failing to realize is that not everyone in the audience may be ready to listen to her speech about nonmedical Adderall use. People might think the topic is boring, irrelevant to them, or for some other reason not worth their time. They might also wonder what makes Katie a credible speaker on the subject. How well you start your speech may determine whether people even listen, and how well you finish your speech can play a major role in determining whether they will remember what you've said.

primacy–recency effect: the tendency to remember the first and last items conveyed orally in a series

One reason the introduction and conclusion are so important is based on what psychologists call the **primacy–recency effect:** We are more likely to remember the first and last items conveyed orally in a series than the items in between.[1] This means listeners are more likely to remember the beginning and ending of your speech than what you say in the body. Another reason stems from the need for listeners to quickly grasp your goal and main points in order to follow along as you present your speech.

In the previous chapter, we described the tasks involved in organizing content to be used in the speech body. In this chapter, we focus on creating an introduction that both gets attention and leads into the body of the speech; creating a conclusion that both summarizes main points and motivates listeners to remember; and completing a formal speech outline, including a speech title and a reference list.

THE INTRODUCTION

Once you have developed the speech body, you need to decide how to introduce it. Because the introduction is so important to success, develop two or three different introductions and then select the one that seems best for the audience you will be addressing. An introduction is generally about 10 percent of the length of the entire speech. In other words, for a 5-minute speech (approximately 750 words), an introduction of about 30 seconds (approximately 60 to 85 words) is appropriate.

An effective introduction achieves four primary goals: it gets attention, conveys listener relevance, establishes speaker credibility, and identifies the thesis statement with main point preview. In our opening scenario, Katie didn't really achieve any of these goals. Rather, she simply identified the topic and then moved right into her first main point.

Get Attention

Whether you are delivering your speech in a face-to-face setting or virtually using a web-based platform, your first goal is to open in a way that arouses curiosity and motivates your audience to want to know more about your topic. Some rhetorical strategies for doing so include startling statements, questions, stories, jokes, personal references, quotations, action, and suspense. You can determine which attention-getting device to use by considering what emotional tone is appropriate for your topic. A humorous attention getter signals a lighthearted tone; a serious one signals a more thoughtful or somber tone. For instance, a speaker who starts with a funny story will put the audience in a lighthearted mood. If that speaker then says, "Now let's turn to the subject of extremist violent terrorism" (or nuclear war or drug abuse), the audience will be confused by the speaker's initial words, which signaled a far different type of subject.

1. A **startling statement** is a shocking expression or example. Chris used this startling statement to get his listeners' attention for his speech about how automobile emissions contribute to global warming:

   Look around. Each one of you is sitting next to a killer. That's right. You are sitting next to a cold-blooded killer. Before you think about jumping up and running out of this room, let me explain. Everyone who drives an automobile is a killer of the environment. Every time you turn the key to your ignition, you are helping to destroy our precious planet.

2. Questions are requests for information that encourage your audience to think about something related to your topic. Questions can be *rhetorical* or *direct*. **Rhetorical questions** don't require an overt response. Notice how this student began his speech on counterfeiting with these three short rhetorical questions:

   What would you do with this $20 bill if I gave it to you? Take your friend to a movie? Treat yourself to a pizza and drinks? Well, if you did either of these things, you could get in big trouble—this bill is counterfeit!

   Unlike a rhetorical question, a **direct question** seeks an overt response from the audience. It might be a "yea" or "nay" or a show of hands (Photo 8.1). For example, here's how Brad Phillips, author of *101 Ways to Open a Speech*, begins his media training and public speaking workshops:

   How many of you absolutely love public speaking? (only a few people raise their hands, provoking laughter)

   How many of you actively volunteer for every chance you get to deliver a presentation? (again almost nobody raises their hands)

startling statement: a shocking expression or example

rhetorical questions: questions phrased to stimulate a mental response

direct question: a question that seeks an overt response from the audience, usually by a show of hands

Photo 8.1 Speakers typically ask for a show of hands when getting attention with a direct question. What is one possible challenge for speakers that do so?

Chapter 8 | The Introduction and Conclusion | 133

Lana used a combination of rhetorical questions and a startling statement to get her listeners' attention for her speech on eating disorders:

Who are five of the most important women in your life? Your mother? Your sister? Your daughter? Your wife? Your best friend? Now which one of them has an eating disorder? Before you disregard my question, listen to what research tells us. One in every five women in the United States has an eating disorder.

story: an account of something that has happened (actual) or could happen (hypothetical)

How many of you believe it would be good for your careers if you could go into a room and deliver a knockout presentation to top leadership, key clients, or major donors? (almost every hand goes up, demonstrating the disconnect between what they feel and what they do).[2]

Direct questions can be helpful in getting audience attention because they require a physical response. However, getting listeners to actually comply with your request can also pose a challenge. One way to overcome this challenge is to begin with "I would like to see a show of hands. . ." while demonstrating a raised hand yourself.

3. A **story** is an account of something that has happened (actual) or could happen (hypothetical). Most people enjoy a well-told story, so it makes a good attention getter (Photo 8.2). One drawback of stories is that they are often lengthy and can take more time to tell than is appropriate for the length of your speech. Use a story only if it is short or if you can abbreviate it so that it is just right for your speech length. Yash Gupta, former dean of the Carey Business School at Johns Hopkins University, used a story to get attention about assumptions, prejudices, and policies about older people:

Imagine this.

You are boarding a routine business flight. As you get on the plane you notice the pilot looks perhaps a bit . . . grandfatherly. In fact, he is only two years away from his FAA-mandated retirement age.

You sit and open a magazine. You know, in advertisements flight attendants always look like the champagne they are pouring: fresh and bubbly. But looking around the cabin at the flight crew the words that instead come to mind are mature and no-nonsense. All three flight attendants are in their 50s.

You are belted comfortably, your seat is in the upright position, and you have just felt the wheels lift off the runway from LaGuardia Airport.

Only a couple minutes into your flight there is a loud bang, followed by another loud bang. Flames shoot out from the plane's two jet engines, and then they both

Photo 8.2 Telling a story is a time-honored way to get attention for a speech. Who do you know that is a really good storyteller?

go silent. Less than 3 minutes later, the pilot makes one terse announcement: prepare for impact.

The next thing you know you're floating on the Hudson River and the flight crew is quickly and efficiently moving you onto the wings of the aircraft. They know their jobs.

Flight attendant Doreen Welsh is 58. She's been flying since 1970—almost 40 years' experience. Sheila Daily is 57. She's been flying since 1980, and the other flight attendant, 51-year-old Donna Dent, has been flying since 1982.

As you watch the rescue boats approach, one thought goes through your mind: At moments like this, who needs fresh and bubbly?

The story of Flight 1549 suggests that in our society perhaps we have been too quick to praise youth, too ready to underestimate the value of age, wisdom, and experience. One thing is certain: as we look forward to the middle years of the 21st century, we are going to have ample opportunity to discover if our assumptions, our prejudices, and our policies about older people are valid—or if perhaps we have some serious reconsidering to do.[3]

4. A **joke** is an anecdote or a piece of wordplay designed to make people laugh (Photo 8.3). A joke can be used to get audience attention when it meets the three Rs test: It must be realistic, relevant, and repeatable.[4] In other words, it can't be too far-fetched, unrelated to the speech purpose, or potentially offensive to some listeners. In his speech about being a person of integrity, for example, Joel Osteen offered this joke to get attention:

    A kindergarten teacher asked one of her students what she was drawing a picture of. The little girl said, "I'm drawing a picture of God." The teacher replied, "Oh honey, nobody knows what God looks like." Without missing a beat, the little girl replied, "They will in a minute . . ."[5]

    When jokes work, they adhere to the three Rs test, but if you decide to use one, be sure to consider how you will handle the situation if nobody laughs.

5. A **personal reference** is a brief account about something that happened to you or a hypothetical situation that listeners can imagine themselves in. In addition to getting attention, a personal reference can be especially effective at engaging listeners as active participants. A personal reference like this one on exercise is suitable for a speech of any length:

    Were you panting when you got to the top of those four flights of stairs this morning? I'll bet there were a few of you who vowed you'd never take a class on the top floor of this building again. But did you ever stop to think that maybe the problem isn't that this class is on the top floor? It just might be that you are not getting enough exercise.

6. A **quotation** is a comment made by and attributed to someone other than the speaker. A particularly vivid or thought-provoking quotation can make an excellent attention getter as long as it relates to your topic. Although it is common to quote famous people, a good quotation from *any* source can create interest in your topic. For instance, notice how Sally Mason, former provost at Purdue University, used the following quotation to get the attention of her audience, the Lafayette, Indiana, YWCA:

    There is an ancient saying, "May you live in interesting times." It is actually an ancient curse. It might sound great to live in interesting times. But interesting times are times of change and

joke: an anecdote or a piece of wordplay designed to make people laugh

personal reference: a brief account about something that happened to you or a hypothetical situation that listeners can imagine themselves in

quotation: a comment made by and attributed to someone other than the speaker

Thaddaeus McAdams/FilmMagic/Getty Images

Photo 8.3 A joke can make a good attention getter as long as it is realistic, relevant, and repeatable. What would you do if nobody laughs?

even turmoil. They are times of struggle. They are exciting. But, at the same time, they are difficult. People of my generation have certainly lived through interesting times and they continue today.[6]

Thanks to the Internet and search engines like Google and Bing, finding compelling and relevant quotations is easier today than it was in the past.

7. An **action** is an attention-getting act designed to highlight and arouse interest in your topic. You can perform an action yourself, as Juan did when he split a stack of boards with his hand to get attention for his speech on karate. Or you can ask volunteers from the audience to perform the action. For example, Cindria used three audience members to participate in breaking a piñata to create interest in her speech on the history of the piñata. If you choose to use audience members, consider soliciting participants ahead of time to avoid the possibility of having no volunteers when you ask during your speech. Finally, you can ask your entire audience to perform some action related to your speech topic. If you'd like to ask your whole audience to perform an action, realistically assess whether what you are asking is something your audience is likely to comply with.

8. To **create suspense**, word your attention getter so that what is described generates uncertainty or mystery and excites the audience. When you get the audience to ask, "What is she leading up to?" you have created suspense. A suspenseful opening is especially valuable when your audience is not particularly interested in hearing about your topic. Consider this suspenseful statement:

It costs the United States more than $116 billion per year. It has cost the loss of more jobs than a recession. It accounts for nearly 100,000 deaths a year. I'm not talking about cocaine abuse—the problem is alcoholism. Today I want to show you how we can avoid this inhumane killer by abstaining from it.

By putting the problem, alcoholism, at the end, the speaker encourages the audience to try to anticipate the answer. And because the audience may well be thinking the problem is drugs, the revelation that it is alcoholism is likely to be that much more effective.

Establish Relevance

Even if you successfully get the attention of your listeners, to *keep* their attention you need to motivate them to listen to your speech. You can do this by creating a clear listener relevance link, a statement of how and why your speech relates to or might affect your audience. Doing this in the introduction and again for each main point helps your audience realize your speech's exigence.[7] Sometimes your attention-getting statement also serves this function, but if it doesn't, you need to provide a personal connection between your topic and your audience. Notice how Tiffany created a listener relevance link for her speech about being a vegetarian:

Although a diet rich in eggs and meat was once the norm in this country, more and more of us are choosing a vegetarian lifestyle to help lower blood pressure, reduce cholesterol, manage weight, and even prevent the onset of some diseases.

When creating a listener relevance link, answer these questions: Why should my listeners care about what I'm saying? In what way(s) might they benefit from hearing about it? How might my speech relate to my listeners' needs or desires for health, wealth, well-being, self-esteem, success, and so forth?

Establish Credibility

If someone hasn't formally introduced you, audience members are going to wonder who you are and why they should pay attention to what you say. So, another goal of your introduction

Reflect on Ethics

ACADAMY AWARDS HOST CHRIS ROCK: ETHICAL OR NOT?

Award show hosts typically provide the introduction for the ceremony in the form of an opening monologue. They also provide transitions between and among presenters and performances, as well as concluding remarks. In essence, they provide the macrostructure for the ceremony.

The weeks prior to the 2016 Academy Awards program were wrought with controversy over the fact that no people of color had been nominated for an Oscar. Many A-list actors boycotted the event and encouraged host Chris Rock to do so as well. Instead, Rock capitalized on the opportunity to showcase the racism controversy in Hollywood.

In Rock's words, Hollywood is not "burning cross racist" but "sorority racist. 'We like you, Rhonda, but you're not a Kappa!'" He dubbed the ceremony "the White People's Choice Awards" and used humor to highlight the racism issue throughout the evening. He quipped that the "In Memoriam" montage for

the year was "just going to be black people who got shot by the cops on the way to the movies" and even commented "And we're Black!" after one commercial break.[8] In addition to peppering his remarks with jokes highlighting the racism issue, he took an opportunity to help his daughters beat the competition by selling Girl Scout cookies to audience members, raising more than $65,000. Finally, he closed the ceremony with Public Enemy's hip-hop anthem "Fight the Power."

1. Do you think Rock's use of humor to put the racism controversy up front at the ceremony was ethical? Why or why not?

2. Do you think using the ceremony as an opportunity for Rock's daughters to sell Girl Scout cookies and beat the competition was ethical? Why or why not?

3. Given what we've talked about in this chapter, do you think closing the awards ceremony with "Fight the Power" was appropriate? Why or why not?

is to begin to build your credibility. **Credibility** is simply the perception your audience has about you as knowledgeable, trustworthy, and personable. The theoretical grounding for this actually dates back to the ancient Greek philosophy of Aristotle in his treatise *Rhetoric*.[9] In it, he asserted that listeners would be motivated to both listen to and believe a speaker based on their perception of his or her *ethos* (competence, good character, and goodwill), *pathos* (appeals to emotions), and *logos* (perception of truthfulness through evidence and reasoning).

credibility: the perception of a speaker as knowledgeable, trustworthy, and personable

To be successful, begin establishing ethos during your introductory remarks. This initial ethos responds to the questions listeners may be thinking, such as: Why should I trust you? What makes you an authority on the subject? Why should I believe you? Do you seem sincere? Do you seem to be a likeable person? Do your words and actions demonstrate respect for me and this occasion? Remember, though, that your goal is to highlight how you are a credible speaker on this topic, one who respects the audience and occasion, not that you are *the* or even *a* final authority on the subject. Carmen Mariano, former principal of Archbishop Williams High School, established credibility and goodwill in a "welcome back students" speech this way:

Ladies and gentlemen, you will hear one word many times this morning. That word is welcome. Please know how much we mean that word. Please know how much I mean that word.

Why will we mean that word so much?

Because without you, this is just a building on 80 Independence Avenue. And with you, this is Archbishop Williams High School. That's right. When you walked through those doors this morning, you made this building a school again.

So welcome back.

And welcome to your school.[10]

State the Thesis

Because audiences want to know what your speech is going to be about, it's important to state your thesis. After Miguel gained the audience's attention and established

SPEECH SNIPPET

In his speech about smoking in public places, Eric established his credibility by saying:

I used to smoke cigarettes and have quit, but not before I did a good deal of research about the effects of smoking and secondhand smoke.

relevance and credibility, he said, "In the next 5 minutes, let's discuss the three elements of romantic love: passion, intimacy, and commitment."

Stating your main points in the introduction is necessary unless you have some special reason for not revealing the details of the thesis. For instance, after getting the attention of his audience, Miguel might say, "In the next 5 minutes, I'd like to explain the three aspects of romantic love," a statement that specifies the number of main points but leaves the details for a preview statement that immediately precedes the main points. Steve Jobs, in his commencement address at Stanford, did so this way: "Today I want to tell you three stories from my life. That's it. No big deal. Just three stories."[11]

Select the Best Introduction

Because the introduction is critical to effective speechmaking, it's worth investing the time to compare different openings. Try working on two or three different introductions, then pick the one you believe will work best for your specific audience and speech goal.

For instance, Jamie created two introductions for her speech on obesity. The first used a personal reference for an attention getter. Notice how she established listener relevance and credibility by citing the US Department of Health and Human Services statistic before offering her thesis statement:

Imagine a table full of all the food you eat in one week. That's a lot of food, right? Now, imagine eating all that food in one day! Believe it or not, there are people who do this. This condition, called binge eating, is contributing to a national epidemic: obesity. According to the US Department of Health and Human Services, obesity may soon overtake tobacco as the leading cause of preventable death. To reduce obesity, let's examine the scope of the problem and its causes, followed by some practical solutions. (90 words)

Her second introduction used a startling statement and rhetorical question to get attention:

Tom is a 135-pound male who enjoys playing computer games and loves pizza. Sounds like an average person, right? Well, what would you think if I told you that Tom is only 6 years old? According to the US Department of Health and Human Services, obesity may soon overtake tobacco as the leading cause of preventable death. Obesity is a serious problem in our society and warrants our attention. To prove my point, let's examine the scope of the problem and its causes, followed by some practical solutions. (88 words)

Which of Jamie's introductions do you prefer? Why?

Your speech introduction should meet all four goals and take no longer than 10 percent of your speaking time. Speech Planning Activity 4E will help you develop three choices for your speech introduction.

4E SPEECH PLANNING

Creating Speech Introductions

1. For the speech body you outlined earlier, write three different introductions—using different rhetorical devices (startling statement, a question, a story, a personal reference, a joke, a quotation, action, or suspense) to get attention—that you believe meet the primary goals of effective introductions and would be appropriate for your speech goal and audience.

4E SPEECH PLANNING *(continued)*

2. Of the three introductions you drafted, which do you believe is the best? Why?

3. Write that introduction in outline form, indicating in parentheses where you are meeting each goal.

SAMPLE STUDENT RESPONSE
Creating Speech Introductions

1. For the speech body you outlined earlier, write three different introductions—using different rhetorical devices (startling statement, a question, a story, a personal reference, a joke, a quotation, action, or suspense) to get attention—that you believe meet the goals of effective introductions and would be appropriate for your speech goal and audience.

   Specific goal: *I would like the audience to understand the three ways to tell if a diamond is real.*

   (1) We are at an age where buying diamonds might be on our minds. I would like to tell you how you can know for sure if your diamond is real.

   (2) Have you ever wondered if you would know if the diamond the jeweler is trying to sell you is real? Nobody wants to be duped into spending a lot of money on a fake. As a geology major, I have studied how to determine whether a diamond is real and would like to share three things you should look for when buying a diamond.

   (3) Calcite, quartz, cubic zirconia, diamond. How can you tell these minerals apart? They are all colorless and can sometimes look alike. But let me give you three ways that you can tell if you are holding a diamond.

2. Of the three introductions you drafted, which do you believe is the best? Why?

   I believe the second one is the best because the rhetorical question and listener relevance link are likely to motivate the audience to listen, I share why they can believe me, and I lead into the body in my thesis statement with main point preview.

3. Write that introduction in outline form, indicating in parentheses where you are meeting each goal.

   I. *Have you ever wondered if you would know if the diamond that the jeweler is trying to sell you is real? (attention getter)*

   II. *Nobody wants to be duped into spending a lot of money on a fake. (listener relevance)*

   III. *As a geology major, I have studied how to determine whether a diamond is real and would like to share three things you should look for when buying a diamond. (speaker credibility and thesis statement with main point preview)*

Photo 8.4 The conclusion offers one final chance to leave a lasting impression. Think of a speech that you remember well. Do you recall what the clincher was?

Purestock/Jupiter Images

THE CONCLUSION

Shakespeare once said, "All's well that ends well." Effective conclusions heighten the impact of a good speech by summarizing the main ideas and leaving the audience with a vivid impression (Photo 8.4). Even though the conclusion is a relatively short part of the speech—seldom more than 5 percent (35 to 45 words for a 5-minute speech)—your conclusion should be carefully planned.

The speech conclusion has two major purposes. First, it summarizes your goal and main points. Second, it provides a sense of closure by driving home the importance of your message in a memorable way. As with your speech introduction, prepare two or three conclusions and then choose the one you believe will be most effective for your audience and occasion.

Summarize Your Goal and Main Points

An effective speech conclusion typically includes an abbreviated restatement of your goal and main points. A summary for an informative speech on how to improve your grades might be, "So I hope you now understand [*informative goal*] that three techniques to improve your grades are to attend classes regularly, to develop a positive attitude toward the course, and to study systematically [*main points*]." A short summary for a persuasive speech on why you should exercise might be, "So you should exercise for at least 30 minutes each day [*persuasive goal*] to improve your appearance as well as your physical and mental health [*main points*]."

Clinch

clincher: a short statement that provides a sense of closure by driving home the importance of the speech in a memorable way

Although a good summary helps your audience remember your main points, a good clincher leaves them with a vivid impression. A **clincher** is a short statement that provides a sense of closure by driving home the importance of your speech in a memorable way. If you can, try to devise a clincher that refers back to your introductory comments in some way. Two effective strategies for clinching are using vivid imagery and appealing to action.

Vivid Imagery

To develop vivid imagery, you can use any of the devices we discussed for getting attention (startling statement, question, story, joke, personal reference, quotation, action, or suspense). For example, in Tiffany's speech about being a vegetarian, she referred back to the personal reference she made in her introduction about a vegetarian Thanksgiving meal:

So now you know why I made the choice to become a vegetarian and how this choice affects my life today. As a vegetarian, I've discovered a world of food I never knew existed. Believe me, I am salivating just thinking about the meal I have planned for this Thanksgiving: fennel and blood orange salad; followed by baked polenta layered with tomato, fontina, and Gorgonzola cheeses; an acorn squash tart; marinated tofu; and what else but pumpkin pie for dessert!

Sounds good, doesn't it? Clinchers that foster vivid imagery are appropriate for both informative and persuasive speeches because they leave listeners with a vibrant picture imprinted in their minds.

Appeal to Action

An appeal to action is a common clincher for persuasive speeches. An **appeal to action** describes the behavior you want your listeners to follow after they have heard your arguments. Notice how Matthew Cossolotto, president and founder of Study Abroad Alumni International, concludes his speech on global awareness and responsibility with a strong appeal to action:

> So, yes, you should have this re-entry program. Yes, you should network and explore international career opportunities. That's all good.
>
> But I also encourage you to Globalize Your Locality. I urge you to Think Global. . . Act Global . . . Be Global.
>
> This is an urgent call to action . . . for you and other study abroad alumni. . . to help us reduce the global awareness deficit.
>
> You can do so by becoming involved with SAAI . . . and other organizations such as the National Council for International Visitors, Sister Cities, or Rotary International.
>
> You can speak to local schools and community organizations about your study abroad experience and the need for more global awareness.
>
> When you studied abroad, I'm sure you were told many times that you would be serving as unofficial ambassadors of the United States . . . your campus . . . and even your community back home.
>
> Now that you're home again, I hope you'll become ambassadors for the value of the study abroad experience and for the need for greater international awareness.
>
> In wrapping up . . . I'd like to leave you with this image . . . just picture in your mind's eye that iconic photograph of planet Earth. I'm sure you've seen it. Taken over four decades ago . . . in December 1968 . . . on the Apollo 8 mission to the moon.
>
> The photograph—dubbed Earthrise—shows our small, blue planet rising above a desolate lunar landscape. This photo was a true watershed in human history . . . marking the first time earthlings . . . fellow global citizens had traveled outside earth's orbit and looked back on our lonely planet.
>
> The widespread publication of Earthrise had a lot to do with launching the worldwide environmental movement. It's no accident that the first Earth Day— on April 22, 1970—took place so soon after the publication of this remarkable photograph.
>
> We're all privileged to inhabit this same planet—truly an island in space. And voices to the contrary notwithstanding . . . whether we want to admit it or not . . . we are all, undeniably and by definition, citizens of the world.
>
> The only question is: will we accept the responsibilities of global citizenship? Your future . . . and perhaps the survival of the planet . . . just may depend on how many of us answer yes to that question.[12]

appeal to action: a statement that describes the behavior you want listeners to follow after they have heard your arguments

Select the Best Conclusion

As with your introduction, create two or three conclusions and then choose the best one for the audience and occasion. For her short speech on Adderall, Katie created the following three variations. Which do you like best?

Adderall is a prescription stimulant that is being used more and more among college students, especially as a study aid, and there are serious risks associated with using the drug illegally. The next time you or a friend considers taking Adderall as a study aid, think again. The potential harm the drug could cause to your body is not worth even a perfect grade point average.

Adderall is a prescription drug that is being abused by college students across the country. The stimulant is meant to treat medical conditions but is now being used illegally as a study aid. The harms in doing so are alarming. So if you've considered taking Adderall as a study aid, I hope you consider what we've talked about today before you do. Not taking it is not only better for you in the long run, just like wearing your seatbelt and not drinking and driving, but it's also obeying the law.

So, Adderall is a stimulant that is prescribed to treat real problems but is now being abused by more and more college students as a study aid, which is, quite frankly, breaking the law. I won't ask for a show of hands this time, but I will ask the question once more. If you've used Adderall illegally as a study aid, will you think twice before you do it again? If you know someone who uses it illegally as a study aid, will you share what you've learned today with that person? I sincerely hope so. It really is a matter of life and health.

Speech Planning Activity 4F will help you develop choices for your speech conclusion.

4F SPEECH PLANNING

Activity

Creating Speech Conclusions

1. For the speech body you outlined earlier, write three different conclusions that review important points you want the audience to remember, and include a clincher that provides closure by leaving the audience with a vivid impression.

2. Which do you believe is the best? Why?

3. Write that conclusion in outline form.

SAMPLE STUDENT RESPONSE

Creating Speech Conclusions

1. For the speech body you outlined earlier, write three different conclusions that review important points you want the audience to remember, and include a clincher that provides closure by leaving the audience with a vivid impression.

   Specific goal: *I would like the audience to understand the three ways to tell if a diamond is real.*

   (1) So, the next time you buy or receive a diamond, you will know how to do the acid, streak, and hardness tests to make sure the diamond is real.

4F SPEECH PLANNING (continued)

> *(2) Before making your final diamond selection, make sure it can pass the acid, streak, and hardness tests. Remember, you want to make sure you're buying a real diamond and not a fake!*
>
> *(3) Now we all know how to tell if a diamond is real. So, folks, if you discover that the gem you're considering effervesces in acid, has a streak that is not clear, or can be scratched, you will know that it is a fake. As a result, none of us will fall victim to being duped by a crook!*

2. Which do you believe is the best? Why?

> *The third one because it restates the characteristics and leaves a vivid impression.*

3. Write that conclusion in outline form.

> I.   *Now we all know how to tell if a diamond is real. (goal restatement)*
>
> II. *If it effervesces, streaks, or scratches, it is a fake. (main point review)*
>
> III. *As a result, none of us will be duped by a crook! (clincher)*

PUBLIC SPEAKING IN THE REAL WORLD

Public Speaking Lessons Learned from Lady Gaga

PETER FOLEY/EPA/Newscom

Ryan Avery is an international professional public speaker who also teaches others to become better communicators. The 2012 World Champion of Public Speaking does keynote speeches and regularly conducts workshops designed to help improve communication among the younger generation. He says he learned a lot about the importance of a strong introduction and conclusion from singer and performer Lady Gaga. Here's what he posted on his blog, AVERYTODAY, after attending one of her concerts:

"Life Lesson: Keep your eyes open for learning new lessons from others. I learned how to be a better speaker from one of the most famous musicians of our time.

- "Strong opening. She opened with a bang! She got the crowed excited and on their feet, and within the first 30 seconds you already want more. What are you doing to grab your audience's attention and have them saying 'Wow, I want more of what this person is giving me'?

- "Strong closing. Cute girls are crying, boys are hugging, hands are in the air, and she sings her last note! You walk out and people are on cloud nine. After 2 hours of dancing, singing, and burning more than 2,000 calories,

people are not tired. They are energized. They were left on a high note and reminded to go for their dreams. How well are you ending your speech or presentation?

"Being a better communicator will help you become a person of influence. Gaga is a great communicator with tremendous influence. Take these lessons and implement them when you give your next speech or presentation."[13]

As Avery points out, a strong introduction and conclusion can make any presentation better, whether that presentation comes in the form of a public speech, professional workshop, or even a musical performance.

1. In what ways do the openings and closings of musical performances like those of Lady Gaga's concerts serve similar functions as speech introductions and conclusions?

2. Why should you spend time preparing them?

COMPLETE FORMAL OUTLINE WITH REFERENCE LIST

formal outline: a complete sentence representation of the hierarchical and sequential relationships among the ideas presented in the speech

After drafting your introduction and conclusion, you have essentially drafted an entire outline of your speech. To complete the **formal outline**, compile a list of the sources you draw from in your speech, create a title (if required), and then review your outline to make sure that it conforms to a logical structure.

Listing Sources

Regardless of the type or length of your speech, you need to prepare a list of sources you use in it. This list allows you to direct audience members to the specific source of any information you used and to quickly find the information at a later date. You also want to use internal references throughout the formal speech outline to help remember what to cite and where during your speech. Doing so will ultimately enhance your credibility and help you avoid unintentional plagiarism.

Many formal bibliographical styles (e.g., MLA, APA, Chicago, CBE) can be used to compile your source list. Exhibit 8.1 gives examples of citations according to the Modern Language Association (MLA) and American Psychological Association (APA) style guides. Which form is "correct" for your topic differs by professional or academic discipline. Check to see if your instructor has a preference about which style you use in class. Speech Planning Activity 4G will help you compile a list of sources used in your speech.

Exhibit 8.1 | Examples of the MLA and APA Citation Formats

	MLA style	APA style
Book	Thebarge, Sarah. *The Invisible Girls: A Memoir.* New York: Jericho Books, 2013.	Thebarge, S. (2013). *The invisible girls: A memoir.* New York: Jericho Books.
Edited book	Pomering, Alan. "Communicating Corporate Social Responsibility." *The Handbook of Communication and Corporate Social Responsibility.* Eds. Ovind Ihlen, Jennifer Bartlett, and Steve May. West Sussex, UK: John Wiley and Sons, 2011. 379–398. Print.	Pomering, A. (2011). Communicating corporate social responsibility. In O. Ihlen, J. Bartlett, & S. May (Eds.), *The handbook of communication and corporate social responsibility* (pp. 379–398). West Sussex, UK: John Wiley & Sons.
Academic journal	Milford, Mike. "Kenneth Burke's punitive priests and the redeeming prophets: The NCAA, the college sports media, and the University of Miami scandal." *Communication Studies* 66.1 (2015): 45–62. Print.	Milford, M. (2015). Kenneth Burke's punitive priests and the redeeming prophets: The NCAA, the college sports media, and the University of Miami. *Communication Studies, 66*(1), 45–62.
Magazine	O'Leary, Kevin. "Krisin Denial." *US Weekly* 16 February, 2015: 38–43. Print.	O'Leary, K. (2015, February 16). Krisin denial. *US Weekly,* 38–43.
Movie	*American Sniper.* Dir. Clint Eastwood. Prod. Bradley Cooper. Warner Brothers, 2014. DVD.	Cooper, B. (Producer), & Eastwood, C. (Director). (2014). *American Sniper* [Motion picture]. United States: Warner Brothers.
Personal interview	Jones, Lucille. Personal interview. 19 March 2016.	APA style dictates that no personal interview is included in a reference list. Rather, cite this type of source orally in your speech, mentioning the name of the person you interviewed and the date of the interview.

(4G) SPEECH PLANNING

Activity

Compiling a List of Sources

1. Review your annotated bibliography and/or research cards, as well as your formal speech outline. Identify each source that you drew information from for your speech.

2. Note on your outline where you'll reference the source during your speech.

3. List the sources used in your speech by copying the bibliographical information recorded on the annotated bibliography and/or research card.

4. Using the style guide required for your class, record the bibliographic citation for each source in an alphabetical list.

SAMPLE STUDENT RESPONSE

Compiling a List of Sources

1. Review your annotated bibliography and/or research cards, as well as your formal speech outline. Identify each source that you drew information from for your speech.

   I used Dixon (1992), Montgomery (2014), Klein & Dutrow (2008), and Shrey & Shigley (2013) in my speech.

2. Note on your outline where you'll reference the source during your speech.

   I placed internal citations on my outline at the points where I drew from each source and will need to cite it orally during my speech.

3. List the sources used in your speech by copying the bibliographical information recorded on the annotated bibliography and/or research card.

   Dixon, D. (1992). The practical geologist. New York: Simon & Shuster.

   Montgomery, C. W. Fundamentals of geology (10th ed.). New York: McGraw-Hill, 2014.

   Klein, C., & Dutrow, B. (2008). Manual of mineral science (23rd ed.). New York: Wiley & Sons.

   Shirey, S. B., & Shigley, J. E. (2013). Recent advances in understanding the geology of diamonds. Gems and Gemology, 49(4). Retrieved online at: http://www.gia.edu/gems-gemology/WN13-advances-diamond-geology-shirey

4. Using the style guide required for your class, record the bibliographic citation for each source in an alphabetical list.

   My instructor wants me to use APA style. My sources in alphabetical order are:

   Dixon, D. (1992). The practical geologist. New York: Simon & Schuster.

   Klein, C., & Dutrow, B. (2008). Manual of mineral science (23rd ed.). New York: John Wiley & Sons.

   Montgomery, C. W. (2014). Fundamentals of geology (10th ed.). New York: McGraw-Hill.

   Shirey, S. B., & Shigley, J. E. (2013). Recent advances in understanding the geology of diamonds. Gems and Gemology, 49(4), Retrieved online at: http://www.gia.edu/gems-gemology/WN13-advances-diamond-geology-shirey

Photo 8.5 You don't always need one, but titles are useful for professional speeches that will be publicized or published. What are some interesting speech titles you've heard or read?

Writing a Title

In most speech situations outside the classroom, it helps to have a speech title that lets the audience know what to expect (Photo 8.5). A title is typically necessary when you will be formally introduced, when your speech will be publicized, or when your speech will be published. A good title encourages audiences to hear what you have to say. Like attention getters, titles should be brief, topical, and creative. For her speech on Adderrall, Katie crafted this title: (Mis)Using Adderall: What's the Big Deal?

Reviewing the Formal Outline

Once you've put all the pieces together into a complete formal outline form, use this checklist to review it.

1. **Have I used a standard set of symbols to indicate structure?** Main points are indicated by Roman numerals, major subpoints by capital letters, sub-subpoints by Arabic numerals, and further subdivisions by lowercase letters.

2. **Have I written main points and major subpoints as complete sentences?**

3. **Do each of my main points contain a single idea?** This guideline ensures that the development of each part of the speech will be relevant to the point. Thus, rather than:

    Organically produced food is good for the environment and for animals.

    divide the sentence so each part is stated separately:

    I. *Organically produced food is good for the environment.*

    II. *Organically produced food is good for animals.*

4. **Does each major subpoint relate to (support) its major point?** This principle, called subordination, ensures that you don't wander off point and confuse your audience. For example:

    I. *Proper equipment is necessary for successful play.*

    A. *Good gym shoes are needed for maneuverability.*

    B. *Padded gloves help protect your hands.*

    C. *A lively ball provides sufficient bounce.*

    D. *And a good attitude doesn't hurt either.*

    Notice that the main point deals with equipment. A, B, and C (shoes, gloves, and ball) all relate to the main point. But D, attitude, is not equipment and should appear somewhere else, if at all.

5. **Have I included potential subpoint elaborations?** Because you don't know how long it might take to discuss each elaboration, you should include more than you are likely to use. During rehearsals and when giving your speech, monitor the time to determine whether to include or skip over them.

Speech Planning Activity 4H will help you write and review a complete-sentence outline of your speech. You may also refer to Katie's complete outline as an example.

4H SPEECH PLANNING

Activity

Completing the Formal Speech Outline

1. Write and review a complete-sentence outline of your speech using material you've developed so far with the Action Steps in Chapters 4 through 8.

SAMPLE STUDENT RESPONSE

(Mis)Using Adderall: What's the Big Deal?

by Katie Anthony, University of Kentucky[14]

General goal: *I want to inform my audience.*

Specific goal: *I would like my audience to understand the uses and abuses of Adderall by college students.*

Thesis statement: *I want to inform you about the growing problem of nonmedical Adderall use by college students, explaining the nature and legal uses of Adderall, its growing popularity as a study aid for college students, and the problems associated with nonmedical Adderall use.*

Introduction

I. *Attention getter: Raise your hand if anyone you know has taken the drug Adderall. Keep your hand raised if the person is doing so without a prescription for the drug.*

II. *Listener relevance: The illegal use of stimulants like Adderall among college students has increased dramatically over the past decade. A 2012 College Life Survey conducted by Vincent, Kasperski, and Caldeira found that nearly 31 percent of college students have used Adderall nonmedically at least once during their college career. Thus, it's quite likely you know someone who is abusing Adderall for nonmedical reasons.*

III. *Speaker credibility: I became interested in this topic my freshman year when my roommate received a call from her mother telling her that her best friend, who was a sophomore at a different college, had died suddenly from an Adderall-induced heart attack. Because I had several friends who were also using Adderall without a prescription but who thought it was safe to do so, I began to read all I could about the drug, its use, and its risks. Not only have I become versed in the written information on Adderall, but I have also interviewed several faculty here who are studying the problem, and I have become an undergraduate research assistant helping one faculty member to collect data on this problem. Today, I want to share with you some of what I have learned.*

IV. *Thesis statement: Specifically, I want to inform you about the growing problem of nonmedical Adderall use by college students, explaining the nature and legal uses of Adderall, its growing popularity as a study aid for college students, and the problems associated with nonmedical Adderall use.*

Body

I. **Adderall is a psychostimulant prescribed to treat three conditions.**

Listener relevance link: Understanding the intended medical uses of the drug Adderall may help you understand why the drug is so widely abused by collegians.

(continued)

A. *According to the US Food and Drug Administration's website, Adderall, the brand name for amphetamine-dextroamphetamine, is a psychostimulant, one of a class of drugs intended to promote concentration, suppress hyperactivity, and promote healthy social experiences for patients.*

1. Adderall stimulates the central nervous system by increasing the amount of dopamine and norepinephrine in the brain. These chemicals are neurotransmitters that help the brain send signals between nerve cells (Faraone, Biederman, Weiffenbach, et al., 2014).

2. Mentally, Adderall brings about a temporary improvement in alertness, wakefulness, endurance, and motivation.

3. Physically, it can increase heart rate and blood pressure and decrease perceived need for food or sleep.

B. *Adderall is prescribed for the medical treatment of attention deficit hyperactivity disorder (ADHD) in children and adults, as well as for narcolepsy and clinical depression.*

1. ADHD is a neurobehavioral developmental disorder characterized by problems of attention coupled with hyperactivity.

   a. According to the Centers for Diseases Control and Prevention (2016) since the mid-1990s, there has been a documented increase in the number of American children diagnosed and treated for ADHD.

   b. According to the Diagnostic and Statistical Manual of Mental Disorders (2013), ADHD symptoms must be present for at least six months for diagnosis and symptoms must be excessive to merit medical treatment.

   c. The drugs Ritalin and Dexedrine are also used to treat ADHD. Adderall, however, remains the most widely prescribed of the ADHD drugs (Spiller, Hays, & Aleguas, 2013).

   d. *According to the Centers for Disease Control and Prevention (2014), approximately 11 percent (6.4 million) of American children have been diagnosed with ADHD since 2011, up from 7.8 percent in 2003.*

2. *Adderall is also prescribed to treat narcolepsy, which occurs when the brain can't normally regulate cycles of sleep and waking.*

   a. Those with narcolepsy experience excessive daytime sleepiness that results in episodes of suddenly falling asleep.

   b. A chronic sleep disorder, narcolepsy affects between 50,000 and 2.4 million Americans (National Heart, Lung, and Blood Institute, 2008).

3. *Adderall can also be used to treat clinical depression.*

   a. Clinical depression is a disorder characterized by low mood, a loss of interest in normal activities, and low self-esteem.

   b. According to the National Institute of Mental Health, 9.5 percent of the adult population—that is, nearly 1.8 million American adults—suffer from clinical depression.

Transition: *Now that we understand the basic properties and medical uses of Adderall, let's assess the increasing level of nonmedical abuse of the drug by college students.*

(4H) SPEECH PLANNING (continued)

Activity

II. Unfortunately, Adderall has become popular among college students who use it as a study aid and for recreational purposes.

Listener relevance link: As college students, we need to be aware of what students believe about Adderall and why they are abusing it.

A. *College students who don't suffer ADHD, narcolepsy, or depression will take Adderall with no prescription because they believe that it will improve their focus and concentration, allowing them to perform better on academic tasks (Nonmedical Use of Adderall on the Rise among Young Adults, 2016).*

  1. Adderall abuse among college students occurs especially at stressful times of the semester when students get little sleep.

     a. DeSantis, Webb, and Noar (2008) found that 72 percent of the students they surveyed reported using the drug to stay awake so that they could study longer when they had many assignments due.

     b. Katherine Stump, a Georgetown University student, reported in the school newspaper that "During finals week here at Georgetown, campus turns into an Adderall drug den. Everyone from a cappella singers to newspaper writers become addicts, while anyone with a prescription and an understanding of the free market becomes an instant pusherman" (Kent, 2013, October 29).

     c. Collegians report using the drug frequently during stressful times of the semester. One student said, "I use it every time I have a major paper due" (Daley, 2004, April 20).

B. *Students also use Adderall for purposes other than academic ones.*

  1. A survey of undergraduate and graduate students revealed that students engage in Adderall abuse for partying, at a frequency just slightly less than they abuse the drug for academic purposes (Prudhomme White, Becker-Blease, & Grace-Bishop, 2006).

  2. Young people also use Adderall to enhance athletic performance (Veliz, Boyd, & McCabe, 2013).

  3. Some college students, especially women, report using the drug as an appetite suppressant for dieting purposes (Holland, 2014).

Transition: *Now that we understand that Adderall abuse is prevalent on university campuses among students, let's focus on the detrimental effects that can accompany nonmedical use of Adderall.*

III. Whether students acknowledge the dangers or not, great risks are involved in nonmedical Adderall use.

Listener relevance link: As we have now discussed the pervasiveness of Adderall abuse, statistically, it is likely that several of you have used this substance without a prescription to either enhance your academic performance or your social outings. Thus, it is important that we all recognize the adverse effects that result from taking Adderall without a prescription.

(continued)

A. *Nonmedical Adderall use can cause negative health effects for individuals not diagnosed with ADHD (Horn, 2014).*

   1. Adderall is reported to cause a heightened risk for heart problems when used inappropriately. Problems include sudden heart attack or stroke, sudden death in individuals with heart conditions, and increased blood pressure and heart rate (FDA, 2010).

   2. Adderall abuse also can result in a myriad of mental problems, including manifestations of bipolar disorder, an increase in aggressive thoughts, and a heightened risk for psychosis similar to schizophrenia (FDA, 2010).

B. *Adderall is highly addictive (Horn, 2014).*

   1. Adderall is an amphetamine, and while amphetamines were once used to treat a variety of ailments, including obesity, in the 1950s and 1960s, the drugs began to be much more closely regulated once their addictive nature was realized (FDA, 2010).

   2. Adderall has similar properties to cocaine, and, as a result, abuse of the drug can lead to substance dependence (FDA, 2010).

C. *Though clear risks are associated with the illegal use of Adderall, unlike other drugs, collegians do not view the inappropriate use of Adderall as harmful or illegal.*

   1. College students typically view stimulant abuse as morally acceptable and physically harmless. In a 2010 study, DeSantis and Hane found that students were quick to justify their stimulant abuse by claiming its use was fine in moderation.

   2. The Kentucky Kernel, the student newspaper at the University of Kentucky, published an editorial of a student who flippantly described the use of Adderall among college students. He states, "If you want to abuse ice cream, amphetamines, or alcohol, then there are going to be serious problems; however, let's not pretend a person using Adderall twice a semester to help them study is in any way likely to die a horrible death or suffer terrible side effects" (Riley, 2010, May 3).

   3. A study assessing the attitudes of college students toward the inappropriate use of stimulants found that "the majority of students who reported misuse or abuse were not concerned about the misuse and abuse of prescription stimulants, and a number of students thought that they should be more readily available" (Prudhomme White, Becker-Blease, & Grace-Bishop, 2006, p. 265).

Transition: *Now that we understand the risks involved in nonmedical Adderall use, hopefully you have a better understanding of why using the drug without a prescription is so dangerous.*

Conclusion

   I. *Restatement of thesis: Adderall is a prescription stimulant that is increasingly being abused by college students.*

  II. *Main point review: We have examined today what the drug Adderall is; its growing popularity among college students, especially as a study aid; and the risks associated with using the drug for nonmedical purposes.*

 III. *Clincher: The next time you or a friend consider taking Adderall as a study aid, think again. The short-term and long-term health consequences are definitely not worth the risk.*

4H SPEECH PLANNING (continued)

References

American Psychiatric Association. (2013). *Diagnostic and statistical manual of mental disorders* (5th ed.). Arlington, VA: Author.

Centers for Disease Control and Prevention. (2016, March 16). Attention-Deficit/Hyperactivity Disorder. Retrieved from http://www.cdc.gov/ncbddd/adhd/data.html

Daley, B. (2004, April 20). Perspective: Miracle drug? Adderall is prescribed for individuals with ADD and ADHD; for nonprescribed users there can be some serious risks. *Daily Pennsylvanian*. Retrieved from http://www.vpul.upenn.edu

DeSantis, A. D., & Hane, A. C. (2010). "Adderall is definitely not a drug": Justifications for the illegal use of ADHD stimulants. *Substance Use & Misuse, 45*, 31–46.

DeSantis, A. D., Webb, E. M., & Noar, S. M. (2008). Illicit use of prescription ADHD medications on a college campus: A multimethodological approach. *Journal of American College Health, 57*, 315–324.

Faraone, S. V., Biederman, J., Weiffenbach, B., Keith, T., Chu, M. P., Weaver, A., . . . Sakai, J. (2014). Dopamine D4 gene 7-repeat allele and attention deficit hyperactivity disorder. *The American Journal of Psychiatry, 156,* 768–770.

Holland, K. (2014, September 30). Adderall and weight loss: What you need to know. *Healthline Media*. Retrieved from http://www.healthline.com/health/adhd/adderall-and-weight-loss#ReadThisNext6

Kent, J. K. (2013, October 29). Adderall: America's favorite amphetamine. *Huffington Post*. Retrieved from http://www.huffingtonpost.com/high-times/adderall-amphetamine_B_4174297.html

National Heart, Blood, and Lung Institute. (2008). "What is narcolepsy?" *National Heart, Blood, and Lung Institute Diseases and Conditions Index*. Retrieved from http://www.nhlbi.nih.gov/health/dci/Diseases/nar/nar_what.html

Prudhomme White, B., Becker-Blease, K. A., & Grace-Bishop, K. (2006). Stimulant medication use, misuse, and abuse in an undergraduate and graduate student sample. *Journal of American College Health, 54*, 261–268.

Riley, T. (2010, May 3). Prescription drug abuse is a personal choice. *Kentucky Kernel*. Retrieved from http://kykernel.com

Spiller, H. A., Hays, H. L., & Aleguas, A. (June 2013). Overdose of drugs for attention-deficit hyperactivity disorder: Clinical presentation, mechanisms of toxicity, and management. *CNS Drugs, 27*(7), 531–543.

US Department of Health and Human Services, Substance Abuse and Mental Health Services Administration, Office of Applied Studies. (2009, April 7). *The NSDUH Report: Nonmedical Use of Adderall among Full-Time College Students*. Rockville, MD: Author.

US Food and Drug Administration. (2010). *Drugs @ FDA: FDA approved drug products*. Retrieved from http://www.accessdata.fda.gov

Veliz, P., Boyd, C., & Esteban McCabe, S. (2013). Adolescent athletic participation and nonmedical Adderall use: An exploratory analysis of a performance-enhancing drug. *Journal of Studies on Alcohol and Drugs, 74*(5), 714–719.

Vincent, K. B., Kasperski, S. J., Caldeira, K. M., et al. (2012). Maintaining superior follow-up rates in a longitudinal study: Experiences from the College Life Study. *International Journal of Multiple Research Approaches, 6*(1), 56–72.

Reflection and Assessment

The final steps in organizing your speech are preparing an introduction and a conclusion and then compiling and reviewing a complete formal outline with a title and a reference list. To assess how well you've learned what we've discussed in this chapter, answer the following questions. If you have trouble answering any of them, go back and review that material. Once you can answer each question accurately, you are ready to move ahead to the next chapter.

1. What are the goals of an effective speech introduction?
2. What are the goals of an effective speech conclusion?
3. How do you go about completing the formal outline and reference list?

MindTap®

Challenge Resource and Assessment Center

Now that you have read Chapter 8, go to your MindTap Communication for *The Challenge of Effective Speaking in a Digital Age* for quick access to flashcards, chapter quizzes, and more.

Applying What You've Learned

1. **Impromptu Speech Activity:** From a basket of thesis statements provided by your instructor, create two introductions and conclusions following the guidelines offered in this chapter. (Be sure to address all the goals of an introduction and conclusion.) Deliver both versions to the class as though you were giving an actual speech on the topic. Ask for feedback regarding which version the class liked better and why.

2. **Assessment Activity A:** Attend a public presentation on campus or in your community or watch and listen to one of the speeches you'll find on your MindTap for *Challenge*. Listen carefully to the speaker's introduction and conclusion. Did the speaker address all the goals identified in this chapter for introductions and conclusions? In your opinion, what could the speaker have done differently to improve and why?

3. **Assessment Activity B:** Complete Action Step 4 for one of the speeches you may give this semester.

9 Presentational Aids

WHAT'S THE POINT?

WHEN YOU'VE FINISHED THIS CHAPTER, YOU WILL BE ABLE TO:

- Identify some reasons for using presentational aids
- Describe different types of presentational aids
- Choose appropriate presentational aids
- Prepare effective presentational aids
- Plan when and how to use presentational aids during your speech

MindTap®

Review the chapter **Learning Objectives** and **Start** with quick warm up activity.

ACTION STEP **5**

Choose, prepare, and use appropriate presentational aids

A. Identify presentational aids that will clarify, emphasize, or dramatize your message.

B. Use a symbol system other than (or in addition to) words in your presentational aids.

C. Make sure your visual aids are large enough to be seen and your audio aids are loud enough to be heard.

D. Prepare and display your presentational aids professionally.

E. Plan when to use your presentational aids and integrate them into your speech.

Ethical communicators demonstrate respect for their audiences by using presentational aids that enhance the verbal message in ways that are not likely to offend.

Scott and Carrie are driving home from an Ignite Phoenix event where engineer Jim St. Leger just gave a 5-minute PowerPoint-aided presentation called "Surprise! Your Child Has Autism. Now What?"[1] (Ignite is a worldwide speaking movement where speakers give 5-minute presentations aided by 20 self-propelling PowerPoint slides.) Carrie exclaims, "Wow, I just can't believe how much we learned in a 5-minute speech. I now know that 1 in 100 children have autism and the numbers are increasing at a rate of 10 to 17 percent per year. I was shocked to learn that Albert Einstein and Bill Gates have autism and that so little is being spent to find a cure. It just goes to show how presentational aids can really help make a speech more effective."

Unlike the "death by PowerPoint" speeches we've all had to suffer through, the speeches given at Ignite events like the one Carrie and Scott saw are great examples of what it takes to be an effective speaker in the technology-saturated digital age in which we live. To reach people today, we must compete for their attention as they check email, Facebook, Twitter, sports scores, and so on while we are speaking. That's why the Ignite motto, "Enlighten Us, But Make it Quick," makes sense. To be effective, we must use multiple communication channels—oral, written, visual, digital—to gain and maintain audience attention throughout the time allotted to us and, in doing so, succeed in helping our audience remember what we say. If you haven't seen an Ignite speech, we encourage you to do so. You can even watch St. Leger's speech, referred to in the chapter-opening vignette, on YouTube. Then you will understand why, in this digital age, presentational aids are far more than aids. Effective presentational aids are integral components of effective public presentations. In fact, as we mentioned in Chapter 6, presentational aids are essentially a form of supporting material you should be looking for as you conduct research to develop your topic. Ultimately, you are likely to use them to get attention in your introduction and to support main points in the body, as well as to clinch in your conclusion.

A **presentational aid** is any visual, audio, audiovisual, or other sensory material used in a speech. **Visual aids** enhance the speech by allowing audience members to see what the speaker is describing or explaining. **Audio aids** enhance the speaker's verbal message with additional sound. **Audiovisual aids** enhance the speech using a combination of visuals and sound. **Other sensory aids** include materials that enhance the speech by appealing to smell, touch, or taste.

BENEFITS OF PRESENTATIONAL AIDS

Research documents several benefits of using presentational aids. First, they clarify and dramatize your verbal message. Second, they help audiences understand and remember your message.[2] Third, they allow you to address the diverse learning style preferences of your audience members.[3] Fourth, they increase persuasive appeal.[4] In fact, some research suggests that speakers who use presentational aids are almost twice as likely to persuade listeners as those who do not.[5] Finally, using presentational aids may help you to feel more competent and confident.[6]

Today, presentational aids are usually developed into computerized slideshows using presentation software such as PowerPoint, MediaPro, Adobe Acrobat, Prezi, or Photodex, and are projected onto a large screen via a computer and LCD projector. Presentation software allows you to embed audio and audiovisual links from local files and the Internet, which makes it fairly simple to create effective multimedia presentations.

presentational aid: any visual, audio, audiovisual, or other sensory material used in a speech

visual aid: a presentational aid that allows the audience to see what the speaker is describing or explaining

audio aid: a presentational aid that enhances the speaker's verbal message with additional sound

audiovisual aid: a presentational aid that enhances the speech using a combination of visuals and sound

other sensory aid: a presentational aid that enhances the speech by appealing to smell, taste, or touch

Whether creating multimedia presentations or developing simpler presentational aids, your purpose for using them is the same: to enhance your message without overpowering it. In this chapter, we describe various types of presentational aids, criteria to consider when choosing and preparing them, and how to use them during your speech.

TYPES OF PRESENTATIONAL AIDS

Presentational aids range from those that are readily available from existing sources you found while conducting your research to those that you custom produce for your specific speech. The most common types are visual, audio, audiovisual, or other sensory aids.

Visual Aids

Visual aids enhance your verbal message by allowing audiences to see what it is you are describing or explaining. They include actual objects, models, photographs, simple drawings, diagrams, maps, charts, and graphs.

Actual Objects

Actual objects are inanimate or animate physical samples of the idea you are communicating. Inanimate objects make good visual aids if they are (1) large enough to be seen by all audience members, (2) small enough to transport to the speech site, (3) simple enough to understand visually, and (4) safe. A set of golf clubs or a Muslim prayer rug would be appropriate in size for audiences of 20 to 30. An Apple iPhone or Samsung Galaxy might be okay if the goal is simply to show what a smartphone looks like, but might be too small if you want to demonstrate how to use any of its specialized functions. A smartboard or Mondopad would work better for this purpose (see Photo 9.1).

On occasion, *you* can be an effective visual aid. For instance, you can demonstrate the motions involved in a golf swing or use your attire to illustrate the native dress of a particular country. Sometimes it can be appropriate to use another person as a visual aid, such as when Jenny used a friend to demonstrate the Heimlich maneuver. Animals can also be effective visual aids. For example, Josh used his AKC obedience

actual objects: an inanimate or animate sample of the idea being communicated

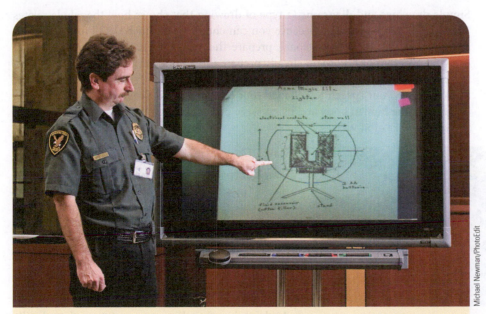

Michael Newman/PhotoEdit

Photo 9.1 Smartboards and Mondopads can make small features on a smartphone large enough for audiences to see. When have you seen someone use either of these devices effectively?

Jose Luis Pelaez Inc/Getty Images

Photo 9.2 When you use a model as a visual aid, it can help your audience understand your topic. How might this model of a wind turbine help the speaker clarify his message?

model: a three-dimensional scaled-down or scaled-up version of an actual object

diagram: a type of drawing that shows how the whole relates to its parts

chart: a graphic representation that distills complex information into an easily interpreted visual format

Lawrey/Shutterstock.com

Photo 9.3 Enlarged photographs can help illustrate people or places, particularly if the person or place is noted in some way. What might be a good photo to share in your upcoming speech?

champion dog to demonstrate the basics of dog training. But keep in mind that animals placed in unfamiliar settings can become difficult to control and may distract from your message, and many people have allergies or phobias involving different animals.

Models

When an actual object is too large or too small for the room where you'll be speaking or to show clearly in your digitally recorded speech, too complex to understand visually, or potentially unsafe or uncontrollable, a model of it can be an effective visual aid. A **model** is a three-dimensional scaled-down or scaled-up version of an actual object that may also be simplified to aid understanding (Photo 9.2). In a speech on the physics of bridge construction, for example, a scale model of a suspension bridge would be an effective visual aid.

Photographs

If an exact reproduction of material is needed, enlarged photographs can be excellent visual aids. In a speech on smart weapons, for example, before and after photos of target sites would be effective in helping the audience understand the pinpoint accuracy of these weapons. When choosing photographs, be sure that the image is large enough for your audience to see, that the object of interest in the photo is clearly identified, and ideally, that the object of interest is in the foreground. For example, if you are giving a speech about your grandmother and project a photo of her with her college graduating class, you might circle her image or use a laser pointer to highlight her image among her classmates in the photo (Photo 9.3).

Simple Drawings and Diagrams

Simple drawings and **diagrams** (a type of drawing that shows how the whole relates to its parts) can be effective because you can choose how much detail to include. To ensure such aids look professional, prepare them using a basic computer software drawing program or find them already prepared in a book, an article, or on the Internet. If you use drawings or diagrams from other sources, however, be sure to credit the source during your speech to enhance your credibility and avoid plagiarism. Andria's diagram of the human body and its pressure points, for example, visually clarified her message (see Exhibit 9.1).

Maps

Simple maps allow you to orient audiences to landmarks (mountains, rivers, and lakes), states, cities, land routes, weather systems, and so on. As with drawings and diagrams, include only the details that are relevant to your purpose. Meteorologists, for example, use maps regularly to explain the weather to viewers (see Photo 9.4).

Charts

A **chart** is a graphic representation that distills complex information into an easily interpreted visual format. Flowcharts, organizational charts, and pie charts are the most common types.

9.1 Diagram

Exhibit

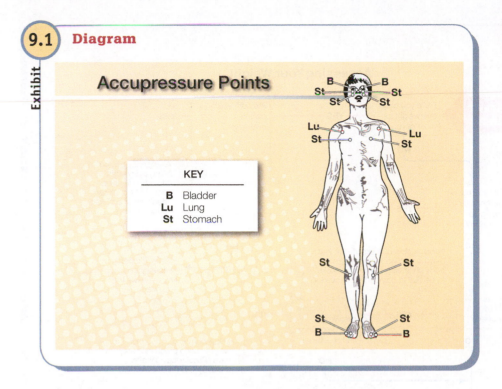

Accupressure Points

KEY

B Bladder
Lu Lung
St Stomach

flowchart: uses symbols and connecting lines to diagram a sequence of steps through a complicated process

organizational chart: shows the structure of an organization in terms of rank and chain of command

pie chart: shows the relationships among parts of a single unit

graph: presents numerical information in visual form

bar graph: uses vertical or horizontal bars to show relationships between or among two or more variables

line graph: indicates changes in one or more variables over time

A **flowchart** uses symbols and connecting lines to diagram a sequence of steps through a complicated process. Tim used a flowchart to help listeners move through the sequence of steps to assess their weight (see Exhibit 9.2). An **organizational chart** shows the structure of an organization in terms of rank and chain of command (see Exhibit 9.3). A **pie chart** shows the relationships among parts of a single unit. Ideally, pie charts have two to five "slices," or wedges—more than eight wedges clutter a pie chart. If your pie chart includes too many wedges, use another kind of chart unless you can consolidate several of the less important wedges into the category of "other," as Tim did to show the percentage of total calories that should come from the various components of food (see Exhibit 9.4).

Graphs

A **graph** presents numerical information in visual form. A **bar graph** uses vertical or horizontal bars to show relationships between or among two or more variables (see Exhibit 9.5). For instance, Jacqueline used a bar graph to compare the amounts of caffeine found in one serving each of chocolate, coffee, tea, and cola. A **line graph** indicates changes in one or more variables over time. In a speech about the US population, for example, the line graph in Exhibit 9.6 was used to illustrate how it has increased, in millions, from 1810 to 2010.

Audio Aids

Audio aids enhance a verbal message through sound. They are especially useful when it is difficult, if not impossible, to describe a sound in words. For example, in David's speech about three types of trumpet mutes and how they alter the trumpet's sound, he played his trumpet so listeners could

Michael Newman/PhotoEdit

Photo 9.4 Meteorologists on TV use maps regularly to explain the weather. Can you imagine understanding their messages without the use of a map?

Exhibit

9.2   **Flowchart**

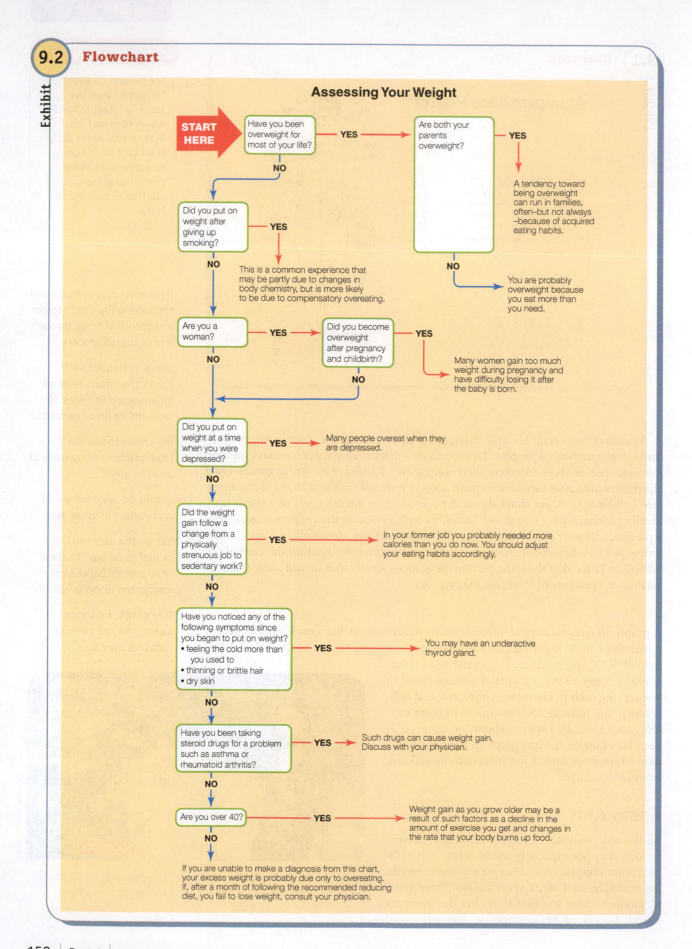

Assessing Your Weight

START HERE

Have you been overweight for most of your life? — **YES** → Are both your parents overweight? — **YES** → A tendency toward being overweight can run in families, often–but not always –because of acquired eating habits.

NO

Did you put on weight after giving up smoking? — **YES** → This is a common experience that may be partly due to changes in body chemistry, but is more likely to be due to compensatory overeating.

NO (from parents) → You are probably overweight because you eat more than you need.

Are you a woman? — **YES** → Did you become overweight after pregnancy and childbirth? — **YES** → Many women gain too much weight during pregnancy and have difficulty losing it after the baby is born.

NO

Did you put on weight at a time when you were depressed? — **YES** → Many people overeat when they are depressed.

NO

Did the weight gain follow a change from a physically strenuous job to sedentary work? — **YES** → In your former job you probably needed more calories than you do now. You should adjust your eating habits accordingly.

NO

Have you noticed any of the following symptoms since you began to put on weight?
• feeling the cold more than you used to
• thinning or brittle hair
• dry skin
— **YES** → You may have an underactive thyroid gland.

NO

Have you been taking steroid drugs for a problem such as asthma or rheumatoid arthritis? — **YES** → Such drugs can cause weight gain. Discuss with your physician.

NO

Are you over 40? — **YES** → Weight gain as you grow older may be a result of such factors as a decline in the amount of exercise you get and changes in the rate that your body burns up food.

NO

If you are unable to make a diagnosis from this chart, your excess weight is probably due only to overeating. If, after a month of following the recommended reducing diet, you fail to lose weight, consult your physician.

9.3 Organizational Chart

Exhibit

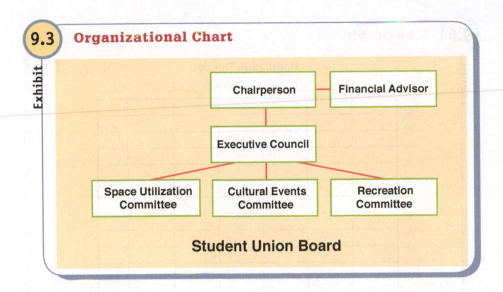

Student Union Board

9.4 Pie Chart

Exhibit

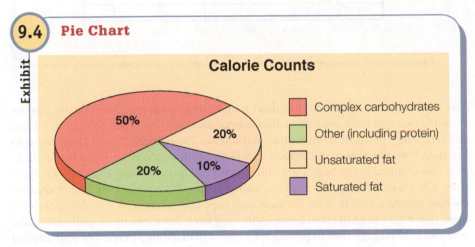

9.5 Bar Graph

Exhibit

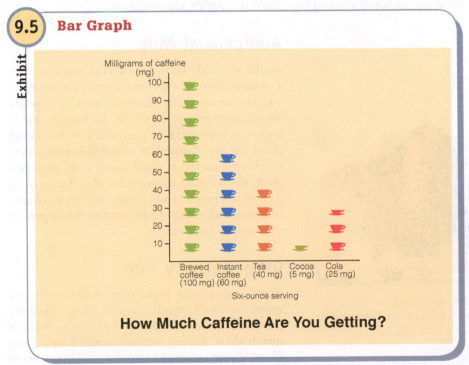

How Much Caffeine Are You Getting?

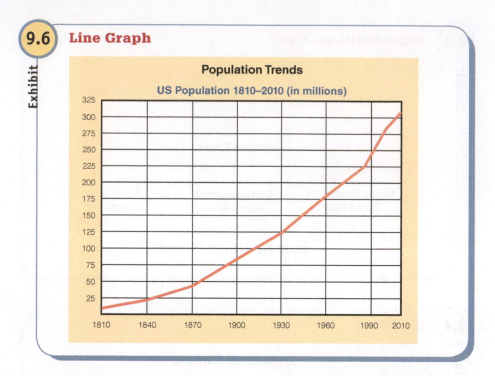

Exhibit

9.6 **Line Graph**

Population Trends

US Population 1810–2010 (in millions)

SPEECH SNIPPET

For his speech on what happens to racehorses after they retire, Paul began by playing a short clip he found on YouTube showing 2015 Triple Crown winner American Pharoah winning the Kentucky Derby.

hear what he meant. If you can't or don't want to make your own sounds, you can use recorded excerpts from sources such as famous speeches, radio programs, interviews, and recordings of music or environmental sounds. For example, Susan chose to begin her speech on the history of the Kentucky Derby with a recording of the bugle call to post that announces the beginning of the race. Chas wrote a song and used a snippet from it as his attention getter and clincher in his speech about following your dreams. He also posted a link to it on his Facebook page and referenced it in his speech for those that might want to listen to the entire song later. Before using an audio aid, make sure you have enough time to present it (no more than about 5 percent of your allotted speaking time) and that you have access to a quality sound system.

Audiovisual Aids

Audiovisual aids enhance a verbal message using a combination of sight and sound. For example, you can use short clips from films and videos that are relatively easy to access on the Internet and to import as hyperlinks in your slides. In his speech about the use of robots in automobile production, Chad, who worked as a technician at the local auto plant, showed a 20-second video clip of a car being painted in a robotic paint booth. As with audio aids, audiovisual aids should take no more than 5 percent of your speaking time.

Other Sensory Aids

Depending on your topic, other sensory aids that appeal to smell, touch, or taste may effectively enhance your speech (Photo 9.5). For example, a speech about making perfume might benefit from allowing your audience to smell scented swatches as

Photo 9.5 Celebrity chefs often ask observers to sample their product to confirm that it really tastes good. Have you ever sampled a product at the grocery store and, if so, did it influence you to purchase it?

Reflect on Ethics

ETHICS AND VISUAL IMAGES IN ADVERTISEMENTS

The International Charter is an organization dedicated to promoting best practices for businesses across the world.[7] Regarding ethical standards in advertising, the organization advocates that:

- Advertisements should not contain statements or visual presentations which offend prevailing standards of decency; and

- Advertisements should not condone any form of discrimination, including that based upon race, national origin, religion, sex, or age, nor should they in any way undermine human dignity.

That said, the ultimate goal of all advertisements is to sell products or services and we all know that sex, humor, and shock appeal sell. This paradox gives rise to an ongoing debate about where to draw the line. Consider the controversial GoDaddy commercial where sexy supermodel Bar Refaeli engages in a sloppy kiss with some smart nerd named Walter; the Volkswagen commercial that came under fire as racist because a white man spoke with a thick Jamaican accent; the Lynx ad's relentless play on the double entendre "balls"; or the Reebok commercial that told viewers to "cheat on your girlfriend, not on your workout." For decades, the ethics line has often been drawn in the court of public opinion. In other words, if an advertisement causes outrage among enough people, the advertisement gets pulled and a public apology is offered. Today, however, even when such advertisements are removed, they remain easily accessible online via a simple Google search.

1. Who should determine whether an advertisement is ethical and in what ways, if any, should advertisers who cross the line be held accountable?

2. Does the fact that ads pulled from publication can still be accessed on social media sites such as YouTube make a difference in where the ethical advertising line should be drawn? Explain your answer.

---

you describe the ingredients used to make the scents. In a speech about Braille, Javier handed out copies of his outline written in Braille for audience members to touch. And in his speech about name brand and generic foods, Greg had his audience members do a taste test of two products.

CHOOSING PRESENTATIONAL AIDS

With so many different types of presentational aids, you have to decide which ones will best illustrate the content you want to highlight, you will feel comfortable using, and you have the time and money to prepare. The additional guidelines that follow can help you make good choices. Choose aids that:

- Illustrate the most important ideas to understand and remember.

- Clarify complex ideas that are difficult to explain verbally.

- Are appropriate for the size of the audience.

- Make dull information and details more interesting.

- Enhance rather than overwhelm the verbal message.

- Demonstrate cultural sensitivity and avoid offending your audience.

PREPARING PRESENTATIONAL AIDS

However simple your presentational aids may be, you still need to produce them carefully. You may need to find or create charts, graphs, diagrams, maps, or drawings. You may need to search for and prepare photographs. You may choose to look for audio, video, or audiovisual clips and then convert them to a format that you can use at your speech site. The goal is to prepare professional-looking and sounding

Photo 9.6 Posters are often used by professionals to help explain research projects. How might a poster be a helpful presentational aid at a career or student activities fair?

presentational aids that will enhance your ethos (perceived competence, credibility, and character) in addition to clarifying your message and making it more memorable. The most common presentational aids used today are prepared as computerized slide shows (e.g., PowerPoint, Prezi). However, you might find yourself preparing a poster (Photo 9.6), particularly if you are giving your speech at a professional conference; using a whiteboard or flip chart if you want to integrate input from your audience during the presentation; or developing a handout to give to audience members after finishing your speech. Here are a few tips to guide you as you prepare them.

1. **Limit the reading required of the audience.** The audience should be listening to you, not reading the presentational aid. So use key words and short phrases rather than complete sentences.

2. **Customize presentational aids from other sources.** As you conduct your research, you will likely find potential supporting material already represented in visual, audio, or audiovisual form. In these cases, simplify your presentational aid to include only the information that is relevant to your speech. For example, Jia Li was preparing a speech on alcohol abuse by young adults. During her research, she found a graph called "Current, Binge, and Heavy Alcohol Use among Persons Aged 12 or Older by Age." Since the graph presented information pertaining to drinkers ages 12 to 65+, she simplified it to include only the information about young adults ages 16 to 29.

3. **Use graphics and type sizes that can be seen easily and a volume and sound quality that can be heard easily by your entire audience.** Check visuals for size by moving as far away from the presentational aid as the farthest person in your audience will be sitting. If you can see the image, read the lettering, and

9.7 The Rule of Thirds

Exhibit

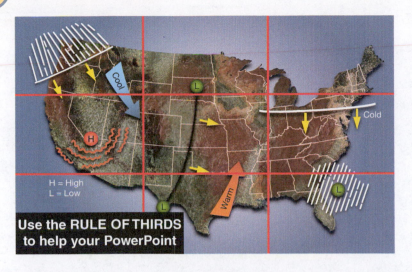

Use the RULE OF THIRDS
to help your PowerPoint

H = High
L = Low

see the pertinent details from that distance, your aid is large enough. If not, create another and check it again. Check audio materials for volume and sound quality in a similar way.

4. **Use a consistent font that is easy to read.** Avoid fancy fonts and stick to one style on all slides. In addition, use uppercase and lowercase letters rather than ALL CAPS; doing the former is actually easier to read.

5. **Make sure information is laid out in an aesthetically pleasing way.** Leave sufficient white space to make each component easy to see. Exercise the "rule of thirds" for effective graphic design by dividing your slide into nine equal parts and placing your key images and labels within the points where those parts intersect.[8] Doing so produces visually pleasing balance. Exhibit 9.7 provides an example of a slide designed using this concept.

6. **Use graphic illustrations in visuals.** To truly enhance a verbal message, a presentational aid should consist of symbols other than or more than just words.[9] Even something as simple as a relevant piece of clip art can make your verbal message more memorable. Of course, clip art can be overdone so be careful not to let your message be overpowered by unnecessary pictures or animations.

7. **Use color strategically.** Although black and white can work well for your visual aids, consider using color strategically to emphasize points. Here are some suggestions for doing so:

   • Use the same background color and theme for all your presentational aids.

   • Use the same color to show similarities, and use opposite colors (on a color wheel) to show differences between ideas.

   • Use bright colors, such as red, to highlight important information. Be sure to avoid using red and green together, however, because audience members who are color-blind may not be able to distinguish them.

   • Use dark colors for lettering on a white background and light colors for lettering on black or deep blue backgrounds.

9.8 **A Cluttered and Cumbersome Visual Aid**

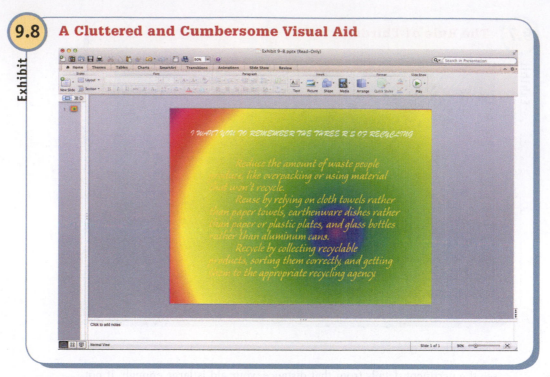

9.9 **A Simple but Effective Visual Aid**

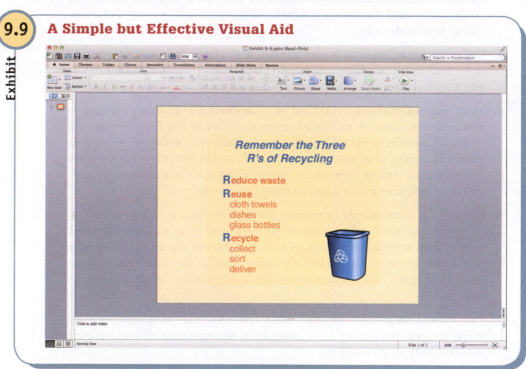

- Use no more than two or three colors on any presentational aid that is not a photograph or video clip.

- Pretend you are your audience. Sit as far away as they will be sitting, and evaluate the colors you have chosen for their readability and appeal.

Let's see if we can put all of these principles to work. Exhibit 9.8 contains a lot of important information, but notice how unpleasant it is to the eye. As you can see, this visual aid ignores all the principles we've discussed. However, with some thoughtful simplification, this speaker could produce the visual aid shown in Exhibit 9.9, which

PUBLIC SPEAKING IN THE REAL WORLD

The Power of Presentational Aids and Ignite Speeches

The first Ignite event was conceived in 2006 as a way for members of the tech community in the Seattle, Washington, area to share their personal and professional passions. An Ignite event typically consists of 15 to 20 speeches by people who submit ideas in advance and are selected to present by event organizers. The rules for presenters are to use 20 self-propelling slides to help tell their story in a formal presentation limited to 5 minutes or less. Since then, Ignite has literally gone global, with events taking place in more than 100 cities around the world. Today, however, Ignite events are no longer limited to tech topics and are open to anyone who submits a good idea. Ignite speeches are also posted online, which means speakers have the potential to reach millions of viewers with their ideas.[10]

Drew Peneton, for instance, is a US Army veteran, business entrepreneur, and finance professional at a Fortune 50 corporation. He speaks regularly at Ignite events across the country to promote Boots to Suits, a nonprofit organization he founded in 2009 to help military veterans reintegrate into the workforce when they return to civilian life. Peneton realizes the value of Ignite public speaking events as a forum for getting the word out about the plight of military veterans when they return from active duty, and as a platform for persuading people to help the cause. Speaking at Ignite events has helped him grow the Boots to Suits nonprofit organization from an online resource for veterans to a nationwide network of volunteers who have helped hundreds of thousands of veterans become gainfully employed.[11]

Ignite speeches resonate with so many people and provide an effective public speech format for several reasons:

- Good Ignite speakers leave audiences both satisfied AND motivated to learn more.
- Good Ignite speakers are less likely to bore audiences because their presentations must be concise. The speakers don't have time to ramble.
- Good Ignite speakers must practice in advance or they won't be able to integrate their verbal message with their self-propelling slides. Practice results in better speeches.
- Good Ignite speakers choose, create, and use presentational aids effectively to enhance the telling of their stories.

As Ignite co-creator Brady Forrest explains: "It's not about slides, it's not even about your words, it's about a performance that marries the two together and lets people walk away with at least one new idea."[12]

1. How might you incorporate the tenets of effective Ignite speeches into your face-to-face speeches?
2. How might you incorporate the tenets of effective Ignite speeches into speeches you present online?

Devon Christopher Adams

---

sharpens the focus by emphasizing the key words (reduce, reuse, recycle), highlighting the major details, and adding clip art for a professional touch.

USING PRESENTATIONAL AIDS

Many speakers think that once they have chosen and prepared good presentational aids, they will have no trouble using them during their speech. However, effective speakers also practice using their aids in advance. Although we will spend more time explaining how to do so in Chapter 11 (Delivery), we present here several guidelines for using presentational aids:

1. Plan carefully when to use each presentational aid and make a note of it on your formal outline and in your speaking notes.

2. Position presentational aids and equipment so all audience members can see and/or hear them before beginning your speech.

> **SPEECH SNIPPET**
>
> In his speech on obesity, Tim created a handout of his flowchart showing how to determine if you are overweight. He created the flowchart on a PowerPoint slide for reference during his speech, saving the handout to distribute afterward.

Photo 9.7 Display visual aids only when you're referring to them. How might you conceal your PowerPoint slides when you are not referring to them?

3. Talk about and visually reference the visual aid while showing it and the audio or audiovisual aid just before and just after playing it (Photo 9.7).

4. Make eye contact with the audience (not the presentational aid) while discussing it.

5. Pass objects and handouts around AFTER rather than during your speech so they do not distract audience members from your message.

5A SPEECH PLANNING

Choosing, Preparing, and Using Presentational Aids

1. Identify key ideas in your speech that could be enhanced with a presentational aid (e.g., create interest, facilitate understanding, foster retention).

2. For each idea, list the type of presentational aid you think would be most appropriate and effective.

3. Decide how you will find and/or design each type of aid you identified in #2.

4. Plan how you will display and reference each aid during your speech.

SAMPLE STUDENT RESPONSE
Choosing, Preparing, and Using Presentational Aids

Speech goal: *I would like my audience to learn to identify common poisonous plants that grow in our area.*

(5A) SPEECH PLANNING *(continued)*

1. Identify key ideas in your speech that could be enhanced with a presentational aid (e.g., create interest, facilitate understanding, foster retention).

    Leaf shape, size, and color; habitat; signs of contact

2. For each idea, list the type of presentational aid you think would be most appropriate and effective.

    I will use two color photographs of each type of plant. The first will show the entire plant; the second will be a close-up of the leaves. I will also use photos to show the habitat in which each plant is usually found. Finally, I will use photographs to show the reactions that occur as a result of contact with the plants. I will have actual plant samples available for closer inspection after my speech and a handout of the types of plants for audience members to take with them as they leave.

3. Decide how you will find and/or design each type of aid you identified in #2.

    I will take photographs of each plant and the habitats in which I find them. I will import them into my PowerPoint slides. I will embed them into my slides in ways that adhere to the rule of thirds. I will also collect samples of each type of plant and bring them with me to the speech, as well as prepare a handout of the types of plants to distribute after the speech.

4. Plan how you will display and reference each aid during your speech.

    I will bring the PowerPoint slides on a memory stick and use the computer and projector that are available at the speaking site. I will reference each slide using a laser pointer because I will be speaking to an audience of more than 50 people. I will transport the plant samples and handouts in my rollerboard suitcase and get them out after finishing my speech.

Reflection and Assessment

Presentational aids are useful when they help audience members understand and remember important information. To assess how well you've learned what we've discussed in this chapter, answer the following questions. If you have trouble answering any of them, go back and review that material. Once you can answer each question accurately, you are ready to move ahead to the next chapter.

1. What are some benefits of using presentational aids in your speech?
2. What are the different types of presentational aids?
3. What are some criteria for choosing appropriate presentational aids?
4. What are some guidelines to follow when preparing presentational aids?
5. What should you consider when planning to use your presentational aids?

MindTap®

Challenge Resource and Assessment Center

Now that you have read Chapter 9, go to your MindTap Communication for *The Challenge of Effective Speaking in a Digital Age* for quick access to flashcards, chapter quizzes, and more.

Applying What You've Learned

1. **Impromptu Speech Activity:** For this "Battle of the Visual Aids," form groups of four or five people. Your instructor will provide you with three sample visual aids that might be used in a speech. Based on the criteria and guidelines you learned in this chapter, evaluate each visual aid and select the best one. At your instructor's request, one member of each team should go to the front of the room and give a 2- to 3-minute speech that makes a case for why the visual aid you selected is the best of the three. After all groups have made their presentations, vote as a class on the best visual aid and discuss why.

2. **Assessment Activity A:** Based on the information and guidelines offered in this chapter, locate a visual, audio, or audiovisual aid example that you believe represents an effective presentational aid and another that represents an ineffective one. Prepare a two- to three-page paper explaining why you assessed them as you did.

3. **Assessment Activity B:** Complete Action Plan Step 5 for one of the speeches you may give this semester.

10

Language and Oral Style

wavebreakmedia/Shutterstock.com

ⓔ Ethical communicators make language choices that demonstrate respect for other individuals and groups.

CoraMax/Shutterstock.com

ACTION STEP 6

Practice oral language and delivery style.

A. Practice to develop an oral style using language that is appropriate, accurate, clear, and vivid.

Nathan asked his friend Josh to read through his formal speech outline and provide suggestions for improvement. After reading the outline on the congenital condition known as Meckel's diverticulum, Josh asked, "What class are you giving this speech for? Isn't it your public speaking class?"

"Yeah, why?" Nathan responded.

"Well," Josh replied, "Don't take this the wrong way, OK? I actually think it would be great for classmates in your human anatomy and physiology class. But it seems awfully technical for classmates who come from all sorts of majors. I'm afraid it might go over their heads."

Nathan sounded bummed as he responded, "Oh, good point. Darn it! I guess I'll have to go back to the drawing board and pick a different topic."

"Actually," said Josh, "I don't think you have to start over. You just need to adjust some of your language to be appropriate and clear for a more general audience. Here, let me show you."

With your outline in hand and presentational aids prepared, you are ready to move to the next step in the preparation process. In other words, you turn your focus from the macrostructure (the overall framework for organizing your speech content) to the microstructure (the specific language and style choices used to verbalize your ideas to a particular audience). In the chapter opening, Josh realizes that Nathan's speech can be adapted to his public speech class audience by choosing appropriate, accurate, clear, and vivid language.

In written communication, effective style evolves through a repetitious process of reading and revising. In a speech, effective style develops through a repetitious process of practicing aloud and revising. In this chapter, we help you do so first by clarifying how oral style differs from written style, as well as how the formal oral style used in public speeches differs from the informal oral style we use in casual conversations. Then, we offer some specific strategies for ensuring that your language is appropriate, accurate, clear, and vivid.

ORAL STYLE

oral style: how one conveys messages through the spoken word

Oral style refers to how we convey messages through the spoken word. An effective oral style differs quite a bit from written style, though when giving a speech, your oral style is still more formal than everyday talk. In fact, the degree of formality required to be an effective public speaker is based on the rhetorical situation. In other words, the goal is to adapt your language to the purpose, audience, and occasion. For example, although your language when speaking to a small audience of colleagues at a business meeting will be more formal than when conversing with a friend at dinner, it will not be as formal as when speaking to an audience of 100 or more at a professional conference or workshop. Still, even in a formal public speaking situation, you must *establish a relationship* with your listeners. Although your oral style is slightly more formal than in everyday conversation, it should still reflect a personal tone that encourages listeners to perceive you to be *having a conversation with them.* Four primary characteristics distinguish an effective oral style from an effective written style.

PUBLIC SPEAKING IN THE REAL WORLD

President Obama's Way with Words

Ryan Rodrick Beiler/Shutterstock.com

In the NPR news story, "The Art of Language, Obama-Style," correspondent Linton Weeks explains that President Barack Obama understands that carefully selected language and oral style are powerful means for reaching the hearts and minds of listeners. How does he do it? He does it by following the guidelines for effective oral style.

First, he relies on simple language. He begins sentences with "look" or "listen" and uses everyday expressions such as "screwed up" and "folks." In other words, "he doesn't use $5 words when nickel ones will suffice."[1] In fact, according to a study that tracked language patterns of presidential candidates from 1948 to 2012 conducted by communication professors Roderick Hart and Kathleen Hall Jamieson,[2] Obama scored lower than anyone else on both "complexity" (average word size) and "embellishment" (number of words used to make a point). As a result, Obama comes across as a "plain spoken Midwesterner."

Second, according to political science professor John Geer, is the President's unique ability to "reach rhetorical heights" by finding the most descriptive words to express his worldview and make his point. In his article published in *The Guardian*, Sam Leith compared the President's brilliant use of rhetorical figures and structures of speech as equivalent to "a greatest hits album knocked out in time for Christmas. All his favourite oratorical devices were on display."[3]

And, he draws upon his "rare gift" and "real strength" for sounding conversational and appearing "comfortable whether scripted or extemporaneous."[4] He does so by using personal pronouns like "we" and "our" as he claims, for example, that "we're going to win this struggle" by working together and "our journey is not complete until."[5]

Whether or not one agrees with his politics, President Obama capitalizes on his own unique language and oral style to appeal effectively to the "folks" in his audience.

1. Do you agree that Obama's language and oral style helps him sound conversational and sincere when he speaks?
2. Why or why not?

1. **An effective oral style tends toward short sentences and familiar language.** Because listeners expect to grasp your main ideas while they listen, choose words that your audience is likely to understand without having to look up definitions. Likewise, opt for short, simple sentences rather than complex ones that require additional time to decipher. We certainly live in a digital age where live public speeches can be recorded and even posted online to be heard multiple times. Even when watching a recorded public speech, however, listeners should not be required to press "pause" to look up word meanings or press "reverse" to replay complex sentences.

2. **An effective oral style features plural personal pronouns.** Using personal pronouns such as "we," "us," and "our" creates a sense of relationship with the audience. It demonstrates respect for the audience as participants in the rhetorical situation. Remember, your goal is to create a perception of conversing *with* your audience rather than presenting *to* or *in front of* them. Personal pronouns help foster that perception.

3. **An effective oral style employs descriptive words and phrases that appeal to the ear in ways that sustain listener interest and promote retention.** By using colorful adjectives and adverbs that appeal to the senses, as well as rhetorical figures of speech (discussed later in this chapter), you will capture the interest of your audience and motivate them to stay focused throughout your speech.

4. **An effective oral style incorporates clear macrostructural elements** (e.g., main point preview, section transitions, and signposts, as discussed in Chapters 7 and 8). Unless your speech is being recorded and posted online for additional viewing, listeners are afforded the opportunity to hear it only once. Consequently, you need to intentionally articulate a preview of your main points so listeners can conceptualize the framework for your main ideas at the outset. Similarly, you need to provide clear section transitions that verbally signal when you are moving from one major idea to the next, and signposts such as "first," "second," "third," and "fourth" to help listeners follow your train of thought as your speech progresses.

Now that we understand the nature of oral style as it differs from written style, let's turn our attention to some specific language choices you should consider as you practice and revise your speech. These include speaking appropriately, accurately, clearly, and vividly.

SPEAKING APPROPRIATELY

speaking appropriately: using language that is adapted to the needs, interests, knowledge, and attitudes of the listener and avoiding language that alienates audience members

verbal immediacy: language that reduces the psychological distance between you and your audience

Speaking appropriately means using language that is adapted to the needs, interests, knowledge, and attitudes of your listeners and avoiding language that might alienate anyone (Photo 10.1). In the communication field, we use the term **verbal immediacy** to describe language that reduces the psychological distance between you and your audience.[6] In other words, speaking appropriately means making language choices that enhance a sense of connection between you and your audience members. In this section, we discuss some specific strategies for making appropriate language choices.

Relevance

Listeners pay attention to and are interested in ideas they perceive as personally relevant (when they can answer the question, "What does this have to do with me?"). Recall from Chapter 5 that you can help the audience perceive your topic as relevant by highlighting its *timeliness*, *proximity*, and *personal impact*. Listeners are more likely to be interested in information they perceive as timely—they want to know how they can use the information *now*. So whenever possible, use present tense as you explain your ideas. Your listeners are also more likely to be interested in information that has proximity, that is, it relates to their "territory" (workplace, neighborhood, city, state, or country). You have probably heard speakers say something like this: "Let me bring this closer to home by showing you . . ." and then make their point by using a local example. In her speech to the local Planned Parenthood organization about the Zika virus, Darla addressed *timeliness* by offering several self-protection steps pregnant women should take and *proximity* by offering statistics about how many people in their city are infected today.

Finally, your listeners are likely to be interested when you present information that can have a personal impact (serious physical, economic, or psychological consequences) on them or their loved ones. Josh, from the opening vignette, suggested that Nathan pique listener interest in this way by pointing out that major

Lou Rocco/Disney ABC Television Group/Getty Images

Photo 10.1 Speaking appropriately means avoiding language that might offend or alienate audience members. Doing so demonstrates respect and bolsters credibility. Do you consider Whoopi Goldberg to be someone who speaks appropriately? Why or why not?

league pitcher Chan Ho Park was diagnosed with Meckel's diverticulum in 2006. Doing so added relevance, since Park pitched for the team located where they were attending school.

Common Ground

Common ground is the combination of background, knowledge, attitudes, experiences, and philosophies that you share with your audience. Use audience analysis to identify areas of similarity, then speak using plural personal pronouns, rhetorical questions, and common experiences to help establish common ground.

1. **Use plural personal pronouns.** One simple way to establish common ground is to use *plural personal pronouns.* You can easily replace "I" and "you" language with "we" language in the macrostructural components of your speech. In your thesis statement, you can say, for example, "let's discuss" rather than "I will inform you," and in your section transitions, you can say "Now that we all have a clearer understanding of" rather than "Now that I've explained." For his Meckel's diverticulum speech, Josh suggested Nathan introduce his thesis and preview using "we" language this way: "In the next few minutes, let's explore the symptoms, diagnosis, and treatment of a fairly unknown defect in the small intestine known as Meckel's diverticulum."

2. **Ask rhetorical questions.** Recall that a *rhetorical question* is one whose answer is obvious to audience members and to which they are not expected to reply. Rhetorical questions create common ground by alluding to experiences that are shared by audience members and the speaker. They are often used in speech introductions but can also be effective in section transitions and in other parts of the speech. For example, here is how Nathan used a rhetorical question in his transition from the second to third main point: "Knowing what the symptoms of Meckel's diverticulum are and how it is diagnosed leads us to another question: how is it treated?"

3. **Draw from common experiences.** You can also develop common ground by sharing personal experiences, examples, and illustrations that embody what you and the audience have in common. For instance, in a speech about television violence, Jesper used a rhetorical question and referred to a common viewing experience:

   At a key moment when you're watching a really frightening scene in a movie, do you ever quickly close your eyes? I vividly remember doing so over and over again during the scariest scenes in The Shining, The Blair Witch Project, *and* Halloween.

Linguistic Sensitivity

Linguistic sensitivity refers to using language that is respectful of others and avoiding the use of potentially offensive language. To demonstrate linguistic sensitivity, avoid generic language, nonparallel language, potentially offensive humor, and profanity and vulgarity.

1. **Generic language** uses words that apply to only one sex, race, or other group as though that group represents everyone. For example, in the past, English speakers used the masculine pronoun *he* to stand for all humans regardless of sex. This example of generic language excluded 50 percent of most audiences.

common ground: the background, knowledge, attitudes, experiences, and philosophies shared by audience members and the speaker

SPEECH SNIPPET

Pete used "we" language to introduce his speech in this way:

Today, we'll see why Tok Pisin of Papua New Guinea should be considered a legitimate language. We'll do this by looking at what kind of language Tok Pisin is, some of the features of the Tok Pisin language, and why this language is necessary in New Guinea.

linguistic sensitivity: using respectful language that doesn't offend others

generic language: language that uses words that apply only to one sex, race, or other group as though that group represents everyone

Photo 10.2 One way to demonstrate linguistic sensitivity is to avoid using generic language when referring to people and groups. Why does referring to these people as policemen fail to demonstrate linguistic sensitivity?

nonparallel language: when terms are changed because of the sex, race, or other group characteristics of the individual

marking: the addition of sex, race, age, or other group designations to a description

irrelevant association: emphasizing someone's relationship to another when that relationship is irrelevant to the point

The best way to avoid generic language is to use plurals: "When we shop, we should have a clear idea of what we want to buy."[7] You can also do so by using terms such as *police officer* instead of *policeman*, *synthetic* instead of *manmade*, *humankind* instead of *mankind*, *flight attendant* instead of *stewardess*, and *server* instead of *waitress* (Photo 10.2).

2. **Nonparallel language** is when terms are changed because of the sex, race, or other group characteristics of the individual. Two common forms of nonparallelism are marking and irrelevant association.

   Marking is the *addition* of sex, race, age, or other group designations to a description. For instance, a doctor is a person with a medical degree who is licensed to practice medicine. Notice the difference between the following two sentences:

   Jones is a good doctor.

   Jones is a good black doctor.

   In the second sentence, use of the marker "black" has nothing to do with doctoring. Marking is inappropriate because it trivializes the person's role by introducing an irrelevant characteristic.[8] The speaker may be intending to praise Jones, but listeners may interpret the sentence as saying that Jones is a good doctor for a black person (or a woman or an aged person).

   A second form of nonparallelism is **irrelevant association**, which is when we emphasize one person's relationship to another when that relationship is irrelevant to our point. For example, introducing a speaker as "Gladys Thompson, whose husband is CEO of Acme Inc., is the chairperson for this year's United Way campaign," is inappropriate. Mentioning her husband's status implies that Gladys Thompson is chairperson because of her *husband's* accomplishments, not her own.

3. **Offensive humor**—dirty jokes and racist, sexist, or other "-ist" remarks—may not be intended to be offensive, but if some listeners are offended, you will have lost verbal immediacy. To be most effective with your formal public speeches, avoid humorous comments or jokes that may be offensive to some listeners. As a general rule, when in doubt, leave it out.

4. **Profanity and vulgarity** are not considered appropriate language. Fifty years ago, a child was punished for saying "hell" or "damn," and adults used profanity and vulgarity only in rare situations to express strong emotions. Today, "casual swearing"—profanity injected into regular conversation—is commonplace in some language communities, including college campuses.[9] As a result, some of us have become desensitized to it (Photo 10.3). However, when giving a public speech, we need to remember that some people in our audience may still be offended by swearing. People who casually pepper their formal speeches with profanity and vulgarity are often perceived as abrasive and lacking in character, maturity, intelligence, manners, and emotional control.[10]

Unfortunately, profanity and vulgarity are habits that are easily acquired and hard to extinguish.

Cultural Diversity

Language rules and expectations vary from culture to culture. One major theory used to explain such similarities and differences is individualism versus collectivism.[11] In general, individualistic cultures tend to use low-context communication, in which information is (1) embedded mainly in the messages transmitted, and (2) presented directly. Collectivistic cultures tend to use high-context communication, in which people (1) expect others to know how they're thinking and feeling, and (2) present some messages indirectly to avoid embarrassing the other person. Thus, speakers from low-context cultures tend to operate on the principle of saying what they mean and getting to the point. Their approach may be characterized by such expressions as "Say what you mean" and "Don't beat around the bush."[12] In contrast, speakers from high-context cultures are likely to use language that is intentionally indirect and listeners are expected to understand the message not only based on the words but also from the context in which they are uttered.

Josh Brasted/Getty Images

Photo 10.3 Some comedians rely on profanity for humor; however, in doing so, they often offend some listeners. Do you consider Louis C.K. to be someone who speaks appropriately? Why or why not?

What does this mean for public speakers? When your audience comprises people from ethnic and language groups different from your own, make an extra effort to ensure that you are being understood. When the first language spoken by your audience members is different from yours, your audience may not be able to understand what you are saying because you may speak with an accent, mispronounce words, choose inappropriate words, or misuse idioms.

Speaking in a second language can sometimes make us feel self-conscious. Most audience members are more tolerant of mistakes made by a second-language speaker than they are of those made by a native speaker. Nevertheless, when speaking in a second language, you can help your audience by speaking more slowly and articulating as clearly as you can. By slowing your speaking rate, you give yourself additional time to pronounce difficult sounds and choose words whose meanings you know. This also gives your audience members additional time to adjust their ears to more easily process what you are saying. You can also use visual aids to reinforce key terms and concepts as you move through your speech. Doing so assures listeners that they've understood you correctly.

One of the best ways to improve when you are giving a speech in a second or third language is to practice in front of friends who are native speakers of that language. Ask them to take note of words and phrases you mispronounce or misuse. Then they can work with you to correct the pronunciation or to choose other words that better express your idea. Also, keep in mind that the more you practice speaking the language, the more comfortable you will become with it.

Speaking Accurately

Using **accurate language** means using words that convey the meaning you intend. On the surface, speaking accurately seems simple enough. In fact, however, speaking accurately is not that simple. Here are three reasons why.

1. **Language is arbitrary.** The **words** we use to represent things are arbitrary symbols. Explained another way, there is not necessarily any literal connection between a word and the thing it represents. For a word to have meaning, it

accurate language: words that convey the meaning you intend

words: arbitrary symbols used to represent things

Reflect on Ethics

INSENSITIVE HUMOR?

What follows is a real-life example of a 2016 wedding toast speech given in England by the best man, Giles Cory, and posted online on the website hitched.com as a great example for using humor.

Hi everyone, before I start could I just get confirmation from the BBC technicians in the other room that the canned laughter is ready to go the moment I crash and burn . . . OK, let's go.

Good afternoon ladies and gentlemen, I'd like to start by thanking Kevin on behalf of the bridesmaids for his kind words. I think they all look beautiful and have done a great job of looking after Gemma today. I would also like to thank everyone here on behalf of the bride and groom, for sharing their wedding day, particularly those who've travelled a long way.

I think it's fair to say that currently I feel like I've moved from the witness bench to the dock as I stand here before you, and yet I'm not the one who has been sentenced here today, sorry! That should be married. Still, as my jury I feel obliged to put the case for my defense before you.

When Kevin asked me to be his best man he dulled the fear I would experience by plying me with a few pints and offering me a tenner. I told him I couldn't be bought, so then he offered me 25 quid, and I asked him if he thought I was cheap. Finally he offered me 50 quid. So good afternoon ladies and gentlemen, my name is Giles and I'm the best man!!

Kevin and I first meet about 7 years ago when we started working in the same company. Back then at work he was always known as a "god"; you would never see him, he was holier than thou, and if he did any work it was a bloody miracle! But times change and it's good to see he's moved on and settled down with someone as wonderful as Gemma.

Apparently, it's my duty to offer a small piece of advice to the groom and Kevin will be pleased to know that a successful marriage can be compared to football, "be fully committed every week and make sure

you score every Saturday." However, Gemma assures me that playing away from home could result in a serious groin injury and is definitely the quickest way onto the transfer list!!

So with all this good advice flying around I decided to ask Kevin what he was looking for in a marriage; he replied love, happiness and a family. When I asked Gemma the same question, she thought for a moment and replied a "perky copulator," sorry, I mean a "coffee percolator."

At this point it's traditional to read a few of the cards,

"Dear Kevin, from all of us at Madame Thrashards spanking emporium we hope you have a great day. P.S. Many thanks for your annual subscription cheque."

"Dearest Kevy Wevy, I miss your strong arms, your tender loving ways, the way you whispered sweet nothings in my ear. I realise I am a loser in love, but I will never forget those wonderful evenings we spent together by the pool. Love forever, Michael Barrymore"

"Dear Kevin & Gemma, Wishing you every happiness on your wedding day, unfortunately owing to unforeseen circumstances I can't be there with you to celebrate your day in person. Lots of love, Al Sama Bin Laden."

It therefore gives me great pleasure to invite you all to charge your glasses, and be upstanding as we toast the new couple, Mr. & Mrs. Meek, the bride and groom, ladies & gentlemen, "the bride and groom."

1. What ethical communication principles do you believe the speaker adhered to in telling this speech? Which do you believe he violated?

2. Do you think the speaker's language choices were appropriate? Why or why not?

---

must be recognized by both or all parties as standing for a particular object, idea, or feeling.[13] In communication studies, we often simply say the *word* is not the *thing*. In their influential book, *The Meaning of Meaning: A Study of the Influence of Language upon Thought and the Science of Symbolism*, I. A. Richards and C. K. Ogden clarify this idea using the semantic triangle.[14] As depicted in Exhibit 10.1, a "referent" is the *thing* (object or idea) we refer to with a word, which is the "symbol" we use to refer to it. Our audience then attaches meaning to that symbol, which is what Richards and Ogden label the "thought of referent." The word D-O-G is nothing more than three letters used together unless all parties agree that it stands for a certain four-legged animal. To clarify, think about the fact that different groups use different word symbols

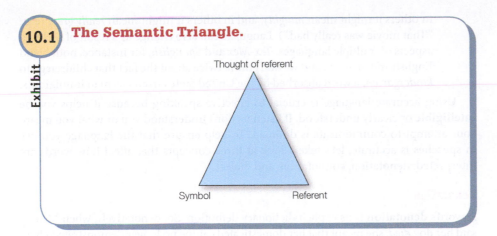

Exhibit 10.1 **The Semantic Triangle.**

Thought of referent

Symbol   Referent

for the same phenomenon. In Spanish, for instance, *el perro* stands for the same thing as *dog* in English. And the storage compartment of an automobile is called a "trunk" in the United States and a "boot" in England.

2. **Language is abstract.** Not only is language arbitrary, but it is also abstract. In the United States, for example, the word "pet" is commonly understood to be an animal kept for companionship. Still, if Rema refers simply to her "pet," Margi may think of a dog, cat, snake, bird, or hamster. Even if Rema specifically mentions her dog, Margi still might think of dogs of various breeds, sizes, colors, and temperaments.

Because language is abstract, two people might interpret the same word quite differently (Photo 10.4). For example, when James tells Chrissie that he liked going to the movie with her, Chrissie might interpret "liked" as enjoying the movie or as spending time with her.

3. **Language changes over time.** New words are constantly being invented and existing words abandoned or assigned new meanings. Just think, for example, of the words that have been invented to represent new technologies, such as *texting, Googling, cyberbullying, tweeting, retweeting, webinar, app, emoticon,* and *emoji.* Some of the new words most recently added to English dictionaries include *vanity sizing* (the deliberate undersizing of clothes), *twirt* (flirt on Twitter), *mankle* (the male ankle), and *cougar* (an older woman in a romantic relationship with a younger man). Did you know that the *Oxford English Dictionary* now also includes *OMG, LOL,* and *<3* as actual words?

Some words become obsolete because the thing they represent becomes obsolete. For example, today we use *photocopiers* and *computers* to make multiple copies of print documents rather than *mimeographs* (low-cost printing presses) and *stencils.* We record audio and video data using *smartphones* rather than *tape recorders, cassette tapes,* and *videotapes.* And we take notes on *electronic tablets* and *laptops* rather than on pads of lined paper that we once organized in three-ring binders and two-pocket file folders.

Sometimes meanings of existing words change. For example, in the United States, the word *gay* once meant *happy* and only that. Today its more common usage references one's sexual orientation. In some communities, *bad* might mean *not good,*

iStockphoto.com/Ursula Alter

Photo 10.4 Depending on where you live, you might call a knitted hat like this one a tuque, a bobble hat, a burglar beanie, a stocking cap, or a toboggan. What would you call it?

in others it might mean *naughty*, and in others it might mean *really great* (e.g., "That movie was really bad."). Language can also change as a result of melding aspects of multiple languages. *Tex-Mex* and *Spanglish*, for instance, both blend English and Spanish, and we don't think twice about the fact that children go to *kindergarten*, a word absorbed by the United States from German immigrants.

Using accurate language is crucial to effective speaking because it helps you be **intelligible** or clearly understood. If listeners don't understand you or what you mean, your attempt to communicate is doomed. To help ensure that the language you use in speeches is accurate, let's take a look at three concepts that affect how words are interpreted: denotation, connotation, and dialect.

intelligible: understandable

Denotation

denotation: dictionary definition

A word's **denotation** is its explicit dictionary definition. So, denotatively, when Melissa said her dog *died*, she meant that her domesticated canine no longer demonstrated physical life. Nathan from the opening vignette offered the dictionary definition of *Meckel's diverticulum* as a congenital defect in the small intestine. Keep in mind that in some situations the denotative meaning of a word may not be clear. Why? One reason is that dictionary definitions reflect current and past practices in the language community. Another reason is that dictionaries often offer more than one definition for a given word. And dictionaries use words (which are abstract) to define words. The end result is that words are defined differently in various dictionaries and may offer multiple meanings.

context: the position of a word in a sentence and its relationship to the words around it

Moreover, meaning may vary depending on the **context**—the position of a word in a sentence and its relationship to the words around it. For example, the dictionary definition of *right* includes both (1) correct (adjective) and (2) a moral or ethical principle (noun). If I say "You're right," the denotative meaning of *right* differs from what I mean when I say "It's your right."

Connotation

connotation: the positive, neutral, or negative feelings we associate with a word

A word's **connotation** is the positive, neutral, or negative feelings we associate with it. For example, consider how your impression of Dave would differ if someone said he was "cheap" versus "frugal." The denotative meaning of both words indicates someone who doesn't like to spend a lot of money, but for most of us "frugal" has a more positive connotation than does "cheap." Connotations can be neutral, positive, or negative, and can be quite different for different people. For example, the word "cop" can conjure up very different connotations for different people based on previous experiences.

Ogden and Richards were among the first scholars to consider the misunderstandings that result from different connotations based on life experiences.[15] For instance, when Melissa told Trish that her dog died, Trish's understanding of the message depends on the extent to which her feelings about pets and death—her connotations of the words—correspond to the feelings Melissa has about pets and death. Whereas Melissa (who sees dogs as truly indispensable friends) may be intending to communicate her overwhelming grief, Trish (who doesn't particularly care for pets in general or dogs in particular) may miss the emotional meaning of Melissa's statement.

Connotations give emotional power to words, so much so that people will even fight and die for them. Consider the connotative meanings people assign to words like *freedom* and *honor* and *justice*. For this reason, connotations can increase the emotional appeal of your message. As you consider language options, be sure to consider audience disposition toward them and steer clear of words that might arouse unintended connotations.

Dialect

dialect: a unique form of a more general language spoken by a specific cultural or co-cultural group

Dialect is a unique form of a more general language spoken by a specific cultural or co-cultural group.[16] These smaller groups that speak a common dialect are called

speech communities. Dialects evolve over time, and the manner in which they differ from the "standard" of the language may be influenced by other languages spoken in the region or by the ethnic group. For instance, in her book *Chicano English in Context*, Carmen Fought explains how the English spoken by some Hispanic people in the Los Angeles area differs from Standard English.[17] Regional differences are also reflected in the words used to represent common things. For example, in some places a car's turn signal is called a "blinker," a seesaw is a "teeter-totter," and a soft drink is a "pop" or a "coke." Some dialects also incorporate what is considered nonstandard grammar, such as "he don't," "I says," "this here book," and "beings as how he was sick." If your audience doesn't share the dialect you normally speak, using it during your speeches can interfere with your intelligibility. Not only that, it can also affect your ethos (the audience's perception of your competence and credibility). Because most audiences are diverse, the best way to ensure being understood by all and conveying positive ethos is to use **Standard English** when speaking to audiences in the United States. Standard English is taught in American schools and detailed in grammar handbooks such as *Hodges Harbrace Handbook*.[18]

speech communities: group of people who speak a common dialect

Standard English: form of English taught in American schools and detailed in English grammar handbooks

SPEAKING CLEARLY

When we take the time to consider denotations, connotations, and dialects, we are well on our way to speaking clearly. Here we offer four specific strategies for improving clarity.

Use Specific Language

Specific language clarifies meaning by using precise words that narrow what is understood from a general category to a particular item or group within that category. For instance, if in her speech Nevah refers to a "blue-collar worker," you might picture any number of occupations that fall within this broad category. If, instead, she says "construction worker," the number of possible images you can picture is reduced. If she is even more specific, she may say "bulldozer operator." Now you are even clearer on the specific occupation.

specific language: words that clarify meaning by narrowing what is understood from a general category to a particular item or group within that category

Choosing specific language is easier when you have a large working vocabulary. As a speaker, the larger your vocabulary, the more choices you have from which to select the word you want. As a listener, the larger your vocabulary, the more likely you are to understand the words used by others. You can use the following strategies to increase your vocabulary:

1. **Study one of the many vocabulary-building books,** such as *Word Smart: How to Build a More Educated Vocabulary*.[19]

2. **Take note of unfamiliar words you read or that people use in conversations and look them up.** For instance, suppose your friend says, "I was inundated with phone calls today!" If you aren't sure what *inundated* means, you can look it up in a dictionary later and discover that it means "overwhelmed" or "flooded." If you then say to yourself, "She was inundated—overwhelmed or flooded—with phone calls today," you are likely to remember its meaning.

3. **Use a thesaurus to identify synonyms that may be more specific options.** But be careful—avoid unfamiliar words that may make you sound intelligent but could reduce your intelligibility. For example, *somnolent* is an interesting word, but most people don't know that it is a synonym for *sleepy*.

Some speakers think that to be effective they must impress their audience with their extensive vocabulary. As a result, instead of looking for specific and precise words, they use words that sound pompous, affected, or stilted to the listener. Speaking precisely and specifically does not mean speaking obscurely. The following story illustrates the problem with pretentious words:

> *A plumber wrote to a government agency, saying that he found that hydrochloric acid quickly opened drainpipes but that he wasn't sure whether it was a good thing to use. A scientist at the agency replied, "The efficacy of hydrochloric acid is indisputable, but the corrosive residue is incompatible with metallic permanence."*
>
> *The plumber wrote back thanking him for the assurance that hydrochloric acid was all right. Disturbed by this turn of affairs, the scientist showed the letter to his boss, another scientist, who then wrote to the plumber: "We cannot assume responsibility for the production of toxic and noxious residue with hydrochloric acid and suggest you use an alternative procedure."*
>
> *The plumber wrote back that he agreed. Hydrochloric acid worked fine. Greatly disturbed by this misunderstanding, the scientists took their problem to the top boss. She wrote to the plumber: "Don't use hydrochloric acid. It eats the hell out of pipes."*

As a general rule, use a more complex word *only* when you believe that it is the very best word for a specific context. Let's suppose you wanted to use a more precise word for *building*. You might select *house, apartment, high-rise,* or *skyscraper,* but not *edifice*. *Edifice* is not more precise, is likely to hurt intelligibility, and is likely to be perceived as affected or stilted.

Choose Familiar Terms

Using familiar terms is just as important as using specific words. Avoid jargon, slang, abbreviations, and acronyms unless (1) you define them clearly the first time they are used, and (2) their use is central to your speech goal.

jargon: unique technical terminology of a trade or profession

Jargon is the unique technical terminology of a trade or profession that is not generally understood by outsiders. We might forget that people not in our same line of work or who do not have the same hobbies may not understand the jargon that is such a part of our daily communication. That's what happened to Nathan in our opening scenario. Josh suggested that Nathan not only say that a technetium-99m scan is the test used to diagnose Meckel's diverticulum, but also what it is. To help listeners understand the technical jargon, Nathan added a sentence to say that technetium-99m is a radioactive material injected into a vein in the arm, which allows a special camera positioned outside the body to detect the deformity.

slang: nonstandard vocabulary and definitions assigned to words by a social group or co-culture

Slang refers to nonstandard vocabulary and definitions assigned to words by a social group or co-culture (Photo 10.5). For example, today the word *wicked*, which has a standard definition denoting something wrong or immoral, can mean quite the opposite in some social groups and co-cultures.[20] You should generally avoid slang in your public speeches not only because you risk being misunderstood but also because slang doesn't sound professional and can hurt your credibility (ethos).

Photo 10.5 Slang that is generally understood within a co-culture may not be clear to all audience members for a public speech. Harley bikers often refer to their motorcycles as "hogs." What are some slang terms that you use?

Overusing and misusing abbreviations and acronyms can also hinder clarity. Even if you think the abbreviation or acronym is a common one, always define it the first time you use it in the speech. For example, in a speech about NASCAR, you should refer to it initially by the organization's full name and then provide the acronym: "National Association for Stock Car Auto Racing, or NASCAR." Providing the full and abbreviated forms of the name will ensure clarity for all listeners.

Provide Details and Examples

Sometimes the word we use may not have a precise synonym. In these situations, clarity can be achieved by adding details or examples. Saying "He lives in a really big house" can be clarified by adding details: "He lives in a 14-room Tudor mansion on a 6-acre estate." You can also share details and examples in the form of presentational aids.

Limit Vocalized Pauses

Vocalized pauses are unnecessary words interjected into sentences to fill moments of silence. Words commonly used for this purpose are "like," "you know," "really," and "basically," as well as "um" and "uh." We sometimes refer to vocalized pauses as "verbal garbage" because they do not serve a meaningful purpose and, when used excessively, actually distract listeners from the message. Although a few vocalized pauses typically don't hinder clarity, practicing your speech aloud will help you eliminate them.

SPEAKING VIVIDLY

Speaking vividly is one effective way to gain and maintain audience interest and help your audience remember what you say. **Vivid language** is full of life—vigorous, bright, and intense. For example, a mediocre baseball announcer might say, "Jackson made a great catch," but a better commentator's vivid account might be, "Jackson leaped and made a spectacular one-handed catch just as he crashed into the center field wall." The words *leaped, spectacular, one-handed catch,* and *crashed* paint an intense verbal

---

SPEECH SNIPPET

As Maren, who is from Minnesota, prepared to practice her speech on the effect drinking sugared sodas has on childhood obesity, she thought about how her roommate would tease her when she referred to "soda" as "pop." As she practiced, she made notes to always say "soda" during her speech.

vocalized pauses: unnecessary words interjected into sentences to fill moments of silence

vivid language: language that is full of life—vigorous, bright, and intense

picture of the action. You can make your ideas come to life by using sensory language and by using rhetorical figures and structures of speech.

Use Sensory Language

Sensory language appeals to the senses of seeing, hearing, tasting, smelling, and feeling. Vivid sensory language begins with vivid thought. You are much more likely to express yourself vividly if you can physically or psychologically sense the meanings you are trying to convey. If you feel the "bite of the wind" or "the sting of freezing rain," if you hear and smell "the thick, juicy sirloin steaks sizzling on the grill," you will be able to describe these sensations. Does the cake merely "taste good" or do your taste buds "quiver with the sweet double-chocolate icing and velvety feel of the rich, moist cake"?

To develop vivid sensory language, begin by considering how you can re-create what something, someone, or some place *looks like*. Consider, too, how you can help listeners imagine how something *sounds*. How can you use language to convey the way something *feels* (textures, shapes, temperatures)? How can language re-create a sense of how something *tastes* or *smells*? To achieve this in your speech, use colorful descriptors. They make your ideas more concrete and can arouse emotions. They invite listeners to imagine details. Here's an example about downhill skiing:

Sight: As you climb the hill, the bright winter sunshine glistening on the snow is blinding.

Touch and feel: Just before you take off, you gently slip your goggles over your eyes. They are bitterly cold and sting your nose for a moment.

Taste: You start the descent and, as you gradually pick up speed, the taste of air and ice and snow in your mouth invigorates you (Photo 10.6).

Sound: An odd silence fills the air. You hear nothing but the swish of your skis against the snow beneath your feet. At last, you arrive at the bottom of the slope.

Ken Redding/Surf/Corbis

Photo 10.6 You can help listeners remember by appealing to the senses. What senses could you appeal to for the topic of your next speech?

Reality hits as you hear the hustle and bustle of other skiers and instructors directing them to their next session.

Smell and feel: You enter the warming house. As your fingers thaw in the warm air, the aroma from the wood stove in the corner comforts you and you drift off into sleep.

By using colorful descriptors that appeal to the senses, you arouse and maintain listener interest and make your ideas more memorable.

Use Rhetorical Figures and Structures of Speech

Rhetorical figures of speech make striking comparisons between things that are not obviously alike to help listeners visualize or internalize what you are saying. **Rhetorical structures of speech** combine ideas in a particular way. Any of these devices can serve to make your speech more memorable as long as they aren't overused. Let's look at some examples.

A **simile** is a direct comparison of dissimilar things using the word *like* or *as*. Clichés such as "He walks like a duck" and "She's as busy as a bee" are similes. If you've seen the movie *Forrest Gump,* you might recall Forrest's use of similes: "Life is like a box of chocolates. You never know what you're going to get" and "Stupid is as stupid does." An elementary school teacher used a simile by saying that being back at school after a long absence "was like trying to hold 35 corks under water at the same time."[21] Similes can be effective because they make ideas more vivid in listeners' minds. But they should be used sparingly or they lose their appeal. Clichés should generally be avoided because their predictability reduces their effectiveness.

A **metaphor** is an implied comparison between two unlike things, expressed without using *like* or *as* Instead of saying that one thing is *like* another, a metaphor says that one thing *is* another. Thus, a problem car is a "lemon" and a leaky roof is a "sieve." Metaphors can be effective because they make an abstract concept more concrete, strengthen an important point, or heighten emotions. Notice how one speaker used a metaphor effectively to explain how one cable company's service differs from the others:

> Most cable providers make you purchase their entire bundled service, which means you have to pay for channels you'll never watch. If you never watch the Golf Channel or Animal Planet, you have to pay for them anyway. Our company is changing that. You pick the channels you want and pay only for what you watch. You might say we're the salad bar of cable providers.[22]

An **analogy** is an extended metaphor. Sometimes, you can develop a story from a metaphor that makes a concept more vivid. If you were to describe a family member as the "black sheep in the barnyard," that's a metaphor. If you went on to talk about the other members of the family as different animals on the farm and the roles ascribed to them, you would be extending the metaphor into an analogy. Analogies can be effective for holding your speech together in a creative and vivid way. Analogies are particularly useful to highlight the similarities between a complex or unfamiliar concept and a familiar one.

Alliteration is the repetition of consonant sounds at the beginning of words that are near one another. Tongue twisters such as "Sally sells seashells by the seashore" use alliteration. In her speech about the history of jelly beans, Sharla used alliteration when she said, "And today there are more than 50 fabulous fruity flavors from which to choose." Used sparingly, alliteration can catch listeners' attention and make a speech memorable. Overuse, however, can hurt the message because listeners might focus on the technique rather than the speech content.

SPEECH SNIPPET

Dan decided to use a metaphor to help explain the complex concept of bioluminescence to his listeners. He said that "bioluminescence is a miniature flashlight that fireflies turn on and off at will."

rhetorical figures of speech: phrases that make striking comparisons between things that are not obviously alike

rhetorical structures of speech: phrases that combine ideas in a particular way

simile: direct comparison of dissimilar things using *like* or *as*

metaphor: implied comparison between two unlike things without using *like* or *as*

analogy: an extended metaphor

alliteration: repetition of consonant sounds at the beginning of words that are near one another

assonance: repetition of vowel sounds in a phrase or phrases

onomatopoeia: words that sound like the things they stand for

personification: attributing human qualities to a concept or an inanimate object

repetition: repeating words, phrases, or sentences for emphasis

antithesis: combining contrasting ideas in the same sentence

Assonance is the repetition of vowel sounds in a phrase or phrases. "How now brown cow" is a common example. Sometimes, the words rhyme, but they don't have to. As with alliteration, assonance can make your speech more memorable as long as it's not overused.

Onomatopoeia is the use of words that sound like the things they stand for, such as "buzz," "hiss," "crack," and "plop." In the speech about skiing, the "swish" of the skis is an example of onomatopoeia.

Personification is attributing human qualities to a concept or an inanimate object. When Madison talked about her truck, "Big Red," as her trusted friend and companion, she used personification. Likewise, when Rick talked about flowers dancing on the front lawn, he used personification.

Repetition is repeating words, phrases, or sentences for emphasis. Martin Luther King Jr.'s "I Have a Dream" speech is a classic example. Professor Nikki Giovanni also used repetition effectively in the speech she gave at a 2007 memorial ceremony for the Virginia Tech shooting victims (Exhibit 10.2).[23]

Antithesis is combining contrasting ideas in the same sentence, as when John F. Kennedy said, "Ask not what your country can do for you. Ask what you can do for your country." Likewise, astronaut Neil Armstrong used antithesis when he first stepped on the moon: "One small step for a man, one giant leap for mankind." Speeches that offer antithesis in the concluding remarks are often very memorable.

Exhibit 10.2

We are Virginia Tech
We are sad today / We will be sad for quite a while
We are not moving on / We are embracing our mourning

We are Virginia Tech

We are strong enough to stand tearlessly
We are brave enough to bend to cry
And sad enough to know we must laugh again

We are Virginia Tech

We do not understand this tragedy / We know we did nothing to deserve it
But neither does the child in Africa / Dying of AIDS
Neither do the Invisible Children / Walking the night away
To avoid being captured by a rogue army
Neither does the baby elephant watching his community / Be devastated for ivory
Neither does the Mexican child looking / For fresh water
Neither does the Iraqi teenager dodging bombs
Neither does the Appalachian infant killed / By a boulder / Dislodged
Because the land was destabilized / No one deserves a tragedy

We are Virginia Tech

The Hokie Nation embraces / Our own / And reaches out / With open heart and mind
To those who offer their hearts and hands / We are strong / And brave
And innocent / And unafraid / We are better than we think / And not yet what we want to be
We are alive to imagination / And open to possibility / We will continue
To invent the future / Through our blood and tears / Through all this sadness
We are the Hokies
We will prevail
We will prevail
We will prevail

We are Virginia Tech

Reflection and Assessment

Your overall goal with regard to language and oral style is to be appropriate, accurate, clear, and vivid. To assess how well you've learned what we've discussed in this chapter, answer the following questions. If you have trouble answering any of them, go back and review that material. Once you can answer each question accurately, you are ready to move ahead to the next chapter.

1. In what ways does oral style differ from written style?
2. What are some guidelines to determine appropriate words for the audience and occasion?
3. How do you choose the most accurate words to convey your ideas?
4. What does it mean to use clear language?
5. What are some examples of vivid language that appeal to the senses or draw on rhetorical devices?

Challenge Resource and Assessment Center   MindTap®

Now that you have read Chapter 10, go to your MindTap Communication for *The Challenge of Effective Speaking in a Digital Age* for quick access to flashcards, chapter quizzes, and more.

Applying What You've Learned

1. **Impromptu Speech Activity:** Draw a nonsensical word from a stack of cards created by your instructor (e.g., photomaniac, alienitus, caninicopia, aquatiphobia). Develop your own definition for this word. Then, prepare and deliver a 2- to 3-minute impromptu speech explaining the meaning of the word using specific language, familiar terms, details, and examples.

2. **Assessment Activity A:** Go online to the *American Rhetoric: Top 100 Speeches* website. Select and listen to one of the speeches posted there. As you listen, take notes regarding the speaker's vivid language choices (sensory language and rhetorical figures and structures of speech). To what degree does the use of them pique your interest and add to the memorability of the message? Explain.

3. **Assessment Activity B:** Select one of these popular television sitcoms: *Modern Family, How I Met Your Mother, Parks and Recreation, Two Broke Girls, Big Bang Theory, The Goldbergs,* or *Family Guy.* Watch an episode and record the following for each of the main characters: use of (a) "we" language, (b) profanity and vulgarity, (c) offensive humor, and (d) linguistic insensitivity. To what degree is each main character portrayed as a role model for viewers? Based on the kinds and number of appropriate and inappropriate language behaviors exhibited and the nature of the character as an intended role model, what message is being sent to viewers about what "appropriate" language usage is?

11 Delivery

CoraMax/Shutterstock.com

WHAT'S THE POINT?

WHEN YOU'VE FINISHED THIS CHAPTER, YOU WILL BE ABLE TO:

• Describe the characteristics of effective delivery

• Use your voice and body effectively to deliver your speech

• Engage in effective speech rehearsals

• Adapt your delivery for face-to-face audiences

• Adapt your delivery for virtual audiences

MindTap®

Review the chapter **Learning Objectives** and **Start** with quick warm-up activity.

Ethical communicators demonstrate respect for their listeners by practicing their delivery in advance.

ACTION STEP 6

Practice oral language and delivery style.

B. Practice until your delivery is conversational, intelligible, and expressive.

C. Practice integrating presentational aids until you can do so smoothly and confidently.

D. Practice until you can deliver your speech conversationally within the time limit.

When Alyssa and Katie finished watching a recording of Alyssa's first speech practice, Alyssa said, "Ugh! That was horrible. I bored myself. I just don't get it. I have all this great information. Why is it so hard to stay focused? My speech is only 5½ minutes long."

Katie responded, "Don't be so hard on yourself, Alyssa. Your speech is good. The topic is interesting and relevant, you cite great evidence, it's well organized, and you use compelling language. You just need to work a bit more on your delivery to make it sound conversational and dynamic. Let's add some delivery cues to your speaking notes to help you remember to emphasize key points with your voice and gestures and to clarify structure with gestures and movement. Then you can practice a few more times until you sound and look spontaneous and conversational."

"OK," Alyssa replied. "After watching that rehearsal, I'll try anything."

What both Alyssa and Katie recognize is that often the difference between a good speech and a great speech is how well it is delivered. In fact, research suggests that listeners are influenced more by delivery than by the content of speeches and that delivery is even more critical when a presentation is online.[1] Of course, a speaker's delivery alone cannot compensate for a poorly researched, organized, or developed speech, but a well-delivered speech can rise above the ordinary and really captivate an audience.

In this chapter, we begin by talking about the characteristics of effective delivery. We then describe the elements of effective delivery: use of voice and use of body. Next, we suggest a process for rehearsing your speech. Finally, we discuss ways to adapt to your audience while speaking in face-to-face settings and in virtual ones.

CHARACTERISTICS OF EFFECTIVE DELIVERY

Think about one of the best speakers you have ever heard. What made this person stand out in your mind? In all likelihood, how the speaker delivered the speech had a lot to do with it. **Delivery** is how a message is communicated nonverbally through your voice and body. **Nonverbal communication** includes all speech elements other than the actual words themselves.[2] Regardless of the channel you use for your speech (face-to-face or digital), effective delivery is both conversational and animated.

Conversational

You have probably heard ineffective speakers whose delivery was overly dramatic and "fake," or stiff and mechanical. In contrast, effective delivery is **conversational**, meaning your audience perceives you as *talking with* them and not *performing in front of* or *reading to* them. The hallmark of a conversational style is spontaneity. **Spontaneity** is the ability to sound natural—as though you are really thinking about the ideas *and* about getting them across to the audience—no matter how many times you've practiced.

Animated

Have you ever been bored by a professor reading a well-structured lecture while mostly looking at the lecture notes or perhaps the PowerPoint slides rather than at the students?

delivery: communicating through the use of voice and body

nonverbal communication: all speech elements other than the words themselves

conversational: sounding spontaneous, as though talking with an audience

spontaneity: sounding natural, no matter how many times a presentation was practiced

Even a well-written speech given by an expert can bore an audience unless its delivery is **animated**, that is, lively and dynamic (Photo 11.1).

You might be wondering how in the world can you sound conversational and animated at the same time? The secret is to focus on conveying the passion you feel about your topic through your voice and body. When we are passionate about sharing something with someone, almost all of us become more animated in our delivery. The goal is to duplicate this level of liveliness when delivering our speeches.

USE OF VOICE AND BODY

Once you've developed your ideas, arranged them in a formal outline, and revised your language to be appropriate, accurate, clear, and vivid, you are ready to practice and revise your delivery until it sounds and looks conversational and animated. Let's look at some specific strategies to employ in our use of voice and body to achieve effective conversational and animated delivery.

iofoto/Shutterstock.com

Photo 11.1 An animated delivery motivates audience members to listen. How will you determine whether your delivery is animated?

animated: lively and dynamic

voice: sound produced by vocal organs

pitch: highness or lowness of vocal sounds

volume: how loudly or softly you speak

rate: speed at which you talk

quality: timbre that distinguishes one voice from others

intelligible: understandable

Use of Voice

Your **voice** is the sound you produce using your vocal organs (your larynx, tongue, teeth, lips, etc.). How your voice sounds depends on its pitch, volume, rate, and quality. **Pitch** is the highness or lowness of the sounds you produce. **Volume** is how loudly or softly you speak. **Rate** is the speed at which you talk. **Quality** is the timbre that distinguishes your voice from others. Your goal in public speaking is to vary your pitch, volume, rate, and quality to achieve a conversational and animated style that is both intelligible and expressive.

Intelligibility

To be **intelligible** simply means to be understandable. All of us have experienced situations when we couldn't understand what was being said because the speaker was talking too softly or too quickly. If you practice your speech using appropriate vocal pitch, volume, rate, and quality, you improve the likelihood that you will be intelligible to your audience.

Appropriate volume is the key to intelligibility. In face-to-face settings, you must speak loudly enough, with or without a microphone, to be heard easily by audience members seated in the back of the room, but not so loudly as to bring discomfort to listeners seated near the front. Similarly, when recording a speech to post online, you want to be heard easily but not sound as though you are shouting.

The rate at which you speak also influences intelligibility. Speaking too slowly gives your listeners' minds time to wander after they've processed an idea. Speaking too quickly, especially when sharing complex ideas and arguments, may not give your listeners enough time to process the information completely. Because nervousness may

Exhibit 11.1 **Commonly Mispronounced Words**

Word	Incorrect	Correct
arctic	ar'-tic	arc'-tic
athlete	ath'-a-lete	ath'-lete
family	fam'-ly	fam'-a-ly
February	Feb'-yu-ary	Feb'-ru-ary
get	git	get
hundred	hun'-derd	hun'-dred
larynx	lar'-nix	ler'-inks
library	ly'-ber-y	ly'-brer-y
nuclear	nu'-kyu-ler	nu'-klee-er
particular	par-tik'-ler	par-tik'-yu-ler
picture	pitch'-er	pic'-ture
recognize	rek'-a-nize	rek'-ig-nize
relevant	rev'-e-lant	rel'-e-vant
theater	thee-ay'-ter	thee'-a-ter
truth	truf	truth
with	wit or wid	with

cause you to speak more quickly than normal, monitor your speaking rate and intentionally slow it down if necessary. This is particularly important when delivering your speeches online, especially if you are doing so using software that doesn't allow listeners to see you as you speak. Many online speeches fail the intelligibility test as a result of the rate at which they are delivered.

Articulation, pronunciation, and accent also affect intelligibility. **Articulation** is using the tongue, palate, teeth, jaw movement, and lips to shape vocalized sounds that combine to produce a word. Many of us suffer from minor articulation and **pronunciation** problems, such as adding a sound where none appears ("ath-a-lete" for *athlete)*, leaving out a sound where one occurs ("ly-ber-y" for *library)*, transposing sounds ("revalent" for *relevant)*, and distorting sounds ("truf" for *truth)*. Exhibit 11.1 lists some words that people commonly mispronounce or misarticulate.

Accent comprises the inflection, tone, and speech habits typical of native speakers of a language. When you misarticulate or speak with a heavy accent during a conversation, your listeners can ask you to repeat yourself until they understand you. But in a face-to-face speech setting, audience members are unlikely to interrupt to ask you to repeat something. And when posting a recording of your speech online, audience members do not even have the option to do so.

Accent can be a major concern for nonnative speakers of a language, as well as for speakers from various regions of a country (Photo 11.2). Natives of a particular city or region in the United States may speak with inflections and tones that they believe are "normal" spoken English—for instance, people from the Northeast who drop the *r* sound (saying "cah" for car), people from the South who elongate their vowels and "drawl," or people from the upper Midwest who elongate certain vowels (e.g., "Min-ne-sooo'-ta"). When these individuals visit a different city or region, they are perceived as having an accent. If your accent is "thick" or very different from that of most of your audience, practice pronouncing key words so that you are easily understood; speak slowly to allow your audience members more time to process your message; and consider using visual

articulation: using the tongue, palate, teeth, jaw movement, and lips to shape vocalized sounds

pronunciation: form and accent of various syllables of a word

accent: inflection, tone, and speech habits typical of native speakers of a language

Photo 11.2 When speaking to people with an accent different from yours, adjust by speaking more slowly, articulating clearly, and using visual aids to reinforce key terms and points. How do you adjust when listening to someone with an accent different from yours?

vocal expression: variety created in the voice through changing pitch, volume, and rate, as well as stressing certain words and using pauses

monotone: a voice in which the pitch, volume, and rate remain constant

aids to reinforce key terms, concepts, and important points. Alyssa from our opening scenario grew up in Arkansas before moving to Lexington to attend the University of Kentucky. Although her accent was similar to most of her classmates, she decided to ask Katie to listen to her speech and point out any words she might want to articulate differently or reinforce on her PowerPoint slides.

Vocal Expression

Vocal expression is achieved by changing pitch, volume, and rate; stressing certain words; and using pauses strategically. Doing so clarifies the emotional intent of your message and helps animate your delivery. Generally, speeding up your rate, raising your pitch, or increasing your volume reinforces emotions such as joy, enthusiasm, excitement, anticipation, and a sense of urgency or fear. Slowing down your rate, lowering your pitch, or decreasing your volume can communicate resolution, peacefulness, remorse, disgust, or sadness. Stressing certain words by saying them with more "punch" and placing strategic pauses before and/or after them can help important ideas stand out.

A total lack of vocal expression produces a **monotone**—a voice in which the pitch, volume, and rate remain constant, with no word, idea, or sentence differing significantly in sound from any other. Although few people speak in a true monotone, many severely limit themselves by using a relatively unchanging volume and rate. An actual or near monotone not only lulls an audience to sleep but, more important, diminishes the chances of audience understanding. For instance, if the sentence "Congress should pass laws limiting the sale of pornography" is presented in a monotone, listeners will be uncertain whether the speaker is concerned with *who* should take action, *what* Congress *should do*, or *what* the laws should be.

Creating vocally expressive messages is a complex process. For example, Nick introduced his speech on legalizing marijuana as a painkiller this way:

Millions of Americans suffer needlessly each year. These people endure unbearable pain because, although our government is capable of helping them, it chooses to ignore their pain. Our government has no compassion, no empathy, no regard for human feeling. I'm here today to convince you to support my efforts toward legalizing marijuana as a painkiller for terminally ill patients.

To reinforce the emotional elements of anger, disgust, and seriousness, Nick gradually slowed his rate, decreased his volume, and lowered his pitch as he emphasized, "Our government has no compassion, no empathy, no regard for human feeling."

He also used **stress**, an emphasis placed on certain words by speaking them more loudly than the rest of the sentence, to shape his meaning. Read the following sentence from Nick's speech:

Millions of Americans suffer needlessly each year.

What did Nick intend the focus of that sentence to be? Without hearing it spoken, it is difficult to say because its focus would change depending on which word Nick chose to stress. Read the sentence aloud several times. Each time, stress a different word, and listen to how your stress changes the meaning. If you stress *millions*, the emphasis is on the number of people affected. When you stress *Americans*, the fact that the problem is on a national scale is emphasized. When you stress *suffer*, notice how much more you feel the pain. When you stress *needlessly*, you can sense Nick's frustration with how unnecessary the suffering is. And when you stress *each year*, the ongoing nature of the unnecessary suffering becomes the focus. Thus, the words you stress in a sentence affect meaning.

Pauses, moments of silence strategically placed to enhance meaning, can also mark important ideas. If you use one or more sentences in your speech to express an important idea, pause before each sentence to signal that something important is coming up, or pause afterward to allow the ideas to sink in. Pausing one or more times within a sentence can add further impact. Nick included several short pauses within and a long pause after his line, "Our government has no compassion (*pause*), no empathy (*pause*), no regard for human feeling" (*longer pause*).

Use of Body

Because your audience can see as well as hear you, how you use your body also contributes to how conversational and animated you are. Body language elements that affect delivery are appearance, posture, poise, eye contact, facial expression, gesture, and movement.

Appearance

Some speakers think that what they wear doesn't influence the success of their speech. But your **appearance**—the way you look to others—does matter. Studies show that a neatly groomed and professional appearance sends important messages about a speaker's commitment to the topic and occasion, as well as the speaker's credibility (ethos).[3] Your appearance should complement your message, not detract from it. Three guidelines can help you decide how to dress for your speech.

1. **Consider your audience and the occasion.** Dress a bit more formally than you expect members of your audience to dress. If you dress too formally, your audience is likely to perceive you as untrustworthy and insincere[4]; if you dress too casually, the audience may view you as uncommitted to your topic or disrespectful of them or the occasion.[5]

2. **Consider your topic and purpose.** In general, the more serious your topic, the more formally you should dress. For example, if your topic is AIDS and you are trying to persuade your audience to be tested for HIV, you will want to look like someone who is an authority by dressing the part. But if your topic is

stress: emphasis placed on certain words by speaking them more loudly than the rest of the sentence

pauses: moments of silence strategically placed to enhance meaning

appearance: the way you look to others

skateboarding and you are trying to convince your audience they would enjoy taking a class at the new campus recreation center, you might dress more casually or even in sportswear.

3. **Avoid extremes.** Your attire shouldn't detract from your speech. Avoid gaudy jewelry, over- or undersized clothing, or sexually suggestive attire. Remember, you want your audience to focus on your message, so your appearance should be neutral, not distracting.

Alyssa would be delivering her speech to an audience of about 15 students sitting in the classroom and another 10–15 students watching online. Because most would probably be wearing anything from pajamas or sweatpants to jeans and t-shirts, she decided to dress a bit more formally in khaki pants and a navy blouse.

Posture

Posture is how you position your body. When giving a speech in a face-to-face setting, an upright stance and squared shoulders communicate a sense of confidence. When giving an speech online from a seated position, be sure to sit up straight in your chair with squared shoulders as well. Speakers who slouch may be perceived as lacking self-confidence and not caring about the topic, audience, and occasion. When delivering your speech from a seated position, whether in a face-to-face setting or via a digital recording, be sure to sit up straight with your feet firmly planted on the ground.

Poise

Poise is a graceful and controlled use of the body that gives the impression that you are self-assured, calm, and dignified. Mannerisms that convey nervousness (swaying from side to side, drumming fingers on the lectern, taking off or putting on glasses, jiggling pocket change, smacking the tongue, scratching the nose, hand, or arm, etc.) distract listeners from your message and should be avoided when giving your speech.

Eye Contact

In face-to-face settings, **eye contact** involves looking at people in all parts of the room throughout the speech. As long as you are looking at someone (those in front of you, in the left rear of the room, in the right center of the room, etc.) and not at your notes or the ceiling, floor, or window, everyone in the audience will perceive you as having good eye contact with them. Generally, you should look at your audience at least 90 percent of the time, glancing at your notes only when you need a quick reference point. When being recorded or streamed online while speaking to a face-to-face audience, treat the camera like another audience member. When recording your speech at your computer, also be sure to treat the camera like your audience. Maintaining eye contact is important for several reasons:

1. **Maintaining eye contact helps audiences concentrate on the speech.** If you do not look at audience members while you talk, they are unlikely to maintain eye contact with you. This break in mutual eye contact often decreases concentration on the message.

2. **Maintaining eye contact bolsters ethos.** In the dominant culture of the United States, eye contact is perceived as a sign of sincerity. Speakers who fail to maintain eye contact with audiences are almost always perceived as ill at ease and often as insincere or dishonest.[6] In some cultures across the world and in some co-cultures within the United States, however, direct eye contact may be perceived as disrespectful. Many Native American nations, such as the Hopi, Cherokee, Navajo, and Sioux, believe indirect eye contact demonstrates humility and respect.[7] Knowing your audience becomes extremely important as you determine what kind of eye contact is most appropriate.

---

posture: position of the body

poise: graceful and controlled use of the body that gives the impression of self-assurance

eye contact: looking at the people to whom you are speaking

SPEECH SNIPPET

As a member of the Cherokee nation, Desiree was raised to avoid direct eye contact as a sign of humility and respect. When speaking to her audience made up of people raised in the dominant American culture, however, she made a special effort to make direct eye contact with them throughout her speech.

3. **Maintaining eye contact helps you gauge audience reaction to your ideas.** Because communication is two-way, public speech audience members in face-to-face settings communicate nonverbally with you while you are speaking. Bored audience members may yawn, look out the window, slouch in their chairs, and even sleep. Confused audience members may look puzzled by furrowing their brows or shaking their heads. Audience members who understand or agree with something may smile or nod their heads. By monitoring your audience's behavior, you can adjust by becoming more animated, offering additional examples, or moving more quickly through a point (Photo 11.3). Unfortunately, we often lose the opportunity to do so when streaming our speeches online or recording them to be posted online later.

Photo 11.3 Maintaining eye contact helps keep your audience engaged as you speak. How can you best do that when delivering your speech online?

When speaking to large (100 or more people) face-to-face audiences, you must create a *sense* of looking all listeners in the eye even though you actually cannot. This process is called **audience contact**. You can create audience contact by mentally dividing your audience into small groups scattered around the room. Then, at random, talk for 4 to 6 seconds with each group. Perhaps start with a Z pattern. Talk with the group in the back left for a few seconds, then glance at people in the far right for a few seconds, and then move to a group in the middle, a group in the front left, a group in the front right, and so forth. Then perhaps reverse the order, starting in the back right. Eventually, you will find yourself using a random pattern to look at all groups over a period of a few minutes. Such a pattern also helps you avoid spending a disproportionate amount of time talking with those in one part of the room.

Facial Expressions

Facial expressions are the eye and mouth movements that convey emotions. When you talk with friends, your facial expressions are naturally animated. Audiences expect your expressions to be similarly animated when giving a speech. Effective facial expressions convey **nonverbal immediacy** by communicating that you are personable and likeable. Audiences respond positively to natural facial expressions that appear to spontaneously reflect what you're saying and how you feel about it. To assess whether you are using effective facial expressions, practice delivering your speech to yourself in front of a mirror or record your rehearsal and evaluate your facial expressions as you watch it (Photo 11.4).

Gestures

Gestures are the movements of your hands, arms, and fingers. Effective gestures emphasize important points and ideas, refer to presentational aids, or clarify structure. For example, as Aaron began to speak about the advantages of smartphone apps, he said, "on one hand" and lifted his right hand face up. When he got to the disadvantages, he lifted his left hand face up as he said, "on the other hand." Some of the most common gestures used by speakers are shown in Exhibit 11.2.

audience contact: creating a sense of looking listeners in the eye when speaking to large audiences

facial expressions: eye and mouth movements that convey emotions

nonverbal immediacy: a perception of being personable and likeable

gestures: movements of hands, arms, and fingers

Photo 11.4 Effective speakers make time to rehearse their speeches several times out loud in advance. How can practicing your speech in front of a mirror help improve your delivery?

Exhibit 11.2 **Commonly Used Hand Gestures**

- The horizontal hand with palm upward to express good humor, frankness, and generalization.

- The vertical hand with palm outward to indicate warding off, pushing from, or a disagreeable thought.

- The clenched hand to reinforce anger or defiance or to emphasize an important point.

- The horizontal hand with palm downward to show superposition or the resting of one thing upon another.

- The index finger to signify or reinforce the first in a sequence of events.

As with facial expressions, effective gestures must appear spontaneous and natural even though they are carefully planned and practiced (Photo 11.5). When you practice and then deliver your speech, leave your hands free so that they will be available to gesture as you normally do.

Movement

Movement refers to changing your body position. During your speech, engage only in **motivated movement**, that is, movement with a specific purpose such as emphasizing an important idea, referencing a presentational aid, or clarifying macrostructure. In face-to-face settings, for example, you might take a few steps to one side of the stage or the other each time you begin a new main point. Or, to emphasize a particular point, you might move closer to your audience. To create a feeling of intimacy before you tell a personal story, you might walk out from behind a lectern and sit down on a chair placed at the edge of the stage. To use motivated movement effectively, practice when and how you will move until you can do so in a way that appears spontaneous and natural while remaining "open" to the audience (not turning your back to them).

Avoid unmotivated movement such as bobbing, weaving, shifting from foot to foot, or pacing from one side of the room to the other, as unplanned movements distract the audience from your message. Because many unplanned movements result from nervousness, you can minimize them by paying mindful attention to your body as you speak. At the beginning of your speech, consciously stand up straight on both feet. Whenever you find yourself fidgeting, readjust and position your body with your weight equally distributed over both feet.

During speech practice sessions, try various methods to monitor or alter your body's action. Video recording provides an excellent means of monitoring your use of your body to determine whether it is enhancing your message or distracting from it. You may also want to practice in front of a mirror to see how you look to others when you speak. Another good method is to get a willing listener to critique your use of body and help you improve. Once you have identified the behavior you want to change, tell your helper what to look for. For instance, you might say, "Raise your hand every time I begin to rock back and forth." By getting specific feedback when the behavior occurs, you can make immediate adjustments.

Photo 11.5 Appropriate facial expressions and gestures animate a speaker's delivery. Why is it important to practice them in advance?

movement: changing the position or location of the entire body

motivated movement: movement with a specific purpose

DELIVERY METHODS

In this section, we explain three common delivery methods: impromptu, scripted, and extemporaneous. Let's look briefly at each one.

Impromptu Speeches

An **impromptu speech** is one that is delivered with only seconds or minutes of advance notice. It is usually presented without referring to notes of any kind. You may have already given an impromptu speech in class, so you know the kind of pressures and problems this type of speaking creates.

Because impromptu speakers must quickly gather their thoughts just before and while they speak, carefully organizing and developing ideas can be challenging. As a result, impromptu speakers may leave out important information or confuse audience members. Delivery can suffer as speakers use "ah," "um," "like," and "you know" to buy time as they scramble to collect their thoughts. That's why the more opportunities you have to use the impromptu method, the better you'll become at doing so.

impromptu speech: a speech delivered with only seconds or minutes of advance notice for preparation

Frank's efforts to stop the city from replacing a four-way stop sign with a traffic light on the street corner where he lived quickly became front-page news. As he left the city council meeting, a local TV reporter stopped him to ask him about the issue. He quickly organized his thoughts, identifying his primary reason for fighting the battle and the three reasons erecting the traffic light was not in the best interests of the community.

Some of the most common situations that require using the impromptu method are during employment and performance review interviews, at business meetings, in class, at social ceremonies, and with the media. In each situation, having practiced organizing ideas quickly and conveying them intelligibly and expressively will bolster your ethos and help you succeed.

You can improve your impromptu performances by practicing "mock" impromptu speeches. For example, if you are taking a class where the professor often calls on students to answer questions, you can prepare by anticipating the questions that might be asked and by practicing giving your answers out loud. Over time, you will become more adept at quickly organizing your ideas and "thinking on your feet."

Scripted Speeches

At the other extreme, a **scripted speech** is one that is prepared by creating a complete written manuscript and delivered by reading from or memorizing it. Obviously, effective scripted speeches take a great deal of time because both an outline and a word-for-word transcript must be prepared, practiced, and then delivered in a way that still sounds both conversational and animated. When you read a scripted speech from a manuscript or teleprompter, you must also become adept at looking at the script with your peripheral vision so that you don't appear to be reading. Although politicians, talk show hosts, and television news anchors are usually good at achieving conversational style while reading from printed manuscripts and teleprompters, most speakers end up sounding like they are reading and find it difficult to sound spontaneous, conversational, and animated (Photo 11.6).

Because of the time and skill required to effectively prepare and deliver a scripted speech, it is usually reserved for significant occasions that have important consequences. Political speeches, keynote addresses, commencement addresses, and CEO remarks at annual stockholder meetings are examples of occasions when a scripted speech might be appropriate and worth the extra effort.

Extemporaneous Speeches

Most speeches, whether in the workplace, in the community, or in class, are delivered extemporaneously. An **extemporaneous speech** is researched and planned ahead of time, but the exact wording is not scripted and will vary somewhat from presentation to presentation. When speaking extemporaneously, you refer to speaking notes as you speak to remind you of key ideas, structure, and delivery cues. Some speakers use their computerized slideshows as speaking notes. If you choose to do so, however, be careful not to include too many words on any given slide, which will ultimately distract listeners from focusing on you as you speak.

REHEARSALS

Effective speakers practice their formal speeches aloud several times before they actually deliver them. In doing so, they are able to revise their use

Peter Kramer/NBCU/Photo Bank/Getty Images

Photo 11.6 News anchors read scripted speeches from a teleprompter but still sound conversational and animated. What can you do to ensure you sound conversational and animated?

Exhibit 11.3 Timetable for Preparing a Speech

7 days before	Select topic; begin research
6 days before	Continue research
5 days before	Outline body of speech
4 days before	Work on introduction and conclusion
3 days before	Finish outline; find additional material if needed; have all presentational aids completed
2 days before	First rehearsal session
1 day before	Second rehearsal session
Due date	Give speech

of voice and body until they are both conversational and animated, and appear to be both spontaneous and professional. **Rehearsing** is the iterative process of practicing your speech aloud. A speech that is not practiced aloud is likely to be far less effective than it would have been had you given yourself sufficient time to revise, evaluate, and mull over all aspects of the speech.[10] Exhibit 11.3 provides a useful timetable for preparing and practicing a classroom speech. In the sections that follow, we describe how to rehearse effectively by preparing speaking notes, handling presentational aids, and engaging in structured practice rounds (practicing aloud, analyzing and adjusting, and practicing aloud again).

Speaking Notes

Prior to your first rehearsal session, prepare a draft of your speaking notes. **Speaking notes** are basically a key-word outline of your speech, and include hard-to-remember information and delivery cues. The best notes contain the fewest words possible written in lettering large enough to be seen instantly at a distance.

To develop your notes, begin by reducing your speech outline to an abbreviated outline of key words and phrases. Then, if there are details you must cite exactly—such

scripted speech: a speech prepared by creating a complete written manuscript and delivered by reading from or memorizing it

extemporaneous speech: a speech researched and planned ahead of time, although the exact wording is not scripted

rehearsing: iterative process of practicing the speech aloud

speaking notes: a key-word outline of the speech, plus hard-to-remember information and delivery cues

---

PUBLIC SPEAKING IN THE REAL WORLD

Anne Hathaway on the Importance of Practicing Your Speech

Sydney Alford/Alamy Stock Photo

In 2013, Anne Hathaway won an Oscar for her best-supporting actress role in *Les Misérables*. If you've ever watched the Academy Awards you know that some actors don't practice their acceptance speeches at all, but Hathaway rehearsed *a lot*. Why? One reason was that her feelings had been hurt by the waves of criticism she received a few weeks earlier after she delivered her acceptance speech at the Golden Globe awards. More importantly, she learned from her experience at the Golden Globes that she needed to practice her Oscar acceptance speech "many, many times."[8] In addition to thanking the academy in her "It Came True!" speech, her goal was to be perceived as "more likeable."[9] Because

appearing personable through delivery is one characteristic of effective public speakers, it appears Hathaway understands the truth in the adage: Practice makes perfect!

1. Do you think award nominees should rehearse their acceptance speeches in advance or wing it spontaneously if they should wind up winning? Why?

2. Would your answer change if the award is less public than the Academy Awards or Golden Globes? Why?

Reflect on Ethics

During her speech at the First National Tea Party Convention, former Alaska Governor Sarah Palin exclaimed that the Tea Party movement is "bigger than any charismatic guy with a teleprompter." She was referring to President Barack Obama, who often uses a teleprompter to deliver scripted speeches. Later, it was revealed in visual recordings of her speech and the question-and-answer session she participated in that she had relied on a "cheat sheet" of notes written on her hand. CNN political editor Mark Preston (among others) criticized Palin as a hypocrite:

> Look, the fact that she wrote on her hand isn't really that big of a deal. We all work

off of notes, certainly in television. But the fact that she was critical of President Obama and called him "that charismatic guy with the teleprompter"—and as you just saw, I looked down at my notes to give that direct quote. It's very hard to be critical of one person when you yourself are using the same kind of aids when you're speaking.[11]

1. Do you agree with Preston's assessment of Palin's use of notes? Explain.

2. Can you think of situations where the delivery method chosen for a speech might raise ethical questions or violate ethical principles? Explain.

as a specific example, quotation, or set of statistics—add these in the appropriate places. You might also use separate "Quotation Cards" for direct quotations. Next, indicate exactly where you plan to share presentational aids. Finally, incorporate delivery cues indicating where you want to make use of your voice and body to enhance intelligibility or expressiveness. For example, indicate where you want to pause, gesture, or make a motivated movement. Capitalize or underline words you want to stress. Use double slash marks (//) to remind yourself to pause. Use an upward-pointing arrow (↑) to remind yourself to increase rate or volume.

As a general rule, you will need one card for your introduction, one for each main point, and one for your conclusion. If your speech contains a particularly important and long quotation or a complicated set of statistics, you can record this information in detail on a separate card. Use your notes during practice sessions just as you will when you actually give the speech. If you will use a lectern, set the notes on the speaker's stand or hold them in one hand and refer to them only when needed. When you use a computerized slideshow, you can also use the "notes" feature for your speaking notes. At the end of this chapter, you can see Alyssa's sample note cards for her presentation.

Presentational Aids

Some speakers think that once they have prepared good presentational aids, they will have no trouble using them in their speech. However, many speeches with good aids have become a shambles because the aids were not well handled. You can avoid problems by following these guidelines.

1. **Carefully plan when to use the presentational aids.** Indicate in your speaking notes exactly when you will reveal and conceal each presentational aid. Practice using your aids until you can do so comfortably and smoothly.

2. **Consider the audience's needs carefully.** As you practice, eliminate any presentational aid that does not contribute directly to the audience's attention to, understanding of, or retention of the key ideas in your speech.

3. **Position presentational aids and equipment before beginning your speech.** Make sure your aids and equipment are where you want them and that everything is ready and in working order. Test electronic equipment to make sure everything from visual displays to sound to hyperlinks work and are cued correctly.

4. **Share a presentational aid only when talking about it.** Presentational aids draw audience attention, so practice sharing them only when you are talking about them and then concealing them when they are no longer the focus of attention. Because a single presentational aid may contain several bits of information, practice only exposing the portion you are currently discussing. On computerized slideshows, you can do so by using the "custom animation" feature to allow only one item to appear at a time, by striking the "B" key for a black screen when you aren't directly referencing the aid, or by inserting blank slides where your ideas are not being supplemented by something on the slideshow.

5. **Display presentational aids so that everyone in the audience can see and hear them.** It's frustrating not to be able to see or hear an aid. If possible, practice in the space where you will give your speech so you can adjust equipment accordingly. If you cannot practice in the space ahead of time, then arrive early enough on the day of the presentation to practice quickly with the equipment you will use.

6. **Reference the presentational aid during the speech.** Because you already know what you want your audience to see in a visual aid, tell your audience what to look for, explain the various elements in it, and interpret figures, symbols, and percentages. For an audio or audiovisual aid, point out what you want your audience to listen for before playing the excerpt. When showing a visual or audiovisual aid, use the "turn-touch-talk" technique.

   - When you display the visual, walk to the screen—that's where everyone will look anyway. Slightly turn to the visual and touch it—that is, point to it with an arm gesture or a pointer. Then, with your back to the screen and your body still facing the audience at a slight 45-degree angle, talk to your audience about it.

   - When you finish making your comments about the visual, return to the lectern or your speaking position and conceal the aid.

7. **Talk to your audience, not to the presentational aid.** Although you want to acknowledge the presentational aid by looking at it occasionally, it is important to maintain eye contact with your audience as much as possible. As you practice, resist the urge to stare at or read from your presentational aid.

8. **Resist the temptation to pass objects among audience members.** People look at, read, handle, and think about whatever they hold in their hands. While they are so occupied, they are not likely to be listening to you. If you are using handouts or objects as presentational aids, distribute them after the speech rather than during it.

Practice Rounds

As with any other activity, effective speech delivery requires practice. Each practice round should consist of (a) practicing aloud, (b) analyzing and making adjustments, and (c) practicing aloud again. The more you practice, the better your speech will be. During each practice round, evaluate your language choices as well as your use of voice, body, and presentational aids. Do as many practice rounds as needed to deliver a speech that is conversational and animated. Let's look at how you can proceed through several practice rounds.

Practice Aloud

1. Record (audio and video) your practice session so you can analyze it and make improvements. You may also want to have a friend sit in on your practice and offer suggestions afterward.

2. Read through your complete formal outline once or twice to refresh your memory. Then, put the outline out of sight and practice using your speaking notes.

3. Make the practice as similar to the speech situation as possible, including using the presentational aids you've prepared. Stand up and face your imaginary audience. Pretend the chairs, lamps, books, and other objects in the room are people.

4. Start the timer on your phone, computer, or stopwatch.

5. Begin speaking. Regardless of what happens, keep going until you have presented your entire speech. If you goof, make a repair and keep going as if you were actually delivering the speech to an audience.

6. Stop the timer and compute the length. If your speech went longer than the allotted speaking time, revise by eliminating some depth or breadth in the body of the speech. If it was too short, add some depth or breadth.

Analyze and Make Adjustments

Watch and listen to your recorded performance while reviewing your complete formal outline. How did it go? Did you leave out any key ideas? Did you talk too long on any one point and not long enough on another? Did you clarify each of your points? Did you adapt to your anticipated audience? Were your notes effective? How well did you do with your presentational aids? If friends sat in, ask for their input as well. Make any necessary changes before your second practice.

Practice Aloud Again

Repeat the six steps listed for the first aloud practice. By practicing a second time right after your analysis, you are more likely to make the kind of adjustments that begin to improve the speech.

Additional Practice Rounds

After you have completed one full practice round, put your speech away for a while. Although you will practice the speech a few more times, you will not benefit from cramming all the practices into one long rehearsal session. You may find that a final practice right before you go to bed will be very helpful; while you are sleeping, your subconscious will continue to work on the speech. As a result, you are likely to notice significant improvement in delivery when you practice again the next day.

ADAPTING WHILE DELIVERING YOUR SPEECH

Even when you've practiced your speech to the point that you know it inside and out, you must be prepared to adapt to your audience and possibly change course a bit as you give your speech. Remember that your primary goal is to generate shared understanding, so pay attention to the audience's feedback as you speak and adjust accordingly. Here are six tips to guide you.

1. **Be aware of and respond to audience feedback.** As you make eye contact with members of your audience, notice how they react to what you say. For instance, if you see quizzical looks on the faces of several listeners, you may need to explain a particular point in a different way. On the other hand, if you

⑥ SPEECH PLANNING

Activity

Rehearsing Your Speech

1. After you have prepared your speaking notes, find a place where you can be alone (or with a friend) to practice and record your speech. Follow the six points of the first practice.

2. Watch and listen to the recording. Review your outline as you do so and then complete a speech evaluation checklist to see how well you delivered your speech. (You can find the Speech Evaluation Checklist: General Criteria on page 16 in Chapter 1, a more detailed checklist in this chapter, and checklists for informative and persuasive speeches in later chapters.)

   List three specific changes you will make in your next practice.

   One: _____

   Two: _____

   Three: _____

3. Go through the six practice steps again. Then assess: Did you achieve the goals you set for the second practice?

Reevaluate the speech using the checklist and do additional practice rounds until you are satisfied with your presentation.

see listeners nodding impatiently, you don't need to belabor your point and can move on. If many audience members look bored, try to rekindle their interest by conveying more emotional expression in your voice and body.

2. **Be prepared to use alternative developmental material.** Your ability to adjust depends on how much additional alternative information you have to share. If you prepared only one example to make a particular point, you won't be ready if your audience is confused and needs another. If you have prepared only one definition for a term, you may be unable to rephrase it if needed.

3. **Correct yourself when you misspeak.** Every speaker makes mistakes. We stumble over words, mispronounce terms, forget information, and mishandle presentational aids. Doing so is normal. If you stumble over a phrase or mispronounce a word, correct yourself and move on. Don't make a big deal of it by laughing, rolling your eyes, or in other ways drawing unnecessary attention to it. If you suddenly remember that you forgot to provide some information, consider how important it is for your audience to have that information. If what you forgot to say will make it difficult to understand an upcoming point, figure out how and when to provide the information later in your speech. Usually, however, information we forget to share is not critical to the audience's understanding and it is better to leave it out and move on.

4. **Adapt to unexpected events.** Maintain your composure if something unexpected happens, such as a cell phone ringing or someone entering the room

while you're speaking. Simply pause until the disruption ceases and then move on. If the disruption causes you to lose your train of thought, take a deep breath, look at your speaking notes, and resume speaking slightly before the point at which the interruption occurred. This will allow both you and your audience to refocus on your speech. You might even acknowledge that you are backtracking by saying something like, "Let's back up a bit and remember where we were."

5. **Adapt to unexpected audience reactions.** Sometimes, you'll encounter listeners who disagree strongly with your message. They might show their disagreement by being inattentive, heckling you, or rolling their eyes when you try to make eye contact with them. If these behaviors are limited to one or two members of your audience, ignore them and focus on the rest of your listeners. If, however, you find that a majority of your audience is hostile to what you are saying, you might acknowledge their feedback and then ask them to suspend their judgment while they listen. For example, you could say something like, "I can see that many of you don't agree with my first point. But let me ask you to put aside your initial reaction and think along with me on this next point. Even if we end up disagreeing, at least you will understand my position."

6. **Handle questions respectfully.** It is rare for audience members to interrupt speakers with questions during a speech. But if you are interrupted, be prepared to respond respectfully. If the question is directly related to understanding the point you are making, answer it immediately. If not, acknowledge the question and indicate that you will answer it later during the question-and-answer period.

question-and-answer period: brief time after a speech designated for addressing audience questions and comments

During the **question-and-answer period**, be honest about what you know and don't know. If an audience member asks a question you don't know the answer to, admit it by saying something like, "That's an excellent question. I'm not sure of the answer, but I would be happy to follow up on it later if you're interested." Then move on to the next question. If someone asks you to state an opinion about a matter you haven't thought much about, it's okay to say, "You know, I don't think I have given that enough thought to have a valid opinion."

Be sure to monitor how much time you have to answer questions. When the time is nearly up, mention that you'll entertain one more question so as to warn listeners that the question-and-answer period is almost over. You might also suggest that you'll be happy to talk more with individuals one on one later—this provides your more reserved listeners an opportunity to follow up with you.

ADAPTING YOUR SPEECH FOR VIRTUAL AUDIENCES

When Plato, Aristotle, and Cicero engaged in public speaking thousands of years ago, the communication event occurred in real time with both the speaker and the audience physically present. Thanks to technology, however, public speeches today may be delivered in both face-to-face and virtual environments. In the opening scenario, for example, Alyssa and Katie would be delivering their speeches in a classroom with some audience members present while simultaneously streaming to several classmates who would be watching online. Their speeches would also be uploaded to the class website so they could watch, critique, and prepare reflective written assessments of themselves later.

Internet accessibility makes it possible to speak publicly to multiple audiences across the country and around the world. For example, Alyssa planned to post her speech to YouTube and link to it from her Facebook and Twitter accounts for extra credit. In doing so, she hoped to reach many more people than just those sitting in the classroom. The bottom line is this. Although public speaking certainly still occurs in traditional face-to-face settings, it is no longer limited by place and time—far from it!

President Franklin Delano Roosevelt (FDR) is credited as one of the first public figures to capitalize on the benefits of electronic media to break through the *place* limitation and reach a wider audience. Throughout his presidency in the 1930s and 1940s, FDR delivered *fireside chats*, weekly radio addresses about issues facing the country.[12] These speeches could be heard by anyone who chose to tune in. American presidents have been offering weekly addresses ever since. As president, Barak Obama posted weekly addresses on YouTube and the White House website.[13]

Perhaps one of the most significant examples of technology overcoming the limitation of *time* comes from Martin Luther King, Jr. Over 200,000 people were at the political rally in Washington, DC, on August 28, 1963, to hear his famous "I Have a Dream" speech in person. More than 50 years later, we can join the 200,000 who made up that first audience to hear King delivery his powerful oration by clicking on any number of websites where it is archived. In fact, a quick *Google* search of it yields more than two million hits.

To reach multiple audiences successfully, we must consider not just those who are informed about the topic, but also those who may not be informed, may be apathetic, and may even be hostile toward it. Those who have analyzed King's speech, for instance, claim he was successful in part because he used a black preacher style while also transcending it to reach broader audiences. To clarify, he began by addressing the grievances of black Americans and then transitioned to focus more broadly on the bedrock of American values. Linking civil rights to the American dream appealed not only to the audience present on the Washington Mall, but also to the millions of uncommitted American who watched the speech on TV.[14] In doing so, his speech transcended time. Today, it continues to resonate as representing core American values and the American dream.

With the proliferation of Internet accessibility comes both additional opportunities and challenges. For example, because speeches today may be easily uploaded to websites like YouTube with or without our permission and then quickly go viral, we also must always be cognizant of possible audiences we never intended to target.

Obviously, we ought to consider how to adapt our delivery for virtual audiences. Although we are only beginning to discover the ways in which to do so, here are a few guidelines to consider:

1. **Adapt your speech to address multiple audiences.** Assume that any speech you give may be recorded and made available to those who are not in your immediate audience. Always consider how your delivery (as well as content and structure) will respectfully address uninformed, apathetic, and oppositional audiences who may view your speech virtually.

2. **Choose presentational aids carefully.** Make sure the visuals and audiovisuals you use can be easily viewed and heard in an online format. Also, be sure to explain them so those who only have audio access or who view them on a small smartphone screen can understand the information on them.

3. **Become proficient with technology in advance.** Technological proficiency is no longer considered a value-added skill. Make it a regular practice to learn how to use the most up-to-date programs and equipment proficiently.

4. **Employ the fundamentals of effective public speaking.** Although it might seem to go without saying, always adhere to the strategies of effective public speaking even when delivering your speech online. The steps regarding topic selection and development, organization, language, and delivery remain fundamental to effective speechmaking for both face-to-face and virtual audiences.

5. **Treat the camera as a person.** As you do so, use your voice and body in ways that are intelligible, conversational, animated, and poised, just as you would if the camera were someone in the room with you.

Speech Assignment & Checklist

Informative Speech with Presentational Aids

Based on the specific assignment of your instructor, prepare a 4- to 6-minute speech by completing the Speech-Planning Action Step activities. You can see an example of Alyssa's outline and speech in the sample speech at the end of this chapter.

Speech Evaluation Checklist

General Criteria

You can use this checklist to critique an informative speech that you hear in class. (You can also use it to critique your own speech.) As you listen to the speaker, consider what makes a speech effective. Then, answer the following questions

Check items that were accomplished effectively.

Content

_____ 1. Was the goal of the speech clear?

_____ 2. Were two to three pieces of evidence provided for each main point (breadth)?

_____ 3. Were some pieces of evidence elaborated on for each main point (depth)?

_____ 4. Were high-quality information and sources used?

_____ 5. Were a variety of kinds of developmental material employed?

_____ 6. Were presentational aids appropriate?

_____ 7. Was common ground established and the content adapted to the audience with listener relevance links?

Macrostructure

1. Did the introduction catch the audience's interest? _____ establish credibility and listener relevance? _____ identify the speech topic/goal?_____ preview the main points?_____

2. Were the main points clear? _____ parallel?_____ in meaningful complete sentences?_____

3. Did section transitions lead smoothly from one point to another? _____

4. Did the conclusion tie the speech together by summarizing the main goal and points?_____ offering a clincher?_____

Microstructure

1. Did the speaker use words (*microstructure*) that were appropriate and inclusive? _____ accurate and clear? _____ vivid and expressive?_____

Speech Assignment & Checklist (continued)

Delivery

_____ 1. Did the speaker appear and sound conversational?

_____ 2. Did the speaker appear and sound animated?

_____ 3. Was the speaker intelligible?

_____ 4. Was the speaker vocally expressive?

_____ 5. Were the speaker's appearance and attire appropriate?

_____ 6. Did the speaker use effective eye/audience contact throughout the speech?

_____ 7. Did the speaker use appropriate facial expressions?

_____ 8. Did the speaker have good posture that communicated poise and confidence?

_____ 9. Were the speaker's gestures and movement appropriate?

_____ 10. Did the speaker conceal and reveal the presentational aids effectively?

_____ 11. Did the speaker reference the presentational aids effectively while discussing them?

Based on these criteria, evaluate the speech as (check one):

_____ excellent _____ good _____ satisfactory _____ fair _____ poor

Explain:

_____

_____

ALYSSA'S INFORMATIVE SPEECH WITH PRESENTATIONAL AIDS

College Student Volunteering and Civic Engagement

By Alyssa Grace Millner, University of Kentucky[15]

Formal Speech Outline

General goal: To inform my audience.

Specific goal: I want my audience to realize the benefits of volunteering in Lexington while we are still students at the University of Kentucky.

INTRODUCTION

Attention getter

Notice how Alyssa uses a famous quotation to get the attention of her audience in a way that also piques interest about the topic.

I. The famous Indian peace activist and spiritual leader Mahatma Gandhi is known for saying "We must become the change we seek in the world." That sounds at first like an awfully tall order, but today I'd like to show you how each of us can do just that and make a difference right here in Lexington, Kentucky.

Listener relevance

II. Think for a moment of a time in your life when you did something kind for someone else. Maybe you helped a child do homework, or a neighbor rake leaves, or even a stranger get groceries from the store to the car. Do you remember how that made you feel? Well, that feeling can be a normal part of your week when you choose to be a volunteer. And for college students like us, it's easy to get involved as volunteers in our local community.

Speaker credibility

Alyssa mentions that she volunteers, which bolsters ethos and establishes her credibility to speak on the topic.

III. Personally, I volunteer at the Lexington Rescue Mission and have reaped many benefits by doing so. (*Show Slide 1: picture of me volunteering at the Mission.*) I've also done extensive research on volunteering and civic engagement.

Thesis statement with main point preview

IV. So, let's spend the next few minutes discussing the benefits volunteering can have for us as college students by focusing on how volunteering helps us get acquainted with the local community, why civic engagement is the responsibility of every one of us, and what volunteering can do to teach us new skills and build our résumés.

Transition

Let's begin by explaining the ways volunteering can connect each of us to our local community.

BODY

I. Volunteering is a great way to become acquainted with a community beyond the university campus.

Listener relevance

A. Most college students move away from the comforts of home to a new and unfamiliar city. Not knowing what there is to do or even how to get around can be overwhelming and isolating. Volunteering is an easy way to quickly become familiar with and begin to feel a part of this new city in addition to the campus community.

B. Volunteering allows you to learn your way around town.

1. In an interview I had with Natalie Cunningham, the volunteer coordinator of the Lexington Rescue Mission, she said, "I've been working with students for several years now. While every group is different, one lingering trend is each group's unawareness of their city. It is easy for the students who live on campus to stay in their 'on-campus bubble.' Volunteering allows students to become acquainted with Lexington and the important issues facing their new home" (personal communication, January 2, 2013).

2. It seems like a silly thing, but knowing your way around town starts to make any city feel like home. Volunteering gets you out into the local area and helps you begin to get acquainted with new people and places.

C. Volunteering can also open your eyes to local social issues and conditions.

1. Many nonprofit organizations and volunteer-centered groups strive to raise awareness of important social issues by getting willing volunteers involved in the local community and issues impacting the area, things like hunger and homelessness (Norris Center, 2013).

2. The second time I showed up to volunteer at the Lexington Rescue Mission, I served food to the homeless. (*Show Slide 2: group of volunteers in the kitchen.*)

a. I served soup and hung out with other volunteers and local homeless people. One of the "veteran" volunteers explained to me that Lexington has approximately 3,000 homeless people. (*Show Slide 3: homelessness statistics in Lexington.*)

b. I was shocked to learn that we had such a large number of men, women, and children without a regular place to sleep. I wouldn't have known about this problem or the organizations working to end homelessness if I hadn't been a volunteer.

Not only is volunteering important because it helps us become familiar with a town and its social issues; frankly, as members of a democratic society, volunteering is our civic responsibility.

II. Giving back to the community through volunteer work is our civic responsibility and a privilege.

Each of us in this room—whether as US citizens or international students—are reaping the benefits of earning college degrees in this democratic society. With that benefit comes the responsibility and privilege of giving back.

A. Volunteering is our civic responsibility.

1. In an article published in 2012 in the *Academy of Management Review*, Grant explains that, without active participation in the local community, civil society becomes deprived.

2. I agree. Giving back by volunteering helps the community in so many ways. (*Show Slides 4 and 5: Volunteers sorting clothes at the mission and then volunteers playing cards with people served at the shelter.*)

Alyssa intersperses actual photos of her and others volunteering throughout the speech. Doing so enhances her verbal message but doesn't replace it. The photos also provide pathos, making her ideas more emotionally compelling.

Transition
Here and throughout the speech, notice how Alyssa uses effective section transitions to verbally tie the point she is wrapping up with an introduction of the point to come. This makes her speech flow smoothly so listeners can follow her train of thought and bolsters her ethos because she sounds prepared.

Listener relevance

B. Volunteering is also a privilege. Making a difference by volunteering ends up making us feel better about ourselves and our role in the world we live in.

    1. In fact, according to the Bureau of Labor Statistics, about 25 percent of the US population volunteered in 2015. What is troubling, however, is that only 18 percent of people aged 20 to 24 volunteered that year (*Show Slide 6: bar graph of demographic comparisons.*)

    2. This seems odd in light of the study of first-year college students done by the Higher Education Research Institute in 2009, which revealed that almost 70 percent of students believe it is *essential* or *very important* to volunteer in order to help people in need (Pryor et al., 2009).

Transition *Certainly, the privilege of giving back as volunteers is our civic responsibility and helps our local community, but we can also reap valuable résumé-building life skills by volunteering.*

III. Volunteering helps teach us new skills.

These new skills and talents can actually make us more marketable for better jobs once we graduate.

Listener relevance

Students want to know how to market themselves to get good jobs. So this main point will help maintain listener interest at a point when minds might tend to wander.

A. Being a consistent volunteer at a nonprofit organization while attending college can strengthen your résumé.

    1. Educational credentials are not enough to ensure college graduates are ready for the workforce. They also need credentials that document their experiences and employability skills. These experiences can be a pathway to getting a job (Spera, Ghertnew, Nerino, and DiTommaso, 2013).

    2. Laura Hatfield, director of the Center for Community Outreach at the University of Kentucky, points out that volunteers can include leadership, teamwork, and listening skills on their résumés because they can document the experiences where they had to use them effectively in the real world.

    3. Andrea Stockelman, another volunteer at the Lexington Rescue Mission, explained some of the new skills she picked up with volunteering. She said, "I learned that there was a lot more that went into preparing food for the homeless than I ever thought possible. It was neat to be a part of that process" (personal communication, April 28, 2010). (*Show Slide 7: photo of Andrea preparing food.*)

B. Volunteering at the Lexington Rescue Mission taught me new skills that bolstered my résumé. (*Show Slide 8: résumé with skills highlighted.*)

    1. I learned to coordinate the schedules of other volunteers.

    2. I also practiced important people skills such as teamwork, empathy, conflict management, and listening.

Thesis statement with main point summary

This very clear thesis restatement with main point summary signals a sense of closure.

CONCLUSION

I. Today we've discussed why volunteering is beneficial to college students by focusing on how volunteering can connect us quickly and easily to our local community, why it's both our responsibility and a privilege to do so, and how volunteering will benefit us after we graduate.

Clincher

Notice how Alyssa ties back to her opening quotation in her clincher. This provides a sense of wrapping up without saying thank you that helps listeners feel like the speech is complete in a memorable way.

II. So, I'm hoping the next time you recall a time you really enjoyed making a difference by helping someone, that memory won't come from the distant past. Instead, I hope you'll be thinking about how you are being the change you seek in the world by volunteering right here in Lexington right now.

REFERENCES

Corporation for National and Community Service. (2006). *College students helping America*. Washington, DC.

Grant, A. (2012). Giving time, time after time: Work design and sustained employee participation in corporate volunteering. *Academy of Management Review, 37*(4), 589–615.

Norris Center. (2013, January 2). *Center for student involvement: Volunteer opportunities*. Northwestern University. Retrieved from http://www.norris.northwestern.edu/csi/community/volunteer-opportunities/

Pryor, J. H., Hurtado, S., DeAngelo, L., Sharkness, J., Romero, L., Korn, W. S., & Tran, S. (2009). *The American freshman: National norms for fall 2008*. Los Angeles: Higher Education Research Institute.

Spera, C., Ghertner, R., Nerion, A., & DiTommaso, A. (2013). *Volunteering as a pathway to employment: Does volunteering increase odds of finding a job for the out of work?* Washington, DC: Corporation for National and Community Service.

United States Bureau of Labor Statistics. (2016, February 25). *Economic news release: Volunteering in the United States, 2015*. Retrieved from http://www.bls.gov/news.release/volun.nr0.htm

Speaking Outline Note Cards

Here is how Alyssa reduced her formal speech outline into a speaking outline consisting of key words, phrases, and delivery cues.

Introduction

PLANT FEET....DIRECT EYE CONTACT....
POISE/ETHOS! ☺ (1)

I. Famous Indian peace activist Mahatma Gandhi: "We must become the change we seek in the world."

Tall order....we can make a difference right here in Lexington, KY

II. Think for a moment....child/homework, neighbor/leaves, stranger/groceries....It's easy for college students like us to get involved.

III. I volunteer at LRM and reaped benefits (Slide 1)

IV. Benefits volunteering....
   a. get acquainted
   b. responsibility & privilege
   c. resumé-building skills

BLANK SLIDE, WALK RIGHT, EYE C.: Let's begin by explaining the ways volunteering can help us connect to our local community.

Body & Conclusion

BLANK SLIDE, WALK RIGHT, EYE C: privilege & responsibility....resume-building.... (3)

III. Life skills
   Article "Employability Credentials: A Key to Successful Youth Transition to Work" by I. Charner—1988 issue of the Journal of Career Development....(Q. CARD #2)

   Laura Hatfield....leadership, teamwork, and listening skills
   Andrea Stockelman, volunteer (SLIDE #7)
   (Q. CARD #3)

   MY RESUMÉ (SLIDE #8)

BLANK SLIDE, WALK TO CENTER, EYE C: Today, we've discussed....get acquainted, responsibility & privilege, resume-building life skills help after grad.

CL: So, I'm hoping the next me you recall....not distant past. Instead, I hope you'll be thinking bout how you ARE being the change you seek in the world by volunteering right here //in Lexington/// right now!

PAUSE, EYE CONTACT, POISE, NOD ☺

Body

(2)

I. GREAT WAY to become acquainted ☺☺

LR: Comforts of home....unfamiliar city....volunteering....easy and quick way....

Natalie Cunningham—May 2nd (Q. CARD #1)

Social issues and conditions

Acc. to a 1991 article published in the J. of Prevention and Intervention in the Community by Cohen, Mowbray, Gillette, and Thompson raise awareness....

My experience at LRM (SLIDES 2 & 3)

BLANK SLIDE, WALK LEFT, EYE C.: Not only is volunteering important....familiar and social issues.... FRANKLY....dem society....

(2a)

II. Civic responsibility AND privilege....LR: We benefit college....give back.

I agree with Wilson and Musick who said in their 1997 article in Social Forces active participation or deprived. (SLIDES 4 & 5)

Also a privilege....make a difference....feel good.... self-actualization (SLIDE #6)

Quotation Card

(4)

#1: "My first group of students needed rides to all the various volunteer sites b/c they had no idea where things were in the city. It was really easy for the students who lived on campus to remain ignorant of their city, but while volunteering they become acquainted with Lexington and the important issues going on here."

#2: "Employers rely on credentials to certify that a young person will become a valuable employee. Credentials document your experiences and employability skills, knowledge, and attitude."

#3: "I learned a lot more went into preparing food for the homeless than I ever thought possible. It was neat to be a part of that process."

Reflection and Assessment

Delivery refers to the use of voice and body in presenting speeches. Effective delivery is conversational and animated. To assess how well you've learned what we've discussed in this chapter, answer the following questions. If you have trouble answering any of them, go back and review that material. Once you can answer each question accurately, you are ready to move ahead to the next chapter.

1. What are the characteristics of effective delivery?
2. How do you use your voice and body effectively?
3. How do you go about rehearsing your speech?
4. What can you do to adapt delivery while giving your speech?
5. What can you do to adapt your delivery for virtual audiences?

Challenge Resource and Assessment Center

MindTap®

Now that you have read Chapter 11, go to your MindTap Communication for *The Challenge of Effective Speaking in a Digital Age* for quick access to flashcards, chapter quizzes, and more.

Applying What You've Learned

1. **Impromptu Speech Activity:** Draw a slip of paper from a container provided by your instructor. The slip of paper will identify an element we've discussed about effective speech preparation (identifying a topic and writing a speech goal, audience analysis and adaptation, locating and evaluating secondary research sources, types of developmental material, conducting primary research, elements of an effective macrostructure, elements of effective microstructure, constructing presentational aids, effective delivery, use of voice, use of body, delivery methods, rehearsal sessions, and so on). Prepare and present a 2- to 3-minute impromptu speech explaining the element with specific examples.

2. **Assessment Activity A:** Select a sample speech from this book, then assess it using the Speech Evaluation Checklist in this chapter. After doing so, provide a brief narrative critique of the speaker's delivery (use of voice and body). Be sure to answer these questions in your assessment: (1) What did the speaker do particularly well and why? (2) What could the speaker do to improve delivery, why, and how? (3) What will you do during your own rehearsal sessions based on your critique of this speaker's delivery?

3. **Assessment Activity B:** Complete Action Step 6 (Rehearsing Your Speech) for a speech you will deliver this term.

12 Informative Speaking

WHAT'S THE POINT?

WHEN YOU'VE FINISHED THIS CHAPTER, YOU WILL BE ABLE TO:

- Explain the characteristics of informative speeches
- Describe the major methods of informing
- Prepare an informative process speech
- Prepare an informative expository speech

MindTap®

Review the chapter **Learning Objectives** and **Start** with quick warm-up activity.

Ethical communicators demonstrate honesty and responsibility by providing listeners with the facts.

As Logan finished his informative speech, the class burst into spontaneous applause. Anna turned to her friend Ryan and whispered, "Wow, when Logan said his speech was going to be on online social networks I thought it would be boring. We all use Facebook, Instagram, Snapchat, and YouTube all the time. What could he possibly teach us? Was I ever wrong."

"I know what you mean," Ryan responded. "I guess Professor Dodd was right. You really can make a familiar topic interesting if you can share new and relevant insight about it."

"Yeah," Anna continued. "Now I'm really glad I don't speak today. I'm going to take another look at my speech tonight to make sure I'm sharing new and relevant insight about online identity theft."

After listening to Logan, Anna and Ryan discovered firsthand what makes informative speeches effective. Effective informative speeches don't just share information. They share information that is both new and relevant for a particular audience. Not only that, Ryan and Anna also learned that even familiar topics can be intellectually stimulating when speakers share new and relevant insights about them. With the amount of information literally at our fingertips via the Internet, however, doing so can be a bit of a challenge. In this chapter, we share some guidelines to help you develop effective informative speeches that do, in fact, offer new information and insight.

An **informative speech** is one whose goal is to explain or describe facts, truths, and principles in a way that stimulates interest, facilitates understanding, and increases the likelihood the audience will remember it. In short, informative speeches are designed to educate audiences. Informative speeches answer questions about a topic, such as those beginning with who, when, what, where, why, how to, and how does. For example, your informative speech might describe who popular singer-songwriter Adele is, define Scientology, compare and contrast the similarities and differences between Twitter and Facebook, narrate the story of golf professional Jordan Spieth's rise to fame, or demonstrate how to create a digital remix of music to make a point and post it on a website like YouTube. Informative speaking differs from other speech forms (such as speaking to persuade, to entertain, or to celebrate) in that your goal is simply to achieve mutual understanding about an object, person, place, process, event, idea, concept, or issue.

In this chapter, we first discuss five distinguishing characteristics of informing. Next, we describe five methods of informing. Finally, we discuss two common types of informative speeches and provide an example of one.

CHARACTERISTICS OF EFFECTIVE INFORMATIVE SPEAKING

We face some unique challenges to gain and sustain listener attention when giving informative speeches. We can address them successfully by attending to five key characteristics of informative speeches.

Intellectually Stimulating

Your audience will perceive information to be **intellectually stimulating** when it is new to them and when it is explained in a way that piques their curiosity and interest (Photo 12.1). By *new*, we mean information that most of your audience

informative speech: a speech whose goal is to explain or describe facts, truths, and principles in a way that stimulates interest, facilitates understanding, and increases the likelihood of remembering

intellectually stimulating: information that is new to audience members and is explained in a way that piques their curiosity

Photo 12.1 You can make familiar topics intellectually stimulating with new and relevant insight. How might you do so when your topic is a familiar one?

is unfamiliar with or that provides fresh insights into a topic with which they are already familiar.

If your audience is unfamiliar with your topic, you should consider how you might tap their natural curiosity. Imagine you are an anthropology major who is interested in prehistoric humans, an interest not shared by most members of your audience. You know that in 1991, the 5,300-year-old body of a man, Otzi, as he has become known, was found surprisingly well-preserved in an ice field in the mountains between Austria and Italy. Even though the discovery was big news at the time, it is unlikely that your audience knows much about it. You can draw on their natural curiosity, however, as you present "Unraveling the Mystery of the Iceman," where you describe scientists' efforts to understand who Otzi was and what happened to him.[1]

If your audience is familiar with your topic, you will need to identify new insight about it. Begin by asking yourself: What things about my topic do listeners probably not know? Answer the question by considering depth and breadth.

- *Depth* has to do with going into more detail than people's general knowledge of the topic. Logan did so by sharing details about the history of online social networks; something his audience of young users probably never thought about before. If you've ever watched programs on the *Food Network*, depth is what its programs provide. Most people know basic recipes, but these programs show new ways to cook the same foods.

- *Breadth* has to do with looking at how your topic relates to associated topics. Trace considered breadth when he informed listeners about type 1 diabetes. He discussed not only the physical and emotional effects on a person with diabetes but also the emotional and relational effects on the person's family and friends, as well as the financial implications of diabetes on society.

Relevant

A general rule to remember when preparing informative speeches is this: Don't assume your listeners will recognize how the information you share is relevant to them.

Remember to incorporate *listener relevance links* throughout your speech. As you prepare each main point, ask and answer the question: How would knowing this information make my listeners happier, healthier, wealthier, wiser, and so forth?

Creative

Your audience will perceive your information to be *creative* when it yields innovative ideas and insights. You may not ordinarily consider yourself to be creative, but that may be because you have never recognized or fully developed your own innovative ideas. Creativity comes from doing good research, taking time, and practicing productive thinking.

Creative informative speeches begin with *good research*. The more you learn about a topic, the more you will have to work with to develop it creatively. Then, for the creative process to work, you have to give yourself *time to think*. Rarely do creative ideas come when we are in a time crunch. Instead, they are likely to come when we least expect it—when we're driving our car, preparing for bed, or daydreaming. Finally, for the creative process to work, you also have to *think productively*. **Productive thinking** occurs when we contemplate something from a variety of perspectives. Then, with numerous ideas to choose from, we can select the ones that are best suited to our particular audience. In the article "A Theory about Genius," author Michael Michalko describes several strategies we can use to become productive thinkers. They include:

productive thinking: to contemplate something from a variety of perspectives

- **Rethink a topic, issue, or problem from many perspectives.** Albert Einstein actually came up with the theory of relativity this way. As you brainstorm, try to think about a possible topic as it might be perceived by many different cultural and co-cultural groups. Then, as you conduct research, try to find sources that represent a variety of perspectives.

- **Make your thoughts visible by sketching drawings, diagrams, and graphs.** Galileo revolutionized science by doing this. Try concept mapping as you generate topics and approaches to them.

- **Set regular goals to actually *produce something*.** The great NHL hockey player Wayne Gretzky put it this way: "You miss every shot you don't take" (Photo 12.2). So take some shots! Thomas Edison actually set a goal to produce an invention every 10 days. J. S. Bach produced one cantata per week. And T. S. Eliot's many drafts of *The Waste Land* eventually became a masterpiece. Don't let writer's block keep you from drafting an initial outline. You need to start somewhere. Getting ideas out of your head and onto paper or a computer screen gives you something to work with and revise. After all, you can't edit air.

- **Combine and recombine ideas, images, and thoughts in different ways.** Austrian monk Gregor Mendel combined mathematics and biology to come up with the laws of heredity, which ground the modern science of genetics. Jennifer's list of possible speech topics included gardening (something she loved to do) and rising college tuition costs. She put the two ideas together and came up with the idea of doing an informative speech about how to

AP Images/Chris O'Meara

Photo 12.2 If you take a shot and write something down, even if it's not very good, you have something to revise. What do you have if you don't?

description: a method of informing that creates a verbal picture of an object, geographic feature, setting, or image

use gardening (services, produce, and products) to raise money to help pay for college.

To come up with creative ways to approach transnational celebrity activism in global politics, Anne Marie not only conducted an extensive library search on several databases, but also researched the topic by reading celebrity gossip magazines and visiting the websites of celebrities known for practicing it. After learning about what people like Angelina Jolie, Matt Damon, George Clooney, Madonna, and others were doing, she gave herself time to let what she had discovered percolate in her mind for a few days and even sketched a concept map to visualize links among her material. Ultimately, she was able to make the topic more interesting for her audience.

Memorable

If your speech is really informative, your audience will hear a lot of new information but will need help remembering what is most important. Emphasizing your specific goal, main points, and key facts are good starting points. Exhibit 12.1 illustrates several memory-enhancing techniques you might use.

Learning Styles

Because audience members differ in how they prefer to learn—whether by feeling, watching, thinking, or doing—you will be most effective when you address the diversity of learning styles. By rounding the learning cycle in this way, all listeners are more likely to both pay attention to and remember the information you share.

- Appeal to people who prefer to learn through the feeling dimension by providing concrete, vivid images, examples, stories, and testimonials.

- Address the watching dimension by using visual aids and by using appropriate facial expressions and gestures (Photo 12.3).

- Address the thinking dimension through clear macrostructure as well as definitions, explanations, and statistics.

- Address the doing dimension by providing your listeners with an opportunity to do something during the speech or afterward.

METHODS OF INFORMING

We inform by describing, defining, comparing and contrasting, narrating, and demonstrating. Let's look at each of these methods more closely.

Description

Description is a method used to create an accurate, vivid, verbal picture of an object, geographic feature, setting, person, event, or image. This method usually answers an overarching "who," "what," or "where" question. Descriptions are most effective when accompanied by a presentational aid, but vivid verbal descriptions can also create informative mental pictures. To describe something effectively, you can explain its size, shape, weight, color, composition, age, condition, and spatial organization.

You can describe size subjectively as large or small or objectively by noting specific numerical measurements. For example, you can describe New York City subjectively as the largest city in the United States or more objectively as home to more than 8 million people with more than 26,000 people per square mile.

Exhibit 12.1

Techniques for Making Informative Speech Material Memorable

Technique	Use	Example
Presentational aids	Provides the opportunity for the audience to retain a visual as well as an aural memory of important or difficult material	A diagram of the process of making ethanol.
Repetition	Gives the audience a second or third chance to retain important information by repeating or paraphrasing it	"The first dimension of romantic love is passion; that is, it can't really be romantic love if there is no sexual attraction."
Transitions	Increases the likelihood that the audience will retain the relationships among the information being presented, including which information is primary and which is supporting	"So the three characteristics of romantic love are passion, intimacy, and commitment. Now let's look at each of the five ways you can keep love alive. The first is through small talk."
Humor and other emotional anecdotes	Creates an emotional memory link to important ideas	"True love is like a pair of socks: you've got to have two, and they've got to match. So you and your partner need to be mutually committed and compatible."
Mnemonics and acronyms	Provides an easily remembered memory prompt or shortcut to increase the likelihood that a list is retained	"You can remember the four criteria for evaluating a diamond as the four Cs: carat, clarity, cut, and color." or "As you can see, useful goals are SMART: S—Specific, M—Measurable, A—Action oriented, R—Reasonable, and T—Time bound. That's SMART."

You can describe shape by reference to common geometric forms such as round, triangular, oblong, spherical, conical, cylindrical, or rectangular, or by reference to common objects such as a book or a milk carton. For example, the lower peninsula of Michigan is often described as a left-handed mitten (Photo 12.4). Shape can also be made more vivid by using adjectives such as *smooth* or *jagged*.

You can describe weight subjectively as heavy or light and objectively by pounds and ounces or kilograms, grams, and milligrams. As with size, you can clarify weight with comparisons. So you can describe a Humvee/Hummer objectively as weighing about 7,600 pounds, or subjectively as about the same weight as three Honda Civics.

You can describe color by coupling a basic color (such as black, white, red, or yellow) with a familiar object. For instance, instead of describing something as puce or ocher, you might describe the object as "eggplant purple" or "lime green."

You can describe the composition of something by indicating what it is made of. So, you can describe a building as

Photo 12.3 When an image or object is very small, you can display a picture or diagram of it in your computerized slideshow to make sure everyone can see what you are talking about. What images or objects might you enlarge in this way for your next speech?

g-stockstudio/Shutterstock.com

Photo 12.4 The shape of the lower peninsula of Michigan can be described as looking like a left-handed mitten. What other states or countries can be described as something they are shaped like?

being made of brick, concrete, wood, or aluminum siding. At times, you might describe something as what it looks like rather than what it is. For example, you might say something looks metallic even though it is actually made of plastic rather than metal. You can also describe something by age and by condition. For example, describing a city as ancient and well-kept produces different mental pictures than does describing a city as old and war torn.

Finally, you can describe spatial organization going from top to bottom, left to right, outer to inner, and so forth. A description of the Sistine Chapel might go from the floor to the ceiling; a description of a painting might proceed from foreground to background; and a description of a NASCAR automobile might go from the body to the engine to the interior (Photo 12.5).

Definition

definition: a method of informing that explains the meaning of something

Definition is a method that explains the meaning of something. There are four ways to define something.

First, you can define a word or idea by classifying it and differentiating it from similar words or ideas. For example, in a speech on vegetarianism, you might use information from the Vegan Society's website to define a vegan: "Veganism is a way of living that seeks to exclude, as far as is possible and practicable, all forms of exploitation of, and cruelty to, animals for food, clothing or any other purpose."[2]

Second, you can define a word by explaining its derivation or history. For instance, the word *vegan* is made from the beginning and end of the word VEG-etariAN and was coined in the United Kingdom in 1944 when the Vegan Society was founded.[3] Offering this etymology will help your audience remember the meaning of vegan.

Third, you can define a word by explaining its use or function. For example, in vegan recipes, you can use tofu or tempeh to replace meat and almond or soy milk to replace cow's milk.

Finally, the fourth and perhaps quickest way to define something is by using a familiar synonym or antonym. A **synonym** is a word that has the same or a similar meaning; an **antonym** is a word that is directly opposite in meaning. So, you could define a *vegan* by comparing it to the word *vegetarian*, which is a synonym with a similar although not identical meaning, or to the word *carnivore*, which is an antonym.

Photo 12.5 You can describe a NASCAR automobile spatially, proceeding from the body to the engine to the interior. What is something you might describe spatially in a similar way?

Sean Gardner/Stewart-Haas Racing /Getty Images

synonym: a word that has the same or a similar meaning

antonym: a word that is directly opposite in meaning

Compare and Contrast

Compare and contrast is a method of informing that focuses on how something is similar to and different from other things. For example, in a speech on veganism, you might tell your audience how vegans are similar to and different from other types of vegetarians. You can point out that like vegetarians, vegans don't eat meat. In contrast, semi-vegetarians eat fish or poultry. Like lacto-vegetarians, vegans don't eat eggs, but unlike this group and lacto-ovo-vegetarians, vegans don't use dairy products. So of all vegetarians, vegans have the most restrictive diet. Because comparisons and contrasts can be figurative or literal, you can use metaphors and analogies as well as make direct comparisons.

compare and contrast: a method of informing that focuses on how something is similar to and different from other things

Narration

Narration is a method that recounts an autobiographical or biographical event, myth, or other story. Narratives usually have four parts:

narration: a method of informing that recounts events

1. First, the narrative orients the listener by describing when and where the event took place and by introducing important characters.

2. Second, the narrative explains the sequence of events that led to a complication or problem.

3. Third, the narrative discusses how the complication or problem affected key characters.

4. Finally, the narrative recounts how the complication or problem was solved.

The characteristics of a good narrative include a strong story line; use of descriptive language and details that enhance the plot, people, setting, and events; effective use of dialogue; pacing that builds suspense; and a strong voice.[4]

Photo 12.6 The TV program *How I Met Your Mother* is an example of informing using the first-person narrative method. How does it capture and maintain audience interest?

demonstration: a method of informing that shows how something is done, displays the stages of a process, or depicts how something works

Narratives can be presented in a first-, second-, or third-person voice. When you use first person, you report what you have personally experienced or observed, using the pronouns *I*, *me*, and *my* (Photo 12.6): "Let me tell you about the first time I tried to water ski". In a second-person narrative, you place your audience "at the scene" by using the pronouns *you* and *your*: "Imagine that you have just gotten off the plane in Hong Kong and can't read Cantonese. You look at the signs and can't understand a thing. Which way is the terminal?" In a third-person narrative, you describe what has happened, is happening, or will happen to other people by using the pronouns *he, her*, and *they*: "When the students arrived in Venice for their study-abroad experience, the first thing they saw was the Rialto Bridge."

Demonstration

Demonstration is a method that shows how something is done, displays the stages of a process, or depicts how something works. Demonstrations range from very simple with a few easy-to-follow steps (such as how to craft a good cover letter) to very complex (such as demonstrating how a nuclear reactor works).

In a demonstration, your experience with what you are demonstrating is critical. Expertise gives you the necessary background to supplement bare-bones instructions with personally lived experiences. Why are TV cooking shows so popular? In such shows, the chef doesn't just read the recipe and do what it says. Rather, while performing each step, the chef shares tips that aren't mentioned in any cookbook. It is the chef's experience that allows him or her to say that one egg will work or how to tell if the cake is really done.

In a demonstration, organize the steps from first to last to help your audience remember the sequence accurately. If there are many steps, grouping them will also help audiences remember. For example, suppose you want to demonstrate the steps in using a touch-screen voting machine. If, rather than presenting 14 separate points, you group them under four headings—(1) get ready to vote, (2) vote, (3) review your choices, and (4) cast your ballot—chances are much higher that your audience will be able to remember them.

Most demonstrations involve actually showing the audience the process or parts of the process. If what you are explaining is relatively simple, you can demonstrate the entire process from start to finish. However, if the process is lengthy or complex, you may choose to prepare material in advance for some of the steps. Although you will show all stages in the process, you will not have to take the time for every single step as the audience watches. For example, many of the ingredients used by TV chefs are already cut up, measured, and placed into little bowls.

Effective demonstrations require practice. Remember that, under the pressure of speaking to an audience, even the simplest task can become difficult. (Have you ever tried to thread a needle with 25 people watching you?) As you practice, you will want to consider the size of your audience and the configuration of the room. Be sure that everyone in your audience will be able to see what you are doing. If you are presenting your speech online, be sure the camera can capture what you are demonstrating or use visual aids to do so.

INFORMATIVE SPEECH TYPES

Two of the most common patterns for organizing the macrostructure of informative speeches are process patterns and expository patterns. In this section, we focus first on process speeches, then look at expository speeches.

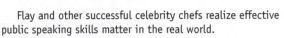
Informative Process Speeches

The goal of a **process speech** is to explain and show how something is done, is made, or works. Effective process speeches require you to carefully delineate the steps and the order in which they occur. The steps typically become the main points and the explanations of each step become the subpoints. Most process speeches rely heavily on the demonstration method of informing.

For example, Allie, a floral designer, was asked to speak on the basics of floral arrangement to a high school art class. The teacher allotted 5 minutes for her presentation. Because Allie could not take her audience through every step in the process in just 5 minutes, she opted to physically demonstrate only parts of the process and to bring additional arrangements in various stages of completion.

Allie began with the first step: choosing the right vase and frog (flower holder). She brought in vases and frogs of various sizes and shapes to show as she explained how to choose one based on the types of flowers used and the desired visual effect. For the second step—preparing the basic triangle of blooms—Allie began to demonstrate how to place the flowers she had brought to form one triangle. Rather than trying to get everything perfect in the few seconds she had, however, she also brought out several other partially finished arrangements that were behind a draped table. These showed other carefully completed triangles that used other types of flowers. For the third step, placing additional flowers and greenery to complete an arrangement and achieve various artistic effects, Allie actually demonstrated how to place several blooms, and then, as she described them, brought out several completed arrangements that illustrated various artistic effects. Even though Allie did not physically perform every part of each step, her visual presentation was an excellent process speech on floral arranging.

Although most process speeches require you to demonstrate, some are not suited to demonstrations. For the latter, you can use visual or audiovisual aids to help your audience "see" the steps in the process. In a speech on remodeling a kitchen, it would not

process speech: an informative presentation that teaches how something is done, is made, or works

12.2

Topic Ideas for Process Speeches

Exhibit

How to do it	How to make it	How it works
Select running shoes	Compost bin	3-D movies
Apply for a loan	Rope knots	Stem cell reproduction
Install a toilet water-saving device	Lefse	Solar energy
Go bouldering/rock climb	Fishing flies	Digital synchronization

be practical to demonstrate the process; however, you could greatly enhance the verbal description by showing pictures before, during, and after a remodeling. Exhibit 12.2 provides some topic examples for process speeches.

Informative Expository Speeches

expository speech: an informative presentation that provides carefully researched in-depth knowledge about a complex topic

The goal of an **expository speech** is to provide carefully researched in-depth knowledge about a complex topic (Photo 12.7). For example, "understanding the gun control debate," "the origins of nursery rhymes," "the sociobiological theory of child abuse," and "rap as poetry" are all topics on which you could give an interesting expository speech.

All expository speeches require speakers to draw from an extensive research base and to use a variety of informative methods (e.g., description, definition, compare and contrast, narration, short demonstration). Expository speeches may explain political, economic, social, religious, or ethical issues; historical events and forces; theories, principles, or laws; and creative works.

Monty Rakusen/Cultura/Getty Images

Photo 12.7 An expository speech, like a classroom lecture, is an informative presentation that provides in-depth knowledge of a subject. Which teachers do you remember because they made their lectures interesting? What techniques did they use to make them interesting?

Speech Assignment & Checklist

Process Speech

Prepare a 4- to 6-minute process speech explaining how something is made, how something is done, or how something works. An adaptation plan and a complete outline are required. To help you prepare your speech and your outline, complete the Speech-Planning Action Step activities. Notice that the sample Process Speech Evaluation Checklist below includes both specific criteria related to process speeches and general criteria that are common to all speeches.

Speech Evaluation Checklist

You can use this checklist to critique a process speech that you hear in class. (You can also use it to critique your own speech.) As you listen to the speaker, consider what makes a speech effective. Then, answer the following questions.

Check items that were accomplished effectively.

General Criteria

_____ 1. Was the goal of the speech clear?

_____ 2. Was the introduction effective in creating interest, as well as introducing the thesis and main points?

_____ 3. Was the macrostructure easy to follow?

_____ 4. Was the language appropriate, accurate, clear, and vivid?

_____ 5. Were the main points developed with appropriate breadth, depth, and supporting material?

_____ 6. Was the conclusion effective in summarizing the thesis and main points, as well as clinching?

_____ 7. Was the speaker's use of voice conversational, intelligible, and expressive?

_____ 8. Did the speaker's use of body (e.g., appearance, posture, eye contact, facial expressions, gestures, and movement) appear poised, spontaneous, appropriate, and effective?

Specific Criteria

_____ 1. Was the specific goal appropriate for a process speech (how to do it, how to make it, how it works)?

_____ 2. Did the speaker show personal expertise with the process?

_____ 3. Did the speaker emphasize the process steps?

_____ 4. If the speaker demonstrated a process or parts of a process, was the demonstration fluid and skillful?

_____ 5. Were presentational aids constructed effectively to help explain the process?

_____ 6. Were presentational aids used effectively to help explain the process and easily seen by all audience members?

Based on these criteria, evaluate the speech as (check one):

_____ excellent _____ good _____ satisfactory _____ fair _____ poor

Explain:

_____

_____

Political, Economic, Social, Religious, or Ethical Issues

In an expository speech, you have the opportunity to help your audience understand the context of an issue, including the forces that gave rise to the issue and continue to affect it. You may also present the various positions held about the issue and the reasoning behind those positions. Finally, you may discuss various attempts made to resolve the issue.

Since the general goal of your speech is to inform (not to persuade), be sure to present the different sides of a controversial issue without advocating which side is better. Also, make a concerted effort to present complex issues in ways that help your audience understand them without oversimplifying them. For example, if you are researching a speech on fracking—a controversial method for extracting oil and natural gas deposits from subterranean rock—be sure to consult articles and experts on all sides of the issue and fairly represent these views in your speech. If time is limited, you might discuss all sides of just one or two of these issues, but you should also at least mention the others, as well. Exhibit 12.3 provides examples of topic ideas for expository speeches about political, economic, social, religious, or ethical issues.

Historical Events and Forces

The philosopher George Santayana wrote, "those who cannot remember the past are condemned to repeat it." So an expositional speech about an historical event or force can be fascinating for its own sake, but it can also be relevant for what is happening today. Because some people think history is boring, you have a special obligation to seek out stories and narratives that can enliven your speech. In doing so, be sure to analyze the event at the time it occurred, as well as the meaning it has for your audience today. For example, most schoolchildren learn about Paul Revere's famous midnight ride warning Americans that the British army was coming. Few know, however, about others who did similar heroic things. In 1777, for instance, 16-year-old Sybil Ludington rode 40 miles through enemy-infested woods in the dark of night, waking men and warning them to prepare for an attack. She succeeded in her mission, returned home safely, and was considered a local heroine.[10] Exhibit 12.4 offers examples of topic ideas for expository speeches about historical events and forces.

Theories, Principles, or Laws

The way we live is affected by natural and human laws and principles that can be explained by various theories. An expository speech can inform us by explaining these important phenomena. The main challenge to you as a speaker is to explain the theory, law, or principle in language that is understandable to your audience. Search for or create examples and illustrations that demystify complicated concepts and terminology. You can also compare unfamiliar ideas with those that the audience already understands. For example, in a speech on the psychological principles of operant

---

Exhibit 12.3

Topic Ideas for Expository Speeches About Political, Economic, Social, Religious, or Ethical Issues

Gay marriage	Stem cell research
Affirmative action	Health care reform
Climate change	School vouchers
Media bias	Digital remixing
Gun control	Home schooling
Immigration	Fracking
Genetic engineering	Celebrity culture

Topic Ideas for Expository Speeches About Historical Events and Forces

Genocide	Gandhi and his movement
The Papacy	The colonization of Africa
Irish immigration	Building the Great Pyramids
Women's suffrage	The Industrial Revolution
The Spanish flu epidemic	The Ming Dynasty
Conquering Mt. Everest	The Vietnam War
Assassination of MLK Jr.	The Crusades
The Balfour Declaration	Space Shuttle *Challenger* explosion

conditioning, a speaker could help the audience understand the difference between continuous reinforcement and intermittent reinforcement in this way:

> When a behavior is reinforced continuously, each time people perform the behavior they get a reward, but when a behavior is reinforced intermittently, a reward is not always given when the behavior is performed. Behavior that is learned by continuous reinforcement stops when the reward is no longer provided. On the other hand, behavior that is learned by intermittent reinforcement might continue for a long period of time, even when no reword is provided. For example, take the behavior of putting a coin into the slot of a machine. If the machine is a vending machine, we expect to be rewarded every time we "play." If the machine doesn't eject the item, we might decide the machine is out of order and even bang on the machine. But suppose the machine is a slot machine. Now how many coins will we "play"? Why the difference? Because we were conditioned to a vending machine on a continuous schedule, but a slot machine "rewards" us on an intermittent schedule.

Reflect on Ethics

WHAT WOULD *YOU* DO?

YOU TOO CAN HAVE SIX-PACK ABS IN ONLY 14 MINUTES A DAY

Body by Jake, Body Dome, Bun & Thigh Max, Smart Abs, Life Fitness, and Body Beast all promise that you can trim and tone your way to a better body in just minutes a day. Besides promising to be the most effective exercise programs ever, what do they have in common? They're the subject of infomercials. Infomercials are TV and online programs designed to look like talk shows when they're actually extended advertisements that offer testimonials as evidence of their effectiveness.

Although some view infomercials with skepticism and derision, others view them as "an example of capitalism at its best."[6] Infomercials have even become sources of entertainment. When "infomercial king" Billy Mays passed away in June 2009, a Facebook page, "RIP Billy Mays," gained 175,000 fans.

Despite their popularity, infomercials are also a controversial subject. Many people claim that they get deceived into buying things they don't need or can't afford, and that don't actually do what they claim to do.[7] One controversial infomercial that targeted teens about abstaining from having sex was posted on the Philippine's Department of Health (DOH) official Facebook page in 2014. The infomercial was removed only hours later because it referred to teens who have sex and become pregnant as "idiots."[8] Kevin Trudeau was actually thrown in jail for misleading the public on his infomercials and books about a weight loss cure "they" don't want you to know about.[9] Nevertheless, infomercials abound on TV and online. Just type "infomercial" into a YouTube search, for example, and you'll get hundreds of thousands of hits.

1. Have you ever purchased a product after seeing an infomercial on it? If so, did the product live up to its promises?

2. Do you think calling these advertisements "info"–mercials is ethical? Why or why not?

Exhibit 12.5

Topic Ideas for Expository Speeches About Theories, Principles, or Laws

Natural selection	Diminishing returns
Gravity	Boyle's law
Number theory	Psychoanalytic theory
Murphy's Law	Intelligent design
Feminist theory	Maslow's hierarchy of needs
Social cognitive theory	Color theory: complements and contrasts
The Peter principle	

Exhibit 12.5 provides examples of topic ideas for expository speeches about theories, principles, or laws.

Creative Works

Courses in art, theater, music, literature, and film appreciation give students tools by which to recognize the style, historical period, and quality of a particular piece or group of pieces. Yet most of us know very little about how to understand a creative work, so presentations designed to explain creative works such as poems, novels, songs, or even famous speeches can be very instructive.

When developing a speech that explains a creative work, try to find information on the work and the artist who created it. Also try to find sources that help you (a) understand the period in which the work was created and (b) learn about the criteria used to evaluate works of its type. For example, if you want to give an expository speech on Frederick Douglass's Fourth of July oration of 1852 in Rochester, New York, orient your audience by first reminding them of who Douglass was. Then, explain the traditional expectations for Fourth of July speakers at the point in history at which Douglass delivered his speech. Next, summarize the speech and perhaps share a few memorable quotations from it. Finally, discuss why the speech is still considered "great" by critics today. Exhibit 12.6 provides examples of topic ideas for expository speeches about creative works.

Exhibit 12.6

Topic Ideas for Expository Speeches About Creative Works

Hip-hop music	Michael Jackson's *Thriller*
Impressionist painting	Kabuki theater
Salsa dancing	Iconography
MLK Jr. National Memorial	*Catcher in the Rye*, a coming-of-age novel
The Hunger Games trilogy	Spike Lee's *Mo' Better Blues*
Van Gogh's *Starry Night*	*Boyhood*, the film
The films of Alfred Hitchcock	

Speech Assignment & Checklist

Expository Speech

Prepare a 5- to 8-minute expository speech. To help you prepare your speech and your outline, complete the Speech-Planning Action Step activities. Notice that the sample Expository Speech Evaluation Checklist that follows includes both specific criteria related to expository speeches and general criteria that are common to all speeches.

Speech Evaluation Checklist

You can use this form to critique an expository speech that you hear in class. (You can also use it to critique your own speech.) As you listen, outline the speech and identify which expository speech type it is. Then, answer the following questions.

Check items that were accomplished effectively.

Type of Expository Speech

_____ Exposition of political, economic, social, religious, or ethical issues

_____ Exposition of historical events or forces

_____ Exposition of theories, principles, or laws

_____ Exposition of creative works

General Criteria

_____ **1.** Was the goal of the speech clear?

_____ **2.** Was the introduction effective in creating interest, as well as introducing the thesis and main points?

_____ **3.** Was the macrostructure easy to follow?

_____ **4.** Was the language appropriate, accurate, clear, and vivid?

_____ **5.** Were the main points developed with appropriate breadth, depth, and supporting material?

_____ **6.** Was the conclusion effective in summarizing the thesis and main points, as well as clinching?

_____ **7.** Was the speaker's use of voice conversational, intelligible, and expressive?

_____ **8.** Did the speaker's use of body (e.g., appearance, posture, eye contact, facial expressions, gestures, and movement) appear poised, spontaneous, appropriate, and effective?

Specific Criteria

_____ **1.** Was the specific speech goal to provide well-researched information on a complex topic?

_____ **2.** Did the speaker effectively use a variety of informative methods?

_____ **3.** Did the speaker emphasize the main ideas and important supporting material?

_____ **4.** Did the speaker use a variety of supporting material?

_____ **5.** Did the speaker present in-depth, high-quality, appropriately cited information?

Based on these criteria, evaluate the speech as (check one):

_____ excellent _____ good _____ satisfactory _____ fair _____ poor

Explain:

_____

_____

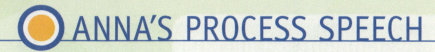

Internet Identity Theft: Self-Protection Steps

By Anna Rankin, University of Kentucky[11]

Preparation Outline

General goal: To inform

Specific goal: I want my audience to understand the steps to protect themselves from online identity theft.

INTRODUCTION

I. **Attention getter:** [I will tell a hypothetical story about someone getting their identity stolen when doing something online.]

II. **Listener relevance:** [I need to find a statistic to show how many people have their identities stolen . . . how common it is]

III. **Speaker credibility:** I have done extensive research on this subject and am also a computer science major.

IV. **Thesis statement with main point preview:** Today, let's discuss several simple steps we can all take to prevent Internet identity theft from phishing, hacking, and pharming.

BODY

I. Phishing

    A. [need listener relevance here yet]

    B. Soliciting personal information by posing as a legitimate company (NCPC, 2013).

    C. Never provide personal information to unknown entities.

    D. Never click on links in emails that come from unknown sources.

    Transition: Now that we know what we can do to protect ourselves when using email, let's talk about how to protect our identities from hacking.

II. Hacking

    A. [need listener relevance here yet]

    B. When a thief gets access to your personal computer to view documents

    C. Password protect all accounts and devices

    D. Wipe all electronic devices clean before selling them or throwing them away

    Transition: [need to write one yet]

III. Pharming

    A. [need listener relevance here yet]

    B. Criminals hack a website (like Amazon.com) and reroute the website to a "poser" website

    C. Look for the "lock" icon on the browser [show a visual aid for this]

D. Look for "https" rather than "http" URLs

E. Use encryption software

CONCLUSION

I. **Thesis restatement and main point summary:** Today we discussed how criminals steal our identities over the Internet and steps we can employ for protection from phishing, hacking, and pharming.

II. **Clincher:** [need to come up with a good clincher yet.]

Formal Outline

INTRODUCTION

I. Imagine this: you are filing your income tax return after starting your first real job after college. After completing the tedious online forms, you hit the "calculate" button. You are ecstatic when the online filing system says you are due a return of a whopping $2,800! Then, imagine hitting "file" to submit your tax return and you get the error message "*Your tax return has already been processed.*" Someone has stolen your identity and pocketed your return.

II. If you think this cannot happen to you, think again! According to the U.S. Government Accountability Office (White, 2015), the IRS reported over $30 billion in tax-related identity theft activity in 2013 and that doesn't even account for the undetected cases.

III. Through my research, I discovered that one out of every four Americans have been victims of identity theft (whitehouse.gov, 2014). Identity theft can happen when someone simply digs through your trash for bank statements so most of us now shred such items before discarding them. Recently, however, Internet identity theft is becoming far more prevalent (US Department of Justice, n.d.). An identity thief who accesses your information online can apply for jobs, loans, and credit cards; can receive medical care or prescription drugs; and can make large purchases all under your name (FTC, 2012).

IV. Today, let's discuss several simple steps we can all take to prevent Internet identity theft (*Show Slide 1: Three Steps to Prevent Identity Theft*). These three steps are designed to help prevent phishing, hacking, and pharming.

BODY

I. The first step in preventing online identity theft is to protect yourself from phishing (*Show Slide 2: Email Phishing [Photo]*).

A. Most likely, everyone in this room receives hundreds of email messages every week. Whether it is an update from our college professors or coupons from our favorite retail stores, we are bombarded with emails that we do not hesitate to open or reply to.

B. Phishing is a process through which identity thieves persuade Internet users to provide personal information by posing as legitimate organizations (NCPC, 2013).

1. Identity thieves might send you an email that appears to be from a legitimate organization.

2. In it, they will ask you to provide personal information such as your bank account numbers, Social Security number, or personal passwords.

Attention getter

Notice how Anna uses a hypothetical example to pique her audience's interest.

Listener relevance

Speaker credibility and listener relevance

Sometimes you can do as Anna did here to combine listener relevance and speaker credibility by sharing statistics about the prevalence of identity theft.

Thesis statement with main point preview

Anna offers a simple thesis statement with main point preview, which she reinforces visually on a slide.

Listener relevance

Anna presents her first main point together with a listener relevance link that all her listeners can relate to.

Although Anna does define phishing here, she could probably make her speech more interesting by sharing a personal narrative from a victim or even a short video clip from the feature film *Identity Thief*.

C. One way to prevent phishing is by never providing personal information online without verifying the legitimacy of the sender.

    1. Always look up the organization's customer service number independent of the email and then call it to verify the legitimacy of the email.

    2. And make it a standard practice to always provide such information over the phone rather than via email (FTC, 2012).

D. Another way to avoid becoming a victim of identity theft through phishing is never to click on links in emails from unknown sources (NCPC, 2013).

    1. Clicking on these links can automatically install software on your computer that reroutes your personal information to the identity thief's personal data collection website.

    2. Once the thief or thieves have this information, they can basically "become you" all over the Internet.

Transition

Notice how smooth Anna's transition statement is as she ties her two main points together.

Now that we all know what we can do to keep our identity safe through good email practices, let's consider how we can prevent identity theft by surfing the Internet wisely.

Listener relevance

II. The second step we can take to protect ourselves from identity theft is to prevent hacking (*Show Slide 3: Computer Hacking [Photo]*).

A. Take a moment to think about all the personal and financial information you have stored on your electronic devices. If someone were to gain open access to your computer, or even to your smartphone for that matter, he or she would be able to steal your identity in a few swipes of the keys.

Again Anna provides a succinct definition. She could make her speech more compelling by using visuals to reinforce it.

Anna does a nice job of proposing steps we can all take to protect ourselves, which appeals to the "doing" on the learning cycle. One thing that could improve her speech is the addition of appeals to the "feeling" dimension of the learning cycle (e.g., stories, narratives, personal accounts, video clips).

B. Hacking refers to a process through which an identity thief gains access to your personal computer to view documents, files, and personal information (NCPC, 2013).

C. Here are a few simple steps you can take to protect yourself from becoming a victim of hacking.

    1. The first step is to password-protect all of your accounts and devices, and to get creative with your passwords (FTC, 2012).

        a. Avoid using personal information such as your name, date of birth, address, or other personal information that is easily discovered by others (NCPC, 2013).

        c. Never use words that are found in the dictionary—some hacking programs can quickly attempt every word found in the dictionary to access your information.

        d. Try creating acronyms that you will always remember. For example, the phrase "I graduate from college in 2016" could turn into the password IgFcI2kl6—a strong and unique password that you can easily remember (*Show Slide 4: Unique Password Examples*)!

        e. Finally, avoid sharing too much information on social networking sites. If an identity thief finds out enough about your personal life, they can easily answer those "challenge" questions you use to keep your accounts and devices protected.

    2. The second step to protect against identity theft from hacking is to be sure you wipe clean any of your electronic devices before selling them or disposing of them (FTC, 2012).

        a. Before you dispose of your laptop or smart phone, eliminate any personal information, including saved passwords, photos, web search histories, and contact information.

b. There are several programs you can use to wipe your hard drive clean. However, the National Crime Protection Council (2005) suggests removing and destroying your computer's hard drive altogether before selling or disposing of your laptop.

So now that we know how to protect our email accounts from phishing and our computers from hacking, let's focus on what we need to do to protect ourselves from the most advanced method of online identity theft.

Transition

III. The third step in protecting ourselves from identity theft is to prevent pharming (*Show Slide 5: Pharming Website Dangers [Photo]*).

Listener relevance

   A. Virtually every day, we engage in online transactions. We may log on to our online banking to make sure we have enough money for dinner with friends, we may purchase a gift for someone through a store's website, or we may pay tuition using the online payment system.

   B. Pharming, one of the online identity theft methods toughest to detect, is a process through which criminals hack established websites and reroute the website to a "poser" website that looks similar and allows them to gather personal information during a transaction (NCPC, 2005).

   C. Although pharming is the most difficult to detect method of identity theft, there are a few steps we can take to protect ourselves when making online transactions.

      1. First, look for the "lock" icon on your Internet browser's status bar. This lock indicates that the website you are on is safe (*Show Slide 6: Internet Browser Safety Features*).

      2. Next, verify that the website is secure by inspecting the URL. A safe website URL will begin with https:// instead of http://.

      3. Finally, you can purchase encryption software that ensures any information you send over the Internet is jumbled and unreadable to others.

Anna was wise to use a screen shot of the "lock" icon to make this piece of information more intelligible and memorable for her audience.

CONCLUSION

I. As you can see, the Internet is literally a gold mine for identity thieves when our personal information is not protected.

Thesis restatement

II. Fortunately, we can take steps to protect ourselves from phishing, hacking, and pharming (*Show Slide 7 [same as slide 1]*).

Main point summary

III. According to a 2011 article in the *New York Times* (Perlroth, 2011), it is extremely difficult to prosecute online identity thieves even though they deserve it. One thing we can do, however, is to put a padlock on our goldmines so these criminals can't access them in the first place!

Clincher
Anna does a nice job of clinching by using analogies of our identities as "goldmines" that we need to "put a padlock on" to keep them safe from these "criminals."

REFERENCES

Federal Trade Commission. (2012). *Identity theft*. Retrieved from http://www.consumer.ftc.gov/features/feature-0014-identity-theft

Koster, C. (n.d.) *Identity theft*. Retrieved from http://ago.mo.gov/publications/idtheft.htm#header3

National Crime Prevention Council. (2013). *Evolving with technology: A comprehensive introduction to cybercrime with links to resources*. Retrieved from http://www.ncpc.org/topics/fraud-and-identity-theft/evolving-with-technology

Perlroth, N. (2011, December 19). A unit to fight cybercrimes. *The New York Times*. Retrieved from http://query.nytimes.com/

Their, D. (2012, February 24). Study: 1 in 20 Americans have been victims of identity theft. *Forbes*. Retrieved from http://www.forbes.com/sites/davidthier/2012/02/24/study-1-in-20-americans-have-been-victims-of-identify-theft/#578112f61141

US Department of Justice. (n.d.). *Identity theft and fraud*. Retrieved from http://www.justice.gov/criminal/fraud/websites/idtheft.html

White, J. R. (2015). *Identity theft (IDT) Refund fraud cost estimates*. (GAO Publication No. GAO-15-119). Washington, DC: US Government Accountability Office. Retrieved from http://www.gao.gov/products/GAO-15-119

Whitehouse.gov (2014, October 17). *FACT SHEET: Safeguarding consumers' financial security*. Retrieved from https://www.whitehouse.gov/the-press-office/2014/10/17/fact-sheet-safeguarding-consumers-financial-security

Speaking Outline Note Cards

Here is how Anna reduced her formal speech outline into a speaking outline of key words/phrases and delivery cues she would use when she delivers her speech.

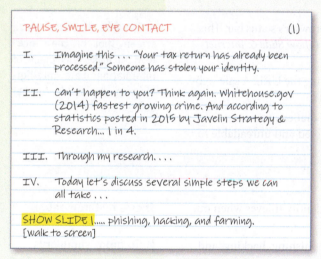

PAUSE, SMILE, EYE CONTACT   (1)

I. Imagine this . . . "Your tax return has already been processed." Someone has stolen your identity.

II. Can't happen to you? Think again. Whitehouse.gov (2014) fastest growing crime. And according to statistics posted in 2015 by Javelin Strategy & Research... 1 in 4.

III. Through my research. . . .

IV. Today let's discuss several simple steps we can all take . . .

SHOW SLIDE 1..... phishing, hacking, and farming.
[walk to screen]

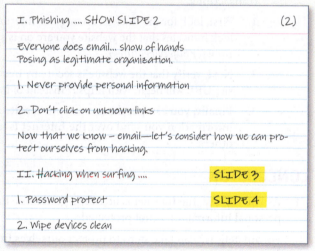

I. Phishing .... SHOW SLIDE 2   (2)

Everyone does email... show of hands
Posing as legitimate organization.

1. Never provide personal information

2. Don't click on unknown links

Now that we know – email—let's consider how we can protect ourselves from hacking.

II. Hacking when surfing ....   SLIDE 3

1. Password protect   SLIDE 4

2. Wipe devices clean

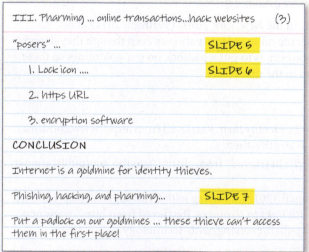

III. Pharming ... online transactions...hack websites   (3)

"posers" ...   SLIDE 5

1. Lock icon ....   SLIDE 6

2. https URL

3. encryption software

CONCLUSION

Internet is a goldmine for identity thieves.

Phishing, hacking, and pharming...   SLIDE 7

Put a padlock on our goldmines ... these thieve can't access them in the first place!

Reflection and Assessment

An informative speech is one with the goal of describing or explaining phenomena in ways that stimulate interest, facilitate understanding, and increase the likelihood that audiences will remember. To assess how well you've learned what we've discussed in this chapter, answer the following questions. If you have trouble answering any of them, go back and review that material. Once you can answer each question accurately, you are ready to move ahead to the next chapter.

1. What are the characteristics of informative speeches?
2. What are the major methods of informing?
3. How do you prepare an informative process speech?
4. How do you prepare an informative expository speech?

Challenge Resource and Assessment Center

MindTap®

Now that you have read Chapter 12, go to your MindTap Communication for *The Challenge of Effective Speaking in a Digital Age* for quick access to flashcards, chapter quizzes, and more.

Applying What You've Learned

1. **Impromptu Speech Activity:** Draw three slips of paper from a container offered by your instructor. Each slip identifies a historical event or historical figure. From the three slips, select one event you'd like to experience or a historical figure you'd like to meet if you could travel back in time. Do a 2- to 3-minute impromptu speech about why you'd like to experience that historical event or meet that historical figure and why.

2. **Assessment Activity A:** Select a current event that's "in the news" today. Learn more about it from three different sources (e.g., a local newspaper, a national news broadcast, and an online blog or social networking site). Compare what you learn from each source and evaluate the ways in which each source cited research, acknowledged fact checking, and established the credentials for its sources. Which source seems to be the most credible and why? Prepare a two- to three-page reflection paper explaining your conclusion. Be sure to attach copies or transcripts of the three sources.

3. **Assessment Activity B:** Identify a celebrity (e.g., television or movie actor, sports star, singer, etc.). Learn more about the person you've identified by visiting his or her personal website or blog, a social networking site devoted to this person, and a celebrity gossip magazine. How does the information shared about this person on each source differ, and how does that shape your understanding of who he or she is? Which one seems most ethical based on the ethical communication principles we discuss in this book and why? Prepare a two- to three-page paper comparing the similarities and differences and your conclusions.

13 Persuasive Messages

B.Christopher/Alamy Stock Photo

Ethical communicators use logos, ethos, and pathos in ways that demonstrate honesty, fairness, and responsibility.

WHAT'S THE POINT?

WHEN YOU'VE FINISHED THIS CHAPTER, YOU WILL BE ABLE TO:

- Describe the nature of persuasion
- Identify and apply logos in persuasive messages
- Identify and apply ethos in persuasive messages
- Identify and apply pathos in persuasive messages

MindTap®

Review the chapter **Learning Objectives** and **Start** with quick warm-up activity.

Rick loves his golden retriever, Trini. He lives in an apartment right downtown and enjoys taking Trini for walks twice a day, but he wishes there was a place nearby where he could let Trini off her leash to run. He decides to try to persuade the city council to fence off an area of a large inner-city park to turn it into a dog park where owners can let their dogs run free. He needs to circulate a petition about the idea, get at least 500 others to sign it, and collect $2,000 in donations to help pay for the fence. Within a few weeks of knocking on doors, Rick easily gathers more than enough signatures. However, he manages to raise less than half of the $2,000 he needs. He wonders what he can do to persuade more people to actually donate money for the cause.

This scenario is not unusual. As with Rick and his campaign for the downtown dog park, whenever we attempt to convince others to agree with our position or behave a certain way, we are actually constructing persuasive messages. **Persuasion** is the process of influencing people's attitudes, beliefs, values, or behaviors. Doing so in a formal public speech is one way of accomplishing this. How successful we are, however, depends on how effectively we employ rhetorical strategies in the microstructure (language and style choices) and arrange them in the macrostructure of our presentation. This chapter focuses on the rhetorical strategies employed in the microstructure of persuasive messages. Chapter 14 focuses on how to arrange these messages in the macrostructure of formal persuasive speeches.

persuasion: the process of influencing people's attitudes, beliefs, values, or behaviors

We begin our two-chapter discussion of persuasive speaking by first describing the nature of persuasive messages and how people process them. Then, we focus specifically on how to use the rhetorical strategies of logos, ethos, and pathos to develop persuasive messages you will use not only in formal speeches but whenever you attempt to influence the attitudes, beliefs, values, or behaviors of others.

THE NATURE OF PERSUASION

Persuasive messages are fundamentally different from informative ones. Whereas the goal of an informative message is to teach, the goal of a persuasive message is to lead. Persuasive speakers are only successful when their audience members are convinced to agree, change their behavior, or take action. In the opening scenario, Rick was successful in convincing others to agree with him, but unsuccessful in getting them to take action.

Persuasive messages are pervasive. Whether we are attempting to convince others or others are attempting to convince us, we are constantly involved in influencing or being influenced. Friends convince us to go to a particular movie or to eat at a certain restaurant, salespeople persuade us to buy a certain sweater or pair of shoes, and advertisements bombard us whenever we turn on the radio or TV, search for information on the Internet, log in to social media, or shop for products online. Once we understand the nature of persuasion and the strategies used to persuade, we can critically examine and evaluate the persuasive messages we receive and create effective and ethical persuasive messages of our own.

Persuasive speaking can be traced to its roots in ancient Greece, where men used it to debate public issues and make important decisions. Thinkers like Aristotle and Plato used the word **rhetoric** to mean using any and all "available means of persuasion."[4] Persuasive speakers achieve their goals by developing solid arguments. An argument, in this context, is not synonymous with "quarrel" as we sometimes define it today. Rather, **argument** means articulating a position with the support of logos, ethos, and pathos.[5]

rhetoric: all available means of persuasion

argument: articulating a position with the support of logos, ethos, and pathos

SUPERBOWL AD ETHICS: WHERE SHOULD THE LINE BE DRAWN?

Professional football is one of the most popular spectator sports in the United States today and the Super Bowl is not just the king of sports TV, it draws more viewers than any TV show in US history. In fact, some 120 million viewers tuned in to watch parts of Super Bowl XLIX, making it the most watched Super Bowl to date.[1] It's no surprise that advertisers were willing to pay an average of $4.5 million per 30-second commercial aired during the event. According to a report in *Forbes*, NBC, the network that aired the game, brought in about $360 million in advertising revenue alone.[2]

Ethical questions come into play when companies struggle to be sure their commercials get noticed and remembered among the competition. For example, the GoDaddy advertisement called "Journey Home" featured a golden retriever puppy name Buddy. Buddy falls out of the back of a truck and arrives home after a perilous journey. His owner exclaims, "Buddy! I'm so glad you made it home because I just sold you on this website I made with GoDaddy." The last scene shows Buddy loaded in the back of a van and being shipped out to a new owner. The ad was pulled as a result of negative feedback from animal advocates; however, it is still accessible online.[3]

1. Do you think ethical standards should be developed and enforced for ads that run during the Super Bowl? Why or why not?

2. Once a company pulls an ad that may damage its reputation, should the ad also be pulled/blocked from Internet viewings? Why or why not?

logos: arguments that use evidence and reasoning to support a position

ethos: arguments about speaker competence, credibility, and good character

pathos: arguments that appeal to emotions

Recall from Chapter 1 that **logos** is a persuasive strategy of constructing logical arguments that use evidence and reasoning to support a position; **ethos** is a persuasive strategy of highlighting your competence, credibility, and good character as a means to convince others to accept and support your position; and **pathos** is a persuasive strategy of appealing to emotions to convince others to support your position.[6]

Processing Persuasive Messages

Do you remember times when you listened thoughtfully about something someone was trying to convince you to agree with before making a deliberate decision? Do you remember other times when you only half listened and made up your mind quickly based on your "gut" feeling? What determines how closely we listen to and how carefully we evaluate the hundreds of persuasive messages we hear each day? Richard Petty and John Cacioppo developed the Elaboration Likelihood Model (ELM) to explain how likely people are to spend more or less time evaluating information (such as the arguments that they hear in a speech) before making their decisions.[7]

The ELM suggests that people process information in one of two ways. The first is the "central route," where we listen carefully, reflect thoughtfully, and maybe even mentally elaborate on the message before making a decision. In doing so, we base our decision primarily on appeals to logic and reasoning (logos). The second way, called the "peripheral route," is a shortcut where we rely on simple cues, such as a quick evaluation of the speaker's competence, credibility, and character (ethos) or a gut check about what we feel (pathos) about the message.

We choose a route based on how important we perceive the issue to be for us. When we believe the issue is important, we are willing to expend the energy necessary to process it using the central route. When we don't see it as important, we take the peripheral route. For example, if you have a serious chronic illness that is expensive to treat, you are more likely to pay attention to and evaluate carefully any proposals to change health care benefits. If you are healthy, you may be more likely to quickly agree with suggestions from someone you perceive to be credible (ethos) or with a proposal that seems compassionate (pathos). The ELM also suggests that when we form attitudes as a result of central processing, we are less likely to change our minds than when we base our decisions on peripheral cues.

When you prepare a persuasive speech (or any persuasive message for that matter), you should use strategies that address both the central and peripheral routes. In other words, be sure to integrate rhetorical strategies that appeal to logos (logic and reasoning), which will be most influential for audience members who use the central processing route. Be sure to also use rhetorical strategies that appeal to both ethos (competence, credibility, and good character) and pathos (emotions) to appeal to audience members using the peripheral processing route. Ultimately, the most compelling persuasive messages offer appeals to all three: logos, ethos, and pathos.

THE RHETORICAL STRATEGY OF LOGOS

Logos strategies are arguments built on logic and reasoning (Photo 13.1). Stephen Toulmin developed a three-part model to describe logos arguments that has stood the test of time. Solid logos argument consists of a claim, support, and warrant.[8]

The **claim (C)** is the conclusion the persuader wants others to agree with. For example, we might *claim:* "Jim's car needs a tune-up." The **support (S)** is the evidence offered as grounds for accepting/agreeing with the claim. You can support a claim with facts, opinions, experiences, and observations. In the car example, we might support our claim with observations that the engine is "missing" at slow speeds" and "stalling at stoplights." The **warrant (W)** is the reasoning process that connects the support to the claim. Sometimes the warrant is verbalized and sometimes it is implied. In the car example, we might offer a warrant such as "missing at slow speeds and stalling at stoplights are *common indications* that a car needs a tune-up." Or we might assume that others already realize these are signs that a car needs a tune-up. When we aren't sure whether audience members will make these connections, we need to verbalize these reasoning warrants to be most effective.

We can connect supporting evidence to the claim using inductive or deductive reasoning warrants. **Inductive reasoning** is arriving at a general conclusion based on several pieces of specific evidence. When we reason inductively, how much our audience agrees with our conclusion depends on the number, quality, and typicality of each piece of evidence we offer. For Jim's car, an inductive reasoning argument might look like this:

> S: *Jim's car engine is "missing" at slow speeds.*
> S: *Jim's car is stalling at stoplights.*
> W: *"Missing" and stalling are common indicators that a car needs a tune-up.*
> C: *Jim's car needs a tune-up.*

Deductive reasoning is arguing that if something is true for everything that belongs to a certain class (**major premise**) and a specific instance is part of that class (**minor premise**), then we must conclude that what is true for all members of the class must be true in the specific instance (claim), as well.

claim (C): conclusion the persuader wants others to agree with

support (S): evidence offered as grounds for accepting the conclusion

warrant (W): reasoning that connects the support to the claim

inductive reasoning: arriving at a conclusion based on a series of pieces of specific evidence

deductive reasoning: arriving at a conclusion based on a major premise and a minor premise

major premise: general principle that most people agree upon

minor premise: specific point that fits within the major premise

Comstock/Comstock Images/Getty Images

Photo 13.1 Logos is making an argument by drawing inferences from factual information to support your conclusion. What logical argument could you make to explain what is happening here?

syllogism: three-part form of deductive reasoning

argue from sign: support a claim by providing evidence that certain events that signal the claim have occurred

argue from example: support a claim by providing one or more individual examples

This three-part form of deductive reasoning is called a **syllogism**. For Jim's car, the deductive reasoning or syllogism might look like this:

> *Major premise: Cars need a tune-up when the engine misses consistently at slow speeds.*
>
> *Minor premise: Jim's car is missing at slow speeds.*
>
> *Claim: Jim's car needs a tune-up.*

With this introduction in mind, let's look at some different types of logical arguments.

Types of Logical Arguments

Although a logical argument *always* includes a claim and support, different types of reasoning warrants can be used to illustrate the relationship between the claim and the support on which it is based. Four common types of logical reasoning arguments are sign, example, analogy, and causation.

Arguing from Sign

You **argue from sign** when you support a claim by providing evidence that certain events that signal the claim have occurred (Photo 13.2). The general warrant for reasoning from sign is: When phenomena that usually or always accompany a specific situation occur, then we can expect that specific situation is occurring (or will occur). For example: "Hives and a slight fever are indicators (signs) of an allergic reaction."

Signs should not be confused with causes: signs accompany a phenomenon but do not bring about, lead to, or create the claim. In fact, signs may actually be the effects of the phenomenon. A rash and fever don't *cause* an allergic reaction; however, they are indications of a reaction.

When arguing from sign, make sure that your reasoning is valid by answering the following questions:

1. **Do these signs usually or always accompany the conclusion (claim) drawn?**

2. **Are a sufficient number of signs present?**

3. **Are contradictory signs also present?**

Photo 13.2 Political campaigns design multiple persuasive messages attempting to convince voters not only that their candidates are the best but also to actually get out and vote for them. Do you typically vote in political elections? Why or why not?

If your answer to either of the first two questions is "no" or your answer to the third is "yes," then your reasoning is flawed.

Arguing from Example

You **argue from example** when examples of the claim you are making are the evidence you use as support (Photo 13.3). The warrant for reasoning from example is: "What is true in the examples provided is (or will be) true in general or in other instances."

Suppose you support Juanita Martinez for president of the local neighborhood council. One of your claims is that "Juanita is electable." In examining her résumé, you find several examples of previous victories. She was elected president of her high school senior class, treasurer of her church council, and president of her college Phi Beta Kappa honor society chapter. Each of these examples supports your claim.

When arguing from example, make sure your reasoning is valid by answering the following questions:

1. **Are enough examples cited?**

2. **Are the examples typical?**

3. **Are negative examples accounted for?**

If your answer to any of these questions is "no," then your reasoning is flawed.

Arguing from Analogy

You **argue from analogy** when you support a claim with a single comparable example that is so significantly similar to the subject of your claim as to be strong proof. The general reasoning warrant is: "What is true in situation A will also be true in situation B, which is similar to situation A" or "What is true for situation A will be true for all similar situations."

Suppose you want to argue that the Taylorsville volunteer fire department should conduct a raffle to raise money for three portable defibrillator units (claim). You could support the claim with an analogy to a single comparable example like this: Jefferson City Fire Department, which is very similar to that of Taylorsville (reasoning warrant), conducted a raffle and raised enough money to purchase four units (support).

When arguing from analogy, make sure that your reasoning is valid by answering the following questions:

1. **Are the two subjects being compared similar in every important way?**

2. **Are any of the ways in which the two subjects are dissimilar important to the claim?**

If your answer to the first questions is "no" or your answer to the second question is "yes," then your reasoning is flawed.

Arguing from Causation

You **argue from causation** when you support a claim by citing events that always (or almost always) bring about or lead to a predictable effect or set of effects (Photo 13.4). The general reasoning warrant is: "If A, which is known to bring about B, has been observed, then we can expect B to occur."

Let's return to Juanita's election campaign one more time. In researching Juanita's election campaign, you might discover that (1) she has campaigned intelligently (support) and (2) she has won the endorsement of key community leaders (support). In the past, these two events have usually been associated with victory (warrant). Thus, Juanita is electable (claim).

Photo 13.3 Lawyers use appeals to logos to make their case for a client's guilt or innocence all the time. Which TV lawyers who are especially good at making appeals to logos can you think of?

argue from analogy: support a claim with a single comparable example that is significantly similar to the subject of the claim

argue from causation: support a claim by citing events that always (or almost always) bring about a predictable effect or set of effects

Photo 13.4 This billboard is making a causal claim. Would you evaluate its reasoning as solid or flawed? Why?

When arguing from causation, make sure your reasoning is valid by answering the following questions:

1. **Are the events alone sufficient to cause the stated effect?**

2. **Do other events accompanying the cited events actually cause the effect?**

3. **Is the relationship between the causal events and the effect consistent?**

If your answer to any of these questions is "no," then your reasoning is flawed.

Reasoning Fallacies

reasoning fallacies: flawed reasoning

As you develop your arguments, make sure that your reasoning is solid. We refer to flawed reasoning as **reasoning fallacies**. Five common fallacies are hasty generalization, false cause, either/or, straw man, and ad hominem.

hasty generalization fallacy: a generalization that is either not supported with evidence or is supported with only one weak example

1. A **hasty generalization fallacy** occurs when a claim is either not supported with evidence or is supported with only one weak example. Enough supporting material must be cited to satisfy the audience that the instances are not isolated or handpicked. For example, someone who argued, "All Akitas are vicious dogs," whose sole piece of evidence was, "My neighbor had an Akita and it bit my best friend's sister," would be guilty of a hasty generalization. It is hasty to generalize about the temperament of a whole breed of dogs based on the single action of one dog. On the other hand, Josh knew a lot of classmates who used or abused substances such as marijuana, Adderall, and anabolic steroids. To make sure he didn't make a hasty generalization that a growing percentage of young American adults are substance abusers, he did an online search for statistics from credible sources such as the National Institute on Drug Abuse, the National Institutes of Health, the US Food and Drug Administration, and the US Department of Health and Human Services.

false cause fallacy: occurs when the alleged cause fails to produce the effect

2. A **false cause fallacy** occurs when the alleged cause fails to produce the effect. The Latin term for this fallacy is *post hoc, ergo propter hoc*, meaning "after this, therefore because of this." Just because two things happen one after the other does not mean that the first necessarily caused the second. An example of a false cause fallacy is claiming that watching violent TV programs, playing violent computer games, or listening to a certain song or musical group causes school shootings. When one event follows another, there may be no connection at all, or the first event might be just one of many things that contribute to the second.

either/or fallacy: argues there are only two alternatives when, in fact, there are many

3. An **either/or fallacy** occurs by suggesting there are only two alternatives when, in fact, others exist. Many such cases are an oversimplification of a complex issue. For example, when Robert argued that "we'll either have to raise taxes or close the library," he committed an either/or fallacy. He reduced a complex issue to one oversimplified solution when many other possible solutions existed.

straw man fallacy: occurs when a speaker weakens the opposing position by misrepresenting it and then attacks that weaker position

4. A **straw man fallacy** occurs when a speaker weakens the opposing position by misrepresenting it in some way and then attacks that weaker (straw man) position. For example, in her speech advocating a 7-day waiting period to purchase handguns, Colleen favored regulation, not prohibition, of gun ownership. Bob countered with "it is our constitutional right to bear arms." In doing so, Bob distorted Colleen's position, making it easier for him to refute it.

Photo 13.5 Ad hominem arguments praise or attack a person rather than focus on the argument. Do you think celebrities enhance the appeal of products they help advertise?

5. An **ad hominem fallacy** attacks or praises the person making the argument rather than addressing the argument itself. *Ad hominem* literally means "to the man." For example, during the 2016 Republican presidential primary campaigns, when Donald Trump called out Carly Fiorina on her looks rather than addressing the substance of her experience, he was committing an ad hominem fallacy. Unfortunately, politicians sometimes resort to ad hominem arguments when they attack their opponent's character rather than their platforms. Bullying in person, over the Internet, and via text messaging is another example of ad hominem attacks that can have dire consequences. Advertisements that feature celebrities using a particular product are often guilty of ad hominem reasoning (Photo 13.5). For example, Tina Fey and Ellen DeGeneres have both appeared in American Express commercials, Gwyneth Paltrow has done ads for Estée Lauder, Kim Kardashian West for T-Mobile, and Liam Neeson for the massive multiplayer online video game *Clash of Clans*. What makes any of these celebrities experts about the products they are endorsing?

ad hominem fallacy: occurs when one attacks or praises the person making an argument rather than the argument itself

THE RHETORICAL STRATEGY OF ETHOS

Not everyone will choose the central processing route to make a decision regarding a persuasive message. One important cue people use when they process information by the peripheral route is ethos. So, you will want to demonstrate good character, as well as say and do things to convey competence and credibility, whenever you are presenting.

Demonstrating Good Character

We turn again to the ancient Greek philosopher Aristotle, who first observed that a speaker's credibility depends on the audience's perception of the speaker's goodwill. Today, we define **goodwill** as a perception the audience forms of a speaker they believe (1) understands them, (2) empathizes with them, and (3) is responsive to them. When audience members believe in the speaker's goodwill, they are more willing to believe what the speaker says. In our opening scenario, Rick was able to convey good character with other dog owners living downtown because he lived there too. So he could talk about sharing their concerns and empathizing with their frustrations.

goodwill: perception the audience forms of a speaker who they believe understands them, empathizes with them, and is responsive to them

You can demonstrate that you understand your audience by personalizing your information, using examples that directly relate to your audience and their experiences. You can also empathizing with your audience. **Empathy** is the ability to see the world through the eyes of someone else. Empathizing with the views of your audience doesn't necessarily mean that you accept their views as your own. It does, however, mean that you acknowledge them as valid. For example, consider what spokespersons lead with when responding to a national emergency or crisis event. They almost always begin by saying something like this: "Our hearts go out to the victims and their loved ones."

Finally, you can demonstrate goodwill by being responsive. **Responsive** speakers show they care about the audience by acknowledging feedback, especially subtle negative cues, in a respectful way. This feedback may occur during the presentation, but it also may have occurred prior to the event.

Here is how former President Obama conveyed good character in the opening remarks of his December 5, 2015, address responding to the families and community of the victims of the San Bernardino shootings:

> *Hi, everybody. This weekend, our hearts are with the people of San Bernardino—another American community shattered by unspeakable violence. We salute the first responders—the police, the SWAT teams, the EMTs—who responded so quickly, with such courage, and saved lives. We pray for the injured as they fight to recover from their wounds.*
>
> *Most of all, we stand with 14 families whose hearts are broken. We're learning more about their loved ones—the men and women, the beautiful lives, that were lost. They were doing what so many of us do this time of year—enjoying the holidays. Celebrating with each other. Rejoicing in the bonds of friendship and community that bind us together, as Americans. Their deaths are an absolute tragedy, not just for San Bernardino, but for our country.[9]*

Conveying Competence and Credibility

Not surprisingly, we are more likely to be persuaded when we perceive a speaker to be competent and credible. We propose the following strategies so that your **terminal credibility**, the audience's perception of your expertise at the end of your speech, is even greater than your **initial credibility**, their perception of your expertise at the beginning of your speech.

1. **Explain your competence**. Unless someone has formally introduced you and your qualifications or your expertise is well known among the group, such as it is for the president of the United States when delivering his or her weekly address, you will need to tell your audience about your expertise. Sending messages about your competence during your speech enhances your **derived credibility** or your audience's perception of your expertise during your speech. You can interweave comments about your expertise into your introductory comments and at appropriate places within the body of your speech.[10] If you've done a good deal of research on your topic, say so. If you have personal experience, say so. It's important for the audience to know why they can trust what you are saying.

2. **Use evidence from respected sources**. You can also increase your derived credibility by using supporting material from well-recognized and respected sources. If you have a choice between using a statistic from a known partisan organization or from a nonpartisan professional association, choose the professional association. Likewise, if you can quote a local expert who is well known and respected by your audience or a national expert your audience may never have heard of, use the local expert's quote.

3. **Use nonverbal delivery cues**. Audience members assess your credibility not only from what they hear about you before you begin speaking but also from what they observe by looking at you. Although professional attire enhances credibility in any speaking situation, it is particularly important for persuasive speeches. Research shows that persuasive speakers who dress professionally are perceived as more credible than those who dress casually or sloppily.[11]

Audience members also notice how confident you appear as you address them. From the moment you rise to speak, convey that you are competent. Plant your feet firmly, glance at your notes, and then make eye contact or audience contact with one person or group before taking a breath and beginning to speak. Likewise, pause and establish eye contact or audience contact upon finishing your speech. Just as pausing and establishing eye contact or audience contact before your speech enhances credibility, doing so upon delivering the closing lines of your speech has the same result.

4. **Use vocal expression**. Research shows that credibility is strongly influenced by how you sound. Speaking fluently, using a moderately fast rate, and expressing yourself with conviction makes you appear intelligent and competent.[12]

THE RHETORICAL STRATEGY OF PATHOS

We are more likely to be involved with a topic when we have an emotional stake in it. **Emotions** are the buildup of action-specific energy.[13] When we experience the tension associated with any emotion, we look for a way to release the energy. For example, consider how people's facial expressions change when they receive good or bad news. Smiling is one way to release built-up feelings of happiness. Crying can be a way to release built-up feelings of sadness or happiness. You can increase audience involvement, then, by stimulating both negative and positive emotions in your speeches.[14]

Evoking Negative Emotions

Negative emotions are disquieting, so when people experience them, they look for ways to eliminate them (Photo 13.6). The five most common negative emotions are fear, guilt, shame, anger, and sadness.

Fear

We experience **fear** when we perceive that we have no control over a situation that threatens us. We may fear physical harm or psychological harm. Fear is reduced when the threat is eliminated or when we escape. If you use examples, stories, and statistics that evoke fear in your audience, they will be more motivated to hear how your proposal can eliminate the source of their fear or allow them to escape from it. For example, in a speech whose goal was to convince the audience that they were at

emotions: the buildup of action-specific energy

negative emotions: disquieting feelings people experience

fear: perceiving no control over a situation that threatens us

Photo 13.6 When appealing to negative emotions, be certain that your choice demonstrates ethical communication. When might it be better *not* to appeal to negative emotions in a persuasive message?

risk of developing high blood pressure, the speaker might use a fear appeal in this way:

> One of every three Americans age 18 and older has high blood pressure. It is a primary cause of stroke, heart disease, heart failure, kidney disease, and blindness. It triples a person's chance of developing heart disease, boosts the chance of stroke seven times, and increases the chance of congestive heart failure six times. Look at the person on your right; look at the person on your left. If they don't get it, chances are you will. Today, I'd like to convince you that you are at risk for developing high blood pressure.

Guilt

We feel **guilt** when we personally violate a moral, ethical, or religious code that we hold dear. We experience guilt as a gnawing sensation that we have done something wrong. When we feel guilty, we are motivated to "make things right" or to atone for our transgression. For example, in a speech designed to motivate the audience to take a turn as a designated driver, a speaker might evoke guilt like this:

> Have you ever promised your mom that you wouldn't ride in a car driven by someone who had been drinking? And then turned around and got in the car with your buddy even though you both had a few? You know that wasn't right. Lying to your mother, putting yourself and your buddy at risk. . . (pause) but what can you do? Well, today I'm going to show you how you can avoid all that guilt, live up to your promises to mom, and keep both you and your buddy safe.

Shame

We feel **shame** when we violate a moral code and our violation is revealed to someone we think highly of. The more egregious our behavior or the more we admire the person who finds out, the more shame we experience. When we feel shame, we are motivated to "redeem" ourselves in the eyes of that person. If in your speech you can evoke feelings of shame and then demonstrate how your proposal can either redeem someone after a violation has occurred or prevent the feeling, then you can motivate the audience to carefully consider your arguments. For example, in a speech advocating thankfulness, the speaker might use a shame-based approach by quoting the old saying, "I cried because I had no shoes until I met a man who had no feet."

Anger

When faced with an obstacle that stands in the way of something we want, we experience **anger**. We may also experience anger when someone threatens to or actually physically or emotionally harms us or someone we love. Speakers who choose to evoke anger in their audience members must be careful that they don't incite so much anger that reasoning processes are short circuited.

If you can rouse your audience's anger and then show how your proposal will help them achieve their goals by stopping or preventing the threat or easing the harm that has occurred, you can motivate them to carefully consider your arguments. For example, suppose you want to convince your audience to support a law requiring community notification when a convicted sex offender moves into the neighborhood. You might arouse their anger to get their attention by personalizing the story of Megan Kanka.

> She was your little girl, just seven years old, and the light of your world. She had a smile that could bring you to your knees. And she loved puppies. So when that nice man who had moved in down the street invited her in to see his new puppy, she didn't hesitate. But she didn't get to see the puppy, and you didn't ever see her alive again. He beat her, he raped her, and then he strangled her. He packaged her body in an old toy chest and dumped it in a park. Your seven-year-old princess would never dig in a toy chest again or slip down the slide in that park. And that hurts. But what makes you really angry is she wasn't his first. But you didn't know that. Because no

one bothered to tell you that the guy down the street was likely to kill little girls. The cops knew it. But they couldn't tell you. You, the one who was supposed to keep her safe, didn't know. Angry? You bet. Yeah, he's behind bars again, but you still don't know who's living down the street from you. But you can. There is a law pending before Congress that will require active notification of the community when a known sex offender takes up residence, and today I'm going to tell how you can help to get this passed.[15]

Sadness

When we fail to achieve a goal or experience a loss or separation, we experience **sadness**. Unlike our reactions to other negative emotions, however, we tend to withdraw and become isolated when we feel sad. Because sadness is an unpleasant feeling, we look for ways to end it. Speeches that help us understand and find answers for what has happened can comfort us and help relieve the unpleasant feeling. For example, after 9/11, many Americans were sad. Yes, they were also afraid and angry, but overlaying it all was profound sadness for those who had been lost and what had been lost. The questions, "Why? Why did they do this? Why do they hate us so?" captured the national melancholy. So, when politicians suggested that they understood the answers to these questions, Americans tended to perk up and listen to what they had to say.

sadness: feeling experienced when we fail to achieve a goal or experience a loss or separation

Evoking Positive Emotions

Just as evoking negative emotions can cause audience members to internalize your arguments, so too can you tap their **positive emotions**, which are feelings that people enjoy experiencing. With negative emotions, the goal is to show how your proposal will reduce or eliminate the feeling. With positive emotions, the goal is to help your audience maintain or even enhance the feeling. Happiness or joy, pride, relief, hope, and compassion are five common positive emotions.

positive emotions: feelings that people enjoy experiencing

Happiness or Joy

Happiness or joy is the buildup of positive energy we experience when we accomplish something, have a satisfying interaction or relationship, or see or possess objects that appeal to us. Think about how you felt when you got accepted into college or when you got a special gift that you had been wanting for a long time. Or think about the birthday when you received that toy you had been dreaming about. As a speaker, if you can show how your proposal will lead your audience members to be happy or joyful, then they are likely to listen and to think carefully about your proposal. For example, suppose you want to motivate your audience to attend a couples' encounter weekend where they will learn how to "rekindle" their relationship with a partner. If you can remind them about how they felt early in their relationship and then suggest how the weekend can reignite those feelings, they may be more motivated to listen.

happiness or joy: the buildup of positive energy

Pride

When we experience satisfaction about something we or someone we care about accomplishes, we feel **pride**. "We're number one! We're number one!" is the chant of the crowd feeling pride in the accomplishment of "their" team. Whereas happiness is related to feelings of pleasure, pride is related to feelings of self-worth. If you can demonstrate how your proposal will help audience members feel good about themselves, they will be more motivated to consider your arguments. For example, suppose you want to persuade your audience to volunteer to work on the newest Habitat for Humanity house being constructed in your community. You might allude to the pride they will feel when they see people moving into the house they helped to build. As Rick revised his persuasive speech campaign to raise money for a dog park, he decided to appeal to pride by focusing on how helping build a park would provide a beautiful green space in the heart of the city and, at the same time, provide a welcome place for family pets to run and play.

pride: feeling of self-satisfaction as the result of an accomplishment

Relief

relief: positive emotion felt when a threatening situation has been alleviated

When a threatening situation has been alleviated, we feel the positive emotion of **relief**. We relax and put down our guard. As a speaker, you use relief to motivate audience members by combining it with the negative emotion of fear. For example, suppose your goal is to convince your audience that they can control their risk for high blood pressure. You might use the same personalization of statistics that was described in the example of fear appeals, but instead of stopping at convincing them that they are at risk, you could also promise relief if they hear you out and do what you advocate.

Hope

hope: feeling that stems from believing something desirable is likely to happen

The emotional energy that stems from believing something desirable is likely to happen is called **hope**. Whereas relief causes us to relax and let down our guard, hope energizes us to take action to overcome the situation. Hope empowers. As with relief, hope appeals are usually accompanied by fear appeals. You can motivate audience members to listen by showing how your proposal provides a plan for overcoming a difficult situation. For example, if you propose adopting a low-fat diet to reduce the risk of high blood pressure, you can use the same personalization of statistics that were cited in the example of fear appeals but change the ending to state: "Today, I'm going to help you to beat the odds by convincing you to adopt a low-fat diet."

Compassion

compassion: feeling of selfless concern for the suffering of another

When we feel selfless concern for the suffering of another person and that concern energizes us to try to relieve that suffering, we feel **compassion**. Speakers can evoke feelings of compassion by vividly describing the suffering endured by someone (Photo 13.7). The audience will then be motivated to listen to see how the speaker's proposal plans to end that suffering. For example, when a speaker whose goal is to have you donate to Project Peanut Butter displays a slide of an emaciated child, claims that 13 percent of all Malawi children die of malnutrition, and states that for $10 you can save a child, he or she is appealing to your compassion.

Photo 13.7 Speakers appeal to compassion by showing how someone is suffering and how we can help. What are some examples of advertisements or campaigns that appeal to compassion?

Guidelines for Appealing to Emotions

You can evoke negative emotions, positive emotions, or both as a way to encourage listeners to internalize your message. In this section, we offer several guidelines for doing so effectively in your speech content, language (microstructure), and delivery.

Tell Vivid Stories

Dramatize your arguments by using stories and testimonials that personalize the issue for listeners by appealing to specific emotions. In his speech on bone marrow donation, David Slater simply could have said, "By donating bone marrow—a simple procedure—you can save lives." Instead, he dramatized both the simplicity of the bone marrow donation procedure and the lifesaving impact with a short story designed to heighten audience members' feelings of compassion.

When Tricia Matthews decided to undergo a simple medical procedure, she had no idea what impact it could have on her life. But more than a year later, when she saw five-year-old Tommy and his younger brother Daniel walk across the stage of the Oprah Winfrey Show, she realized that the short amount of time it took her to donate her bone marrow was well worth it. Tricia is not related to the boys, who suffered from a rare immune deficiency disorder treated by a transplant of her marrow. Tricia and the boys found each other through the National Marrow Donor Program, or NMDP, a national network which strives to bring willing donors and needy patients together. Though the efforts Tricia made were minimal, few Americans made the strides she did. Few of us would deny anyone the gift of life, but sadly, few know how easily we can help.[16]

Notice how David used a compelling example to appeal to his listeners' emotions and personalize the information for them.

Similarly, Ryan Labor began his speech on shaken baby syndrome with the following vivid story designed to raise feelings of fear, anger, and sadness:

Last winter, two-year-old Cody Dannar refused to eat or play. He had a headache. Doctors said he just had the flu. After a couple weeks home with his mother, Cody felt better. Days later . . . Cody's headaches returned. Coming home from work the next afternoon, his parents found the babysitter frantically calling 911 and Cody lying rigid and unconscious on the floor. He didn't have the flu; in fact, he wasn't sick at all. The babysitter had caused his headaches. To quiet Cody down, she had shaken him, damaging the base of Cody's brain that now risked his life as he lay on the ground.[17]

Use Startling Statistics

Statistics don't have to be boring. When used strategically, they can evoke strong emotions. To provoke emotions, statistics need to be startling. A statistic may surprise because of its sheer magnitude. For example, in a speech urging attendance at a local protest march organized by the Mobilization for Global Justice, Cory used the following statistic to shame and anger his audience about the global problem of unequal wealth distribution: "Did you know that the USA has 25.4 percent of the world's wealth? And of that, the top 10 percent of Americans control 71 percent?"

Sometimes, by comparing two statistics, you can increase their emotional impact. For example, during his second main point, Cory used the following comparative statistic to highlight wealth disparity. "In the United States, not only does the top 10 percent control 71 percent of the wealth, but the bottom 40 percent of Americans control less than 1 percent!"

In Ryan's speech on shaken baby syndrome, he strengthened his emotional appeal by following his vivid story with these startling statistics:

Unfortunately, Cody isn't alone. Over one million infants and young children suffer from shaken baby syndrome annually while thousands die. . . . Only 15 percent survive without damage. The remaining children suffer from blindness, learning disabilities, deafness, cerebral palsy, or paralysis.[18]

Incorporate Listener Relevance Links

You can also appeal to emotions by integrating listener relevance links, as emotions are stronger when listeners feel personally involved. At a later point in Ryan's shaken baby syndrome speech, he appealed to emotions through listener relevance. Notice how he brings the problem close to each listener by suggesting the universality of the problem.

Jacy Showers, director of the first National Conference on Shaken Baby Syndrome, says "Shaking occurs in families of all races, incomes, and education levels" and "81 percent of SBS offenders had no previous history of child abuse." The reason? The offenders were so young, either babysitters or new parents.

Choose Striking Presentational Aids

Because "a picture is worth a thousand words," consider how you can reinforce your verbal message with dramatic presentational aids. Still pictures and short video clips can at times create an emotional jolt that is difficult to achieve with words alone. Jonna used several before-and-after pictures of female celebrities Nicole Richie, LeeAnn Rimes, and Mary Kate Olsen to reinforce her point that emaciated celebrities were contributing to an eating disorder epidemic among teenage girls. Likewise, Anton used a 15-second video clip from the documentary *Zoned for Slavery: The Child Behind the Label*[19] to dramatize the problem of child labor in the global textile industry. His goal was to shame his audience members into sending one postcard to the manufacturer of their favorite brand of clothing asking about the working conditions of those who manufacture their clothing. As part of his dog park campaign, Rick solicited help from a graphic designer to provide an artist's rendering of what the empty space would look like once the dog park was finished.

Use Descriptive and Provocative Language

When developing your speech, include persuasive punch words—words that evoke emotion—where you can. Here's how Ryan used persuasive punch words to strengthen his emotional appeal:

> *The worst of all epidemics is a silent one. With the majority of all victims either infants or young children, shaken baby syndrome can be classified as a stealthy plague . . . . When shaken, the brain is literally ricocheted inside the skull, bruising the brain and tearing blood vessels coming from the neck . . . cutting off oxygen and causing the eyes to bulge.*

Use Nonverbal Delivery Cues

Even the most eloquently phrased emotional appeal will lose its impact unless the non-verbal parts of delivery heighten and highlight the emotional content of the message. Practice using your voice to emphasize what you are saying, employing pauses and modifying your volume and pitch to heighten and highlight the emotional content of

IMPROMPTU SPEECH CHALLENGE

Select a product advertisement from YouTube, a magazine or newspaper, or a billboard. Create a short 1- to 2-minute speech evaluating its use of appeals to logos, ethos, and pathos.

Jerod Harris/FilmMagic/Getty Images

PUBLIC SPEAKING IN THE REAL WORLD

Charlize Theron: Award-Winning Actress *and* Powerful Persuasive Speaker

Many people may know Charlize Theron as an Academy award-winning actress who takes on difficult roles, such as a serial killer in *Monster*, a sexual harassment activist in *North Country*, and an evil stepmother in *Snow White and the Huntsman*. What is less well known, however, is that Theron has a genuine fear of public speaking. In fact, she nearly passed out on the first day of filming *North Country* because she had to give a public speech. She is quoted as saying "I get this really strange sensation (when public speaking) where everything goes black, and I see white spots, and I break out in hives. It's probably the most frightening thing you can make me do."[20] Nevertheless, Theron is an outspoken activist, designated by the United Nations as a "Messenger of Peace," who travels across the globe giving persuasive speeches focused on eliminating violence against women, creating a better life for impoverished families in South Africa, promoting HIV prevention, and endorsing same-sex marriage.[21] In spite of her fear, Theron is an effective persuasive speaker determined to get her message across to all who will listen.

1. Does it surprise you to learn that Theron experiences fear of public speaking? Why or why not?

2. Why do you suppose Theron continues to speaking in public in spite of her fear?

your message. A dramatic pause before a startling statistic can magnify its emotional effect. Similarly, lowering or raising the volume or pitch of your voice at strategic places can create an emotional response. If you experiment as you practice aloud, you will find a combination of vocal elements that can enhance emotional appeal when delivering your speech.

Use Gestures and Facial Expressions to Highlight Emotions

Your message will lose its emotional impact if you deliver it with a deadpan expression or if your demeanor contradicts the emotional content of your message. So, if you want your audience to feel angry, you should model this feeling by looking annoyed or livid or furious. You might clench your fists, furrow your brow, and frown. When you want to foster feelings of joy in your audience, you can smile, nod, and use other nonverbal gestures that are natural for you when you experience joy. Remember, as an ethical speaker, you are appealing to emotions that you yourself feel about the situation, so allow yourself to experience these emotions as you practice. Then, when you give your speech, you will be more comfortable displaying your feelings for your audience.

Reflection and Assessment

Persuasion is the process of influencing people's attitudes, beliefs, values, or behaviors. Persuasive speaking is doing so in a public speech. Persuasive messages differ from informative messages in that their primary goal is to seek agreement and sometimes to incite action. To assess how well you've learned what we've discussed in this chapter, answer the following questions. If you have trouble answering any of them, go back and review that material. Once you can answer each question accurately, you are ready to move ahead to the next chapter.

1. What is the nature of persuasive messages and how do people process them?
2. What is the role of logos in persuasive messages?
3. What is the role of ethos in persuasive messages?
4. What is the role of pathos in persuasive messages?

MindTap®

Challenge Resource and Assessment Center

Now that you have read Chapter 13, go to your MindTap Communication for *The Challenge of Effective Speaking in a Digital Age* for quick access to flashcards, chapter quizzes, and more.

Applying What You've Learned

1. **Impromptu Speech Activity:** Draw a common household product from a box of products your instructor provides. Products in the box might range from nonperishable foods (soup, cereal, snacks, etc.), to cleaning supplies (window cleaner, hand soap, dishwashing liquid), to paper products (toilet paper, paper towels, napkins). Prepare a 2- to 3-minute speech identifying how the product you selected appeals to logos, ethos, and pathos.

2. **Assessment Activity A:** Select a product and watch a TV commercial for it that airs on a cable news network, sports network, and family-oriented network. Identify similar and different rhetorical appeals used in the commercials. Offer possible reasons based on the ELM for using similar and different appeals. Prepare a one- to two-page reflection paper describing what you discovered and the assessment you drew from it.

3. **Assessment Activity B:** Consider an interaction you had recently with a friend or family member who convinced you (a) *to do something* you hadn't planned on doing (e.g., go to a movie, attend an event) or (b) *not to do something* you had intended to do (e.g., a household chore, homework). What rhetorical strategies can you identify that influenced your decision? Prepare a one- to two-page paper documenting examples of logos, ethos, and pathos that persuaded you.

14 Persuasive Speaking

AP Images/UCLA Daily Bruin, Tiffany Michalka

Ethical communicators demonstrate responsibility by considering implications of their persuasive message on their audience.

WHAT'S THE POINT?

WHEN YOU'VE FINISHED THIS CHAPTER, YOU WILL BE ABLE TO:

- Determine an appropriate persuasive speech goal based on the rhetorical situation
- Identify some persuasive speech patterns
- Follow ethical communication guidelines when preparing persuasive speeches

MindTap®

Review the chapter **Learning Objectives** and **Start** with quick warm-up activity.

As Tomeka finished her speech on "Taking Back the Neighborhood: Get Out the Vote!" the audience stood up and began to chant, "No more! No more! No more! No more!" It was clear to her that she had made an impact. Not only had she convinced her audience, but she could also see that some of them were visibly angry and ready for action. As she was leaving the platform, she heard a member of the audience shout out, "You heard her. It's time! Voting won't do any good. Let's go take what is ours. Take to the streets! Get yours!" In the riot that ensued, three neighborhood shops were ransacked, ten cars were set on fire, and 23 people were arrested. The next day as she toured the neighborhood and saw firsthand the wreckage her speech had led to, all she could think was, "This wasn't what I meant. This isn't what I wanted."

In the previous chapter, we focused on how persuasive messages employ what Aristotle called all available means of persuasion (logos, ethos, and pathos) to seek agreement or to encourage action. In this chapter, we focus on how to organize those rhetorical appeals into persuasive speeches that are both effective and ethical. We do so via a three-step process:

1. First, determine an appropriate persuasive speech goal.

2. Second, organize the speech content using an appropriate persuasive speech pattern.

3. Finally, refine the speech based on ethical guidelines for persuasive speeches.

In the opening vignette, Tomeka's speech was certainly effective in not only convincing her audience to agree with her, but also leaving them so emotionally charged that that they took action. However, those actions went well beyond what Tomeka wanted them to do.

PERSUASIVE SPEECH GOALS

proposition: a declarative sentence that clearly indicates the position the speaker will advocate

Persuasive speech goals are stated as propositions. A **proposition** is a declarative sentence that clearly indicates the position you advocate. For example, "I want to convince my audience that pirating (downloading from the Internet) copyrighted media without paying for it is wrong" is a proposition. Notice how a persuasive proposition differs from an informative speech goal on the same subject: "I want to inform my audience about the practice of pirating copyrighted media." In the informative speech, you achieve your goal if the audience understands and remembers what you talk about. In the persuasive speech, however, they must not only understand and remember, but also agree with your position and possibly even take action. The three types of propositions are fact, value, or policy.

Types of Propositions

proposition of fact: a statement designed to convince the audience that something did or did not exist or occur, is or is not true, or will or will not occur

A **proposition of fact** is a statement designed to convince your audience that something:

- did, probably did, probably did not, or did not exist or occur;
- is, probably is, probably is not, or is not true; or
- will, probably will, probably will not, or will not occur.

Although propositions of fact may or may not be true—both positions are arguable—they are stated as though they are, without question, true. For example, whether or not Princess Diana's death was an unfortunate car accident or an assassination is debatable. So you could argue a proposition of fact in two ways: "Princess Diana's death was nothing more than a tragic car accident" or "Princess Diana's death was, in fact, a successful assassination attempt." Examples of propositions of fact concerning the present are "God exists" or "There is no God"; and "Cell phone use causes brain cancer" or "Cell phone use does not cause brain cancer." Claims of fact concerning the future are predictions. For example, "Thanks to the Internet, paper-bound books will eventually cease to exist" and "The New York Yankees will surely win the World Series next year" are both propositions of fact concerning the future.

A **proposition of value** is a statement designed to convince your audience that something is good or bad; desirable or undesirable; fair or unfair; moral or immoral; sound or unsound; beneficial or harmful; or important or unimportant.[1] You can attempt to convince your audience that something has more value than something else, or you can convince your audience that something meets valued standards. "Running is a better form of exercise than bicycling" is an example of the former and "The real value of a college education is that it creates an informed citizenry" is an example of the latter.

A **proposition of policy** is a statement designed to convince your audience that a particular rule, plan, or course of action should be taken. Propositions of policy will implore listeners using words such as "do it/don't do it," "should/shouldn't," or "must/must not." "All college students *should* be required to take a public speaking course," "The United States *must* stop deep sea oil drilling," "*Don't* text while driving," and "Water packaged in plastic bottles *should* be taxed to pay for the cost associated with recycling empties" are propositions of policy. Tomeka's speech focused on a proposition of policy as well: "We must get out and vote." Exhibit 14.1 provides several examples of how propositions of fact, value, and policy can be developed from the same topic idea.

As you begin working on your persuasive speeches, you can use the Speech-Planning Action Steps to help you organize and develop them, although some of the steps will be modified to provide you with guidance that is particular to persuasive speeches. You can use Activity 1Ep and the sample student response to help you develop a specific goal for a persuasive speech stated as a proposition.

proposition of value: a statement designed to convince the audience that something is good, bad, desirable, undesirable, fair, unfair, moral, immoral, sound, unsound, beneficial, harmful, important, or unimportant

proposition of policy: a statement designed to convince the audience that they should take a specific course of action

---

Exhibit 14.1 **Example of Persuasive Speech Propositions**

Propositions of fact	Propositions of value	Propositions of policy
Mahatma Gandhi was the father of passive resistance.	Mahatma Gandhi was a moral leader.	Mahatma Gandhi should be given a special award for his views on passive resistance.
Pharmaceutical advertising to consumers increases prescription drug prices.	Pharmaceutical advertising of new prescription drugs on TV is better than marketing new drugs directly to doctors.	Pharmaceutical companies should be required to refrain from advertising prescription drugs on TV.
Using paper ballots is a popular method for voting in US elections.	Using paper ballots is better than using electronic voting machines.	Using paper ballots should be required for US elections.

1Ep SPEECH PLANNING

Activity

Writing a Specific Goal as a Persuasive Proposition

1. Identify your topic and tentatively phrase your goal.

2. Check whether you believe that your target audience is opposed to, has no opinion of, or is in favor of your position, and why they might feel that way.

3. Rephrase your goal as a proposition of fact, value, or policy appropriately tailored to the attitude of your target audience.

SAMPLE STUDENT RESPONSE

1. Identify your topic and tentatively phrase your goal.

   I want to convince my audience not to download copyrighted music from the Internet without paying for it.

2. Check whether you believe that your target audience is opposed to, has no opinion of, or is in favor of your position, and why they might feel that way.

   Although some students may be opposed to or in favor of this proposition, I think the majority are undecided.

3. Rephrase your goal as a proposition of fact, value, or policy appropriately tailored to the attitude of your target audience.

   Because my audience is neutral, I will phrase my goal as a proposition of value: Downloading copyrighted music from the Internet without paying for it is wrong.

Tailoring Propositions to Your Target Audience

Because it is difficult to convince people to change their minds, what you can hope to accomplish in one speech depends on where your audience stands on your topic. So you'll want to analyze your audience and tailor your proposition based on their initial attitude toward the topic.

Audience members' attitudes can range from highly favorable to strongly opposed and can be visualized as lying on a continuum like the one pictured in Exhibit 14.2. Even though an audience will include individuals whose opinions fall at nearly every point along the continuum, generally audience members' opinions tend to cluster in one area of it. For instance, the opinions of the audience represented in Exhibit 14.2 cluster around "mildly opposed," even though a few people are more hostile and a few have favorable opinions. This cluster point represents your **target audience**, the group of people you most want to persuade. Based on your target audience, you can classify your audience's initial attitude toward your topic as "opposed" (holding an opposite point of view), "no opinion" (uninformed, neutral, or apathetic), or "in favor" (already supportive).

target audience: the group of people you most want to persuade

Exhibit 14.2

14.2 Sample Opinion Continuum

Highly opposed	Opposed	Mildly opposed	Neither in favor nor opposed	Mildly in favor	In favor	Highly in favor
2	2	11	1	2	2	0

Tailoring Your Speech for an "Opposed" Target Audience

It is unrealistic to believe you will be able to change your target audience's attitude from "opposed" to "in favor" in only one short speech. Instead, seek **incremental change**, that is, attempt to move them only a small degree in your direction, hoping for additional movement later. For example, if your target audience is opposed to the goal "I want to convince my audience that recreational marijuana should be legal," you might rephrase your goal as "I want to convince my audience that medical marijuana should be legal to help terminally ill patients ease their pain." Then brainstorm potential objections, questions, and criticisms that might arise and shape your speech to address them.

Tailoring Your Speech for a "No Opinion" Target Audience

If your target audience has no opinion for or against your topic, consider whether they are uninformed, neutral, or apathetic. If they are **uninformed**—that is, they do not know enough about the topic to have formed an opinion—provide the basic arguments and information needed for them to become informed. For example, if your target audience is uninformed about marijuana, you might begin by highlighting what it is, the forms it comes in, and what effect it has on the mind and body. If your target audience is **neutral**, that is, they know the basics about your topic but not enough to have formed an opinion, provide evidence and reasoning illustrating why your position is superior to others (Photo 14.1). Perhaps your target audience knows what marijuana is and what it does to the mind and body, but needs to understand the benefits in legalizing it as a recreational substance. When target audiences have no opinion because they are **apathetic**, find ways to show how your topic relates to them or their needs. For the marijuana example, address possible questions such as, "I'm not interested in using marijuana, so why should I care?" You can do this by including strong listener relevance links for each main point.

Tailoring Your Speech for an "In Favor" Target Audience

If your target audience is only mildly in favor of your proposal, your task is to reinforce and strengthen their beliefs. Audience members who favor your position may become further committed to it after hearing new reasons and more recent evidence supporting it. When your target audience strongly agrees with your position, then consider a goal that moves them to act on it.

incremental change: attempting to move your audience only a small degree in your direction

uninformed: an audience that doesn't know enough about a topic to have formed an opinion

neutral: an audience that has some information about a topic but does not really understand why one position is preferred and so still has no opinion

apathetic: an audience that is uninterested in, unconcerned about, or indifferent toward a topic

Photo 14.1 Audiences believe reasons when there is strong evidence to support them. Do you believe the claim made on this sign? Why or why not?

PUBLIC SPEAKING IN THE REAL WORLD

"Let us be outraged, let us be loud, let us be bold."

When most of us think of Brad Pitt, we probably think of the guy who seems to have it all, for instance, the six-time Oscar-nominated actor and producer, the two-time recipient of *People*'s "Sexiest Man Alive," or the happy family man in the Pitt–Jolie clan. What we might not think of is Brad Pitt the human rights and social issues activist. Some of his more famous speech quotations include "heartthrobs are a dime a dozen," "you must lose everything in order to gain anything," and "success is a beast. It actually puts the emphasis on the wrong thing." Perhaps that's why for over a decade, he has devoted so much time to publicly supporting causes he believes in, such as stem-cell research and same-sex marriage, as well as combating AIDS and poverty in developing countries.[2] His courage for doing so in the face of critics who question his sincerity is grounded in what we talk about in this chapter: being genuinely committed to

your message. In his own words:

"Let us be the ones who say we do not accept that a child dies every three seconds simply because he does not have the drugs you and I have. Let us be the ones to say we are not satisfied that your place of birth determines your right to life. Let us be outraged, let us be loud, let us be bold."[3]

1. Do you believe Brad Pitt is a credible speaker on this topic? Why?

2. Do you find other celebrities who stand behind human rights causes credible? Why?

To continue with the marijuana example, if your target audience strongly favors the idea of legalizing recreational marijuana, then your goal might be "I want my audience to email or write letters to their state representatives urging them to support legislation to legalize recreational marijuana." In the opening vignette, Tomeka's audience was already in favor of her proposition so she focused on motivating them to act.

PERSUASIVE SPEECH PATTERNS

speeches to convince: a speech designed to seek agreement about a belief, value, or attitude

speeches to actuate: a speech designed to incite action

statement of reasons: a straightforward organization in which the best-supported reasons are presented in a meaningful order

Persuasive speeches are organized as **speeches to convince** (to reinforce or change an audience's belief or attitude) or **speeches to actuate** (to take action). Let's look more closely at some of them.

Speeches to Convince

Most speeches to convince follow one of four organizational patterns: statement of reasons, comparative advantages, criteria satisfaction, and refutative. The following paragraphs describe each pattern and show how Tomeka's speech to convince her audience to agree with her about how they should vote on a school tax proposition might be arranged using it.

Statement of Reasons

The **statement of reasons** pattern is used to confirm propositions of fact by presenting the best-supported reasons in a meaningful order. For a speech with three reasons or more, place the strongest reason last because this is the reason you believe the audience will find most persuasive. Place the second strongest reason first because you want to start with a significant point. Place the other reasons in between.

Proposition of fact: *The proposed school tax levy is necessary.*

   I. *The income is needed to restore vital programs.* [second strongest]

  II. *The income is needed to give teachers cost of living raises.*

 III. *The income is needed to maintain local control.* [strongest]

Comparative Advantages

The **comparative advantages** pattern attempts to convince others that something has more value or is better than the any of the alternatives.[4] A comparative advantages approach to the school tax proposition might look like this:

Proposition of value: *Passing the school tax levy will be better than not passing it.* [compares the value of change to the status quo]

   I. *New income from a tax levy will afford schools the means to reintroduce important programs that had been cut.* [advantage 1]

  II. *New income from a tax levy will provide much needed salary increases for teachers and avert a strike.* [advantage 2]

 III. *New income from a tax levy will make it possible to retain local control of our schools, which will be lost to the state if additional local funding is not provided.* [advantage 3]

Criteria Satisfaction

The **criteria satisfaction** pattern seeks agreement on the criteria that should be considered when evaluating a particular proposition and then shows how the proposition satisfies those criteria. A criteria satisfaction pattern is especially useful when your audience is opposed to your proposition, as it approaches the proposition indirectly by first focusing on criteria that the audience will probably agree with before introducing the specific proposition (Photo 14.2). A criteria satisfaction organization for the school tax proposition might look like this:

Proposition of value: *Passing a school tax levy is a good way to fund our schools.*

   I. *We all agree that the funding method we select must meet three key criteria*:

      A. *The funding method must provide resources needed to reinstate important programs.* [criteria 1]

      B. *The funding method must provide funds to pay teachers.* [criteria 2]

      C. *The funding method must generate enough income to maintain local control.* [criteria 3]

  II. *Passing a local school tax levy will satisfy each of these criteria.*

      A. *A local levy will allow us to fund important programs again.* [satisfaction]

      B. *A local levy will provide needed revenue for teacher raises.* [satisfaction]

      C. *A local levy will generate enough income to maintain local control.* [satisfaction]

Refutative

The **refutative** pattern arranges main points according to opposing arguments and then both challenges those arguments and bolsters your own. This pattern is particularly useful when your target audience opposes your position. Begin by acknowledging the merit of opposing arguments and then showing their flaws. Once your listeners understand the flaws, they will be more receptive to the arguments you present to

Draw a slip of paper from a stack provided by your instructor. Read the issue identified on it (e.g., school uniforms, capital punishment, the draft, climate change, college tuition costs). Create a short 1- to 2-minute impromptu speech explaining how you would phrase a specific goal as a proposition of fact, value, and policy.

comparative advantages: an organization that shows that a proposed change has more value than any of the alternatives

criteria satisfaction: an indirect organization that seeks audience agreement on criteria that should be considered when evaluating a proposition and then shows how the proposition satisfies those criteria

SPEECH SNIPPET

Because Molly knew some members of her audience probably engaged in the practice of "hooking up," and others probably didn't care one way or the other, she decided to organize her persuasive speech to convince them using a comparative advantages pattern.

refutative: an organization that persuades by both challenging the opposing position and bolstering one's own

support your proposition. A refutative pattern for the school tax proposition might look like this:

Proposition of value: *A school tax levy is the best way to fund our schools.*

I. *Some opponents of the tax levy argue that the tax increase will fall only on property owners.* [opposing argument]

    A. *Landlords will recoup property taxes in the form of higher rents.* [refutation]

    B. *Thus, all people will be affected.* [refutation]

II. *Some opponents of the tax levy also argue that there are fewer students in the school district, so schools should be able to function on the same amount of revenue.* [opposing argument]

    A. *Although there are fewer pupils, costs continue to rise.* [refutation]

        1. *Salary costs are increasing.*

        2. *Energy costs are increasing.*

        3. *Maintenance costs are increasing.*

        4. *Costs from unfunded federal and state government mandates are increasing.*

    B. *Although there are fewer pupils, there are many aging school buildings that need replacing or renovating.* [refutation]

III. *Some opponents of the tax levy also argue that parents should be responsible for the costs of educating their children.* [opposing argument]

    A. *Historically, our nation flourished under a publicly funded education system.* [refutation]

    B. *Parents today already pay more for their children's education than parents in previous generations did.* [refutation]

        1. *Activity fees*

        2. *Lab fees*

        3. *Book fees*

        4. *Transportation fees*

    C. *Of school-age children today in this district, 42 percent live in families that are below the poverty line and have limited resources.* [refutation]

Speeches to Actuate

Implicit in speeches to actuate is the assumption that there is a problem that audience members can help solve by taking certain actions. As a result, most actuation persuasive speeches follow one of three organizational frameworks: problem–solution, problem–cause–solution, and the motivated sequence.

Problem–solution

The **problem–solution** pattern explains the nature of a problem and proposes a solution. This pattern is particularly effective when the audience is neutral or agrees only that there is a problem but has no opinion about a particular solution. A problem–solution

Photo 14.2 If your audience is opposed to your position, you can appeal to them by establishing criteria they are likely to agree with and then introduce your proposition as it relates to the agreed-upon criteria. What criteria can you come up with for your persuasive speech?

AP Images/Cyrena Chang

problem–solution:
persuasive pattern that reveals the nature of a problem and proposes a solution

speech usually has three main points. The first examines the problem, the second presents the solution(s), and the third suggests what action the listener should take.

To convince the audience that there is a problem, you need to explore the breadth and depth of the issue, as well as provide listener relevance links. You provide breadth by showing the scope or scale of the problem, for example, by giving the number of people it affects and proving upward trends over time, including forecasted trends if the problem is not solved. You might provide depth by showing the gravity of the problem. Both breadth and depth may be described through stories and startling statistics. When you describe the solution, you should be detailed enough for the audience to understand how and why it will solve the problem (Photo 14.3). Your call to action should provide your audience with specific steps that they ought to take to help implement the solution(s).

Photo 14.3 You arrange the main points for a speech on a topic differently depending on your proposition. What would convince you to support a raise in taxes for improving local schools?

A problem–solution organization for Tomeka's speech about the school tax levy proposition might look like this:

Proposition of policy: *We must solve the current fiscal crisis in the school district.*

1. *Current funding is insufficient.* [statement of the problem]
    A. *The schools have had to cut important programs.*
    B. *The teachers have not had a cost-of-living raise in 5 years.*
    C. *The state could take over control.*

II. *The proposed tax levy will address these problems.* [proposed solution]
    A. *The schools will be able to reinstate important programs.*
    B. *The teachers will receive raises.*
    C. *The district will be able to maintain control.*

III. *We must do our part to make this happen.* [call to action]
    A. *Vote "yes" next week.*
    B. *Encourage your friends and neighbors to vote "yes" next week.*

Problem–Cause–Solution

A **problem–cause–solution** pattern is similar to a problem–solution pattern, but differs from it by adding a main point that reveals the causes of the problem and then proposes a solution designed to address those causes. This pattern is particularly useful for seemingly intractable problems that have been dealt with unsuccessfully in the past as a result of treating symptoms rather than underlying causes. A problem–cause–solution pattern for the school tax levy proposition might look like this:

problem–cause–solution: persuasive pattern that examines a problem, its cause(s), and the solutions designed to eliminate or alleviate the underlying cause(s)

Proposition of policy: *We must solve the current fiscal crisis in the school district.*

   I. *Current funding is insufficient.* [statement of the problem]

      A. *The schools have had to cut important programs.*

      B. *The teachers have not had a cost-of-living raise in 5 years.*

      C. *The state could take over control.*

  II. *We can trace these problems to several key things.* [causes]

      A. *Government support continues to dwindle.*

      B. *Operating expenses continue to rise.*

 III. *The proposed tax levy will address these issues.* [solutions]

      A. *The levy will supplement inadequate government support.*

      B. *The levy will fill the gap in operating expense needs.*

 IV. *Each one of us is responsible for making sure the tax levy proposition passes.* [call to action]

      A. *Vote "yes" next week.*

      B. *Encourage your friends and neighbors to vote "yes" next week.*

Motivated Sequence

motivated sequence: a persuasive organization that combines a problem–solution pattern with explicit appeals designed to motivate the audience to act

The **motivated sequence** pattern combines a problem–solution pattern with explicit appeals designed to motivate the audience to act. The motivated sequence pattern consists of a five-step sequence:

attention step: piques the audience's curiosity, identifies the goal, and previews main points

1. The **attention step** is essentially the introduction. It should begin by piquing the audience's curiosity about the problem or issue, as well as referring to the knowledge and experiences that build your credibility. As in any introduction, clearly identify your goal, which should be stated as a proposition in your thesis statement, and preview the main points of your speech.

need step: explores the nature of the problem

2. The **need step** explores the nature of the problem and why something needs to change. In it, point out the breadth and depth of the unsatisfactory conditions using statistics, examples, and expert opinions to bolster your arguments. Then, describe the implications or ramifications of the problem. What is happening/might happen if the condition is allowed to continue? Finally, allude to how the audience can be instrumental in changing the situation.

satisfaction step: explains the proposed solution to the problem

3. The **satisfaction step** explains the proposed solution to the problem. Explain point by point how what you are proposing will satisfy each of the needs that you articulated in the previous step. If there are other places where your proposal has been tried successfully, mention them as support for the feasibility of your solution to solve the problem. Be sure to also integrate refutations regarding anticipated objections to the proposed solution.

visualization step: asks the audience to imagine what will happen if the proposed solution to the problem is or is not implemented

4. The **visualization step** asks the audience to imagine the future if your proposed solution is implemented successfully, as well as if your proposal is not adopted. The movie *It's a Wonderful Life* uses visualization to show leading character George Bailey (as well as viewers) what it would be like if he had never been born.

5. The **action step** is essentially the conclusion. In it, emphasize the specific action(s) you advocate. These should come in the form of appeals at broad, local, and individual levels. Be sure to offer a very direct call to action indicating what your listeners are to do, when, where, and how.

action step: the conclusion

A motivated sequence pattern for the school tax levy proposition might look like this:

Proposition of policy: We must solve the current fiscal crisis in the school district.

I. **Attention step:** *Today we are at a critical crossroads. Our decisions will impact the future of the world as we know it.*

   A. *Comparisons of worldwide test scores in math and science show the United States continues to lose ground.*

   B. *I've made an extensive study of this problem, and today I'm going to convince you to join with me to take actions to stop it. To do so, I'll start by describing the problem, then clarify what we can and must do to stop it, and finally reveal what the future will look like for our schools, our community, and our kids when we do so.*

II. **Need step:** *The local schools are underfunded.*

   A. *Current funding is insufficient and has resulted in serious cuts to important program at all levels.*

   B. *Excellent teachers are leaving because of stagnant wages.*

   C. *A threatened state takeover of local schools would lead to more bureaucracy and less learning.*

III. **Satisfaction step:** *The proposed local tax levy is large enough to solve these problems.*

   A. *Important programs will be restored.*

   B. *Excellent teachers will get well-deserved raises and stay.*

   C. *We will retain local control.*

   D. *We will retain pride in our community.*

IV. **Visualization step:** *Imagine the best, and imagine the worst.*

   A. *What it will be like if we pass the levy.*

   B. *What it will be like if we don't pass the levy.*

V. **Action step:** *Vote "yes" for the levy in November.*

   A. *Passing the tax levy will demonstrate that we accept our civic responsibility to help United States schools regain their status as educational role models for the rest of the world.*

   B. *Come join me. I'm registered, I'm ready, I'm voting for the levy.*

   C. *If you haven't done so yet, do register today and do vote for the levy next week.*

   D. *They say it takes a village. Now is our chance. Together we can make a difference for our kids, for our community, and for our country by demonstrating our commitment to our schools. Cast your "yes" vote for the school tax levy next Tuesday!*

> **SPEECH SNIPPET**
>
> Daniel decided to arrange his speech to actuate about ending the practice of deep-sea oil drilling using the motivated sequence. He did so because he wanted to spend a good deal of time visualizing a positive and negative future to help persuade his listeners to lobby legislators to create and vote for laws to stop the practice.

Speech Assignment & Checklist

Persuasive Speech to Actuate

1. Prepare a 5- to 7-minute persuasive speech to actuate. To help you prepare your speech and your outline, complete the Speech-Planning Action Step activities.

2. As an addendum to your outline, write a persuasive speech adaptation plan in which you describe:

   a. Your target audience's initial attitude and background knowledge.

   b. Organizational pattern you will use and why.

   c. Arguments you will make to support your proposition (logos).

   d. How you will demonstrate competence, credibility, and good character (ethos).

   e. How you will appeal to emotions (pathos).

Speech Evaluation Checklist

You can use this checklist to critique a persuasive speech to actuate that you hear in class. (You can also use it to critique your own speech.) As you listen to the speaker, consider what makes a speech effective. Then, answer the following questions

General Criteria

_____ 1. Was the introduction effective in creating interest, involving the audience in the speech, and previewing the main points?

_____ 2. Were section transitions used to help you follow the organization of the main points?

_____ 3. Did the conclusion summarize the thesis and main points in a memorable way?

_____ 4. Was the language appropriate, accurate, clear, and vivid?

_____ 5. Was the speech delivered conversationally, intelligibly, expressively, and convincingly?

Specific Criteria

_____ 1. Was the specific goal clear and phrased as a proposition of policy?

_____ 2. Was the speech organized into an appropriate actuation persuasive speech framework, and if so, which one?

   _____ Problem–solution

   _____ Problem–cause–solution

   _____ Motivated sequence

_____ 3. Did the speaker use logos effectively?

   _____ Used strong evidence

   _____ Used reasoning to link evidence to claims

   _____ Avoided fallacies

_____ **4.** Did the speaker use ethos effectively?

      _____ Established expertise

      _____ Demonstrated trustworthiness

      _____ Conveyed goodwill

_____ **5.** Did the speaker use pathos effectively?

      _____ Appealed to negative emotions (if so, check all that were tapped)

            _____ fear _____ guilt _____ anger _____ shame _____ sadness

      _____ Appealed to positive emotions (if so, check all that were tapped)

            _____ happiness/joy _____ pride _____ relief _____ hope _____ compassion

_____ **6.** Did the speaker offer a compelling call to action?

Based on these criteria, evaluate the speech as (check one):

      _____ excellent _____ good _____ average _____ fair _____ poor

Explain:

_____

_____

ETHICAL GUIDELINES FOR PERSUASIVE SPEECHES

Throughout this book, we have discussed the fundamental behaviors of ethical communicators. At this point, we want to look at six ethical guidelines speakers should follow when their specific goal is to convince the audience to agree with a proposition or to move the audience to action.

1. **Ethical persuasive speeches advocate the genuine beliefs of the speaker.** Sometimes people get excited about playing devil's advocate—that is, arguing for a belief or action just to stir up discussion. However, it is unethical to give a speech on a proposition that you do not genuinely endorse.

2. **Ethical persuasive speeches provide choice.** Ethical persuasive speeches let audiences evaluate what is said before making up their own minds.

3. **Ethical persuasive speeches use representative supporting information.** You can probably find a piece of "evidence" to support any claim, but ethical speakers make sure the evidence they cite is representative of all the evidence that could be used. It is unethical to misrepresent what a *body* of evidence (as opposed to a single item) would show if all of it were presented to the audience.

4. **Ethical persuasive speeches use emotional appeals conscientiously.** Emotional appeals are a legitimate strategy to get an audience involved in your persuasive speech. However, using excessive emotional appeals as the basis of persuasion, without strong evidence and reasoning, is unethical.

5. **Ethical persuasive speeches honestly present the speaker's credibility.** Ethical speakers present their expertise and trustworthiness honestly (Photo 14.4). It is unethical to act as if you know a great deal about a subject when you do not. Ethical speakers also disclose interests that may influence their stance on an issue. You might say, for example, "I work for the Literacy Project as a paid intern, so my experiences there do influence my position on what must be done regarding illiteracy in this country."

Photo 14.4 Ethical persuasion requires speakers to admit their expertise and trustworthiness honestly. What can you say to help your listeners trust you?

The section that follows presents a sample speech to actuate given by a student, including a preparation outline, a formal outline, and a speaking outline/notes using the "notes" feature available for PowerPoint slides.

Reflect on Ethics

WHAT WOULD *YOU* DO?

DAVID ORTIZ'S EMOTIONAL PREGAME SPEECH SPARKS DEBATE

Shortly after the horrific Boston Marathon bombings on April 15, 2013, the city of Boston went on lockdown while law enforcement officials searched for the terrorists. The city, the nation, and the world followed breaking stories throughout the unprecedented manhunt and breathed a collective sigh of relief when it finally ended with one perpetrator dead and the other arrested. Boston residents could come out of their homes and resume their lives.

On April 20, 2013, fans made their way back to Fenway Park to watch their beloved Boston Red Sox. A pregame ceremony was held to honor the victims, the law enforcement responders, and the people of Boston; it was branded *Boston Proud*. David Ortiz, designated hitter for the Red Sox, was handed the microphone, and he said when he looked out "at the faces in the crowd . . . he felt what they were feeling."[5] His short speech rocked the house by precisely capturing their emotions.

He clinched his speech with conviction, saying, "This is our [expletive] city, and nobody is going to dictate our freedom. Stay strong." Though emotionally compelling and clearly representative of the passionate feelings of those in his audience, Ortiz's clincher sparked controversy. Why? Because Ortiz, who is also known as Big Papi, dropped an F-bomb at a family-friendly event, which was also broadcast on national television. Later, Ortiz apologized, saying, "It just came out. If I offended anyone, I apologize."[6]

The Federal Communications Commission (FCC), which is tasked with policing such profanity in broadcasting, also did something unprecedented. It chose not to fine Major League Baseball, the Boston Red Sox, or Ortiz.[7] In fact, FCC Chair Julius Genachowski tweeted: "David Ortiz spoke from the heart at today's Red Sox game. I stand with Big Papi and the people of Boston – Julius."[8]

1. What, if any, ethical communication principles did Ortiz violate in his speech?

2. Does the fact that he apologized later make a difference? Why or why not?

3. Do you think the FCC's decision not to fine Ortiz, the Boston Red Sox, or Major League Baseball was ethical? Why or why not?

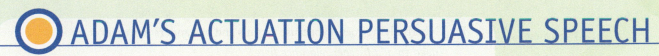

Together, We Can Stop Cyberbullying

By Adam Parrish, University of Kentucky[9]

Read the speech adaptation plan, outline, and transcript of a speech given by Adam Parrish in an introductory speaking course. You can identify some of the strengths of Adam's speech by preparing an evaluation checklist and an analysis. You can then compare your answers with those of the authors.

Preparation Outline

General goal: To persuade

Specific goal: To convince my audience to take action to help stop cyberbullying.

Proposition: We must confront and stop the devastating abuse of cyberbullying.

INTRODUCTION

I. [tell the story of someone that committed suicide as a result of being cyberbullied . . . maybe Phoebe Prince or Tyler Clementi? . . . maybe show a photo of the victim]   **Attention getter**

II. Many of us know someone who has been bullied in school. With the advent of communication technologies, cyberbullying is becoming a real problem, as well. Cyberbullying is basically using electronic technologies to tease, harass, threaten, and intimidate others [maybe show this definition on a slide]. It's particularly pervasive because bullies can now follow their victims wherever they go . . . even into their bedrooms.   **Listener relevance**

III. I tutor and mentor high school students and have witnessed cyberbullying first hand. I've also done a lot of research and feel compelled to share it.   **Speaker credibility**

IV. Cyberbullying is a devastating and violent form of abuse that we must confront and stop.   **Thesis statement (phrased as a proposition)**

V. We will examine the harmful nature of the cyberbullying problem, discover how and why it persists, and propose solutions we must engage in to stop it.   **Main point preview**

   [need to add a transition here]   **Transition**

BODY

I. Cyberbullying is a dangerous practice that is becoming more pervasive every day.   **The problem**

   Many of us have read rude, insensitive, or nasty statements posted about us or others on social media. [maybe have a visual of this?]

   A. Cyberbullying is a worldwide problem. (Ipsos for Reuters News global research company statistics from 24 countries)

   B. Here in the United States, cyberbullying is particularly pervasive among middle-school and high school students.   **Listener relevance**

   C. Cyberbullying can have devastating psychological effects on victims.

   [need to add a transition here]   **Transition**

	II. Cyberbullying goes on because victims and bystanders don't report it.
The cause(s)	
Listener relevance	*[need to add listener relevance here]*
	A. Cyberbullies are often anonymous.
	B. When we don't report known cyberbullying, we are enabling the attackers.
The solution(s)	III. To stop the madness, cyberbullying must be confronted on national, local, and personal levels.
Listener relevance	A. Forty-nine states have antibullying laws but only 18 include cyberbullying. Our state is one that doesn't include it.
	B. Local communities must organize and mobilize at multiple levels.
	C. We must know the warning signs and report cyberbullying.

CONCLUSION

<table>
<tr><td>Thesis (proposition) restatement</td><td>I. Cyberbullying is a horrible form of abuse that we must confront and stop.</td></tr>
<tr><td>Main point summary</td><td>II. This pervasive problem is perpetuated by silence and must be addressed through antibullying legislation with clear consequences, community organization and mobilization, and personal actions by each one of us.</td></tr>
<tr><td>Call to action and clincher</td><td>III. I implore you to do your part to help stop cyberbullying.

[need to flesh out this call to action more]</td></tr>
</table>

Formal Outline

INTRODUCTION

<table>
<tr><td>Attention getter
Adam uses actual quotes from family and friends of Phoebe Prince to get his audience's attention.</td><td>I. "I'll miss just being around her." "I didn't want to believe it." "It's such a sad thing." These quotes are from the friends and family of 15-year-old Phoebe Prince, who, on January 14, 2010, committed suicide by hanging herself. Why did this senseless act occur? The answer is simple: Phoebe Prince was bullied to death.</td></tr>
<tr><td>Listener relevance</td><td>II. Most of us know someone who was bullied in school. Perhaps they were teased in the parking lot or in the locker room. In the past, bullying occurred primarily in face-to-face settings in and around schools. However, with the proliferation of communication technologies today, such as cell phones with text messaging capability, instant messaging, emails, blogs, and social networking sites, bullies can now follow their victims anywhere and attack at any time, even in the bedrooms of victims, day or night. Using electronic communications to tease, harass, threaten, and intimidate another person is called cyberbullying.</td></tr>
<tr><td>Speaker credibility</td><td>III. As a tutor and mentor to young students, I have witnessed cyberbullying firsthand, and by examining current research, I believe I understand the problem, its causes, and how we can help end cyberbullying. I feel compelled to share what I've learned with you today.</td></tr>
<tr><td>Thesis statement (stated as proposition)</td><td>IV. Cyberbullying is a devastating form of abuse that we must confront and stop.</td></tr>
<tr><td>Preview</td><td>V. Today, we will examine the widespread and harmful nature of cyberbullying, discover how and why it persists, and propose some simple solutions that we must engage in to thwart cyberbullies and comfort their victims.</td></tr>
<tr><td>Transition</td><td>Let's begin by tackling the problem head on.</td></tr>
</table>

BODY

I. Cyberbullying is a pervasive and dangerous behavior.

Many of us have read rude, insensitive, or nasty statements posted about us or someone we care about on social networking sites like Twitter, Snapchat, and Facebook. Whether or not those comments were actually intended to hurt another person's feelings, they are perfect examples of cyberbullying.

A. Cyberbullying takes place all over the world through a wide array of electronic media.

   1. According to a poll conducted in 24 countries for Reuters News by the global research company Ipsos, 38% of parents are aware of cyberbully occurring with their children or with children in their communities (Ipsos Poll, 2012).

   2. According to *Statisticbrain.com*, as of 2012, 52 percent of American middle-school students had experienced instances of cyberbullying ranging from hurtful comments to threats of physical violence (Statisticbrain.com, 2012).

   3. A 2011 study reported in the journal *Pediatrics* noted that instances of bullying via text messages have risen significantly since 2006 (Ybarra, Mitchell, & Korchmaros, 2011).

   4. The Internet and cell phones are the tools most commonly used by bullies to harass, torment, and threaten young people in North America, Europe, and Asia.

   5. A particularly disturbing incident occurred in Dallas, Texas, where an overweight student with multiple sclerosis (MS) was targeted on a school's social networking page. One message read, "I guess I'll have to wait until you kill yourself, which I hope is not long from now, or I'll have to wait until your disease kills you" (Keith & Martin, 2005, p. 226).

Clearly, cyberbullying is a widespread problem. What is most disturbing about cyberbullying, however, is its effects upon victims, bystanders, and perhaps even upon the bullies themselves.

B. Cyberbullying can lead to traumatic psychological injuries upon its victims.

   1. According to a 2012 article in the *Children and Youth Services Review*, 50 percent of the victims of cyberbullies are also harassed by their attackers in school (Mishna, Khoury-Kassabri, Gadall, & Daciuk, 2012).

   2. For example, the Dallas student with MS had eggs thrown at her car and a bottle of acid thrown at her house (Keith & Martin, 2005).

   3. Victims of cyberbullying experience such severe emotional distress that they often exhibit behavioral problems that lead to poor grades, truancy, detentions, and suspensions (Wang, Nansel, Iannotti, 2011). Smith et al. (2008) suggested that even a few instances of cyberbullying can have these long-lasting and heartbreaking results.

Now that we realize the devastating nature, scope, and effects of cyberbullying, let's look at its causes.

The problem

Listener relevance
Adam offers listener relevance to maintain audience attention.

Adam offers statistics to support his claim that cyberbullying is pervasive not just in the United States but all over the world.

Transition

Transition
Adam's transition is clear and simple.

The cause(s)

Listener relevance

II. Cyberbullying is perpetuated because victims and bystanders do not report their abusers to authorities.

Think back to a time when you may have seen a friend or loved one being harassed online. Did you report the bully to the network administrator or other authorities? Did you console the victim? I know I didn't. If you are like me, we may unknowingly be enabling future instances of cyberbullying.

A. Cyberbullies are cowards who attack their victims anonymously.

1. Ybarra et al. (2007) discovered that 13 percent of cyberbullying victims did not know who was tormenting them.

2. This is an important statistic because traditional bullying takes place face to face and often ends when students leave school. However, today, students are subjected to cyberbullying in their own homes.

3. Perhaps the anonymous nature of cyberattacks partially explains why only 1 in 10 teens tells a parent if they have been a cyberbully victim (Webster, 2012).

Adam does a nice job countering the argument that it will do no good to report cyberbullying with the fact that 49 states have passed antibullying legislation and 18 have specific mentions of cyberbullying.

B. Victims and bystanders who do not report attacks from cyberbullies can unintentionally enable bullies.

1. According to De Nies, Donaldson, and Netter of *ABCNews.com* (2010) several of Phoebe Prince's classmates were aware that she was being harassed but did not inform the school's administration.

2. Li (2007) suggested that victims and bystanders often do not believe that adults will actually intervene to stop cyberbullying.

3. However, 49 states now have antibullying laws, although only 18 of them include cyberbullying in their legislation (Clark, 2013).

Transition

Now that we realize that victims of cyberbullies desperately need the help of witnesses and bystanders to report their attacks, we should arm ourselves with the information necessary to provide that assistance.

The solution(s)

Adam offers breadth and depth to his solutions by appealing to what the federal government should do, local communities and schools should do, and what each person in his audience can and should do to help.

Listener relevance

III. Cyberbullying must be confronted on national, local, and personal levels.

Think about the next time you see a friend or loved one being tormented or harassed online. What would you be willing to do to help?

A. There should be a comprehensive national law confronting cyberbullying in schools. Certain statutes currently in state laws should be amalgamated to create the strongest protections for victims and the most effective punishments for bullies possible.

1. According to a 2013 *governing.com* article by Maggie Clark entitled "49 States Now Have Anti-Bullying Laws. How's That Working Out?" only 18 state-level bullying laws include cyberbullying.

2. Furthermore, only 12 states include criminal sanctions for bullying.

3. All 49 state antibullying laws do require schools to set up school policies, as well as work with the victim and attacker in the form of education, training, and counseling. Legislating punishment for bullies is difficult. As Limber and Small (2003) noted, zero-tolerance polices often perpetuate violence because at-risk youth (bullies) are removed from all of the benefits of school, which might help make them less abusive.

4. A comprehensive anti-cyberbullying law should incorporate the best aspects of these state laws and find a way to punish bullies that is both punitive and has the ability to rehabilitate abusers.

B. Local communities must organize and mobilize to attack the problem of cyberbullying.

   1. Communities need to support bullying prevention programs by conducting a school-based bullying survey for individual school districts. We can't know how to best protect victims in our community without knowing how they are affected by the problem.

   2. Local school districts should create a Coordinating Committee made up of "administrators, teachers, students, parents, school staff, and community partners" to gather bullying data and rally support to confront the problem (Greene, 2006, p. 73).

   3. Even if your local school district is unable or unwilling to mobilize behind this critical cause, there are some important actions you can take personally to safeguard those you love against cyberbullying.

C. Take note of these cyberbullying warning signs posted on the Centers for Disease Control and Prevention website (Violence Prevention, 2016).

   1. Victims of cyberbullies often use electronic communication more frequently than do people who are not being bullied.

   2. Victims of cyberbullies have mood swings and difficulty sleeping.

   3. Victims of cyberbullies seem depressed and/or become anxious.

   4. Victims of cyberbullies become withdrawn from social activities and fall behind in scholastic responsibilities.

D. If you see a friend or loved one exhibiting any of these signs, I implore you not to ignore them. Rather take action. Get involved. Do something to stop it.

   1. According to Raskauskas and Stoltz (2007), witnesses of cyberbullying should inform victims to take the attacks seriously, especially if the bullies threaten violence.

   2. Tell victims to report their attacks to police or other authority figures.

   3. Tell victims to block harmful messages by blocking email accounts and cell phone numbers (Raskauskas & Stoltz, 2007).

   4. Tell victims to save copies of attacks and provide them to authorities.

   5. If you personally know the bully and feel safe confronting him or her, do so! Bullies will often back down when confronted by peers.

   6. By being a good friend and by giving good advice, you can help a victim report his or her attacks from cyberbullies and take a major step toward eliminating this horrendous problem.

So, you see, we are not helpless to stop the cyberbullying problem as long as we make the choice NOT to ignore it.

Transition

CONCLUSION

I. Cyberbullying is a devastating form of abuse that must be reported to authorities.

II. Cyberbullying is a worldwide problem perpetuated by the silence of both victims and bystanders. By paying attention to certain warning signs, we can empower ourselves to console victims and report their abusers.

Thesis (proposition) restatement

Main point summary

Call to action and clincher

III. Today, I implore you to do your part to help stop cyberbullying. I know that you agree that stopping cyberbullying must be a priority.

  A. First, although other states have cyberbullying laws in place, ours does not. So I'm asking you to sign this petition that I will forward to our district's state legislators. We need to make our voices heard that we want specific laws passed to stop this horrific practice and to punish those caught doing it.

  B. Second, I'm also asking you to be vigilant in noticing signs of cyberbullying and then taking action. Look for signs that your friend, brother, sister, cousin, boyfriend, girlfriend, or loved one might be a victim of cyberbullying and then get involved to help stop it! Phoebe Prince showed the warning signs, and she did not deserve to die so senselessly. None of us would ever want to say, "I'll miss just being around her," "I didn't want to believe it," "It's such a sad thing" about our own friends or family members.

  C. We must work to ensure that victims are supported and bullies are confronted nationally, locally, and personally. I know that, if we stand together and refuse to be silent, we can and will stop cyberbullying.

REFERENCES

Cyber-Bullying Statistics (2012). Retrieved from http://www.statisticbrain.com/cyber-bullying-statistics/

De Nies, Y., Donaldson, S., & Netter, S. (2010, January 28). Mean girls: Cyberbullying blamed for teen suicides. *ABCNews.com*. Retrieved from http://abcnews.go.com/GMA/Parenting/girls-teen-suicide-calls-attention-cyberbullying/story?id=9685026

Greene, M. B. (2006). Bullying in schools: A plea for measure of human rights. *Journal of Social Issues, 62*(1), 63–79.

Keith, S., & Martin, M. (2005). Cyber-bullying: Creating a culture of respect in the cyber world. *Reclaiming Children and Youth, 13*(4), 224–228.

Li, Q. (2007). New bottle of old wine: A research of cyberbullying in schools. *Computers in Human Behavior, 23*, 1777–1791.

Limber, S. P., & Small, M. A. (2003). State laws and policies to address bullying in schools. *School Psychology Review, 32*(3), 445–455.

Raskauskas, J., & Stoltz, A. D. (2007). Involvement in traditional and electronic bullying among adolescents. *Developmental Psychology, 43*(3), 564–575.

Smith, P. K., Mahdavi, J., Carvalho, M., Fisher, S. Russel, S., & Tippett, N. (2008). Cyberbullying: Its nature and impact in secondary school pupils. *Journal of Child Psychology and Psychiatry, 49*(4), 374–385.

Violence Prevention. (2016, March 21). *Centers for Disease Control and Prevention*. Retrieved from http://www.cdc.gov/ViolencePrevention/index.html

Ybarra, M. L., Diener-West, M., & Leaf, P. J. (2007). Examining the overlap in Internet harassment and school bullying: Implications for school intervention. *Journal of Adolescent Health, 41*, S42–S50.

Ybarra, M. L., Mitchell, K. J., Wolak, J., & Finkelhor, D. (2006). Examining characteristics and associated distress related to Internet harassment: Findings from the second Youth Internet Safety Survey. *Pediatrics, 118*, 1169–1177.

Ybarra, M. L., Mitchell, K. M., & Korchmaros, J. D. (2011). National trends in exposure to and experiences of violence on the Internet among children. *Pediatrics*. Retrieved from http://pediatrics.aappublications.org/content/early/2011/11/16/peds.2011-0118

Speaking Outline Note Slides

Here is how Adam used the "notes" feature in PowerPoint to prepare his speaking outline notes. Notice how they include only key words/phrases and delivery cues.

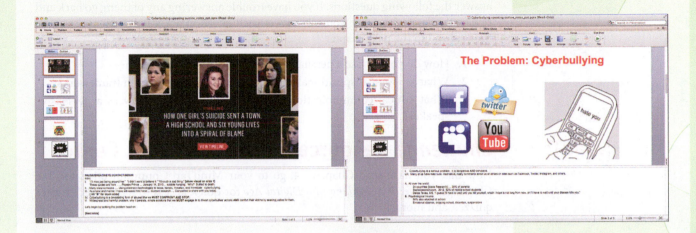

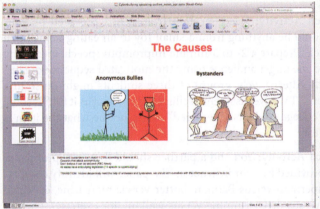

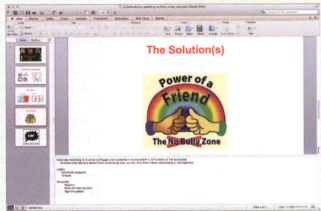

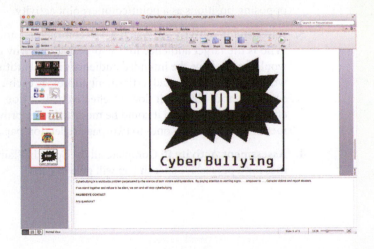

Reflection and Assessment

Persuasive speeches are designed to influence the attitudes, beliefs, values, or behaviors of audience members. This chapter focused on creating effective and ethical persuasive speeches. To assess how well you've learned what we've discussed in this chapter, answer the following questions. If you have trouble answering any of them, go back and review that material. Once you can answer each question accurately, you are ready to move ahead to the next chapter.

1. How do you phrase a persuasive speech goal as a proposition?
2. What are some dispositional and actuation persuasive speech frameworks?
3. What ethical communication guidelines should you follow as a persuasive speaker?

MindTap®

Challenge Resource and Assessment Center

Now that you have read Chapter 14, go to your MindTap Communication for *The Challenge of Effective Speaking in a Digital Age* for quick access to flashcards, chapter quizzes, and more.

Applying What You've Learned

1. **Impromptu Speech Activity:** Select an item from a box provided by your instructor. Items could be anything from a small toy to an eating utensil to a tool to a knickknack. Prepare a 2- to 3-minute impromptu speech attempting to "sell" the item to the target audience using the motivated sequence organizational framework. Alternatively, groups of three students might do so in a role-play impromptu "TV advertisement," selling the product as it fulfills some "unique need" for college students. The "need" might not be what the item is typically intended for.

2. **Impromptu Speech Activity:** You and a partner should draw a slip of paper from a container provided by your instructor. The paper will identify competing topics (e.g., Superman versus Batman, butter versus margarine, eat eggs/don't eat eggs, fly versus drive, running versus walking for exercise). Each of you will prepare a 1- to 2-minute persuasive impromptu speech advocating opposing positions as a point/counterpoint activity.

3. **Assessment Activity A:** Watch a TV commercial and identify the following: Who is the target audience for the product, and why do you believe so? What would you believe the intended audience's initial attitude is to the product and why? Identify how the advertisement addresses each element of the motivated sequence and whether it does so effectively. If it does not address an element effectively, suggest how it could be modified to improve. Write up your assessment in the form of a one- to two-page reflection paper.

4. **Assessment Activity B:** Complete all the Speech-Planning Action Steps activities for a persuasive speech you will give in class.

15 Ceremonial Speaking

WHAT'S THE POINT?

WHEN YOU'VE FINISHED THIS CHAPTER, YOU WILL BE ABLE TO:

- Determine what you should include in a speech of welcome
- Identify why a speech of introduction should be brief
- Prepare a speech of nomination
- Know when you might be expected to give a speech of recognition
- Determine key things to say in a speech of acceptance
- List some common types of speeches of tribute
- Identify additional types of ceremonial speeches

MindTap®

Review the chapter **Learning Objectives** and **Start** with quick warm-up activity.

Ethical communicators demonstrate respect for their audiences by considering the context for the ceremonial speech they'll be giving.

Because Ben didn't know his biological father, his grandfather had been like a father to him. He and his grandfather used to spend hours playing ball, fishing, or simply watching TV together. Although Ben's grandfather had lived a long and fruitful life, Ben found it difficult to say goodbye. Still, he wanted to give the eulogy at the funeral. How could he find the right words to do justice to his grandfather's memory?

On special occasions, such as weddings, funerals, etc., we may be called on to "say a few words." Because our audience has distinct expectations for what they will hear, we need to understand how these expectations affect the way we will shape our speech.

The goal of ceremonial speaking lies somewhere between informing and persuading. In ceremonial speeches, we invite listeners to agree with us about the value of a person, object, event, or place. Another characteristic of most ceremonial speeches is brevity: Ceremonial speeches are generally—although not always— fewer than 5 minutes long. This chapter describes six common types of ceremonial speeches: speeches of welcome, introduction, nomination, recognition, acceptance, and tribute. For each speech type, we describe the typical expectations to keep in mind as you prepare.

SPEECHES OF WELCOME

speech of welcome: an address that greets and expresses pleasure for the presence of a person or an organization

A **speech of welcome** greets and expresses pleasure for the presence of a person, group, or organization. We typically give a speech of welcome as the representative of a group. Thus, we must be familiar with the group we are representing and the occasion. This sometimes means we must do some research about the group and occasion in advance. A speech of welcome is generally not more than 2 to 4 minutes long.

A speech of welcome invites listeners to agree that the occasion is friendly and their attendance is appreciated. You accomplish this by respectfully catching attention, and after expressing appreciation on behalf of the group, providing a brief description of the group and setting to which the audience members are being welcomed. The conclusion should briefly express your hope for the outcome of the visit, event, or relationship. A typical speech of welcome might be as simple as this:

> *Today, I want to welcome John Sheldon, who is joining us from the North Thurston Club. John, as you are aware, we are a newer club, having been established in 2007. At that time, we had only ten members. But we had big hopes. Today, we are 127 members strong, and we raised more than $250,000 last year to support local children's organizations. We hope our talks today will lead to closer cooperation between the North Thurston Club and ours here in Yelm.*

master of ceremonies: an individual designated to set the mood of the program, introduce participants, and keep the program moving

On some occasions, you may be asked to serve as a **master of ceremonies**, an individual designated to welcome guests, set the mood for the program, introduce participants, and keep the program moving. (Either a woman or a man can be referred to as a master of ceremonies.) Year-end honorary banquets, corporate dinner meetings, and local charity events typically use someone in this role. As master of ceremonies, you might be asked to give a speech that both welcomes and introduces a speaker. When this is the case, the speech can be a bit longer than a speech of welcome and should also include the type of information described in the next section.

SPEECHES OF INTRODUCTION

speech of introduction: establishes a supportive climate for the main speaker, highlights the speaker's credibility, and generates enthusiasm for listening

A **speech of introduction** introduces the main speaker by establishing a supportive climate, highlighting pertinent biographical information, and generating enthusiasm for listening to the speech. Sometimes you will be provided with a résumé or brief biography of the speaker; at other times, you may need to research the speaker's background yourself. Regardless of what you learn, you should also try to contact the speaker directly and ask what points the speaker would like you to emphasize. Generally, a speech of introduction is not more than 3 to 5 minutes long.

The beginning of a speech of introduction should quickly establish the nature of the occasion, the body of the speech should focus on three or four things the audience ought to know about the person being introduced, and the conclusion should mention the speaker by name and briefly identify the topic and title of the speech. If the person is well known, you might simply say something like, "Ladies and gentlemen, the president of the United States." If the person is less well known, however, then mentioning his or her name specifically during the speech of introduction and especially at the end is imperative.

Speeches of introduction should honestly represent the person being introduced. You should not hype a speaker's credentials or overpraise the speaker. If you set the audience's expectations too high, even a good speaker may have trouble living up to them. For instance, an overzealous introducer can doom a competent speaker by saying, "This man [woman] is undoubtedly one of the greatest speakers of our time. I have no doubt that what you are about to hear will change your thinking." Although this introduction is meant to be complimentary, it does the speaker a grave disservice. A typical speech of introduction might look like the following:

> *It is my pleasure to introduce our speaker, Ms. Susan Wong, the new president of the finance club. I've worked with Susan for 3 years and have found her to have a gift for organization, insight into the financial markets, and an interest in aligning student organizations with leaders in our community. Susan, as you may not know, has spent the past two summers working as an intern at Salomon Smith Barney and has now laid the groundwork for more college internships for students from our university. She is a finance major with a minor in international business. Today, she is going to talk with us about the benefits of summer internships. Let's give a warm welcome to Susan Wong!*

SPEECHES OF NOMINATION

A **speech of nomination** proposes a nominee for an elected office, honor, position, or award. Every 4 years, the Democratic and Republican parties have speeches of nomination at their national conventions. Those speeches are rather long, but most speeches of nomination are brief, lasting only about 2 to 4 minutes.

The goal of a speech of nomination is to highlight the qualities that make the nominee the most credible candidate (Photo 15.1). To do so, first clarify the importance of the position, honor, or award by describing the responsibilities involved, related challenges or issues, and the characteristics needed to fulfill it. Second, list the candidate's personal and professional qualifications that meet those criteria. Doing so links the candidate with the position, honor, or award in ways that make him or her appear to be a natural choice. Finally, formally place the candidate's name in nomination, creating a dramatic climax to clinch your speech. A speech of nomination could be as simple and brief as this:

> *I am very proud to place in nomination for president of our association the name of one of our most active members, Ms. Adrienne Lamb.*
>
> *We all realize the demands of this particular post. It requires leadership. It requires vision. It requires enthusiasm and motivation. And, most of all, it requires a sincere love for our group and its mission.*
>
> *Adrienne Lamb meets and exceeds each one of these demands. It was Adrienne Lamb who chaired our visioning task force. She led us to articulate the mission*

speech of nomination: proposes a nominee for an elected office, honor, position, or award

Chip Somodevilla/Getty Images

Photo 15.1 Common speeches of nomination occur when candidates' names are placed in nomination for an open political office. Can you recall hearing a particularly compelling speech of nomination?

statement we abide by today. It was Adrienne Lamb who chaired the fund-raising committee last year when we enjoyed a record drive. And it was Adrienne Lamb who acted as mentor to so many of us, myself included, when we were trying to find our place in this association and this community. This association and its members have reaped the benefits of Adrienne Lamb's love and leadership so many times and in so many ways. We now have the opportunity to benefit in even greater ways.

It is truly an honor and a privilege to place in nomination for president of our association Ms. Adrienne Lamb!

SPEECHES OF RECOGNITION

speech of recognition: acknowledges someone, usually accompanied by the presentation of an award, prize, or gift

A **speech of recognition** acknowledges someone and usually presents them with an award, prize, or gift. You have probably watched speeches of recognition during the presentation of lifetime achievement awards on the Academy Awards, the Grammys, or the Golden Globes. Speeches of recognition may be a bit longer depending on the prestige of the award, but are more often quite brief (fewer than 3 minutes long).

Because the audience wants to know why the recipient is being recognized, your speech of recognition should recount the nature and history of the award, the recognition criteria, and how the recipient met the criteria (Photo 15.2). If the recognition is based on a competition, this might include the number of contestants and the way the contest was judged. If the recipient earned the award through years of achievement, describe the specific milestones that were passed. Sometimes the recognition is meant to be a surprise. If so, deliberately omit the name of the recipient in what you say, building to a climax when the name is announced.

Keep two special considerations in mind when you prepare a speech of recognition. First, refrain from overpraising; do not explain everything in superlatives as this can make the presentation seem to lack sincerity and honesty. Second, in the United States, it is traditional to shake hands with recipients as awards are received. So, if you

Photo 15.2 When presenting an award, discuss the nature of the award and the recipient's accomplishments. What might you include in a speech honoring a student for an outstanding scholastic achievement?

have a certificate or other tangible award to hand to the recipient, be careful to hold it in your left hand and present it to the recipient's left hand. That way, you will be able to shake the right hand in congratulations. A typical speech of recognition might look like this:

> *I'm honored to present this year's Idea of the Year Award to Ryan Goldbloom from the installation department. As you may remember, we have been giving this award since 1985 to the employee who has submitted an idea that resulted in the largest first-year cost savings for the company. Ryan's idea to equip all installation trucks with prepackaged kits for each type of job has resulted in a $10,458 savings in the first 12 months of implementation. And in recognition of this contribution to our bottom line, I am pleased to share our savings with Ryan in the form of a check for $2,091.60, one-fifth of what he has saved us. Good work, Ryan.*

SPEECHES OF ACCEPTANCE

A **speech of acceptance** acknowledges receipt of an honor or award. As the recipient, your goal is to sincerely convey your appreciation for the honor. You should briefly thank the person or group bestowing the honor, acknowledge the competition, express gratitude about receiving the award, and thank those who contributed to your success. To be effective, your speech should be brief, humble, and gracious. Remember that your goal is to convey appreciation in a way that makes the audience feel good about you receiving the award. Rarely, as in the case of a politician accepting a nomination, a professional accepting the presidency of a national organization, or a person receiving a prestigious award that is the focus of the gathering, an audience will expect a longer speech. Generally, however, acceptance speeches are no longer than 1 to 2 minutes.

Acceptance speeches that don't adhere to expectations often have disastrous results. If you have ever watched award programs such as the Academy Awards, MTV Music Awards, People's Choice Awards, or Grammys, you no doubt have observed an award

IMPROMPTU SPEECH CHALLENGE

Draw a slip of paper from a stack provided by your instructor. Prepare a 2- to 3- minute speech of recognition to a classmate for the award identified on it. Criteria for evaluation include identifying what the award is for, the criteria for winning it, and what the person did to meet the criteria.

speech of acceptance: acknowledges receipt of an honor or award

Reflect on Ethics

LANGUAGE OKAY FOR THE OCCASION?

When actor and comedian Steve Carell won the People's Choice Award for favorite TV comedy actor in 2010, his acceptance speech was filled with sexual innuendos. For example, he said, "Wow! I can't believe it. This is much *bigger* than I thought it would be," and "I'm going to go home, and I'm going to find a special place to *put* this," and "I'm glad I *came.*" You can search for and watch Carell's speech on YouTube.

1. What, if any, expectations for an acceptance speech did Carell violate?
2. What, if any, ethical communication principles did Carell violate?
3. Do you think Carell's speech offended any members in the live or TV audience? Explain.

---

winner who gave an overly long or otherwise inappropriate acceptance speech. Among the most famous of them:

- Sally Field's 1985 acceptance of the Best Actress Oscar, when she chose to say "you like me, right now, you really like me" rather than to humbly and graciously thank the Academy for honoring her

- Michael Moore's 2003 acceptance of the Best Documentary Film Oscar, when he used the occasion to chastise then-President George W. Bush by saying "shame on you Mr. Bush, shame on you" rather than to focus on humbly and graciously thanking the Academy

- Melissa Leo's 2011 acceptance of the Best Supporting Actress Oscar, when she said, "It looked so f—kin' easy" in her speech rather than graciously saying thank you. It became all anyone ended up remembering.

So, when you have the opportunity to give an acceptance speech, focus your remarks on the recognition you have been given or on the position you are accepting. It is inappropriate to use an acceptance speech to advocate for an unrelated cause. The following is an example of an appropriate speech of acceptance:

> *I would like to thank the hospital for hosting this beautiful luncheon today. It is absolutely lovely! Thank you, too, to the chef, cooks, and wait staff. You have really made this event memorable in so many ways. In all honesty, I must admit I am a bit stunned and also truly honored to be recognized today as this year's Volunteer of the Year. As I look out at all of you here today, I am humbled to think of the countless hours you all spend giving freely of your time, and your love for the hurting children in our community. I am grateful to count myself among such amazing, selfless servant leaders. Each one of you deserves this trophy. I want to also thank my husband, Terry, for encouraging me to join Big Hearts, Big Hands and for supporting me when I became involved as a volunteer. You are my rock and I love you! Thank you, again, for this award. I will treasure it forever.*

SPEECH SNIPPET

When Renee accepted her award for "outstanding community service," she began by acknowledging how much she admired the work of the three other nominees before saying how honored she was to receive the award.

SPEECHES OF TRIBUTE

speech of tribute: praises or celebrates a person, group, or event

A **speech of tribute** praises or celebrates a person, a group, or an event. You might be asked to pay tribute to a person or persons on the occasion of a birthday, wedding, anniversary, oath of office, retirement, or funeral. Although the type of speech of tribute will vary based on the specific special occasion it is meant for, the goal in any of them is to invite listeners to truly appreciate the person, group, or event by arousing their sentiments. This is achieved by focusing on the most notable characteristics or achievements of the person, group, or event, using vivid stories, examples, and language that arouses sentiments. Speeches of tribute can vary in length from very brief to lengthy, depending on the nature of the occasion. Let's take a closer look at three types of tribute that you are likely to be asked to give at some point in your life.

Toasts

A **toast**, usually offered at the start of a reception or meal, pays tribute to an occasion or a person. On most occasions, a toast is expected to be very brief (lasting less than a minute), comprising only a few sentences and focusing on a single characteristic of the person or occasion. Usually, a short example is used to support or illustrate the characteristic. Wedding toasts, given at a rehearsal dinner or reception by a family member or member of the wedding party, are generally longer speeches (3 to 4 minutes) that may use humor but should not embarrass the persons at whom they are directed.

A toast should be sincere and express a sentiment that is likely to be widely shared by those in attendance. Generally, the person giving the toast and all other attendees have a drink in hand, which they raise and sip from at the conclusion of the toast (Photo 15.3). So, before offering a toast, it is customary to make sure that drinks are refreshed so that all can participate. If particular people are being toasted, the toast is drunk in their honor, so they do not drink. A typical toast by a daughter given to honor her mother's college graduation might be:

> *Tonight, I'd like to offer a toast to a woman I admire, respect, and love. My mom has always supported my brother and me. So, when she told me that she wanted to go back and finish college, I was worried about how we'd all manage. But I shouldn't have worried. Mom not only finished her degree in less than 2 years, but she also continued to work full time, and, what's more, she's even had time to coach my brother's Little League team. Here's to you, Mom—you're amazing!*

Roasts

One unique type of tribute speech is given as part of a **roast**, which is an event where family and friends share short speeches in honor of one person. In these short speeches, guests might offer good-natured insults or anecdotes, heartwarming or outlandish

toast: offered at the start of a reception or meal to pay tribute to the occasion or a person

roast: an event where guests provide short speeches of tribute, developed with humorous stories and anecdotes, about the featured guest.

SPEECH SNIPPET

Tim wasn't able to travel to attend the milestone birthday roast for his longtime buddy, Tom. He and several others used Adobe Connect to participate along with those who were able to attend in person. That way, they each got to share their roasts of Tom too.

IMPROMPTU SPEECH CHALLENGE

Draw a slip of paper from a stack provided by your instructor. Prepare a 2- to 3-minute roast speech for the person identified on it. Criteria for evaluation include how well you identify and develop the person's laudable characteristics and accomplishments in the form of good-natured humorous anecdotes, stories, and examples.

Photo 15.3 Weddings, birthdays, and retirements often call for a toast to pay tribute to the occasion or honored person(s). Have you ever been called on to give a toast?

image100/Alamy Stock Photo

Photo 15.4 Ethical communicators offer only good-natured jokes and stories that respect the individual being honored at a roast. Have you ever been offended by remarks made at a roast?

personal stories, or uplifting accolades. Roasts became mainstream in popular culture when Dean Martin hosted a series of celebrity roasts on television during the 1970s. Some of the most famous celebrity roasts have been of William Shatner, Pamela Anderson, Frank Sinatra, Hugh Hefner, Johnny Carson, and Muhammad Ali. The key when offering a speech of tribute during a roast is to demonstrate the ethical communication principles of respect and integrity by offering only jokes, stories, and anecdotes that do not offend the featured guest (Photo 15.4). The point, after all, is to honor and laud the guest.

Eulogies

A **eulogy** is a speech of tribute presented at a funeral or memorial service that praises someone's life and accomplishments. You might recall from our opening scenario that Ben was preparing a eulogy for his grandfather (Photo 15.5). Your goal when giving a eulogy is to comfort the mourners by focusing on positive memories of the deceased person. Based on what you know about the person, you should select three or four positive personal characteristics of the person to use as the main points, then use personal stories about the person to develop each main point. Your audience will enjoy hearing new stories that exemplify the person's characteristics as well as revisiting widely shared stories. Incidents that reveal how a personal characteristic helped the person overcome adversity will be especially powerful.

eulogy: speech of tribute given during a funeral or memorial service, which praises the life and accomplishments of the deceased

SPEECH SNIPPET

In the eulogy for his grandfather, "Gramps," Ben highlighted three character traits in Gramps that he admired. One trait was Gramps' patience, which Ben highlighted by telling stories of how Gramps had handled Ben's mistakes during three different incidents. In each instance, Gramps had taught Ben a life lesson by sharing a story from his own boyhood rather than reprimanding him.

Photo 15.5 At some point you may be asked to pay tribute to someone you love by giving the eulogy. How would you prepare your remarks?

OTHER CEREMONIAL SPEECHES

Other occasions that call for ceremonial speeches include graduations, holidays, and anniversaries of major events, and special events.

- A **commencement address**, for example, praises graduating students and attempts to inspire them to reach for their goals.

- A **commemorative address** celebrates national holidays or anniversaries of important events. For example, the president of the United States might give a commemorative speech on Martin Luther King day or on the anniversary of the 9/11 attacks.

- A **keynote address** both sets the tone and generates enthusiasm for the topic of a conference or convention. It is usually delivered by a well-known and well-regarded person in a field within the theme of the conference.

- A **dedication** honors a worthy person or group by naming a structure such as a building, monument, or park after the honoree.

- A **farewell** honors someone who is leaving an organization.

- A **speech to entertain** is a humorous speech that makes a serious point. Late night talk show hosts typically do a speech to entertain in the form of an opening monologue.

- An **elevator pitch** introduces and enlists interest in a concept, product, or practice in 3 minutes or less. The key is to be brief, but still thorough enough to get through to the listeners in a way that encourages them to ask questions.

commencement address: praises graduating students and attempts to inspire them to reach for their goals

commemorative address: celebrates national holidays or anniversaries of important events

keynote address: both sets the tone and generates enthusiasm for the topic of a conference or convention

dedication: honors a worthy person or group by naming a structure, monument, or park after them

farewell: honors someone who is leaving an organization

speech to entertain: a humorous speech that makes a serious point

elevator pitch: introduces and enlists interest in a concept, product, or practice in 3 minutes or less

PUBLIC SPEAKING IN THE REAL WORLD

Jason LaVeris/Contributor/Getty Images

10 Things Kristen Stewart Can Teach Us About Public Speaking

By now you know that effective public speaking is a skill that anyone can learn and that the skill improves with practice. Quite frankly, even those who have an aptitude for performing in front of audiences can't just "wing it" and expect to be effective public speakers. Just ask *Twilight* motion picture star Kristen Stewart. As Kelsey Manning, writer of the blog *The Grindstone*, points out, "K-Stew is the epitome of what not to do when public speaking" based on her many public speaking fiascos. Here they are:

- Don't act like those you are speaking to are beneath you. No one wants to listen to someone who acts like she has better places to be.

- Don't excessively touch your face. Classic Kristen Stewart move. Even if you're nervous, don't do this unless you're about to sneeze on someone.

- Don't bite your lip. Another classic. It's not cute, coy, or sexy; you just look like you're a little kid trying to tell his mom he broke a vase.

- Avoid "like," "um," "uh," or any other interjection that means nothing. The best thing to do is to try to eliminate such words in all conversation, which will make it easier to avoid using them when giving speeches too.

- Don't trail off at the end of sentences.

- Don't turn declarative sentences into questions.

- Look at the person you're speaking to (not at the floor).

- Avoid long pauses.

- Don't curse or make jokes that will make people feel awkward. Throwing in a curse word does not make you sound more casual and curse words are particularly jarring in speeches.

- Don't end speeches with "So . . . there you go," "So . . . yeah," "'Kay, bye," or any derivative thereof. These are actual quotes from the ends of some of Kristen Stewart's speeches. Just don't.[1]

If you've ever heard Stewart introduce or accept an award, you'll probably agree with Manning: we can learn a lot from Kristen Stewart about what *not* to do when giving speeches.

1. Which of these ten traps do you fall victim to when speaking in public?

2. How will you work to overcome them?

Reflection and Assessment

In addition to informative and persuasive speeches, you are likely to have occasion to give speeches to welcome, introduce, nominate, recognize, accept, and pay tribute. To assess how well you've learned what we've discussed in this chapter, answer the following questions. If you have trouble answering any of them, go back and review that material. Once you can answer each question accurately, you are ready to move ahead to the next chapter.

1. What should you include in a speech of welcome?
2. Why should a speech of introduction be brief?
3. What is your goal in a speech of nomination?
4. When might you be expected to give a speech of recognition?
5. What are the key elements of an effective acceptance speech?
6. What are some common types of speeches of tribute?
7. What are some other types of ceremonial speeches?

MindTap®

Challenge Resource and Assessment Center

Now that you have read Chapter 15, go to your MindTap Communication for *The Challenge of Effective Speaking in a Digital Age* for quick access to flashcards, chapter quizzes, and more.

Applying What You've Learned

1. **Impromptu Speech Activity:** Consider what you would like people to remember or know about you if you were to die tomorrow. Prepare a 2- to 3-minute impromptu eulogy based on the expectations detailed in this chapter.

2. **Assessment Activity A:** Watch the opening segment to a popular late-night TV program such as *Saturday Night Live, The Tonight Show Starring Jimmy Fallon,* or *Late Night with Seth Meyers* or to a talk show such as *The Ellen DeGeneres Show* or *The View*. Consider the guidelines for a speech of welcome as described in this chapter. In what ways does the host of the show follow or not follow the guidelines suggested in this chapter? How effective do you believe the host to be and why? Write up your assessment in the form of a one- to two-page reflection paper.

3. **Assessment Activity B:** Attend a professional public speaking event on campus or in your community. Assess the ways in which the master of ceremonies follows or does not follow the guidelines for a speech of introduction as described in this chapter. Do you believe the speech of introduction was effective in meeting the goals described in this chapter? Why or why not?

16

Group Communication and Presentations

WHAT'S THE POINT?
WHEN YOU'VE FINISHED THIS CHAPTER, YOU WILL BE ABLE TO:

- Share leadership responsibilities in groups
- Manage conflict among group members
- Engage in the steps of the systematic problem-solving process
- Communicate more effectively in virtual groups
- Present group findings in different formats
- Evaluate group dynamics and presentations

MindTap®

Review the chapter **Learning Objectives** and **Start** with quick warm-up activity.

ⓔ Ethical communicators demonstrate respect for other group members by resolving interpersonal conflict through collaboration, encouraging input, and acknowledging all sides of an issue.

WORK SESSION 1: Julio, Kristi, Luke, Bryn, and Nick have been asked to work as a small group to prepare a persuasive presentation that will count for one-third of the grade in the course. As the other members see it, Nick is a troublemaker because he has contradicted the instructor several times during previous class sessions. Nick has also been absent a number of times and seems less than fully committed to earning a good grade. In short, the other members are worried that Nick will cause them to earn a lower grade than they would earn without him in their group.

WORK SESSION 2: After the instructor refused to move Nick to another group, Julio, Kristi, Luke, and Bryn decide to restrict Nick's participation by not asking him for substantive help even though that means he'll get a better grade than he deserves. As the full group begins discussing their topic—gun control—Nick explains that he has a lot of material on it since he is a fairly vocal opponent of this proposal. Kristi, Julio, and Luke become disgruntled because they plan to argue in support of the proposal, and as they suspected, Nick opposes it. Kristi asks Bryn: "How do YOU feel about this conflict?" Much to Kristi's surprise, Bryn replies, "Actually, I'd like to hear more from Nick before I decide. Nick, tell us more." Nick goes on to share highly relevant information that would eventually be used to strengthen the group's speech. The group soon realizes the hastiness of their judgments about Nick.

Perhaps you have already been part of a group whose task was to prepare a joint presentation. If so, the opening scenario might sound familiar. In fact, when asked to work in small groups on a class or work project, many people respond—as Julio, Kristi, Luke, and Bryn did—with resistance. Their reasons usually focus on concerns that a few members will end up doing most of the work, that the group process will slow them down, that they'll earn a lower grade than if they worked alone, or that they will be forced to work on a topic that they aren't interested in or take a position they don't agree with.

Although working in a group to develop and deliver a presentation has its disadvantages, it is the preferred approach in business and industry.[1] **Problem-solving groups** (usually composed of five to seven people) are formed to carry out a specific task or solve a particular problem. Whether you want to or not, you can expect to work in a problem-solving group or team in your professional life, sometimes in face-to-face settings and often in virtual settings through email, chat rooms, discussion boards, and video conferences.[2] Leaders in business and industry have come to realize that the advantages of groups (e.g., deeper analysis of problems, greater breadth of ideas and of potential solutions, improved group morale, increased productivity) far outweigh the disadvantages.

This book includes a chapter on problem-solving groups because these groups typically present their findings in formal presentations, for example, as progress reports, sales presentations, proposals, or staff reports.[3] In this chapter, we begin by talking about effective leadership and the responsibilities of group members in achieving it, as well as in managing conflict among members. Then we explain an effective problem-solving method first described by educational philosopher John Dewey. From there, we turn our attention to particular strategies for effective communication in virtual groups. Finally, we describe several formats for communicating your findings publically and evaluating group effectiveness both in terms of group dynamics and presentations.

problem-solving groups: five to seven people who work together to complete a specific task or solve a particular problem

LEADERSHIP

Leadership is a process "whereby an individual influences a group of individuals to achieve a common goal."[4] When we think of leadership, we often think of a person who is in charge. In fact, scholars once thought leaders were "born"—that some people inherited traits that made them naturally suited to be leaders. This trait theory approach was called "The Great Man Theory of Leadership."[5] Later, scholars believed that different leadership styles were more or less effective based on the goal and situation. These classic theories suggest that *leadership* is enacted by one person. Today, however, we understand leadership as a set of communication functions performed by different group members at various times based on each person's unique strengths and expertise.[6] So, although a group may have a **formal leader** (a person designated or elected to oversee the group process), a series of **informal emergent leaders** (members who help lead the group to achieve different leadership functions) make for the most effective leadership in groups.

Shared leadership functions are the sets of roles you and other members perform to facilitate the work of the group and to help maintain harmonious relations among members. A **role** is a specific communication behavior group members perform to address the needs of the group at any given point in time. When roles are performed effectively, the group functions smoothly. Shared leadership functions may be categorized as task, procedural, and maintenance roles.

1. **Task leadership roles** help the group acquire, process, or apply information that contributes directly to completing a task or goal. Task leaders are good at finding pertinent research related to the goal and sharing it with the group. They may also be good at summarizing group discussions in ways that pull them together toward the group goal.

2. **Procedural leadership roles** provide logistical support and record the group's decisions and accomplishments (Photo 16.1). Procedural leaders are usually good at arranging a time and place for face-to-face meetings or setting up links for access to teleconferences or videoconferences. They may also be good at taking notes and keeping track of group decisions.

leadership: a process whereby an individual influences a group of individuals to achieve a common goal

formal leader: a person designated or elected to oversee the group process

informal emergent leaders: members who engage in different leadership functions

shared leadership functions: the sets of roles group members perform to facilitate the work of the group and to help maintain harmonious relations among members

role: a specific communication behavior group members perform to address group needs at any given point in time

task leadership roles: help the group acquire, process, or apply information that contributes directly to completing a task or goal

procedural leadership roles: provide logistical support and record the group's decisions and accomplishments

Blend Images/John Fedele/Vetta/Getty Images

Photo 16.1 Procedural leaders are good at making logistical arrangements and keeping track of group decisions and accomplishments. Which leadership roles are you best at performing?

maintenance leadership roles: help the group to develop and maintain cohesion, commitment, and positive working relationships

synergy: when the result of group work is better than what one member could achieve alone

When Luke and Kristi began talking during the group work session about attending the upcoming football game, Bryn gently reminded them that the group had only 30 minutes to figure out how to proceed and to assign tasks for the speech that would be due the next week.

3. **Maintenance leadership roles** help the group to develop and maintain cohesion, commitment, and positive working relationships. Maintenance leaders are good at encouraging others to share ideas and praising them for sharing, as well as intervening when conflict is threatening to harm the group process.

When problem-solving groups work well, the product they produce is better than what any one member could have accomplished alone. This is known as **synergy**. This synergy occurs when all members adhere to the five critical shared leadership responsibilities shown in Exhibit 16.1.

1. **Be committed to the group goal.** Being committed to the group goal means finding a way to align your expertise with the agreed-upon goal of the group.

   In addition to demonstrating responsibility, being committed to the group goal also conveys both integrity and respect. So, for a class project, this might mean working together on a topic that wasn't your first choice. Once the decision has been agreed to, it is no longer appropriate to dredge up old issues that have already been settled. For example, although Drew wanted to do a dance-a-thon to raise money, once the group agreed to do a raffle instead, he offered to ask the bookstore manager about donating some prizes.

2. **Keep discussions on track.** It is every member's responsibility to keep the discussion on track by offering only comments that are relevant and by gently reminding others to stay focused if the discussion starts to get off track. It is unproductive to talk about personal issues during the team's work time. Moreover, it is unethical to try to get the discussion off track because you disagree with what is being said.

3. **Complete individual assignments on time.** One potential advantage of group work is that tasks can be divided among members. However, each member is responsible for completing his or her tasks thoroughly and on time.

Exhibit 16.1 **Responsibilities of Group Members**

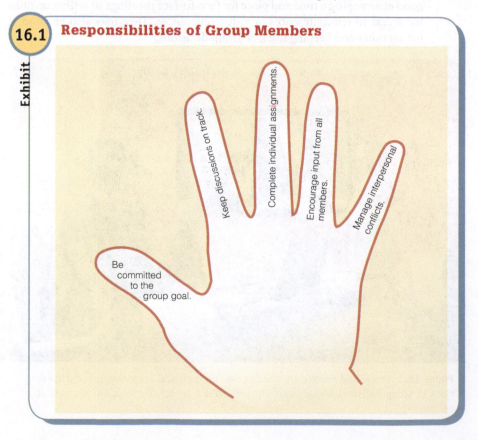

4. **Encourage input from all members.** All too often, extroverts overshadow quiet group members. Sometimes, outspoken members misinterpret this silence as the quieter members having nothing to contribute or not wanting to contribute. On the contrary, all members have valuable perspectives. If you are an extrovert, you have a special responsibility to refrain from dominating the discussion and to ask others for their opinions. Likewise, if you tend to be an introvert, you should make a conscious effort to express yourself. You might write down what you want to share or even raise your hand to get the attention of other members in an unobtrusive way.

5. **Manage interpersonal conflicts.** All small groups experience some **conflict**— disagreements or clashes among ideas, principles, or people. If managed appropriately, conflict can actually be beneficial to the group goal by stimulating thinking, fostering open communication, encouraging diverse opinions, and enlarging members' understanding of the issues.[7] Doing your part to manage conflict demonstrates the ethical principles of responsibility and respect for others. Because managing conflict effectively is so essential to successful group work, we focus specifically on conflict management and resolution in the next section.

> **conflict:** disagreements among ideas, principles, or people

CONFLICT IN GROUPS

As we have already mentioned, all small groups experience some conflict. When managed effectively, conflict enhances synergy.[8] In fact, groups that *don't* experience some conflict risk the problem of **groupthink**—when group members accept information and ideas without subjecting them to critical analysis.[9] Behaviors that signal groupthink include:

> **groupthink:** when group members accept information and ideas without subjecting them to critical analysis

- Avoiding conflict to prevent hurting someone's feelings;

- Pressuring members who do not agree with the majority of the group to conform;

- Reaching "consensus" without the support of all members;

- Discouraging or ignoring disagreements; and

- Rationalizing a decision without testing it.

If effective groups actually experience conflict, how do they manage it successfully? Effective groups do so when all members understand their personal conflict management styles and follow certain guidelines when addressing potentially conflict-arousing situations. Let's begin by discussing several potential sources of conflict and then five of the most common conflict management styles as they function in groups.

> **pseudo-conflict:** when group members who actually agree about something believe they disagree due to poor communication

Sources of Conflict

1. **Pseudo-conflict** occurs when group members who actually agree about something believe they disagree due to poor communication. Since *pseudo* means *fake*, the perceived conflict is actually a misperception.

2. **Issue-related conflict** occurs when two or more group members' goals, ideas, or opinions about a topic are incompatible. Issue-related conflict can be a good thing when handled effectively because, without it, groupthink is far more likely to occur.

> **issue-related conflict:** when two or more group members' goals, ideas, or opinions about a topic are incompatible

3. **Personality-related conflict** occurs when two or more group members become defensive because they feel as though they are being attacked. Typically, personality-related conflicts are rooted in a power struggle.[10]

> **personality-related conflict:** when two or more group members become defensive because they feel as though they are being attacked

4. **Culture-related conflict** occurs when the communication norms of group members are incongruent. For example, people who identify with

> **culture-related conflict:** when the communication norms of group members are incongruent

Photo 16.2 Group members demonstrate ethical communication behavior by managing conflict, collaborating, perception checking, and paraphrasing. What kinds of conflict do you find most difficult to manage?

individualistic cultural norms tend to use direct communication to manage conflict, whereas those who identify with collectivist norms tend to use indirect nonverbal means for doing so.[11]

5. **Virtual group-related conflict** arises as a result of meeting through technology-enhanced channels. For example, most technology-enhanced channels reduce our ability to send and receive subtle nonverbal messages, particularly those related to emotions and relational issues. Many of us use emoticons and emojis to represent missing nonverbal cues; however, a smiley face can be offered sincerely or sarcastically and it can be difficult for the receiver to ascertain the difference. Unfortunately, conflict often goes unresolved in virtual groups because we cannot see the nonverbal reactions of frustration that are visible when interacting in person.[12] When communication is effective, however, the bonds among members of virtual groups can be even stronger than those in face-to-face groups.[13] Effective members of virtual groups make a conscious effort to communicate both what they *think* and how they *feel* about a topic.

We can deal with these sorts of conflict in several ways. We can manage disagreements by separating the issues from the people involved, keeping our emotions in check, and phrasing our comments descriptively, not judgmentally (Photo 16.2). Rather than calling a particular idea stupid, for example, you might ask for clarification about why members of your group think or feel the way they do. Seek first to understand.

We can also employ perception checking or paraphrasing, using "I language" that phrases our interpretations and opinions as our own rather than as defense-arousing "you language."[14] In other words, our language needs to reflect the fact that we are responsible for our feelings.[15] We can also diffuse potential conflicts by using "I" and "we" statements (See Exhibit 16.2).

virtual group-related conflict: arises as a result of meeting through technology-enhanced channels

Exhibit 16.2 **Reframing "You" Statements into "I" Statements**

"You" Statement	"I" Statement
"You hurt my feelings."	"I feel hurt when you don't acknowledge what I say."
"You're so irresponsible."	"I feel my efforts don't matter when you come to the meeting unprepared."
"Don't be so critical."	"I feel disrespected when you say my opinion is stupid."
"I can't believe you said that!"	"I feel humiliated when you mention my problems in front of others."

Steve Cheny/Corbis

Perception checking is a verbal statement that reflects your understanding of another's behavior. It is a process of describing what you have seen and heard and then asking for feedback. A perception check statement consists of three parts:

1. In a nonevaluative way, describe what you observed or sensed from someone's behavior.

2. Offer two possible interpretations.

3. Ask for clarification.

Paraphrasing is putting your understanding of another person's verbal message into your own words. It is a four-step process:

1. Listen carefully to the message.

2. Notice what images, ideas, and feelings you experience from the message.

3. Determine what the message means to you.

4. Share your interpretation and ask for confirmation that you did so correctly.

Exhibit 16.3 provides examples of perception checking and paraphrasing as they may be applied to avoid personality conflict.

perception checking: a verbal statement that reflects your understanding of another's behavior

paraphrasing: putting a message into your own words

16.3 **Avoiding Personality Conflict Through Perception Checking and Paraphrasing**

Exhibit

Situation	Perception check	Paraphrase
As you are offering your idea about who the group might interview to get more information on your topic, Tomika says, "Whatever. . ." and begins reading a message on her cell phone.	Tomika, I see you are checking your messages. I sense that you don't like my suggestion. Is that an accurate read or are you just expecting an important message? Or is it something else?	From your "whatever" response, I sense that either you don't really agree with my suggestion, you aren't really committed to the project, or you just don't respect me. Or is it something else?
Over the term, Jose has been quick to volunteer for the easiest assignments and has never taken on a difficult piece of work. Today the group was finalizing who would deliver which part of the group presentation and Jose quickly volunteered, saying: "I'll be the master of ceremonies and introduce our topic and each speaker."	Jose, I have been noticing that you have been quick to volunteer and you usually choose the least time consuming and simplest tasks, and now you're offering to take a role in the presentation that will again require little effort. Are you really overextended in your other classes or trying to take the easy way out? Or is there some other explanation?	Jose, it seems to me like you are again volunteering to do the part of the presentation that will be the least amount of work. Are you really overextended with other courses or not committed to doing your share? Or is there some other reason that you want to be the master of ceremonies?
Today is the day that Madison is supposed to lead the group's discussion, as she was responsible for the research on this part of the group's project. As the group waits for her to begin, she avoids eye contact and rummages through her backpack, finally looking up and saying, "Well, I guess that you all are going to be kind of mad at me."	Madison, I'm noticing you don't seem like you want to get the meeting started, are avoiding eye contact, and have been rummaging around in your bag. I get the sense that you don't feel prepared for today. Did you lose your homework? Were you able to complete it? Am I on target or is it something else?	Madison, from what you said, I understand that you are not prepared to lead the meeting. I'm wondering if you did your homework and lost it. Or is there something else?

Conflict Management Styles

Perception checking and paraphrasing are useful strategies for resolving conflict. Members also can succeed at resolving conflicts when they understand conflict management styles and employ the most effective ones when working in groups. Research reveals five common conflict management styles: avoiding, accommodating, competing, compromising, and collaborating.[16]

avoiding: physically or psychologically removing oneself from the conflict

Avoiding involves physically or psychologically removing yourself from the conflict. For instance, in our opening scenario, if Nick decided to leave the first group session and then not show up at others because he perceived other members didn't agree with him, he would be managing conflict by avoiding. Similarly, if he attended the work sessions, but didn't share his input, he would also be avoiding. When a group member engages in avoiding as a conflict management style, the whole group suffers because everyone is not committed to the group goal and every member's input is not being considered. We label this a lose-lose conflict management style.

accommodating: accepting others' ideas while neglecting your own, even when you disagree with the views of the others

Accommodating is accepting others' ideas and opinions while neglecting your own, even when you disagree with the views of the others. If we continue with the example of Nick and his group members, we could say that Nick is engaging in accommodating if he goes along with Kristi, Julio, and Luke, who want to support increased gun control, even though he personally opposes that view. When a group member engages in accommodating as a conflict management style, the whole group suffers because not all potential ideas are being weighed in the discussion. We label this a lose-win conflict management style.

competing: satisfying one's own needs without concern for the needs of the others or for the harm it does to the group dynamics or problem-solving process

Competing is satisfying your own needs without concern for the needs of others or for the harm it does to the group dynamics or problem-solving process. When one member dominates the group discussion by forcing his or her opinions without considering other views or even allowing them to be expressed, the whole group suffers because input from all group members is not being heard. If two or more members engage in competing conflict styles, the whole group suffers, not only because all ideas are not being heard, but also because the discussion gets off track, interpersonal conflicts are not being managed, and the arguments may even impede the completion of individual assignments. If Nick and Luke engage in competing behavior over the gun control issue, other input is squelched and the group process comes to a halt. We label this a lose-lose conflict management style.

Reflect on Ethics

WHAT WOULD *YOU* DO?

MODELING GROUP DYNAMICS ON TV TALK SHOWS

ABC's *The View* is a popular daytime talk show. The program has garnered several daytime Emmy Awards since it first aired in 1997. It features a team of several female cohosts of different ages and backgrounds who discuss current events and issues. What do *The View* and similar programs convey to viewers about engaging in group discussion? We can begin to answer this question by observing comments posted online about the show:

- KellyKKelly wrote: "I realized that every time I catch excerpts from the thing, I wind up with a headache. They talk over each other, Whoopi yells. . . "

- Sanbur posted this comment: "I am all for free speech. . . I want to hear all opinions, but I expect

them to be informed, to be respectful, and to be open to the FACT that there are always two sides to a story."[17]

If you haven't seen *The View,* watch an episode of it, and then answer the following questions:

1. In what ways, if any, does this program violate the guidelines for effective group dynamics discussed in this chapter?

2. What would you do if you found yourself interacting in a group functioning as these cohosts do?

16.4 Collaborative Conflict Management Tips

Initiating collaboration	Responding collaboratively
1. Identify the problem as your own using "I" language. "I could really use your help here."	1. Disengage to avoid a defensive response.
2. Describe your observations in terms of behavior, consequences, and feelings. "When I see you checking your email, I feel we're missing out on your ideas for the project, and I get frustrated."	2. Respond empathically with genuine interest and concern by first describing the behavior you observe. "I see you checking your email, and I wonder if you're angry or frustrated with something."
3. Refrain from blaming or accusing.	3. Paraphrase your understanding of the problem and ask questions to clarify issues. "Is there something bothering you or something we're overlooking?"
4. Find common ground. "Figuring this out is really tough. I know I feel overwhelmed about it sometimes."	4. Seek common ground. "I know that trying to come to one goal and solution seems impossible at times."
5. Mentally rehearse so you can state your request briefly.	5. Ask the other person to suggest alternative solutions. "What other ideas do you have that we might consider?"

Compromising occurs when individuals give up part of what they want to provide at least some satisfaction to others in the group. If group members can't find an ideal time to meet outside of class because they all have busy schedules, they might compromise on a time to meet that isn't particularly ideal for any of them or decide to meet virtually by posting to a blog. In terms of coming to a solution, one drawback of this style is that the quality of the decision is probably affected when someone "trades away" a better solution to reach a compromise. We label this a partial lose-lose conflict management style.

compromising: giving up part of what you want to satisfy others in the group

Collaborating occurs when people work through the problem together to discover a mutually acceptable solution. We label this a win-win conflict management style. A win-win solution occurs when input from all members is heard, valued, and evaluated honestly and fairly until the group reaches consensus about how to proceed. Consider the tips in Exhibit 16.4 to achieve effective collaborative conflict management.

collaborating: discussing the issues, describing feelings, and identifying the characteristics of an effective solution before deciding what the ultimate solution will be

SYSTEMATIC PROBLEM SOLVING

When you meet with your classmates, coworkers, or community members to work on a project, you will be trying to solve a problem. To be effective, your group will need to follow a concrete process for analyzing the problem and coming up with a productive solution in a short amount of time. One effective means for doing this is the **systematic problem-solving method**.[18] This six-step process, first described by John Dewey in 1933 and since revised by others, remains a tried and true method for individual and group problem solving.[19]

systematic problem-solving method: a six-step method for finding an effective solution to a problem

1. **Identify and define the problem.** The first step is to identify the problem and define it in a way all group members understand and agree with. Even when a group is commissioned by an outside agency that provides a description of the problem, the group still needs to understand precisely what is at issue and what needs to be resolved. Often, what appears to be a problem is only a symptom of

Questions to Guide Problem Analysis

- What are the symptoms of this problem?
- What are the causes of this problem?
- Can this problem be subdivided into several smaller problems, each of which may have individual solutions?
- What have others who have faced this problem done?
- How successful have others been with the solutions they attempted?
- How is our situation similar to and different from theirs?
- Does this problem consist of several smaller problems? If so, what are their symptoms, causes, previously tried solutions, and so forth?
- What would be the consequences of doing nothing?
- What would be the consequences of trying something and having it fail?

a problem; if the group focuses on solutions that eliminate only that symptom, the underlying problem will remain.

Groups might begin by coming up with a number of problems and then narrowing them to a particular one. You can also identify and define a problem by posing questions such as: What is the problem? What is its history? Who is affected by it, and how does it affect them? How many people are affected, in what ways, and to what degree? These questions help a group to realize what kinds of information must be gathered to help define the problem. To ensure that your group is focusing on the problem itself and not just the symptoms of the problem, don't rush through this step.

2. **Analyze the problem.** To analyze the problem, you must find out as much as possible about it. Most groups begin with each member sharing information he or she already knows about the problem. The group then determines what additional questions need to be answered and searches for additional information to answer them. You might consider questions such as those in Exhibit 16.5.

criteria: standards used for judging the merits of proposed solutions

3. **Determine criteria for judging solutions. Criteria** are standards used for judging the merits of proposed solutions—a blueprint for evaluating them. Research suggests that when groups develop criteria before they think about specific solutions, they are more likely to come to a decision that all members can accept.[20] Without clear criteria, group members may argue for their preferred solution without thoughtfully considering whether it will adequately address the problem or whether it is truly feasible. Exhibit 16.6 poses questions that can help groups think about the types of criteria a solution might need to meet.

4. **Generate a host of solutions.** Arriving at a good solution depends on having a wide variety of possible solutions to choose from. Many groups fail at generating a variety of possible solutions because they criticize the first ideas expressed, which discourages members from taking the risk to offer their ideas for the group to consider. One way to encourage input is to use the brainstorming technique. **Brainstorming**, you'll recall, is an uncritical, nonevaluative process of generating associated ideas. It involves group members verbalizing ideas as they come to mind without stopping to evaluate their merits. At least one member should record all solutions as they are suggested. To ensure that creativity is not stifled, no solution should be ignored, and members should build on the ideas presented by others. Brainstorming may generate 20 or more potential solutions. As a minimum, the group should try to come up with eight to ten potential solutions before moving to the next step.

brainstorming: an uncritical, nonevaluative process of generating associated ideas

Exhibit 16.6 Questions to Guide Discussion of Solution Criteria

- What are the quantitative and qualitative measures of success that a solution must be able to demonstrate?
- Are there resource constraints that a good solution must meet (costs, time, manpower)?
- Is solution simplicity a factor?
- What risks are unacceptable?
- Is ease of implementation a consideration?
- Is it important that no constituency be unfairly harmed or advantaged by a solution?

5. **Evaluate solutions based on the criteria and select one.** Using the criteria established by the group in step 3, evaluate the merits of each potential solution generated in step 4. Consider each solution as it meets the criteria, and eliminate solutions that do not meet them adequately. In addition to applying the criteria, the group might also ask questions such as the following: How will the solution solve the problem? How difficult will it be to implement? What problems might be caused as a result of implementing the solution? Once each potential solution has been thoroughly evaluated based on the criteria, the group must select the best one(s).
6. **Implement the agreed-upon solution and assess it.** Finally, the group should implement the agreed-upon solution or, if the group is presenting the solution to others for implementation, make recommendations for how the solution should be implemented. What tasks are required by the solution(s)? Who will carry out these tasks? What is a reasonable time frame for implementation generally and for each of the tasks specifically? Because the agreed-upon solution may or may not prove effective, the group should determine a point at which they will revisit and assess the success of the solution(s). Doing so builds in an opportunity to revise or replace the solution if warranted.

SPEECH SNIPPET

In their report about gang violence, Matt, Shannon, Pam, and Michelle created implementation plans for parental accountability and for the government to crack down on the illegal gun market. They also provided implementation strategies for churches, businesses, and service groups to offer alternative programs for area youth. Thus, they didn't merely offer solutions; they provided plans for implementing them.

COMMUNICATING EFFECTIVELY IN VIRTUAL GROUPS

Virtual groups that convene using phone or computer technology are becoming increasingly popular for many reasons (Photo 16.3). First, members need not be physically present. Before these technologies became available, groups had to meet face-to-face to exchange information, solve problems, and make decisions. But today, group members can interact while in different cities, states, and countries. Second, **asynchronous virtual groups**—those whose members can post and respond to messages at any time, although usually within a few days—allow people to participate across time. Busy people often struggle to find a meeting time that works with everyone's schedule. So a group can "meet" via a threaded discussion instead. Third, virtual meetings can save money. Before these technologies, people often had to travel to a meeting site. That often also meant paying for travel, accommodations, meals, parking, and even meeting space rental. Because virtual meetings can be conducted over the phone or Internet, meeting costs are reduced for both participants and hosts.

virtual groups: groups that convene using telephone or computer technology

asynchronous virtual groups: those whose members can post and respond to messages at any time, although usually within a few days

The benefits of virtual groups also come with potential costs. For example, research has found that communication problems can impact both task and relational outcomes.[21] Face-to-face groups are often more dedicated to completing the task,[22] to

Photo 16.3 As virtual groups become more prevalent, we must take care to adhere to effective communication practices in them. What are some tips offered in this chapter that you will follow when meeting virtually with a group?

Monty Rakusen/Newscom

netiquette: etiquette rules applicable to communicating over computer networks

fostering positive relationships among members,[23] and to building cohesion[24] than are virtual groups. Thus, we offer a few guidelines to follow for effective communication when working in a virtual group.

1. **Train members to use the technology.** Do not assume everyone is adept at using the technology needed to conduct the work session. Provide training if needed.

2. **Create ice-breaker and team-building opportunities.** Just as face-to-face groups benefit from getting to know and trust one another, so do members of virtual groups. You can do so, for example, by encouraging members to share personal websites, photos, and self-introduction narratives. Members can also become Facebook friends and follow one another on Twitter accounts.

3. **Develop group ground rules.** Just as rules need to be clarified for face-to-face groups, they need to be articulated for virtual groups. For example, set rules regarding expected message response time, turn-taking, and **netiquette** (etiquette rules applicable to communicating over computer networks). Netiquette include such things as being courteous and respectful, use of emoticons and emojis, keeping messages short, refraining from the use of all capital letters, thinking before posting, being patient with new users, obeying copyright laws, and keeping personal information private.[25]

4. **Provide clear structure.** Virtual groups perform best when a clear structure is provided. A formal task leader ought to clearly lay out not only the goal but also the systematic process the group will follow to achieve it.

5. **Use synchronous technology if possible.** Although threaded discussions allow people to interact at their own convenience, these formats offer limited means for conveying nonverbal, emotional, and social cues. So, whenever possible, use regularly scheduled synchronous teleconference or videoconference meetings.

6. **Create opportunities to meet outside the virtual environment.** Members of virtual groups can feel closer if they can also have side conversations. One way to accomplish this is to set up an instant messaging system that allows members to contact each other for short conversations during and between meetings.

7. **Schedule regular opportunities to assess the pros and cons of the technology and make adjustments as warranted.** Survey the group regularly to discover emerging problems and work together to correct them before they undermine the quality of the group's work.

Group communication in virtual settings poses an additional set of challenges to ensure an effective outcome. As more and more people opt to engage in virtual groups, it is critical to continuing developing and engaging in communication strategies that will promote effective outcomes.

GROUP PRESENTATION FORMATS

deliverables: products of the work provided to someone else

Once a group has completed its deliberations, it typically must communicate its results. **Deliverables** are the products of your work you provide to someone else. Although some deliverables are objects, typically the deliverables from problem-solving groups come in the form of communicating the information, analyses, and recommendations of the group. These deliverables can be communicated in written, oral, or virtual formats.

Written Formats

1. A **written brief** is a short document that describes the problem, background, process, decision, and rationale so that the reader can quickly understand and evaluate the group's product. Most written briefs are one or two pages long. When preparing a brief, begin by describing your group's task: What problems are you attempting to solve and why? Then briefly provide the background information the reader will need to evaluate whether the group has adequately studied the problem. Present solution steps and timelines for implementation as bullet points so that the reader can quickly understand what is being proposed. Close with a sentence or short paragraph that describes how the recommendation will solve the problem, as well as any potential side effects.

2. A **comprehensive report** is a written document that provides a detailed review of the problem-solving process used to arrive at the recommendation. A comprehensive report is usually organized into sections that parallel the problem-solving process.

Because comprehensive reports can be long, they usually include an executive summary. An **executive summary** is a one-page synopsis of the report. This summary contains enough information to acquaint readers with the highlights of the full document without reading it. Usually, it contains a statement of the problem, some background information, a description of any alternatives, and the major conclusions.

Oral Formats

1. An **oral brief** is similar to a written brief. It is a short presentation delivered by one group member that describes the problem, background, process, decision, and rationale so that the audience can quickly understand and evaluate the group's product. Typically, an oral brief can be delivered in less than 10 minutes.

2. An **oral report** is similar to a comprehensive report. It delivers to an audience a detailed review of a group's problem-solving process. Oral reports can range from 30 to 60 minutes.

3. A **panel discussion** is a structured problem-solving discussion held by a group in front of an audience. One group member serves as moderator, introducing the topic and providing structure by asking a series of planned questions that panelists answer. The panelists' answers and the interaction among them provide the supporting evidence. A well-planned panel discussion seems spontaneous and interactive but requires careful planning and rehearsal to ensure that all relevant information is presented and that all speakers are afforded equal speaking time. After the formal discussion, the audience is often encouraged to question the participants. Perhaps you've seen or heard a panel of experts discuss a topic on a radio or TV talk show like *SportsCenter, Meet the Press,* or *The Doctors.*

4. A **symposium** is a set of prepared oral reports delivered sequentially by group members before a gathering of people who are interested in the work of the group. A symposium may be organized so that each person's speech focuses on one step of the problem-solving process, or it may be organized so that each speaker covers all of the steps in the problem-solving process as they relate to one of several issues that the group worked on or recommendations the group made. In a symposium, the speakers usually sit together at the front of the

written brief: a short document that describes the problem, background, process, decision, and rationale so that the reader can quickly understand and evaluate the group's product

comprehensive report: a written document that provides a detailed review of the problem-solving process used to arrive at the recommendation

executive summary: a one-page synopsis of a comprehensive report

oral brief: a short presentation delivered by one group member that describes the problem, background, process, decision, and rationale so that the audience can quickly understand and evaluate the group's product.

oral report: an oral presentation that provides a detailed review of the problem-solving process used to arrive at the recommendation

panel discussion: a structured problem-solving discussion in front of an audience

symposium: a set of prepared oral reports delivered sequentially by group members

room. One group member acts as moderator, offering the introductory and concluding remarks and providing transitions between speakers. When introduced by the moderator, each speaker may stand and walk to a central spot, usually a lectern. Speakers who use a computerized slideshow should coordinate their slides so that there are seamless transitions between speakers. Symposiums often conclude with a question-and-answer session facilitated by the moderator, who directs one or more group members to answer based on their expertise. Questions can be directed to individuals or to the group as a whole.

Virtual Formats

remote access report: a computer-mediated audiovisual presentation of the group's process and outcome

1. A **remote access report (RAR)** is a computer-mediated audiovisual presentation of the group's process and outcome that others can receive through email, Web posting, or other online transmission. Prepared by one or more members of the group, the RAR is prepared using PowerPoint or other computer slideshow software and provides a visual overview of the group's process, decisions, and recommendations. Effective RARs typically consist of no more than 15 to 20 slides. Slides are titled and content is presented in outline or bullet-point phrases or key words (rather than complete sentences or paragraphs), as well as through visual representations of important information. For example, a budget task force might have a slide with a pie chart depicting the portions of the proposed budget that are allocated to operating expenses, salaries, fundraising, and travel (see Exhibit 16.7). RARs may be self-running so that the slides automatically forward after a certain number of seconds, but it is better to let the viewer choose the pace and control when the next slide appears. RARs can be silent or narrated. When narrated, a voice-over accompanies each slide, providing additional or explanatory information.

streaming video: a recording that is sent in compressed form over the Internet

2. A **streaming video** is an audiovisual recording that is sent in compressed form over the Internet. You are probably familiar with streaming video from popular websites such as YouTube. Streaming videos are a great way to distribute oral briefs, but they also can be used to distribute recordings of oral reports, symposiums, or panel presentations. Streaming videos are useful when it is inconvenient for some or all the people who need to know the results of the group's work to meet at one time or in one place.

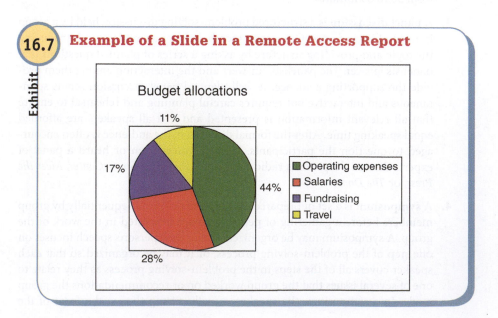

Exhibit 16.7   **Example of a Slide in a Remote Access Report**

Budget allocations

- Operating expenses 44%
- Salaries 28%
- Fundraising 17%
- Travel 11%

EVALUATING GROUP EFFECTIVENESS

Just as preparing and presenting are a bit different for group speeches than for individual speeches, so is the process of evaluating effectiveness. Evaluations should focus on group dynamics during the preparation process as well as on the effectiveness of the actual presentation.

Group Dynamics

To be effective, groups must work together as they define and analyze a problem, generate solutions, and select a course of action. They also need to work together as they prepare their written report, as well as when they prepare and practice their oral presentation if warranted. These communication interactions among members to achieve a goal are known as **group dynamics**.

You can evaluate group dynamics by judging the merit of each member's efforts in terms of the five group-member responsibilities discussed earlier in this chapter. In addition, each group member could prepare a "reflective thinking process paper," which details in paragraph form what each member did well and what each could improve upon in terms of the five group-member responsibilities. In the final paragraph of the paper, each member should provide a self-evaluation of what he or she did and what he or she could do to improve the group process in future sessions.

Like the evaluations business managers make of employees, these evaluations serve to document the efforts of group members. They can be submitted to the instructor, just as they would be submitted to a supervisor. In business, these documents provide a basis for determining promotion, merit pay, and salary adjustments. In the classroom, they can provide a basis for determining one portion of each member's grade.

group dynamics: how individuals work together as a team toward a common goal

Group Presentations

Effective group presentations depend on quality individual presentations as well as quality overall group performance. So evaluations of group presentations should consist of both an individual and a group component. Exhibit 16.8 provides a form you can use as a model to evaluate the effectiveness of a group presentation.

Evaluating Your Effectiveness

Effective group presentations depend on the combined efforts of individuals. So it's also a good idea to conduct a self-evaluation to determine whether you could be doing something better during the group problem-solving process, while preparing the group presentation, and when giving your portion of the group speech. Exhibit 16.9 is an example of a form you can use to evaluate your own efforts.

Speech Assignment

Public Group Presentation

Following your instructor's directions, form groups of four to six. Prepare a symposium or a panel discussion of a topic. Use the problem-solving process to guide your work as a group. Each group member must help identify an appropriate issue, participate in the problem-solving process, and take part in the presentation. Your instructor will provide more details of the expectations for this assignment.

Exhibit 16.8 — Sample Evaluation Form for Group Presentations

Group Member Name: _____

Critic (your name): _____

Directions: Evaluate the effectiveness of each group member according to the following criteria for effective presentations individually and as a group.

Rating Scale:

1	2	3	4	5	6	7
(poor)						(excellent)

INDIVIDUAL PERFORMANCE CRITIQUE

_____ **Content** (Breadth and depth and listener relevance)

(rating)   Critique (Provide a rationale for the rating you gave):

_____

_____ **Structure** (Macrostructure and microstructure/language)

(rating)   Critique (Provide a rationale for the rating you gave):

_____

_____ **Delivery** (Use of voice and use of body)

(rating)   Critique (Provide a rationale for the rating you gave):

_____

GROUP PERFORMANCE CRITIQUE

_____ **Content** (Thematic? Focused? Thorough? Construction of presentational aids?)

(rating)   Critique (Provide a rationale for the rating you gave):

_____

_____ **Structure** (Balanced? Transitions? Flow? Attn/Clincher?)

(rating)   Critique (Provide a rationale for the rating you gave):

_____

_____ **Delivery** (Teamwork? Cooperation? Fluency? Use of aids?)

(rating)   Critique (Provide a rationale for the rating you gave):

_____

Overall Comments:

_____

Exhibit 16.9 — Sample Self-Critique Form for Group Presentations

1. In terms of content, I did the following things well in my oral presentation:
   a.
   b.

2. In terms of structure, I did the following things well in my oral presentation:
   a.
   b.

3. In terms of delivery, I did the following things well in my oral presentation:
   a.
   b.

4. If I could do my portion of the oral presentation over again, I would do the following things differently:
   a.
   b.

5. In terms of my role as a group member, I am most proud of how I:

   _____

6. In terms of my role as a group member, I am least proud of how I:

   _____

7. Overall, I would give myself a grade of _____ for the group speech because:

   _____

Reflection and Assessment

Today, the ability to work and speak in groups is a necessity not only in the classroom but also in business and industry. Effective problem-solving groups produce better solutions than do individuals on their own. To assess how well you've learned what we've discussed in this chapter, answer the following questions. If you have trouble answering any of them, go back and review that material. Once you can answer each question accurately, you will have a basic understanding of how to master the challenge of effective speaking in a digital age.

1. Why is shared leadership so critical when working in groups?
2. What can you do to manage conflict effectively in groups?
3. What are the steps in the systematic problem-solving method?
4. What are some special guidelines to follow when communicating in virtual groups?
5. What are some formats for group presentations?
6. How can you evaluate group dynamics and presentations?

Challenge Resource and Assessment Center   MindTap®

Now that you have read Chapter 16, go to your MindTap Communication for *The Challenge of Effective Speaking in a Digital Age* for quick access to flashcards, chapter quizzes, and more.

Applying What You've Learned

1. **Impromptu Speech Activity:** Your instructor will place you in a group with three of your classmates. Your group should brainstorm a list of at least ten topic ideas for its group presentation. Then, each member of the group should select one of the topics (no duplicates allowed) and quickly prepare a 2- to 3-minute impromptu speech with the goal of convincing the other group members that his or her topic should be the one the group selects for the group's panel or symposium. After members have presented their speeches to the other group members, all members should individually rank order their preference for each topic. Groups should compile these results and use them as they decide on a topic.

2. **Assessment Activity A:** Watch a TV talk show program that is presented as a panel discussion, for example, *SportsCenter, Fox and Friends,* or *Morning Joe.* Evaluate the group dynamics process based on the five responsibilities of group members described in this chapter. Be sure to offer specific examples supporting your evaluation as to how each member of the panel performed and what each could do to improve.

3. **Assessment Activity B:** Assess how well your group functioned for this project by completing a one- to two-page reflection paper. Indicate what each member did well according to the five responsibilities and why, what each member could do to improve and why, and what your role is in that process. Also assess how well you performed according to each of the five responsibilities and why, as well as what you could do to improve, why, and how.

Notes

Chapter 1 Foundations of Public Speaking

1. Deardorff, K., & Hollingsworth, C. (2015, March 11). 2013 Information and communication technology survey. US Census Bureau. Retrieved from http://www.census.gov/econ/ict/xls/2013/full_report.html

2. Morreale, S., Hugenberg, L., & Worley, D. (2006). The basic communication course at U.S. colleges and universities in the 21st century: Study VII. *Communication Education, 55*(4), 415–437.

3. Cooper, L. (trans.) (1932/1960). *The rhetoric of Aristotle.* Englewood Cliffs, NJ: Prentice-Hall.

4. Koncz, A. (2008). *Job outlook 2009.* Bethlehem, PA: National Association of Colleges and Employers.

5. Hansen, R. S., & Hansen, K. (n.d.). What do employers *really* want? Top skills and values employers seek from job-seekers. Retrieved from http://www.quintcareers.com/job_skills_values.html

6. Parker, A., Lenhart, A., & Moore, K. (2011, August 28). The digital revolution and higher education. *The Pew Research Center: Internet, Science and Tech.* Retrieved from http://www.pewinternet.org/2011/08/28/the-digital-revolution-and-higher-education/

7. McCullen, C. (2003, November–December). Tactics and resources to help students avoid plagiarism. *Multimedia Schools,* 40–43.

8. Johannesen, R. L., Valde, K. S., & Whedbee, K. E. (2008). *Ethics in human communication* (6th ed.). Long Grove, IL: Waveland.

9. Montgomery, B. (2008, February 17). TV chef spiced up his past exploits. *Tampa Bay Times.* Retrieved from: http://www.sptimes.com/2008/02/17/Southpinellas/TV_chef_spiced_up_his.shtml

10. Cragen, J. F., & Shields, D. C. (1998). *Understanding communication theory: The communicative forces for human action.* Boston: Allyn & Bacon; Frey, L. R., Botan, C. H., & Kreps, G. L. (2000). *Investigating communication: An introduction to research methods* (2nd ed.). Needham Heights, MA: Allyn & Bacon.

11. Littlejohn, S. W., & Foss, K. A. (2011). *Theories of human communication* (10th ed.). Longrove, IL: Waveland.

12. Kellerman, K. (1992). Communication: Inherently strategic and primarily automatic. *Communication Monographs, 59,* 288–300.

13. Ibid.; Knapp, M., & Daly, J. (2002). *Handbook of interpersonal communication.* Thousand Oaks, CA: Sage.

14. Poole, M. S. (1998). The small group should be the fundamental unit of communication research. In J. Trent (Ed.), *Communication: Views from the helm for the twenty-first century* (p. 94). Needham Heights, MA: Allyn & Bacon; Beebe, S., & Masterson, J. (2006). *Communicating in groups: Principles and practice* (8th ed.). Boston: Pearson; Hirokawa, R., Cathcart, R., Samovar, I., & Henman, I. (Eds.). (2003). *Small group communication theory and practice* (8th ed.). Los Angeles: Roxbury.

15. Devine, D. J., Clayton, L. D., Phillips, J. L., Dunford, B. B., & Melner, S. B. (1999). Teams in organizations: Prevalence, characteristics, and effectiveness. *Small Group Research, 30,* 678–711.

16. Forsythe, D. R., & Burnette, J. L. (2005). The history of group research. In S. A. Wheelen (Ed.), *The handbook of group research*

and practice. Thousand Oaks, CA: Sage; Knapp, M. L., & Daly, J. A. (Eds.). (2011). *The SAGE handbook of interpersonal communication* (4th ed.). Thousand Oaks, CA: Sage; Wazlawick, P., Bavelas, J., & Jackson, D. (1967). *Pragmatics of human communication: A study of interactional patterns, pathologies, and paradoxes.* New York: Norton.

17. Cooper, *Rhetoric.*

18. Bitzer, L. F. (1995). The rhetorical situation. In Covino, W. A., Jolliffe, D. A. (Eds.), *Rhetoric: Concepts, definitions, boundaries.* Boston: Allyn & Bacon.

19. Ibid.

20. Exigence. (2009). In *Microsoft Encarta world English dictionary* (North American edition). Retrieved from http://encarta.msn.com/dictionary_1861609760/exigency.html

21. Sandy Hook Promise website. Retrieved from http://www.sandyhookpromise.org/

22. Cooper, *Rhetoric.*

23. The Stuttering Foundation. (1991–2012). *Famous people.* Retrieved from www.stutteringhelp.org/famous-people

24. Ibid.

Chapter 2 Your First Speech

1. Fear of Public Speaking Statistics. (2013, November 23). 2013 Statistic Brain Research Institute, publishing as Statistics Brain. Retrieved from http://statisticbrain.com/fear-of-public-speaking-statistics/

2. Richmond, V. P., & McCroskey, J. C. (2000). *Communication apprehension, avoidance, and effectiveness* (5th ed.). Scottsdale, AZ: Gorsuch Scarisbrick.

3. Phillips, G. M. (1977). Rhetoritherapy versus the medical model: Dealing with reticence. *Communication Education, 26,* 37.

4. Motley, M. (1997). COM therapy. In J. A. Daly, J. C. McCroskey, J. Ayres, T. Hopf, & D. M. Ayres (Eds.), *Avoiding communication: Shyness, reticence, and communication apprehension* (2nd ed., p. 382). Cresskill, NJ: Hampton Press.

5. Phillips, Rhetoritherapy, 37.

6. Richmond & McCroskey, *Communication.*

7. Behnke, R. R., & Carlile, L. W. (1971). Heart rate as an index of speech anxiety. *Speech Monographs, 38,* 66.

8. Beatty, M. J., & Behnke, R. R. (1991). Effects of public speaking trait anxiety and intensity of speaking task on heart rate during performance. *Human Communication Research, 18,* 147–176.

9. Taken from the PRCA-24, subscale Public Speaking. See Rich, V. P., & McCroskey, J. C. (1997). *Communication apprehension, avoidance, and effectiveness.* Scottsdale, AZ: Gorsuch Scarisbrick.

10. McCroskey, J. C. (2012). 5.0 Oral communication apprehension: A reconceptualization. *Communication Yearbook, 6*(6), 136.

11. Beatty, M. J., McCroskey, J. C., & Heisner, A. D. (1998, September). Communication apprehension as temperamental expression: A communibiological paradigm. *Communication Monographs, 65,* 200.

12. Richmond & McCroskey, *Communication.*

13. Bandura, A. (1973). *Social learning theory.* Englewood Cliffs, NJ: Prentice Hall.

14. Daly, J. A., Caughlin, J. P., & Stafford, L. (1997). Correlates and consequences of social-communicative anxiety. In J. A. Daly, J. C. McCroskey, J. Ayres, T. Hopf, & D. M. Ayres (Eds.), *Avoiding communication: Shyness, reticence, and communication apprehension* (2nd ed., p. 27). Cresskill, NJ: Hampton Press.

15. Dunn, J. (2008, April). Tina Fey: Funny girl. *Reader's Digest Magazine* [online]. Retrieved from http://www.rd.com/advice/tina-fey-interview/

16. Burke, B., Cameron, K., Cooper, J., Johnson, S., & Miller, K. (2014). The correlation between computer mediated communication and communication apprehension. *Meta-communicate, 3*(2). Retrieved from http://journals.chapman.edu/ojs/index

17. Motley, COM therapy, 382.

18. Ibid., 380.

19. Dwyer, K. K. (2012). *iConquer speech anxiety: A workbook to help you overcome your nervousness about public speaking.* Omaha, NE: KLD Publications.

20. Scott, P. (1997, January–February). Mind of a champion. *Natural Health, 27*, 99.

21. Bourne, E. J. (1990). *The anxiety and phobia workbook.* Oakland, CA: New Harbinger Publications.

22. Davis, M., Echelon, E., & McKay, M. (1988). *The relaxation and stress workbook.* Oakland, CA: New Harbinger Publications.

23. Friedrich, G., & Goss, B. (1984). Systematic desensitization. In J. A. Daly & J. C. McCroskey (Eds.), *Avoiding communication.* Beverly Hills, CA: Sage.

24. Richmond & McCroskey, *Communication.*

25. Ibid.

26. Griffin, K. (1995, July). Beating performance anxiety. *Working Woman*, 62–65, 76.

27. Dwyer, K. K. (2000, January). The multidimensional model: Teaching students to self-manage high communication apprehension by self-selecting treatments. *Communication Education, 49*, 79.

28. Thomas, B. (2000, February 28). In normal conversation. Associated Press.

29. Bailey, E. (2008, August 7). Celebrities with anxiety: Harrison Ford: Fear of public speaking. *Health Central*. Retrieved from http://www.healthcentral.com/anxiety/c/22705/36519/celebrities-public

30. IMDb. Biography for Harrison Ford. Retrieved from http://www.imdb.com/name/nm0000148/bio

31. Richmond & McCroskey, *Communication.*

32. Study shows how sleep improves memory. (2005, June 29). *Science Daily.* Retrieved from http://www.sciencedaily.com/releases/2005/06/050629070337.htm

33. *Rhetorica ad herennium.* (1954) (H. Caplan, Trans.). Cambridge, MA: Harvard University Press.

34. Bitzer, L. (1968). The rhetorical situation. *Philosophy and Rhetoric, 1*(1), 1–14.

35. Cooper, L. (trans.) (1932/1960). *The rhetoric of Aristotle.* Englewood Cliffs, NJ: Prentice-Hall.

36. Efrati, A., & Lublin, J. S. (2012, May 13). Thompson resigns as CEO of Yahoo. *The Wall Street Journal.* Retrieved from http://www.wsj.com/articles/SB10001424052702304192704577402224129006022

37. Ricker, S. (n.d.). "I lied about my job because . . ." *CareerBuilder.com.* Retrieved from http://advice.careerbuilder.com/posts/i-lied-about-my-job-because

Chapter 3 Listening

1. Donaghue, P. J., & Seigal, M. E. (2005). *Are you really listening? Keys to successful communication.* Notre Dame, IN: Sorin Books.

2. Imhof, M. (2010). The cognitive psychology of listening. In A. S. Wolvin (Ed.), *Listening and human communication in the 21st century* (pp. 97–126). Boston: Blackwell.

3. Bodie, G. D., Cyr, K. S., Pence, M., Rold, M. I., & Honeycutt, J. (2012). Listening competence in initial interactions I: Distinguishing between what listening is and what listeners do. *International Journal of Listening, 26*(1), 1–28.

4. Janusik, L. A., & Wolving, A. D. (2009). 24 hours in a day: A listening update to the time studies. *International Journal of Listening, 23*, 104–120. doi:10.1080/10904010903014442

5. International Listening Association. (2003). *Listening factoid.* Retrieved from http://www.listen.org/pages/factoids/html

6. Brownell, J. (2013). *Listening: Attitudes, principles, and skills* (5th ed.). New York: Routledge.

7. DeWine, S., & Daniels, T. (1993). Beyond the snapshot: Setting a research agenda in organizational communication. In S. A. Deetz (Ed.), *Communication yearbook 16* (pp. 252–230). Thousand Oaks, CA: Sage.

8. Salopek, J. J. (1999). Is anyone listening? *Training and Development, 53*(9), 58–60.

9. Brownell, *Listening.*

10. Watson, K. W., Barker, L. L., & Weaver, J. B. III. (1995). The listening styles profile (LSP-16): Development and validation of an instrument to assess four listening styles. *International Journal of Listening, 9*, 1–13.

11. Gearhart, C. C., Denham, J. P., & Bodie, G. D. (2014). Listening as a goal-directed activity. *Western Journal of Communication, 78*(5), 668–684. doi:10.1080/10570314.2014.910888

12. O'Shaughnessy, B. (2003). Active attending or a theory of mental action. *Consciousness and the World, 29*, 379–407.

13. Wolvin, A., & Coakley, C. G. (1996). *Listening* (5th ed.). New York: McGraw-Hill.

14. Dukette, D., & Cornish, D. (2009). *The essential 20: Twenty components of an excellent health care team* (pp. 72–73). Pittsburgh, PA: RoseDog Books; Turning into digital goldfish. (2002, February 22). *BBC News.* Retrieved from http://news.bbc.co.uk/2/hi/science/nature/1834682.stm

15. Sharpening your listening skills. (2002, October). *Teller Vision* 0895–1039, 7.

16. Bonaguro, A. (2009, September 13). Kanye West steals Taylor Swift's thunder at MTV Video Music Awards. Retrieved from http://blog.cmt.com/2009-09-13/kanye-west-steals-taylor-swifts-thunder-at-mtv-video-music-awards/

17. Melas, C. (2012, August 30). Kanye West will not apologize to Taylor Swift at VMAs. *Hollywood Life.* Retrieved from http://hollywoodlife.com/2012/08/30/kanye-west-taylor-swift-vmas-video/

18. Bueno, A. (2015, February 9). Beck on Kanye's GRAMMY speech interruption: "I still love him and think he's a genius." *ETOnline.* Retrieved from http://www.etonline.com/awards/grammys/beck_on_conye_grammy_speech_interruption/

19. Lee, A., & Couch, A. (2015, February 8). Grammys: Kanye West rails against Beck, explains stage rush, bashes show. *The Hollywood Reporter.* Retrieved from http://www.hollywoodreporter.com/news/grammys-2015-kanye-west-rails-771636

20. Estes, W. K. (1989). Learning theory. In A. Lesgold & R. Glaser (Eds.). *Foundations for a psychology of education* (pp. 1–49). Hillsdale, NJ: Lawrence Erlbaum Associates.

21. Wolvin & Coakley, *Listening;* Dunkel, P., & Pialorsi, F. (2005). *Advanced listening comprehension: Developing aural and notetaking skills.* Boston: Thomson Heinle.

22. Bill Clinton has a superpower, and mastering it can make you successful beyond belief. (2013, August 8). *Huffington Post,* Retrieved from http://www.huffingtonpost.com/2013/08/08/bill-clinton_n_3718956.html

23. Killingsworth, M. A., & Gilbert, D. T. (2010, November 12). A wandering mind is an unhappy mind. *Science, 330*(6006), 932.

24. Carnegie, D. (1936). *How to win friends and influence people.* New York: Simon and Schuster. Dale Carnegie Training. [website] Retrieved from www.dalecarnegie.com

Chapter 4 Determining an Appropriate Speech Goal

1. Berger, C. R. (1988). Uncertainty reduction and information exchange in developing relationships. In S. Duck, D. Hay, S. Hobfoll, W. Ickes, & B. Montgomery (Eds.), *Handbook of interpersonal relationships: Theory, research, and interventions* (pp. 239–255). New York: Wiley.

2. Trenholm, R. (2015, October 18). "Steve Jobs" writer Aaron Sorkin says "my conscience is clear" on film's accuracy. C|net. Retrieved from http://www.cnet.com/news/steve-jobs-writer-aaron-sorkin-says-my-conscience-is-clear-on-films-accuracy/

3. Aaron Sorkin: The Writer Behind "The Newsroom," interview by Terry Gross, *Fresh Air*, NPR, July 16, 2012, http://www.npr.org/2012/07/16/156841165/aaron-sorkin-the-writer-behind-the-newsroom

4. Callison, D. (2001). Concept mapping. *School Library Media Activities Monthly, 17*(10), 30–32.

Chapter 5 Adapting to Audiences

1. Blumer, H. (1969). *Symbolic interactionism.* Englewood Cliffs, NJ: Prentice-Hall.

2. Thamel, P. (2012, October 1). The full Manti. *Sports Illustrated.* Retrieved from http://www.si.com/vault/2012/10/01/106238739/the-full-manti

3. Barbe, W., & Swassing, R. H. (1979). *The Swassing-Barbe Modality Index.* Columbus, OH: Waner-Bloser; Canfield, A. A. (1980). *Learning styles inventory manual.* Ann Arbor, MI: Humanics, Inc.; Dunn, R., Dunn, K., & Price, G. E. (1975). *Learning styles inventory.* Lawrence, KS: Price Systems; Gardner, H. (1983). *Frames of mind: The theory of multiple intelligences.* New York: Basic Books; Kolb, D. A. (1984). *Experiential learning: Experience as the source of learning and development.* Upper Saddle River, NJ: Prentice Hall.

4. Kolb, D. A. (1984). *Experiential learning: Experience as the source of learning and development.* Upper Saddle River, NJ: Prentice-Hall.

5. Dewey, J. (1938/1997) *Experience and education.* New York: Macmillan.

6. Kolb, *Experiential learning.*

7. Celebrity lessons in selling. (2010). *Inc.* Retrieved from http://www.inc.com/ss/celebrity-lessons-selling#0

8. Tannen, D. (1998, June 8). Oprah Winfrey: The TV host. *Time.* Retrieved from http://www.time.com/time/magazine/article/0,9171,988512-2,00.html

Chapter 6 Topic Development

1. Dave, P. (2015, August 19). Why NASA scientists are excited about Matt Damon film "The Martian." *Los Angeles Times.* Retrieved from http://www.latimes.com/science/la-fi-martian-movie-science-20150820-story.html

2. Munger, D., & Campbell, S. (2013). *What every student should know about researching online* (2nd ed.). New York: Pearson.

3. Tengler, C., & Jablin, F. M. (1983). Effects of question type, orientation, and sequencing in the employment screening interview. *Communication Monographs, 50,* 261.

4. Biagi, S. *Interviews that work: A practical guide for journalists* (2nd ed., p. 94). Belmont, CA: Wadsworth.

5. Frances, P. (1994). Lies, damned lies. *American Demographics, 16,* 2.

6. Ibid.

7. International Data Corporation. *Big Data and Analytics.* Retrieved from: http://www.idc.com/prodserv/4Pillars/bigdata

8. Shalala, D. (1994, May 15). Domestic terrorism: An unacknowledged epidemic. *Vital Speeches,* 451.

9. Durst, G. M. (1989, March 1). The manager as a developer. *Vital Speeches,* 309–310.

10. Becherer, H. (2000, September 15). Enduring values for a secular age: Faith, hope and love. *Vital Speeches,* 732.

11. Opheim, C. (2000, November 1). Making democracy work: Your responsibility to society. *Vital Speeches,* 60.

12. Kreps, D. (2009, September 16). Satriani's "Viva La Vida" copyright suit against Coldplay dismissed. *Rolling Stone.* Retrieved from http://www.rollingstone.com/rockdaily/inde.php/2009/09/16satrianis-viva-la-vida-copyright-suit-against-coldplay-dismissed/

Chapter 7 Organizing and Outlining the Speech Body

1. Fisher, W. (1987). *Human communication as narration: Toward a philosophy of reason, value, and action.* Columbia, SC: University of South Carolina Press.

2. Barribeau, T. (2012, March 26). *Fortune* names Steve Jobs "greatest entrepreneur of our time." *Fortune.* Retrieved from http://fortune.com/2012/03/26/fortune-names-steve-jobs-the-greatest-entrepreneur/

3. Barber, C. (2010, September 29). Steve Jobs: Chunk structure helps engage Stanford audience. *The Vivid Method for Public Speaking.* Retrieved from http://vividmethod.com/a-good-structure-helps-steve-jobs/

4. Kids' book gets pulled. (2006, January 31). *Associated Press.* Retrieved from http://www.canada.com/topics/entertainment/story.html?id=45761b54-245c-4c76-9618-212c645f9800&k=23104

5. Deahl, R. (2006, January 31). Blue Apple to cancel book. *Publishers Weekly.* Retrieved from http://www.publishersweekly.com/article/CA6303375.html

Chapter 8 The Introduction and Conclusion

1. Trenholm, S. (1989). *Persuasion and social influence.* Englewood Cliffs, NJ: Prentice-Hall; Crano, W. D. (1977). Primacy versus recency in retention of information and opinion change. *The Journal of Social Psychology, 101,* 87–96.

2. Phillips, B. (2015). *101 ways to open a speech: How to hook your audience from the start with an engaging and effective beginning.* Washington, DC: SpeakGood Press.

3. Gupta, Y. (2010, February). Beyond wisdom: Business dimensions of an aging America. *Vital Speeches,* 69–75.

4. Humes, J. C. (1988). *Standing ovation: How to be an effective speaker and communicator.* New York: Harper & Row.

5. Osteen, J. (2012). Best jokes of Joel Osteen. *Better Days TV.* Retrieved from http://www.betterdaystv.net/play.php?vid=247

6. Mason, S. (2007, April). Equality will someday come. *Vital Speeches,* 159–163.

7. Bitzer, L. F. (1995). The Rhetorical Situation. In W. A. Covino & D. A. Jolliffe (Eds.), *Rhetoric: Concepts, definitions, boundaries.* Boston: Allyn and Bacon.

8. Sepinwall, A. (2016, February 29). Review: Chris Rock dives into #OscarsSoWhite Controversy as Academy Awards host. *HitFix.* Retrieved from http://www.hitfix.com/whats-alan-watching/review-chris-rock-dives-into-oscarssowhite-controversy-as-academy-awards-host

9. Aristotle. (W. Rhys Roberts, Trans.). (1954). *Rhetoric.* New York: Modern Library.

10. Mariano, C. (2010, January). Unity, quality, responsibility: The real meaning of the words. *Vital Speeches,* 20–22.

11. Jobs, S. (2005, 15 June). You've got to find what you love. *Stanford University News.* Retrieved from http://news.stanford.edu/news/2005/june15/jobs-061505.html

12. Cossolotto, M. (2009, December). An urgent call to action for study abroad alumni to help reduce our global awareness deficit. *Vital Speeches,* 564–568.

13. Avery, R. (2013, February 6). 9 lessons learned from Lady Gaga. Blog. *AveryToday* 2013. Retrieved from http://averytoday.com/9-public-speaking-lessons-learned-from-lady-gaga/

14. Used with permission of Katie Anthony.

Chapter 9 Presentational Aids

1. St. Leger, J. (2010, November 5). Surprise! You child has autism. Now what? Retrieved from https://www.youtube.com/watch?v=HtdvCqn5RuQ

2. Garcia-Retamero, R., & Cokely, E. T. (2013). Communicating health risk with visual aids. *Current Directions in Psychological Science, 22*(5), 392–399. doi: 10.1177/0963721413491570

3. Rogers, L. (2013). *Visual supports for visual thinkers: Practical ideas for students with autism spectrum disorders and other special education needs.* London: Jessica Kingsley Publishers.

4. Krauss, J. (2012). Infographics: More than words can say. *Learning and Leading with Technology, 39*(5), 10–14.

5. Hanke, J. (1998). The psychology of presentation visuals. *Presentations, 12*(5), 42–47.

6. Campbell, S. (2015). Presentation anxiety analysis: Comparing face-to-face presentations and webinars. *Journal of Case Studies in Education, 7,* 1–13.

7. International Charter. (1997–2012). *EAS-405: Ethical advertising standard.* Retrieved from http://www.icharter.org/standards/eas405/index.html

8. Peterson, B. (2015). *Learning to see creatively: Design, color, and composition in photography* (3rd ed.). New York: Amphoto Books.

9. Booher, D. D. (2003). *Speak with confidence: Powerful presentations that inform, inspire, and persuade (electronic resources).* New York: McGraw-Hill.

10. Ristor, A. (2012, October 31). What is an Ignite presentation and why should you try it? Blog. *Six Minutes: Speaking and Presentation Skills.* Retrieved from http://sixminutes.dlugan.com/ignite-presentations/; VanGrove, J. (2010, March 1). 10 reasons you should attend or watch a Global Ignite Week event. Mashable, Inc. Retrieved from http://mashable.com/2010/03/01/global-ignite-week/

11. Connecting Veterans to Career Opportunities. (2013). Retrieved from http://boots-to-suits.com/

12. Forrest, B. (2009). Speaker confessions. True tales from a veteran public speaker. O'Reilly Media, Inc. Retrieved from http://www.speakerconfessions.com/press/

Chapter 10 Language and Oral Style

1. The art of language, Obama style?, by Linton Weeks, *NPR Politics,* NPR, February 11, 2009, http://www.npr.org/templates/story/story.php?storyId=100525275

2. Hart, R., & Jamieson, K. H. (2012). *Campaign mapping project.* The Annette Strauss Institute for Civic Life at the University of Austin Texas. [Funding support from the Ford Foundation and Carnegie Foundation of New York]. Retrieved from http://communication.utexas.edu/strauss/campaign-mapping-project

3. Leith, S. (2013, January 21). Barack Obama inauguration speech: A greatest hits of rhetorical tricks. *The Guardian.* Retrieved from http://www.guardian.co.uk/world/2013/jan/21/barack-obama-speech-greatest-hits-rhetoric

4. Weeks (2009).

5. Leith (2013).

6. Mazer, J. P. (2015). Teacher immediacy in the classroom. *The International Encyclopedia of Interpersonal Communication,* pp. 1–5.

7. Stewart, L. P., Cooper, P. J., Stewart, A. D., & Friedley, S. A. (2003). *Communication and gender* (4th ed., p. 63). Boston: Allyn & Bacon.

8. Treinen, K., & Warren, J. (2001). Antiracist pedagogy in the basic course: Teaching cultural communication as if whiteness matters. *Basic Communication Course Annual, 13,* 46–75.

9. DuFrene, D. D., & Lehman, C. M. (2002, March). Persuasive appeal for clean language. *Business Quarterly, 65,* 48.

10. Ward, F. (2014, July 15). Profanity. Curse words. Speeches. Motivational speakers. Blog. *Francine D. Ward.* Retrieved from https://francineward.com/profanity/

11. Gudykunst, W. B., & Matsumoto, Y. (1996). Cross-cultural variability of communication in personal relationships. In W. B. Gudykunst, S. Ting-Toomey, & T. Nishida (Eds.), *Communication in personal relationships across cultures* (p. 21). Thousand Oaks, CA: Sage.

12. Levine, D. (1985). *The flight from ambiguity* (p. 28). Chicago: University of Chicago Press.

13. Duck, S. W. (1994). *Meaningful relationships.* Thousand Oaks, CA: Sage; See also Shotter, J. (1993). *Conversational realities: The construction of life through language.* Newbury Park, CA: Sage.

14. Richards, I. A., & Ogden, C. K. (1923). *The meaning of meaning: A study of the influence of language upon thought and the science of symbolism.* Orlando, FL: Harcourt.

15. Ibid.

16. O'Grady, W., Archibald, J., Aronoff, M., & Rees-Miller, J. (2001). *Contemporary linguistics* (4th ed.). Boston: Bedford/St. Martin's.

17. Fought, C. (2003). *Chicano English in context* (pp. 64–78). New York: Pallgrave MacMillan.

18. Glenn, C., & Gray, L. (2013). *Hodges Harbrace handbook* (18th ed.) Boston: Wadsworth, Cengage Learning.

19. Princeton Review (2012). *Word smart: How to build a more educated vocabulary* (5th ed.). Princeton, NJ: Princeton Review, Inc.

20. Rader, W. (2007). *The online slang dictionary.* Retrieved from http://www.ocf.berkeley.edu/~wrader/slang/b.html

21. Hensley, C. W. (1995, September 1). Speak with style and watch the impact. *Vital Speeches of the Day,* p. 703.

22. Phillips, B. (2015). *101 ways to open a speech: How to hook your audience from the start with an engaging and effective beginning.* Washington, DC: SpeakGood Press.

23. Giovanni, N. (2007, April 17). *We are Virginia Tech.* [speech]. Retrieved from http://www.americanrhetoric.com/speeches/nikkigiovannivatechmemorial.htm

Chapter 11 Delivery

1. Gallo, C. (2014). *Talk like TED: The 9 public-speaking secrets of the world's top minds.* New York: St. Martin's Press.

2. Watzlawick, P., Bavelas, J. B., & Jackson, D. D. (1967). *Pragmatics of human communication.* New York: Norton.

3. Bates, B. (1992). *Communication and the sexes.* Prospect Heights, IL: Waveland Press; Cherulnik, P. D. (1989). *Physical attractiveness and judged suitability for leadership,* Report No. CG 021 893. Paper presented at the Annual Meeting of the Midwestern Psychological Association, Chicago (ERIC Document Services No. ED 310 317); Lawrence, S. G., & Watson, M. (1991). Getting others to help: The effectiveness of professional uniforms in charitable fund raising. *Journal of Applied Communication Research, 19,* 170–185; Malloy, J. T. (1975). *Dress for success.* New York: Warner; and Temple, L. E., & Loewen, K. R. (1993). Perceptions of power: First impressions of a woman wearing a jacket. *Perceptual and Motor Skills, 76,* 339–348.

4. Phillips P. A., & Smith, L. R. (1992). *The effects of teacher dress on student perceptions,* Report No. SP 033 944 (ERIC Document Services No. ED 347 151).

5. Morris, T. L., Gorham, J., Cohen, S. H., & Huffman, D. (1996). Fashion in the classroom: Effects of attire on student perceptions of instructors in college classes. *Communication Education, 45,* 135–148.

6. Burgoon, J. K., Coker, D. A., & Coker, R. A. (1986). Communicative effects of gaze behavior: A test of two contrasting explanations. *Human Communication Research, 12,* 495–524.

7. Chiang, L. H. (1993). *Beyond the language: Native Americans' nonverbal communication*. Paper presented at the Annual Meeting of the Midwest Association of Teachers of Educational Psychology, Anderson, IN (ERIC Document Services No. ED 368540).

8. Boardman, M. (2013, February 26). Anne Hathaway acceptance speech: Best supporting actress winner practiced a lot. *Huffington Post*. Retrieved from http://www.huffingtonpost.com/2013/02/26/anne-hathaway-acceptance-speech-best-supporting-actress_n_2767270.html

9. Exclusive: Anne Hathaway practiced her Oscar speech a lot to be more likable. (2013, February 26). *Us Weekly*. Retrieved from http://www.usmagazine.com/celebrity-news/news/anne-hathaway-practiced-her-oscar-speech-a-lot-to-be-more-likable-2013262

10. Menzel, K. E., & Carrell, L. J. (1994). The relationship between preparation and performance in public speaking. *Communication Education, 43*, 23.

11. Palin's "cheat sheet" on hand. *CNN.com*. Retrieved from http://www.cnn.com/video/#/video/politics/2010/02/08/lemon.palin.cheat.sheet.cnn?iref=allsearch

12. Mankowski, D., & Jose, R. (2012). MBC flashback: The 70th anniversary of FDR's fireside chats. *The Museum of Broadcast Communications*. Retrieved from http://www.museum.tv/exhibitionssection.php?page=79

13. Obama, B. (n.d.). Your weekly address. *The White House*. Retrieved from http://www.whitehouse.gov/briefing-room/weekly-address/

14. Thomas, W. G. (2004). Television news and the civil rights struggle: The views in Virginia and Mississippi. *Southern Spaces*. Retrieved from http://southernspaces.org/2004/television-news-and-civil-rights-struggle-views-virginia-and-mississippi

15. Used with permission of Alyssa Grace Millner.

Chapter 12 Informative Speaking

1. Otzi, the ice man. (n.d.). *Dig: The archaeology magazine for kids*. Retrieved from http://www.digonsite.com/drdig/mummy/22.html

2. The Vegan Society. (2016, May 8). *Definition of veganism*. Retrieved from http://www.vegansociety.com/go-vegan/definition-veganism

3. Vegan Society website. Retrieved from http://www.vegansociety.com

4. Based on "Narrative" by Baerwald, D., & Northshore School District. Retrieved from http://ccweb.norshore.wednet.edu/writingcorner/narrative.html

5. Bonanno, G. (2012, December 11). Public speaking tips from chef Bobby Flay. *SelfGrowth.com*. Retrieved from http://www.selfgrowth.com/print/6214941

6. Billy Mays, the death of the infomercial king (2009, July 1). *Pulp Magazine*. Retrieved from http://pulpmagazine.co.uk/2009/07/01/billy-mays-the-death-of-the-infomercial-king/index.html

7. Crain, R. (2009, May 4). Deceitful financial infomercial tars entire advertising industry. *Advertising Age, 80*(16), 17.

8. Marcus, V. (2014, December 1). Controversial DOH infomercial calls teens with unwanted pregnancies "idiots." *Kicker Daily News*. Retrieved from http://kickerdaily.com/posts/2014/12/controversial-doh-infomercial-calls-teens-with-unwanted-pregnancies-idiots/

9. Nolan, H. (2013, November 13). Infomercial scam diet pitchman jailed. *Gawker*. Retrieved from http://gawker.com/infomercial-scam-diet-pitchman-jailed-1463606625

10. Dacquino, V. T. (2000). *Sybil Ludington: The call to arms*. Fleischmanns, NY: Purple Mountain Press.

11. Used with permission of Anna Rankin.

Chapter 13 Persuasive Messages

1. Pallotta, F. (2015, February 2). Super Bowl XLIX posts the largest audience in TV history. *CNN Money*. Retrieved from http://money.cnn.com/2015/02/02/media/super-bowl-ratings/index.html

2. Phillips Erb, K. (2015, February 1). Salaries, ads, and security: What's the real cost of Super Bowl XLIX? *Forbes*. Retrieved from http://www.forbes.com/sites/kellyphillipserb/2015/02/01/salaries-ads-security-whats-the-real-cost-of-super-bowl-xlix/#448bdb4c1b29

3. Greenwood, A. (2015, January 25). GoDaddy pulls 2015 Super Bowl ad after slew of negative feedback from animal advocates. *Huffington Post*. Retrieved from http://www.huffingtonpost.com/2015/01/28/godaddy-2015-super-bowl-ad_n_6557548.html

4. Solmsen, F. (Ed.). (1954). *The rhetoric and the poetics of Aristotle* (p. 24). New York: The Modern Library.

5. Perloff, R. M. (1993). *The dynamics of persuasion*. Hillsdale, NJ: Lawrence Erlbaum.

6. Kennedy, G. A. (1980). *Classical rhetoric and its Christian and secular tradition from ancient to modern times*. Chapel Hill: The University of North Carolina Press.

7. Petty, R. E., & Cacioppo, J. T. (1986). *Communication and persuasion: Central and peripheral routes to attitude change*. New York: Springer-Verlag.

8. Toulmin, S. (1958). *The uses of argument*. Cambridge, England: Cambridge University Press.

9. Obama, B. (2015, December 5). WEEKLY ADDRESS: We will not be terrorized. Washington, DC: Office of the Press Secretary, The White House. Retrieved from https://www.whitehouse.gov/the-press-office/2015/12/05/weekly-address-we-will-not-be-terrorized

10. Stewart, R. (1994). Perceptions of a speaker's initial credibility as a function of religious involvement and religious disclosiveness. *Communication Research Reports, 11*, 169–176.

11. Morris, T. L., Gorham, J., Cohen, S. H., & Huffman, D. (1996). Fashion in the classroom: Effects of attire on student perceptions of instructors in college classes. *Communication Education, 45*, 135–148; Treinen, K. (1998). *The effects of gender and physical attractiveness on peer critiques of a persuasive speech*. Unpublished master's thesis, North Dakota State University, Fargo, ND.

12. Perloff, *Dynamics of persuasion*.

13. Petri, H. L., & Govern, J. M. (2012). *Motivation: Theory, research, and application* (6th ed.). Belmont, CA: Wadsworth.

14. Nabi, R. L. (2002). Discrete emotions and persuasion. In J. P. Dillard & M. Pfau (Eds.), *The persuasion handbook: Developments in theory and practice* (pp. 291–299). Thousand Oaks, CA: Sage.

15. Megan's law. Retrieved from http://www.meganslaw.com/

16. Slater, D. (1998). Sharing life. In *Winning orations* (pp. 63–66). Mankato, MN: Interstate Oratorical Association.

17. Labor, R. (1998). Shaken baby syndrome. The silent epidemic. In *Winning orations* (pp. 70–72). Mankato, MN: Interstate Oratorical Association.

18. Ibid.

19. National Labor Committee. (1995). *Zoned for slavery: The child behind the label*. Pittsburgh, PA: Institute for Global Labour and Human Rights.

20. Theron tackles public speaking fears in new film. (2005, October 26). *Contact Music.com*. Retrieved from http://www.contactmusic.com/news-article/theron-tackles-public-speaking-fears-in-new-film

21. Hall, K. (2009, September 17). Charlize Theron: I won't get married until my gay friends can. *Huffington Post*. Retrieved from http://www.huffingtonpost.com/2009/09/17/charlize-theron-i-wont-ge_n_290073.html; Messengers of Peace (n.d.). United Nations. Retrieved from http://outreach.un.org/mop/

Chapter 14 Persuasive Speaking

1. Van Eemeren, F. H., Garrsen, B., Karabbe, F. C. W., Henkemans, A. F. S., Verheij, B., & Wagemans, J. H. M. (2014). *Handbook of argumentation theory*. New York: Springer.

2. Cheadle, D., & Prendergast, J. (2007). *Not on our watch: The mission to end genocide in Darfur and beyond*. New York: Hyperion.

3. Pitt, B. (n.d.). Brad Pitt quotes with pictures. *QuotesPapa*. Retrieved from http://www.quotespapa.com/authors/brad-pitt-quotes.html

4. Ziegelmueller, G. W., Kay, J., & Dause, C. A. (1990). *Argumentation: Inquiry and advocacy* (2nd ed., p. 186). Englewood Cliffs, NJ: Prentice Hall.

5. Benbow, J. (2013, April 21). David Ortiz's speech caps emotional ceremony. *Boston Globe*. Retrieved from http://www.bostonglobe.com/sports/2013/04/20/david-ortiz-impassioned-speech-caps-emotional-red-sox-pregame-ceremony/Ushx2LJ6b8ozPsz1u71cPM/story.html

6. Perry, D. (2013, April 20). The FCC has no problem with David Ortiz's speech. *CBSSports.com*. Retrieved from http://www.cbssports.com/mlb/blog/eye-on-baseball/22111863/the-fcc-has-no-problem-with-david-ortizs-speech

7. Ibid.

8. Schwartz, N. (2013, April 21). FCC overlooks Ortiz's passionate, profane speech to Red Sox fans. *USA Today*. Retrieved from http://www.usatoday.com/story/gameon/2013/04/20/david-ortiz-boston-red-sox-speech-fcc/2100051/

9. Used with permission of Adam Parrish.

Chapter 15 Ceremonial Speaking

1. Manning, K. (2012, June 4). 10 things we can learn about public speaking from Kristen Stewart (because she is the worst). *The Grindstone*. Retrieved from http://www.thegrindstone.com/2012/06/04/career-management/dos-and-dontsstrategy/10-things-we-can-learn-about-public-speaking-from-kristen-stewart-597/

Chapter 16 Group Communication and Presentations

1. O'Hair, D., O'Rourke, J., & O'Hair, M. (2001). *Business communication: A framework for success*. Cincinnati, OH: South-Western; Snyder, B. (2004). Differing views cultivate better decisions. *Stanford Business*. Retrieved from http://www.gsb.stanford.edu/NEWS/bmag/sbsm0405/feature_workteams_gruenfeld.shtml; *Harvard Business Review on teams that succeed*. (2004). Boston: Harvard Business School Press.

2. Tullar, W., & Kaiser, P. (2000). The effect of process training on process and outcomes in virtual groups. *Journal of Business Communication, 37*, 408–427.

3. Lesikar, R., Pettit Jr., J., & Flately, M. (1999). *Basic business communication* (8th ed.). New York: McGraw-Hill.

4. Northouse, G. (2007). *Leadership theory and practice* (4th ed.). Thousand Oaks, CA: Sage.

5. Kippenberger, T. (2002). *Leadership styles*. New York: John Wiley and Sons.

6. Fairhurst, G. T. (2001). Dualism in leadership. In F. M. Jablin & L. M. Putnam (Eds.), *The new handbook of organizational communication* (pp. 379–439). Thousand Oaks, CA: Sage; Frey, L., & Sunwulf. (2005). The communication perspective on group life. In S. A. Wheelen (Ed.), *The handbook of group research and practice* (pp. 159–186). Thousand Oaks, CA: Sage.

7. Rahim, M. A. (2001). *Managing conflict in organizations* (3rd ed.). Westport, CT: Greenwood Press.

8. Bradley, B. H., Postlethwaite, B. E., Klotz, A. C., Hamdani, M. R., & Brown, K. G. (2012). Reaping the benefits of task conflict in teams: The critical role of team psychological safety climate. *Journal of Applied Psychology, 97*(1), 151–158.

9. Janis, I. L. (1982). *Groupthink: Psychological studies of policy decision and fiascos* (2nd ed.). Boston: Houghton Mifflin.

10. Sell, J., Lovaglia, M. J., Mannix, E. A., Samuelson, C. D., & Wilson, R. K. (2004). Investigating conflict, power, and status within and among groups. *Small Group Research, 35*, 44–72.

11. Ting-Toomey, S., & Chung, L. C. (2012). *Understanding intercultural communication* (2nd ed.). New York: Oxford University Press.

12. Bordia, P., DiFonzo, N., & Change, A. (1999). Rumor as group problem-solving: Development patterns in informal computer-mediated groups. *Small Group Research, 30*, 8–28.

13. Jiang, L., Bazarova, N. N., & Hancock, J. T. (2011). The disclosure-intimacy link in computer-mediated communication: An attributional extension of the hyperpersonal model. *Human Communication Research, 37*, 58–77; Wang, Z., Walther, J. B., & Hancock, J. T. (2009). Social identification and interpersonal communication in computer mediated communication: What you do versus who you are in virtual groups. *Human Communication Research, 35*, 59–85.

14. Godamer, H. (1989). (J. Weinsheimer & D. G. Marshall, Trans.). *Truth and method* (2nd ed.). New York: Crossroad.

15. Braithwaite, D. O., & Eckstein, N. (2003). Reconceptualizing supportive interactions: How persons with disabilities communicatively manage assistance. *Journal of Applied Communication Research, 31*, 1–26.

16. Conrad, C., & Poole, M. S. (1998). *Strategic organizational communication: Into the twenty-first century* (4th ed.). Fort Worth, TX: Harcourt Brace College Publishers.

17. *The View*. Retrieved from http://www.tv.com/the-view/show/1676/summary.html

18. Dewey, J. (1933). *How we think*. Boston: Heath.

19. Duch, B. J., Groh, S. E., & Allen, D. E. (Eds.). (2001). *The power of problem-based learning*. Sterling, VA: Stylus; Edens, K. M. (2000). Preparing problem solvers for the 21st century through problem-based learning. *College Teaching, 48*(2), 55–60; Levin, B. B. (Ed.). (2001). *Energizing teacher education and professional development with problem-based learning*. Alexandria, VA: Association for Supervision and Curriculum Development.

20. Young, K. S., Wood, J. T., Phillips, G. M., & Pedersen, D. J. (2007). *Group discussion: A practical guide to participation and leadership* (4th ed.). Long Grove, IL: Waveland Press.

21. Andres, H. P. (2002). A comparison of face-to-face and virtual software development teams. *Team Performance Managements: An International Journal, 8*–1/2, 39–48.

22. Olson, J., & Teasley, S. (1996). Groupware in the wild: Lessons learned from a year of virtual collocation. In *CSCW '96 proceedings of the 1996 ACM Conference on Computer Supported Cooperative Work*. New York: Association for Computing Machinery, pp. 419–427.

23. Warkentin, M. E., Sayeed, L., & Hightower, R. (1997). Virtual teams versus face-to-face teams: An exploratory study of a Web-based conference system. *Decision Sciences, 28*(4), 957–996.

24. Huang, W. W., Wei, K. K., Watson, R. T., & Tan, B. C. Y. (2003). Supporting virtual team-building with a GSS: An empirical investigation. *Decision Support Systems, 34*, 359–367.

25. Shoemaker-Galloway, J. (2007, August 6). Top 10 netiquette guidelines. *Suite 101*, Retrieved from http://suite101.com/article/netiquette-guidelines-a26615

Glossary

abstract a short paragraph summarizing the research findings

accent inflection, tone, and speech habits typical of native speakers of a language

accommodating accepting others' ideas while neglecting your own, even when you disagree with the views of the others

accurate language words that convey the meaning you intend

accurate sources attempt to present unbiased information and often include a balanced discussion of controversial topics

action an attention-getting act designed to arouse interest in the topic

action step the conclusion

action-oriented listeners focus on the ultimate point the speaker is trying to make

active listening the deliberate and conscious process of attending to, understanding, remembering, evaluating, and responding to messages

actual objects an inanimate or animate sample of the idea being communicated

ad hominem fallacy occurs when one attacks or praises the person making an argument rather than the argument itself

alliteration repetition of consonant sounds at the beginning of words that are near one another

analogy an extended metaphor

anecdotes brief, often amusing stories

anger feeling experienced when we are faced with an obstacle in the way of something we want

animated lively and dynamic

annotated bibliography a preliminary record of relevant sources

antithesis combining contrasting ideas in the same sentence

antonym a word that is directly opposite in meaning

apathetic an audience that is uninterested in, unconcerned about, or indifferent toward a topic

appeal to action a statement that describes the behavior you want listeners to follow after they have heard your arguments

appearance the way you look to others

argue from analogy support a claim with a single comparable example that is significantly similar to the subject of the claim

argue from causation support a claim by citing events that always (or almost always) bring about a predictable effect or set of effects

argue from example support a claim by providing one or more individual examples

argue from sign support a claim by providing evidence that certain events that signal the claim have occurred

argument articulating a position with the support of logos, ethos, and pathos

articulation using the tongue, palate, teeth, jaw movement, and lips to shape vocalized sounds

assonance repetition of vowel sounds in a phrase or phrases

asynchronous virtual groups those whose members can post and respond to messages at any time, although usually within a few days

attending process of intentionally perceiving and focusing on a message

attention step piques the audience's curiosity, identifies the goal, and previews main points

audience adaptation the ongoing process of tailoring a speech to the needs, interests, and expectations of its listeners

audience the specific group of people to whom the speech is directed

audience analysis the study of the intended audience for your speech

audience contact creating a sense of looking listeners in the eye when speaking to large audiences

audience diversity the range of demographic and subject-related differences represented in an audience

audio aid a presentational aid that enhances the speaker's verbal message with additional sound

audiovisual aid a presentational aid that enhances the speech using a combination of visuals and sound

avoiding physically or psychologically removing oneself from the conflict

bar graph uses vertical or horizontal bars to show relationships between or among two or more variables

blogs websites that provide a forum for the personal viewpoints of their authors

brainstorming an uncritical, nonevaluative process of generating associated ideas

canons of rhetoric five general rules for effective public speeches

channels both the route traveled by a message and the means of transportation

chart a graphic representation that distills complex information into an easily interpreted visual format

chronological following an order that moves from first to last

claim (C) conclusion the persuader wants others to agree with

clincher a short statement that provides a sense of closure by driving home the importance of the speech in a memorable way

closed questions narrowly focused questions that require only very brief answers

cognitive restructuring an anxiety-reduction method of systematically replacing negative self-talk with positive coping statements

collaborating discussing the issues, describing feelings, and identifying the characteristics of an effective solution before deciding what the ultimate solution will be

commemorative address celebrates national holidays or anniversaries of important events

commencement address praises graduating students and attempts to inspire them to reach for their goals

common ground the background, knowledge, attitudes, experiences, and philosophies shared by audience members and the speaker

communication the process of creating shared meaning

communication context the environment in which communication occurs

communication orientation viewing public speaking as a conversation with a number of people about an important topic and getting the message across

communication orientation motivation (COM) adopting a "communication" rather than a "performance" orientation toward speeches

comparative advantages an organization that shows that a proposed change has more value than any of the alternatives

compare and contrast a method of informing that focuses on how something is similar to and different from other things

comparisons illuminate a point by showing similarities

compassion feeling of selfless concern for the suffering of another

competing satisfying one's own needs without concern for the needs of the others or for the harm it does to the group dynamics or problem-solving process

comprehensive report a written document that provides a detailed review of the problem-solving process used to arrive at the recommendation

compromising giving up part of what you want to satisfy others in the group

concept mapping a visual means of exploring connections between a subject and related ideas

conflict disagreements among ideas, principles, or people

connotation the positive, neutral, or negative feelings we associate with a word

constructive critique an evaluative response that identifies what was effective and what could be improved in a speech

content-oriented listeners focus on and evaluate the facts and evidence

content the information and ideas you present

context the position of a word in a sentence and its relationship to the words around it

contrasts illuminate a point by highlighting differences

conversational sounding spontaneous, as though talking with an audience

create suspense wording an attention getter so that what is described generates initial uncertainty or mystery and excites the audience

credentials experiences or education that qualifies a presenter to speak with authority on a specific subject

credibility the perception of a speaker as knowledgeable, trustworthy, and personable

criteria standards used for judging the merits of proposed solutions

criteria satisfaction an indirect organization that seeks audience agreement on criteria that should be considered when evaluating a proposition and then shows how the proposition satisfies those criteria

culture-related conflict when the communication norms of group members are incongruent

cyberplagiarism presenting material found on the Internet as one's own by failing to credit the source

decoding the process of interpreting messages

dedication honors a worthy person or group by naming a structure, monument, or park after them

deductive reasoning arriving at a conclusion based on a major premise and a minor premise

definition a statement that clarifies the meaning of a word or phrase (Ch. 6); a method of informing that explains the meaning of something (Ch. 12)

deliverables products of the work provided to someone else

delivery communicating through the use of voice and body

demonstration a method of informing that shows how something is done, displays the stages of a process, or depicts how something works

denotation dictionary definition

derived credibility perception of a speaker's expertise during the speech

description a method of informing that creates a verbal picture of an object, geographic feature, setting, or image

diagram a type of drawing that shows how the whole relates to its parts

dialect a unique form of a more general language spoken by a specific cultural or co-cultural group

direct question a question that seeks an overt response from the audience, usually by a show of hands

either/or fallacy argues there are only two alternatives when, in fact, there are many

elevator pitch introduces and enlists interest in a concept, product, or practice in 3 minutes or less

emotions the buildup of action-specific energy

empathy the ability to see the world through the eyes of someone else

encoding the process of creating messages

ethics moral principles that a society, group, or individual hold that differentiate right from wrong

ethnography a form of primary research based on fieldwork observations

ethos arguments about speaker competence, credibility, and good character

eulogy speech of tribute given during a funeral or memorial service, which praises the life and accomplishments of the deceased

evaluating critically analyzing the message

evidence any information that clarifies, explains, or otherwise adds depth or breadth to a topic

examples specific instances that illustrate or explain a general factual statement

executive summary a one-page synopsis of a comprehensive report

exigence a real or perceived specific need that a speech might help address

expert a person recognized as having mastered a specific subject

expert opinions interpretations and judgments made by authorities in particular subject areas

expository speech an informative presentation that provides carefully researched in-depth knowledge about a complex topic

extemporaneous speech a speech researched and planned ahead of time, although the exact wording is not scripted

eye contact looking at the people to whom you are speaking

facial expressions eye and mouth movements that convey emotions

facts statements whose accuracy can be verified as true

factual statements information that can be verified

false cause fallacy occurs when the alleged cause fails to produce the effect

farewell honors someone who is leaving an organization

fear perceiving no control over a situation that threatens us

feedback the receivers' reactions and responses that indicate how a message is interpreted

flowchart uses symbols and connecting lines to diagram a sequence of steps through a complicated process

formal leader a person designated or elected to oversee the group process

formal speech outline a complete sentence representation of the hierarchical and sequential relationships among the ideas presented in the speech

general goal the overall intent of the speech

generic language language that uses words that apply only to one sex, race, or other group as though that group represents everyone

gestures movements of hands, arms, and fingers

glossophobia the fear of public speaking

goodwill perception the audience forms of a speaker who they believe understands them, empathizes with them, and is responsive to them

graph presents numerical information in visual form

group dynamics how individuals work together as a team toward a common goal

groupthink when group members accept information and ideas without subjecting them to critical analysis

guilt feeling experienced when we personally violate a moral, ethical, or religious code that we hold dear

happiness or joy the buildup of positive energy

hasty generalization fallacy a generalization that is either not supported with evidence or is supported with only one weak example

hearing the physiological process that occurs when the brain detects sound waves

hope feeling that stems from believing something desirable is likely to happen

hypothesis an educated guess about a cause-and-effect relationship between two or more things

hypothetical examples specific instances based on reflections about future events

impromptu speech a speech delivered with only seconds or minutes of advance notice for preparation

incremental change attempting to move your audience only a small degree in your direction

inductive reasoning arriving at a conclusion based on a series of pieces of specific evidence

inferences assertions based on the facts presented

informal emergent leaders members who engage in different leadership functions

informative speech a speech whose goal is to explain or describe facts, truths, and principles in a way that stimulates interest, facilitates understanding, and increases the likelihood of remembering

initial audience disposition the knowledge and opinions listeners have about your topic before they hear you speak

initial credibility perception of a speaker's expertise at the beginning of the speech

intellectually stimulating information that is new to audience members and is explained in a way that piques their curiosity

intelligible understandable

interference/noise any stimulus that interferes with the process of achieving shared meaning

Internet search a way to generate a variety of potential topic ideas on a subject area

interpersonal communication communication between two people who have an identifiable relationship with each other

interview a highly structured conversation where one person asks questions and another answers them

interview protocol the list of questions to be asked

intrapersonal communication communicating with yourself (self-talk)

irrelevant association emphasizing someone's relationship to another when that relationship is irrelevant to the point

issue-related conflict when two or more group members' goals, ideas, or opinions about a topic are incompatible

jargon unique technical terminology of a trade or profession

joke an anecdote or a piece of wordplay designed to make people laugh

keynote address both sets the tone and generates enthusiasm for the topic of a conference or convention

leadership a process whereby an individual influences a group of individuals to achieve a common goal

leading questions questions phrased in a way that suggests the interviewer has a preferred answer

learning style a person's preferred way of receiving information

line graph indicates changes in one or more variables over time

linguistic sensitivity using respectful language that doesn't offend others

listener relevance link statement alerting listeners about how a main point or subpoint is relevant to them

listening the cognitive process of receiving, attending to, constructing meaning from, and responding to messages

listening apprehension the anxiety we feel about listening

listening style the favored and usually unconscious approach to listening

logical reasons order organizing the main points according to reasons for accepting the thesis as desirable or true

logos arguments that use evidence and reasoning to support a position

macrostructure the overall organizational framework of your speech content

main points complete sentence statements of the two to four central ideas the audience needs to understand to achieve the speech goal

maintenance leadership roles help the group to develop and maintain cohesion, commitment, and positive working relationships

major premise general principle that most people agree upon

marginalizing ignoring the values, needs, and interests of some audience members, leaving them feeling excluded

marking the addition of sex, race, age, or other group designations to a description

mass communication communication produced and transmitted via mass media to large audiences

master of ceremonies an individual designated to set the mood of the program, introduce participants, and keep the program moving

mediated channels technology-enhanced auditory and visual channels

messages the verbal utterances, visual images, and nonverbal behaviors used to communicate

metaphor implied comparison between two unlike things without using *like* or *as*

microstructure the specific language and style you use within your sentences

minor premise specific point that fits within the major premise

mnemonic device associates a special word or very short statement with new and longer information

model a three-dimensional scaled-down or scaled-up version of an actual object

monotone a voice in which the pitch, volume, and rate remain constant

motivated movement movement with a specific purpose

motivated sequence a persuasive organization that combines a problem–solution pattern with explicit appeals designed to motivate the audience to act

movement changing the position or location of the entire body

multiple-response items survey items that give respondents several alternative answers from which to choose

narration a method of informing that recounts events

narrative order organizing the main points as a story or series of stories

narratives accounts, personal experiences, tales, or lengthier stories

need step explores the nature of the problem

negative emotions disquieting feelings people experience

netiquette etiquette rules applicable to communicating over computer networks

neutral an audience that has some information about a topic but does not really understand why one position is preferred and so still has no opinion

neutral questions questions phrased in a way that does not direct a person's answers

nonparallel language when terms are changed because of the sex, race, or other group characteristics of the individual

nonverbal communication all speech elements other than the words themselves

nonverbal immediacy a perception of being personable and likeable

occasion the expected purpose of and setting (location) for the speech

online social networks websites where communities of people interact with one another

onomatopoeia words that sound like the things they stand for

open questions broad-based queries

open-ended items survey items that encourage respondents to elaborate on their opinions without forcing them to answer in a predetermined way

oral brief a short presentation delivered by one group member that describes the problem, background, process, decision, and rationale so that the audience can quickly understand and evaluate the group's product.

oral footnotes references to an original source, made at the point in the speech where information from that source is presented

oral report an oral presentation that provides a detailed review of the problem-solving process used to arrive at the recommendation

oral style how one conveys messages through the spoken word

organizational chart shows the structure of an organization in terms of rank and chain of command

organizing the process of arranging the speech content

other sensory aid a presentational aid that enhances the speech by appealing to smell, taste, or touch

panel discussion a structured problem-solving discussion in front of an audience

parallel structure when the main points follow the same structural pattern, often using the same introductory words

paraphrasing putting a message into your own words

participants individuals who assume the roles of senders and receivers during an interaction

passive listening the habitual and unconscious process of receiving messages

pathos arguments that appeal to emotions

pauses moments of silence strategically placed to enhance meaning

people-oriented listeners focus on the feelings the speakers may have about what they are saying

perception checking a verbal statement that reflects your understanding of another's behavior

performance orientation believing in the need to impress a hypercritical audience with knowledge and delivery

periodicals magazines and journals published at regular intervals

personableness the extent to which you project a pleasing personality

personal impact serious physical, economic, or psychological consequences for listeners or their loved ones

personal pronouns "we," "us," and "our"—pronouns that directly link the speaker to members of the audience

personal reference a brief account about something that happened to you or a hypothetical situation that listeners can imagine themselves in

personality-related conflict when two or more group members become defensive because they feel as though they are being attacked

personification attributing human qualities to a concept or an inanimate object

persuasion the process of influencing people's attitudes, beliefs, values, or behaviors

pie chart shows the relationships among parts of a single unit

pitch highness or lowness of vocal sounds

plagiarism the unethical act of representing another person's work as your own by failing to credit the source

plagiarize presenting the ideas, words, or created works of another as one's own by failing to credit the source

poise graceful and controlled use of the body that gives the impression of self-assurance

positive emotions feelings that people enjoy experiencing

posture position of the body

preparation outline a draft of main points and supporting ideas

presentational aid any visual, audio, audiovisual, or other sensory material used in a speech

pride feeling of self-satisfaction as the result of an accomplishment

primacy–recency effect the tendency to remember the first and last items conveyed orally in a series

primary questions introductory questions about each major interview topic

primary research collecting data about a topic directly from the real world

problem–cause–solution persuasive pattern that examines a problem, its cause(s), and the solutions designed to eliminate or alleviate the underlying cause(s)

problem–solution persuasive pattern that reveals the nature of a problem and proposes a solution

problem-solving groups five to seven people who work together to complete a specific task or solve a particular problem

procedural leadership roles provide logistical support and record the group's decisions and accomplishments

process speech an informative presentation that teaches how something is done, is made, or works

productive thinking to contemplate something from a variety of perspectives

pronunciation form and accent of various syllables of a word

proposition a declarative sentence that clearly indicates the position the speaker will advocate

proposition of fact a statement designed to convince the audience that something did or did not exist or occur, is or is not true, or will or will not occur

proposition of policy a statement designed to convince the audience that they should take a specific course of action

proposition of value a statement designed to convince the audience that something is good, bad, desirable, undesirable, fair, unfair, moral, immoral, sound, unsound, beneficial, harmful, important, or unimportant

proximity the relevance of information to the listener's personal space

pseudo-conflict when group members who actually agree about something believe they disagree due to poor communication

public communication communication with more than ten people by one primary sender to multiple receivers

public speaking a sustained formal presentation by a speaker to an audience

quality timbre that distinguishes one voice from others

question a statement designed to clarify information or get additional details (Ch. 3); requests for information (Ch. 8)

question-and-answer period brief time after a speech designated for addressing audience questions and comments

quotation a comment made by and attributed to someone other than the speaker

rapport-building questions nonthreatening questions designed to put the interviewee at ease and demonstrate respect

rate speed at which you talk

reasoning fallacies flawed reasoning

receivers participants who interpret messages sent by others

refutative an organization that persuades by both challen–ging the opposing position and bolstering one's own

rehearsing iterative process of practicing the speech aloud

relaxation exercises the use of breathing techniques and progressive muscle relaxation to reduce anxiety

relevance adapting information in ways that help audience members realize its importance to them

reliable sources have a history of presenting valid and accurate information

relief positive emotion felt when a threatening situation has been alleviated

remembering retaining and recalling information at a later time

remote access report a computer-mediated audiovisual presentation of the group's process and outcome

repetition repeating words, phrases, or sentences for emphasis

research cards individual index cards or electronic facsimiles identifying a piece of information, the key word or theme it represents, and its bibliographic data

responding providing feedback to the speaker

responsive when speakers show that they care about the audience by acknowledging feedback

rhetoric all available means of persuasion

rhetorical figures of speech phrases that make striking comparisons between things that are not obviously alike

rhetorical questions questions phrased to stimulate a mental response from the audience

rhetorical situation the intersection of the speaker, audience, and occasion

rhetorical structures of speech phrases that combine ideas in a particular way

roast an event where guests provide short speeches of tribute, developed with humorous stories and anecdotes, about the featured guest.

role a specific communication behavior group members perform to address group needs at any given point in time

sadness feeling experienced when we fail to achieve a goal or experience a loss or separation

satisfaction step explains the proposed solution to the problem

scaled items survey items that measure the direction and/or intensity of an audience member's feeling or attitude toward something

scripted speech a speech prepared by creating a complete written manuscript and delivered by reading from or memorizing it

secondary questions follow-up questions designed to probe the answers given to primary questions

secondary research locating information that has been discovered by other people

section transitions complete sentences that bridge the major parts of a speech

self-talk intrapersonal communication regarding perceived success or failure in a particular situation

senders participants who form and transmit messages

sensory language appeals to the senses of seeing, hearing, tasting, smelling, and feeling

setting the location where the speech will be given

shame feeling that arises when we violate a moral code and our violation is revealed to someone we think highly of

shared leadership functions the sets of roles group members perform to facilitate the work of the group and to help maintain harmonious relations among members

signposts words, phrases, or visual cues that connect pieces of supporting material to the main point or subpoint they address

simile direct comparison of dissimilar things using *like* or *as*

skimming rapidly going through a work to determine what is covered and how

slang nonstandard vocabulary and definitions assigned to words by a social group or co-culture

small group communication interaction that occurs in a group of approximately three to ten people

speaker the originator of the speech

speaking appropriately using language that is adapted to the needs, interests, knowledge, and attitudes of the listener and avoiding language that alienates audience members

speaking notes a key-word outline of the speech, plus hard-to-remember information and delivery cues

specific goal a single statement that identifies the exact response the speaker wants from the audience

specific language words that clarify meaning by narrowing what is understood from a general category to a particular item or group within that category

speech communities group of people who speak a common dialect

speech goal a specific statement of what you want your audience to know, believe, or do

speech of acceptance acknowledges receipt of an honor or award

speech of introduction establishes a supportive climate for the main speaker, highlights the speaker's credibility, and generates enthusiasm for listening

speech of nomination proposes a nominee for an elected office, honor, position, or award

speech of recognition acknowledges someone, usually accompanied by the presentation of an award, prize, or gift

speech of tribute praises or celebrates a person, group, or event

speech of welcome an address that greets and expresses pleasure for the presence of a person or an organization

speech plan a strategic method for achieving your effective speech goal

speech to entertain a humorous speech that makes a serious point

speeches to actuate a speech designed to incite action

speeches to convince a speech designed to seek agreement about a belief, value, or attitude

spontaneity sounding natural, no matter how many times a presentation was practiced

stance an author's attitude, perspective, or viewpoint on a topic

Standard English form of English taught in American schools and detailed in English grammar handbooks

startling statement a shocking expression or example

statement of reasons a straightforward organization in which the best-supported reasons are presented in a meaningful order

statistics numerical facts

stereotyping assuming all members of a group have similar knowledge, behaviors, or beliefs simply because they belong to that group

story an account of something that has happened (actual) or could happen (hypothetical)

straw man fallacy occurs when a speaker weakens the opposing position by misrepresenting it and then attacks that weaker position

streaming video a recording that is sent in compressed form over the Internet

stress emphasis placed on certain words by speaking them more loudly than the rest of the sentence

structure the framework that organizes the speech content

subject a broad area of knowledge

subpoints statements that elaborate on a main point

support (S) evidence offered as grounds for accepting the conclusion

supporting material evidence and reasoning used to develop the main points

survey a canvassing of people to get information about their ideas and opinions about a specific topic

syllogism three-part form of deductive reasoning

symposium a set of prepared oral reports delivered sequentially by group members

synergy when the result of group work is better than what one member could achieve alone

synonym a word that has the same or a similar meaning

systematic desensitization an anxiety-reduction method of gradually visualizing and then engaging in increasingly more frightening speaking events while remaining calm

systematic problem-solving method a six-step method for finding an effective solution to a problem

target audience the group of people you most want to persuade

task leadership roles help the group acquire, process, or apply information that contributes directly to completing a task or goal

terminal credibility perception of a speaker's expertise at the end of the speech

thesis statement one- or two-sentence summary of the speech that incorporates the general and specific goals and previews the main points

time order organizing the main points in sequence or by steps in a process

time-oriented listeners prefer brief and hurried conversations

timeliness showing how information is useful now or in the near future

toast offered at the start of a reception or meal to pay tribute to the occasion or a person

topic a narrow aspect of a subject

topical order organizing the main points by categories or divisions of a subject

topical following an order of interest

transcribe word-for-word translation into written form of the interview

transitions words, phrases, or sentences that bridge two ideas

trustworthiness the extent to which the audience can believe that what you say is accurate, true, and in their best interests

two-sided items survey items that force respondents to choose between two answers

understanding accurately interpreting a message

uninformed an audience that doesn't know enough about a topic to have formed an opinion

valid sources report factual information that can be counted on to be true

verbal immediacy language that reduces the psychological distance between you and your audience

virtual group-related conflict arises as a result of meeting through technology-enhanced channels

virtual groups groups that convene using telephone or computer technology

virtual presence simulated presence made possible through the use of digital technology

visual aid a presentational aid that allows the audience to see what the speaker is describing or explaining

visualization a method to reduce anxiety by picturing yourself giving a masterful speech

visualization step asks the audience to imagine what will happen if the proposed solution to the problem is or is not implemented

vivid language language that is full of life—vigorous, bright, and intense

vocal expression variety created in the voice through changing pitch, volume, and rate, as well as stressing certain words and using pauses

vocalized pauses unnecessary words interjected into sentences to fill moments of silence

voice sound produced by vocal organs

volume how loudly or softly you speak

warrant (W) reasoning that connects the support to the claim

words arbitrary symbols used to represent things

written brief a short document that describes the problem, background, process, decision, and rationale so that the reader can quickly understand and evaluate the group's product

Index

A

Abdominal breathing, 28*e*

Abstract(s), 97

Abstractness
    of language, 177, 177*f*

Accent(s), 189–190

Acceptance
    speech of, 277–278

Accommodating
    as conflict management style, 290

Accurate language, 175–179, 177*e*, 177*f*
    abstractness of, 177, 177*f*
    changes over time, 177–178
    connotation and, 178
    defined, 175
    denotation and, 178
    dialect and, 178–179

Accurate sources, 97

Action(s)
    appeal to
        in conclusion, 141
    defined, 136
    in getting attention, 136

Action-oriented listeners, 46

Action step
    in motivated sequence pattern, 261

Active listening
    attending and, 47–48, 47*e*, 48*f*
    defined, 46
    strategies in, 47–50, 47*e*, 48*f*
    understanding and, 47*e*, 48–49

Actual objects
    as visual aids, 155–156, 155*f*

Actuate
    speeches to, 258–263, 259*f* (*See also*
        Persuasive speech(es), to actuate)

Adaptation
    audience (*See* Audience adaptation)
    of speech
        during delivery, 200–202
        for virtual audiences, 202–203

Adaptation phase, 24, 24*e*

Address(es)
    farewell, 281
    keynote, 281

Ad hominem fallacy, 241, 241*f*

Advertising
    ethical standards in, 161

Affective processes
    in listening, 44

Aid(s)
    presentational, 153–168 (*See also specific
        types and* Presentational aids)

Alliteration, 183

Analogy, 183
    argue from, 239

Anecdote(s), 106–107, 107*f*

Anger
    as negative emotion, 244–245

Animated delivery, 187–188, 188*f*

Annotated bibliography, 108

Anticipation phase, 24, 24*e*

Antithesis, 184

Antonym, 219

APA citation formats
    examples of, 144*e*

Apathetic audience, 255

Appeal to action
    in conclusion, 141
    defined, 141

Appearance
    of speaker, 191–192

Appreciative listening, 45, 45*f*

Apprehension
    listening, 45, 45*f*
    public speaking, 22–42
        causes of, 25–26, 26*f*, 27*f*
        developing effective speech plan,
            31–36 (*See also* Speech plan,
            developing)
        managing, 26–31, 28*e*, 28*f*, 29*e*, 30*f*
        personal report (score sheet) of,
            24, 25*e*
        phases of, 24, 24*e*
        symptoms of, 24, 24*e*, 25*e*
        understanding nature of, 23–26, 24*e*,
            25*e*, 26*f*

Arbitrary
    language as, 175–176, 177*e*

Argue from analogy, 239

Argue from causation, 239–240, 240*f*

Argue from example, 238–239, 239*f*

Argue from sign, 238, 238*f*

Argument(s)
    defined, 235
    logical
        types of, 238–240, 248*f*–240*f* (*See also*
            Logical arguments)

Aristotle, 10

Articles
    for secondary research, 95–96, 96*f*

Articulation, 189

Artifact(s)
    original
        for primary research, 102, 102*f*

Assonance, 184

Asynchronous virtual groups
    communicating in, 293

Attending, 47–48, 47*e*, 48*f*

Attention
    getting
        in introduction, 132–136, 133*f*–135*f*
            action, 136
            ask questions, 133–134, 133*f*
            create suspense, 136
            personal reference, 135
            quotations, 135–136
            startling statement, 133
            tell joke, 135, 135*f*
            tell story, 134–135, 134*f*

Attention step
    in motivated sequence pattern, 260, 261

Attitude(s)
    of audience, 61, 63, 64*f*

Audience(s)
    adapting to, 78–91 (*See also* Audience
        adaptation)
    in ancient Greece, 10
    apathetic, 255
    attitude of, 61, 63, 64*f*
    defined, 12
    neutral, 255
    tailoring propositions to, 254–256, 255*e*,
        255*f*
    uninformed, 255
    virtual
        adapting speech for, 202–203

Audience adaptation, 78–91
    common experiences and, 81
    common ground and, 80–81
    cultural differences and, 88
    culturally appropriate supporting material
        and, 88
    defined, 12, 33, 57
    in developing speech plan, 33
    information comprehension and retention
        and, 84–87, 85*e*, 87*f*
    initial audience disposition and, 79, 80*f*
    knowledge/expertise and, 82–83
    language in
        specific/familiar, 86
    learning styles awareness and, 84–86, 85*e*
    personableness and, 83–84
    personal impact and, 82